Divided Only by Distance & Allegiance

The Bulloch/Roosevelt Letters: 1861-1865

Divided Only by Distance and Allegiance

The Bulloch/Roosevelt Letters: 1861-1865

Connie M. Huddleston
&
Gwendolyn I. Koehler

The Bulloch Letters Volume 3

Divided Only by Distance & Allegiance
The Bulloch/Roosevelt Letters: 1861-1865

Second Edition: 2021
Interpreting Time's Past Press

Text and cover photograph copyright © 2017
by Connie M. Huddleston and Gwendolyn I. Koehler.
All rights reserved. No part of this book may be used or reproduced in any manner whatsoever without written permission except in the case of brief quotations embodied in critical articles and reviews. For information, please address Connie Huddleston at Interpreting Time's Past, LLC, 450 Old Richmond Road, South, Crab Orchard, KY 40419.

Cover design by Interpreting Time's Past, LLC
Cover photograph and photograph of Daniel Stuart Elliott's tombstone by
Connie M. Huddleston
Authors' photographs courtesy of Duane Stork at Stork AV Productions.

ISBN-13: 979-8-9852672-0-4
LCCN: 2020920009

Publisher's Cataloging-in-Publication data

Names: Huddleston, Connie M., author. | Koehler, Gwendolyn I., author.
Title: Divided only by distance and allegiance : the Bulloch/Roosevelt Letters: 1861-1865 / Connie M. Huddleston and Gwendolyn I. Koehler.
Series: The Bulloch/Roosevelt Letters
Description: Includes bibliographical references. | Second edition. | Crab Orchard, KY: Interpreting Time's Past Press, 2021.
Identifiers: LCCN: 2020920009 | ISBN: 979-8-9852672-0-4
Subjects: LCSH Roosevelt, Martha Bulloch--Correspondence. | Roosevelt, Theodore, 1831-1878--Correspondence. | United States--History--19th century. | United States--19th century--Biography. | BISAC HISTORY / United States / 19th Century | HISTORY / United States / Civil War Period (1850-1877) | BIOGRAPHY & AUTOBIOGRAPHY / Historical
Classification: LCC E468 .H83 v.3 2021 | DDC 973.7--dc23

Table of Contents

List of Figures vi
Dedication viii
Acknowledgments ix
Preface xi
Chapter 1: Setting the Stage 1
Chapter 2: January through June of 1861 23
Chapter 3: July through October of 1861 41
Chapter 4: November of 1861 59
Chapter 5: December of 1861 89
Chapter 6: January of 1862 117
Chapter 7: February of 1862 129
Chapter 8: March through July of 1862 165
Chapter 9: August through October of 1862 189
Chapter 10: November & December of 1862 211
Chapter 11: January through April of 1863 235
Chapter 12: May through August of 1863 253
Chapter 13: October of 1863 271
Chapter 14: November & December of 1863 289
Chapter 15: 1864 & 1865 319
Epilogue 341
Endnotes 353
Bibliography 375
List of Persons 383
Appendix A: A Brief History of Bulloch Friends
   and Family Who Served the Confederacy 393
Appendix B: Relevant Union and Confederate Officers
   and Leaders 399
Appendix C: Undated Notes from Mrs. Abraham
   Lincoln 409
Appendix D: Daniel Stuart Elliott's Will 411
Index 413
About the Authors 425

List of Figures

Martha Stewart Elliott Bulloch xviii
Bulloch Hall. 8
Martha *Mittie* Bulloch Roosevelt 11
Anna Bulloch. 12
Bulloch Family Tree 13
Roosevelt Family Tree. 14
Theodore *Thee* Roosevelt 16
Map of New York City. 20
Daddy Luke Monroe and *Maum* Grace 36
Laird's Mansion House. 39
Laird's Dining Room 39
New York Avenue Presbyterian Church 71
James Dunwoody Bulloch 84
Pontoon Bridge 105
P.G.T. Beauregard. 107
Daniel A. Butterfield 107
Fortress Monroe. 128
Grand Ball at the White House 136
At the Grand Ball, Mrs. McClellan, Mrs. Lincoln,
   and Mrs Crittenden. 137
Contraband Camp. 140
Raphael J. DeCordova 144
General George and Mary McClellan. 156
Willie and Tad Lincoln. 157
Ladies' Caps 161
Barnum's City Hotel. 168
A Churchyard Gate 187
Irvine Bulloch 188
Unidentified Union Drummer Boy 194
Fashionable Gown 195
Niagara Falls. 204

Paper Needle Folder 206
Stuart Elliott's Tombstone 215
"Preparing for the Christmas Party" 234
General Tom Thumb's Wedding 240
Omnibus 244
Sorrel-Weed House. 269
Winslow Homer Engraving of the Russian Ball 295
Dancing at the Russian Ball 296
The Sinking of the C.S.S. Alabama. 331
Tombstones of Anna Bulloch Gracie, James Gracie,
    and Martha Bulloch 347
West Family Graves 347

Dedication

We dedicate this book
to
Major Charles V. Huddleston
(U.S. Army retired)
and
Arthur C. Koehler

Without their love and support
we would have never accomplished
these three volumes.

Acknowledgments

Our project began nine years ago when the family of Clarece Martin donated her research collection and writings to the Bulloch Hall Archives. This sparked the project that led to the publication of the Bulloch and Roosevelt family letters. Both families, one significant in the South and one in the North, played important roles in the development of our country. The opportunity to learn about their lives and times through their own words has been fascinating. With the enthusiastic and/or financial support of many individuals and groups, especially the Friends of Bulloch Inc., the three volume collection is now available.

The authors especially thank Heather Cole, Curator of the Theodore Roosevelt Collection, Houghton Library, Harvard University, and Pam Billingsley, Bulloch Hall Site Director for their assistance.

Bulloch Hall's staff, volunteers, family, and friends have listened *ad nauseam* to our endless stories, and assisted, supported, and encouraged us along the way. Without the skills of Amy C. Davis, Connie's daughter, our ebook versions would have never happened. It is hard to describe the role Sherron Lawson has played in the eventual publication of these letters. She is our skilled editor, patient mediator, and above all, dear friend. Her humor lightened many intense moments.

First readers are tasked with ferreting out errors of all kinds. Dr. Deborah Posser, Dean of Libraries, University of North Georgia, and Sara Harwood, Bulloch Hall docent diligently forged through the first draft. Second readers Walter E. Wilson, author, fact checker, and friend, and Ina Born, Bulloch Hall docent, helped polish and put the final touches on the second and final draft.

Our most sincere thanks and heartfelt gratitude goes to all of these wonderful people.

Preface

This book is the third in the Bulloch Letters Series. If you read *Mittie & Thee*, or *Between the Wedding and the War* you may wish to proceed directly to Chapter 1. However, this section incorporates some new information.

Bulloch Hall (Roswell, Georgia) is the antebellum home of James Stephens Bulloch and Martha Bulloch. Built in the late 1830s, this Greek Revival town home served as one of the Bulloch children's many homes and was their last in the South. Today, Bulloch Hall is operated as a house museum and is owned and administered by the City of Roswell. The Friends of Bulloch, Inc., (501(c)3) actively works to assure Bulloch Hall is well cared for and funded. In addition to the main house, the site features a reproduction farmhouse welcome center and museum shop, a summer house, two reproduction slave quarters (one of which holds administrative offices), a reproduction carriage house, two reproduction privies, two restored well houses, a pond, gardens, a nature trail, and a large pavilion used for events.

In 2008, Bulloch Hall's archives received forty-eight boxes from the estate of a local historian filled with miscellaneous papers, memorabilia, print clippings, and copies of newspaper articles covering a wide variety of topics related to Roswell's history. Copies of Bulloch and Roosevelt family letters, some complete and others simply random pages, were scattered throughout the boxes. After reading through a few of the pages, we (the authors) realized we possessed a treasure trove of family information and stories. Initially, we did not have a clear idea of the letters' source. Later in our search, we found partial lists of letters that had been obtained from the Theodore Roosevelt Collection housed in Harvard University's Houghton Library.

In 2014, we traveled to Harvard to examine that collection and locate additional letters and/or find missing pages. Curator Heather Cole provided invaluable assistance as we explored the entire Bulloch family-related collection and found further letters and documents that helped complete the story.

At Bulloch Hall, university interns, volunteers, docents, and staff helped sort the contents of each box. They matched pages whenever possible, and the arduous years-long task of transcribing began. The letters were originally written on small, almost transparent paper with pen and ink, requiring the transcriber to determine if a mark on the page was intentional punctuation or merely an ink blot. Copies of some letters were faint and high intensity lighting and computer enhancement aided in their interpretation. Some words simply remained indecipherable. A few of the letters were incomplete. We came to every new letter with feelings of anticipation and delight, as each revealed new insights about the family members.

Transcribing letters written in the nineteenth century poses a fascinating set of problems. There were no standard rules of punctuation or capitalization, and alternate word spellings and meanings were often used. For example Mittie referred to her fiancé as *Thee, Thee-a-te, Thee-ate, Thee a te,* and *Theeate*. *Myown, atlast,* and *atall* were almost always written as one word, an indication of personal style. Some individuals used hyphens inconsistently. *Grandmother* would also be written as *grand mother* or *grand-mother*. Letter formation varied greatly from writer to writer (if you can't read cursive you can't read old letters). Individual handwriting changed with age, stress, and circumstance. Writers often inserted words above the text (presented here as superscript) and did not capitalize days of the week or months. It took each transcriber considerable time and patience to become comfortable with individual writing styles. Some writers commonly used dashes between sentences. We found unfamiliar vocabulary words, *quondam* and *philopena*, for instance, which sent us to the dictionary.

We thought the word *waitor* was a misspelling of waiter, as it sometimes was, but learned it was "a tray on which something was carried." Our writers did not use periods after Mr, Mrs, or Dr. We have maintained the original spelling of all words as written as well as the original punctuation.

Letter writers of the nineteenth century used a variety of stationery. Sometimes the writer folded a sheet of paper in half. They might begin writing on the outside left panel, then on the inside right panel, next on the inside left panel, and finally on the outside left panel. When the writer ran out of room, they sometimes turned the paper 90 degrees and continued writing in the margin or even perpendicular to and over their previous words.

Occasionally, letters were not dated or only the year was missing. This created another mystery as we needed to transcribe the letters and use clues to figure out where in the sequence these letters belonged. One such letter from Lucy Elliott should have been included in the previous volume, *Between the Wedding & the War*. We had assigned the year 1862, in error, and present it here.

Marietta August 7th

My Dear Mother -
    Stuart has been writing you so frequently - that I have scarcely thought it necessary for me to write also - I suppose he has told you every thing in regard to our plans - which we are so anxious to put into execution - but the difficulty of getting servants will detain us at this miserable place for some time - Stuart is dreadfully disgusted at every thing - and sometimes he fears that I will never be satisfied but I am sure in our own house, with occupation that I will never be lonely - I am the only lady in the Hotel and as this spot is the scene of many rows and drunken fights I require Stuart to be constantly with me - this he does very cheerfully as he knows how timid I am in such scenes - the fact is we are both disgusted with our situation now - and only await the servants to go to our Place -I have seen more drunken

men since I have been here than I have seen before. Whisky is the cure of the country together with slavery - I am fast becoming - not an abolitionist exactly - ^but favorable to white or free labor - I suppose you have heard how much trouble we have had with one nurse - Diana ~~first~~ ^She was a wretched creature - At first Stuart thought he could make her behave - by having her punished - but I always objected especially to keep a nurse who required such treatment - and then she constantly kept him excited - I persuaded him therefore to dispatch her to Savannah and altho for a few days I had to attend to Johnnie myself - I felt so pleased to have her away - She was such a disolute character - that I could not bear to see Johnnie in her arms - Well After the greatest trouble Stuart got me an old woman an excellent nurse - but she is most unfortunately devoted to her husband and will go home every evening after ten - Consequently both Stuart and myself are obliged to sit up in our room every evening - I cannot tell you - my dear Mother how much trouble we have had about servants -I am looking about for another nurse - completely worn out from attending to Johnnie so much - then I have been so uneasy about Stuart - he has had a dreadful cough - I expected every moment to see him spit blood - I persuaded him to take Ayer's Pectoral after great difficulty - which relieved his cough somewhat - but still suffered intense pain in his sides and chest - I was up several nights trying to give him relief - I put mustard plaster on - but it gave only temporary relief - I begged and entreated him to send for a Dr - but no he would not - he said he would rather die than take these drugs - the {___} pain - that which made him uneasy in any position - has left - but he still has a constant dull pain - and he has lost a great deal in weight - I am so anxious to get him something that he can eat - indeed neither of us can eat the fare here - I wish you would persuade him when he suffers with that pain - to do something - for I am afraid of its becoming fixed we have been very forlorn - until the other day -I got positively {___} - and only think - Oh all - dont exclaim until I tell you how it was - I was so weak myself before dinner—that

I asked Stuart to get me a bottle of ale which he did - and as we have been entirely without spirits of any kind this summer I drank it off freely - the consequence was I was very jolly - but was sick afterwards - Stuart says I laughed all the time - he seemed so amused as I had given him a temperance lecture the night previous - he says I watch him so closely - I really can say - that I believe he is one of the most absteminious men any where - more so this summer - than he has ever been before - I always notice however whenever he takes anything - for these things upon {p___} upon one - Stuart says that if a gentleman were inclined to drink - he sees so much of the disgusting part of it here - that of itself would {____} him - I have met many of your friends here - Mrs Mary Robert always asks very kindly for you - I find her so pleasant - that I frequently drop in to see her There are a good many Savannah people at the other Hotel - Mr & Mrs James Hunter - who also enquired for you - and desired to be remembered - I think the Kings from Roswell are there ł Young Dr King was married to Miss MacLeod last week I think they are to reside in Atlanta {_____} with the prickler heat I keep flour on it - to cool him Give much love to all the family with you Tell Mittie that I will write her very soon - Tell her I will write her to get something out of the rest of the $95.00 - check I sent on last winter {who} I would like to know if she received it -she acknowledged the contents of this letter but not the check - I told Stuart - I felt a delicacy in asking for her to get me anything until I knew - With much love dear Mother - believe me your attached daughter
                                    Lucy Elliot
Johnnie sends a kiss to grandma Do write me all that is going on at {Turkers} [Tuckers] - especially if there are any Theatricals -

    In so many letters, the Victorian convention of calling everyone by their surname, unless family or extremely close friend, often made identification of persons mentioned impossible. Sometimes, a name was mentioned in two or more letters and only from context could we properly identify the person of interest. This created more problems when the name could not be deciphered due to incorrect spelling or commonality, such as Elliott, Scott, et cetera.

Our process involved Gwen and two additional individuals interpreting each letter. The first interpreter transcribed by hand. Then a second set of eyes proofed the results. The letter was then typed, compared to the original, and proofed again. Gwen performed the fourth and final proofing.

Corinne Robinson's *My Brother Theodore Roosevelt* contains several excerpts from family letters. Our transcriptions sometimes differ widely from Corinne's. We believe Corinne selected and used particular portions of the letters to suit her purpose instead of publishing the entire letter in its original form.

Transcribing many letters from a particular individual is a deeply personal experience. The transcribers came to know the correspondents intimately, imagining each writer was watching to ensure accuracy in content and tone. These Bulloch and Roosevelt letters provide a singular window into personal lives of the nineteenth century and a pivotal moment in American history. The courtship letters are the focus of the first book, *Mittie & Thee: An 1853 Roosevelt Romance*, while *Between the Wedding and the War: The Bulloch/Roosevelt Letters 1854-1860* provides a detailed look at relationships and social mores of those transitional years as some of the family members moved north. This final volume encompasses all the letters preserved from the beginning of the Civil War until the War's end.

To increase reader enjoyment and understanding of these letters, we have researched those individuals mentioned and discussed within each letter. Within the letters, we simply inserted last or full names where necessary for understanding. In order to not interrupt the flow of the original letters, a glossary of individuals is provided after the endnotes. Our intent is to provide the reader with basic birth and death dates, and family relationships, where possible. When we could not identify an individual to great accuracy, we provide no further information than did our letter writers. It should be noted that some individuals did not have middle names, such as Martha *Mittie* Bulloch and Theodore *Thee* Roosevelt. Middle names are present when applicable. Other individuals had nicknames, often several, such as *Sudie* and *Tudie* for Susan Elliott West. Daniel Stewart (Stuart) Elliot officially changed his name from Stewart to Stuart in December of 1853. It seems he wished to be called Stuart; however, as family will do, his siblings continued to call him *Brother Dan* in many of these letters.

While transcribing the letters, we often felt it necessary to include information within the letter, such as a person's name or translation of a misspelled word. Our intrusions into the letters are always presented in brackets [ ]. A { } set of brackets may contain an underline to represent an illegible word or even letters of a partially recognizable word. When {?} is used, it denotes that we are unsure of the previous word's transcription.

During the period of 1860-1865, when these letters were written, African-Americans or Blacks were commonly referred to as *Negroes*. This term is used throughout these volumes as it was the name used by these women and men in their letters.

Following the endnotes and bibliography is our List of Persons which presents an alphabetical listing of individuals prominent in this volume. Appendix A contains a brief history of military service of Bulloch family and friends who served the Confederacy. Appendix B is a alphabetical listing of Union and Confederate officers and leaders encountered in this volume. It begins with a list of the U.S. Army rank structure. At the end is a table showing the Union and Confederate names for important battles in the Civil War. Appendix C presents two undated notes from First Lady Mary Todd Lincoln to the Roosevelts. Appendix D is a transcription of Daniel Stuart Elliott's will.

Martha Stewart Elliott Bulloch, age unknown,
Courtesy of the Theodore Roosevelt Collection,

Chapter I: Setting the Stage

In some stories, the narrative needs to begin well before the main characters are introduced. This is such a story. As with *Mittie & Thee* and *Between the Wedding & the War*, to understand and appreciate these letters, written between 1861 and 1865, the reader needs to meet the principal characters much earlier in their lives. The following brings new readers into the history and connections of these two prominent families, allowing for a thorough understanding of their letters.

The Bulloch Family

This story's Southern families established themselves with the early settlement of Savannah, Georgia, and South Carolina. These first immigrants would later settle the coastal counties of Georgia, help win the Revolutionary War, and create a vibrant plantation community in Liberty and surrounding counties as well as a successful trading harbor at Savannah. We begin our narrative some years later, after the birth of our principal letter writer.

In 1817, a complicated tale of romance, oft told, yet undocumented, commenced. In that year, according to family lore, amidst the rural cotton and rice plantations of Liberty County, twenty-four-year-old James Stephens Bulloch, business man, planter, and veteran of the War of 1812, proposed to eighteen-year-old Martha Stewart, daughter of Revolutionary War General Daniel Stewart. Despite her reputed love for this young man whom she had known since early childhood, she did as the fashion of the time dictated and refused his offer. Tradition indicated she could expect another offer from him. However, much to her dismay, James instead proposed to her friend, Hester Elliott (b. 1797), daughter of neighbor John Elliott. Hester readily accepted his offer and made wedding plans. Meanwhile, Martha - a noted beauty - received an offer of marriage from that same John Elliott, age 44, a Yale graduate, lawyer, and plantation owner, some 26 years her senior.

James and Hester *Hettie* married on 31 December 1817, followed quickly by the marriage of Martha and John on 6 January 1818. Both weddings took place in the Midway Congregational Church in Liberty County. Thus, Martha became James' stepmother-in-law. Liberty County society saw Martha's marriage as one of prestige and advantage for the couple. Perhaps an added attraction was the anticipation that John Elliott, a Yale-trained lawyer, was a likely candidate for the United States Senate.

History has not revealed the nature of James and Hettie's relationship; however, it was not uncommon for young women to marry for status instead of love. James was quite a catch. The residents of Liberty County and Savannah (Chatham County) already recognized this young man for his family connections. His grandfather Archibald Bulloch was the first *president* of Georgia and the man who initially read the Declaration of Independence to the citizens of the colony. Additionally, James had by this time established himself as a gentleman investor, public servant, and factor[1] in Savannah.

James and Hettie resided in Savannah on Broughton Street. Hettie bore James at least two children of whom only one lived to maturity, James Dunwoody Bulloch (1823-1901). Their first son, named John Elliott for her father, died at age two years and 10 months in Burke County, Georgia, in late September 1821.[2]

Though marrying a man old enough to be her father, Martha embraced the role of stepmother to John's three daughters who remained at home; Caroline Matilda (a 22-year-old spinster, who died before 1827), Jane Elizabeth (age 9), and Corinne Louisa (age 5). Martha's first child, John

Whitehead Elliott, was born on 7 November 1818. Her life changed greatly when the Georgia legislature appointed her husband to the U.S. Senate in 1819. John took his young wife to Washington, where she charmed residents with her stylish and gracious ways. Tragedy struck the family in November 1820 when her firstborn son died. Another son, Charles William, born in 1824, would survive a mere three years. The infant mortality rate was high in the 1820s. Only three children from this union would live to maturity: Susan Ann (1820-1895), Georgia Amanda (1822-1848), and Daniel Stewart (1826-1862).[3]

Historical records show that the two families were much entwined, with James, John, and their wives often traveling together for business and pleasure. Years passed with James and Hettie residing in Savannah, while John and Martha split their time between his Liberty County plantation, their new expansive Savannah home, and Washington, D.C. and Philadelphia while the Senate was in session.

In 1824, with John's term of office completed, they returned south and later rejoiced at the birth of son Daniel Stewart (1826). However, on 9 August 1827, John Elliott died prematurely in Savannah of dysentery which he had contracted while tending the slaves at one of his plantations. John's death left a grieving 28-year-old Martha with four small children from their union, including nine-month-old Daniel, and two stepdaughters, Jane Elizabeth, age 18, and Corinne Louisa, age 14, to raise. Compounding the family's grief was the death of three-year-old Charles, one month after his father's death.[4]

It seems this shared grief brought James, Hettie, and Martha even closer together. At age 55 and in robust health, no doubt expecting to live many more years, John Elliott died *intestate*. James became the executor of John's estate. Managing John's extensive plantation and other business holdings occupied a tremendous amount of James' time in the coming years. That first year, both families lived in *full mourning*. Then, for half a year, the families continued in *half mourning*, attending only small social events and seldom traveling.

On 1 May 1828 following her father's death by not quite nine months, Jane Elizabeth Elliott married John Stevens Law, a physician from Liberty County. Sadly, Jane enjoyed only eleven months of marital bliss. The *Savannah Georgian* on 18 April 1829 reported a fire at their residence. On 30 April, the *Georgian* posted an article documenting her death only three days after the fire. Jane's passing, falling so soon after the fire, presumably at their home, leaves the nature of her death to speculation.

It seemed Martha's period of mourning would never end, as one month later on 27 May 1829, Martha's father General Daniel Stewart died at his plantation in Liberty County. Within a two-year period, Martha lost her husband and young son, her stepdaughter, and her father.

Nevertheless, life went on. Martha inherited a substantial amount from her father's estate. Her personal wealth also increased with her inheritance from her husband's estate, insuring a comfortable lifestyle. Steamship records of the time show that Martha traveled, with her children and a few servants, once to the North during the South's hottest months of summer, and more often to Charleston, South Carolina. James, Hettie, and their small son, James, Martha's step-grandson accompanied her on the trip to New York in 1829.

Hettie's health deteriorated, and at some point in 1830, James, Hettie, and their seven-year-old son moved in with Martha at her Savannah home. On 21 February 1831, Hettie succumbed to what was described as a "protracted and painful" illness.[5] Life now found Martha and James, living as "*brother and sister*"[6] while raising children from three marriages. On 12 January 1832, Martha's stepdaughter Corinne Elliott married family friend Robert Hutchison.

Hutchison, born in Scotland in 1802, migrated to Savannah and quickly moved up from a clerk's position to become one of Savannah's wealthiest and most respected citizens. His marriage to Corinne Elliott, some ten years younger, would not have seemed unusual and was no doubt considered an excellent match for Corinne.

One year and two months after Hettie's death, on 8 May 1832, James and Martha married. Savannah resident and nineteenth-century diarist, Mary Telfair, wrote to her friend Mary Few of Virginia that a good deal of buzzing was taking place over a match among members of the church. It was said that "the church would weep over such a marriage."[7] She described Mrs. John Elliott as a woman of exalted piety. But clearly she had misgivings about this upcoming marriage:

> . . . she married in the first instance a Man old enough to be her father and no doubt sacrificed feeling to ambition. She made a most exemplary Wife & (hardest of all duties) an excellent Step Mother. For four years she has acted the part of a dignified Widow which of all characters (Step Mother excepted) is the most difficult to support, and now she is about marrying her husband's daughter's husband — he has been living in the house with her ever since the death of his wife and I thought viewed by her with sisterly regard. I begin to think with Miss Edgeworth that propinquity is dangerous and beyond the relationship of Brother and Sister mutual dependence is apt to create sentiment more tender than platonic. . . It does not strike me as a criminal connection, but one highly revolting to delicacy. . .[8]

Mary Telfair went on to expound about how the late Mr. Elliott's surviving daughter's feelings "were very much enraged." Telfair stated that this daughter, Corinne Louisa, was devotedly attached to her stepmother, but now refused to have any interaction with James.[9] Mary Telfair ended with "I feel sorry for Mrs. Elliott, she had in her first marriage to practice an Apprenticeship to self denial, in order to conciliate the good will of daughters as old as herself — by a noble and disinterested course of conduct she received their confidence and affection and fulfilled her duties as a wife as faithfully as if she had married from Love."[10]

Martha and James lived in Savannah, on Liberty County plantations, and in Hartford, Connecticut, in the following years. Their first child Anna Louisa, born in 1833, joined the family while in one of their southern residences. It was during their extended stay in Hartford, where James Dunwoody Bulloch, age 14, Susan Elliott, age 15, Georgia Elliott, age 13, and Daniel Elliott, age nine, were attending school that *Mittie* was born on 8 July 1835.[11]

In the spring of 1838, Martha, James, and four of their children (Susan, Georgia, Anna, and Mittie) left Savannah for the "colony" at Roswell, Georgia.[12] Fifteen-year-old James Dunwoody Bulloch and eleven-year-old Daniel did not make the trip with the rest of the family, as both still attended boarding school in Middletown, Connecticut. James Bulloch had invested in the Roswell Manufacturing Company, newly established in the town, and had received acreage for a home as part of the deal. Located in Georgia's Piedmont region, Roswell sprang into being due to the efforts of Roswell King and his son Barrington. In the early 1830s, Roswell King had initiated a plan to build a cotton mill on Vickery Creek on what was then Cherokee land. He and his son purchased land lots, started recruiting investors, and began building the mill and other business concerns. James Bulloch invested in the company early in its conception.

It is believed that six slaves joined James and Martha on the journey. These were most likely *Daddy* Luke Moumar,[13] the butler and handyman, and his wife *Maum* Charlotte, the housekeeper, along with *Daddy* Stephen, the coachman, *Maum* Rose, the cook, *Daddy* William, and *Maum* Grace, the nursemaid.[14] Taking along oxcarts of belongings, the family traveled first by sloop or steamship to Augusta, and then by coach across eastern Georgia to the Chattahoochee River, and finally on to Roswell.

The family lived in an abandoned Cherokee cabin, which they called *Clifton Farm*, while their new home was under construction. Clifton lay approximately four miles east of what would become Bulloch Hall. Willis Ball, a Connecticut skilled-builder, designed and built their new Roswell town house. Historic preservation architects agree he based his work on the widely-used Asher Benjamin books such as *The Architect, or Practical House Carpenter* and *The American Builder's Companion*. With Tuscan columns across its wide veranda, the lovely home sat at the end of a long lane leading to the town square.[15]

In late 1838 or early 1839, their family expanded with the birth of Charles Irvine. He was baptized by the visiting Reverend Nathaniel A. Pratt during his first trip to the colony on 20 October 1839, the same day the Roswell Presbyterian Church was organized. Two years later, in 1841, Charles Irvine Bulloch died at age two years and nine months of scarlet fever. The family buried him in the new town cemetery, now known as *Founders Cemetery*. In 1842, Martha delivered her ninth and last child, Irvine Stephens Bulloch.

The family worshiped at the Presbyterian Church, only a short walk down Mimosa Boulevard from their home. Anna, Mittie, and Irvine attended the Academy, Roswell's school, built directly north of the church. They socialized with the colony's other prominent founders, the Barrington King family, the Archibald Smith family, the Reverend Nathaniel A. Pratt family, and their cousins, the family of John Dunwoody. John had married James Stephens Bulloch's sister Jane in 1808. They raised five sons and one daughter. The Dunwoodys occupied Phoenix Hall (now called Mimosa Hall[16]) directly adjoining the Bulloch property. The family frequently traveled to the coast to visit friends and relatives. The Bullochs were wealthy, well educated, and well traveled.

At the time of the family's move to Roswell, tragedy struck again. In June of 1838, headed north for the summer, Robert Hutchison, his wife, and their two small daughters boarded the Steamship *Pulaski* in Savannah. Just off the coast of Palmetto Bluff, South Carolina, during the night, the *Pulaski's* boiler exploded killing Corinne and their youngest daughter immediately. Robert survived the explosion, clinging to debris with others for several days. His oldest daughter also survived for a period of time, but was swept from his arms into the ocean during a storm not long before their rescue. Robert, along with 58 others, lived. Approximately 100 men, women, and children perished.[17] Despite the loss of his wife and daughters, Robert continued his relationship with the Bulloch/Elliott family.

Bulloch Hall, circa 1934,
Historic American Buildings Survey

Years passed, children grew, and life in Roswell for the Bulloch family was filled with social events, church, school, and trips south to Savannah. James Dunwoody Bulloch entered the U. S. Navy as a midshipman in 1839.[18] In 1848, Georgia Amanda Elliott died of consumption, known today as tuberculosis. Georgia left her portion of her father's estate to her sister Susan, her brother Daniel, and her mother Martha. Soon after Georgia's death, Susan Ann Elliott accepted a proposal of marriage from Hilborne West (1818-1907) of Philadelphia, and they married in a quiet ceremony the following January in Bulloch Hall. Susan was almost 29, and Hilborne was two years older.

Hilborne West was the son of James (1785-1867) and Rebecca West, who resided at 1316 Walnut Street in Philadelphia. James had married Rebecca Coe (1791-1882) on 30 October 1816. The city's 1830 directory listed James as a "Gentleman."[19] James' family had owned wharves and ships in Philadelphia for at least three generations back to James West (1658-1701), a shipwright, who had emigrated from England before 1683.[20] The term *gentleman* denoted a level of financial independence and status. James was listed with this designation for most of his adult life. He took up residence at 366 Walnut Street as early as 1849, and lived at 1316 Walnut Street from 1859 until his death in 1867.[21]

In February 1849, James Stephens Bulloch died while teaching Sunday school at the Roswell Presbyterian Church. Martha lived exclusively in Roswell, visiting Savannah and Liberty County only occasionally. Susan and Hilborne continued to reside with her and her children for several years, although they traveled to Philadelphia on occasion to visit his family. Daniel Stewart Elliott, Martha's son from her first marriage, attended Princeton for three years before returning home. He often traveled to Europe for extended periods with her former step-son-in-law and family friend Robert Hutchison.

As Anna and Mittie grew to be young women, Martha sent them to Barhamville, South Carolina, to Dr. Marks' South Carolina Female Academy, often called Barham's Academy, to further their education. Dr. Marks located his academy near Columbia, South Carolina, and named the area Barhamville. A physician by training but educator by choice, Dr. Marks opened his academy on 1 October 1828. His original idea was a place with "scale of economy" that would make it affordable to those of moderate circumstances.[22] The school offered four years of studies built on a collegiate basis and soon attracted the daughters of many of central South Carolina's wealthiest planters. The girls studied the ornamental arts, the Classics, music, dancing, and languages such as French, Italian, Spanish, and Latin. Marks and his wife, fellow educator Jane Barham (1788-1827), the area and the school's namesake, thought studying these subjects would create a so-called *accomplished lady*. After the death of Jane Barham, Marks hired and later married Julia Pierpont Warne, head of a flourishing girls' school at Sparta, Georgia.[23]

Mittie and Anna lived at the school for two terms each year. They were well attended with servants to draw baths, tend fires, and see to their needs. School rules required them to write home on the first day of each month. The staff inspected all incoming letters, and those deemed of a "trifling nature" were frowned upon. The girls were not even permitted to converse with a young man without the written permission of their parents. By the early 1850s, the school had more than 100 young ladies in attendance, and bookkeeping had been added as a new course.[24] It is not clear how long the girls attended the Academy; however, they were in attendance in the fall of 1849.

On 11 July 1849, their half-brother, James Dunwoody Bulloch, *Brother Jimmie*, a midshipman in the United States Navy, wrote of his stepmother and half-sisters:

> Mother bears her weight of years most stoutly & with the meekness woman only knows, regards her cares & sorrows as the will of her maker. With my two little sisters I am delighted. They have grown up fine full graceful girls, intelligent & full of loving kindness. Though differing in many respects, they are each quite perfect in their peculiar style. 'Mitty' as we call the younger is a black haired bright eyed lassie lively in her disposition with a ready tongue, she does everything by impulse and with an air of perfect self confidence, but she is a warm hearted little darling. Annie is a sensitive confiding little creature, all heart & soul with large soft slowly winking eyes & great long lashes. She does every thing with gentleness &

has a way of nestling by her brothers side which is truly touching.[25]

Martha *Mittie* Bulloch Roosevelt, age 22,
Courtesy of the Theodore Roosevelt Collection,
Houghton Library, Harvard University

Anna Louisa Bulloch, age unknown,
Courtesy of the Theodore Roosevelt Collection,
Houghton Library, Harvard University

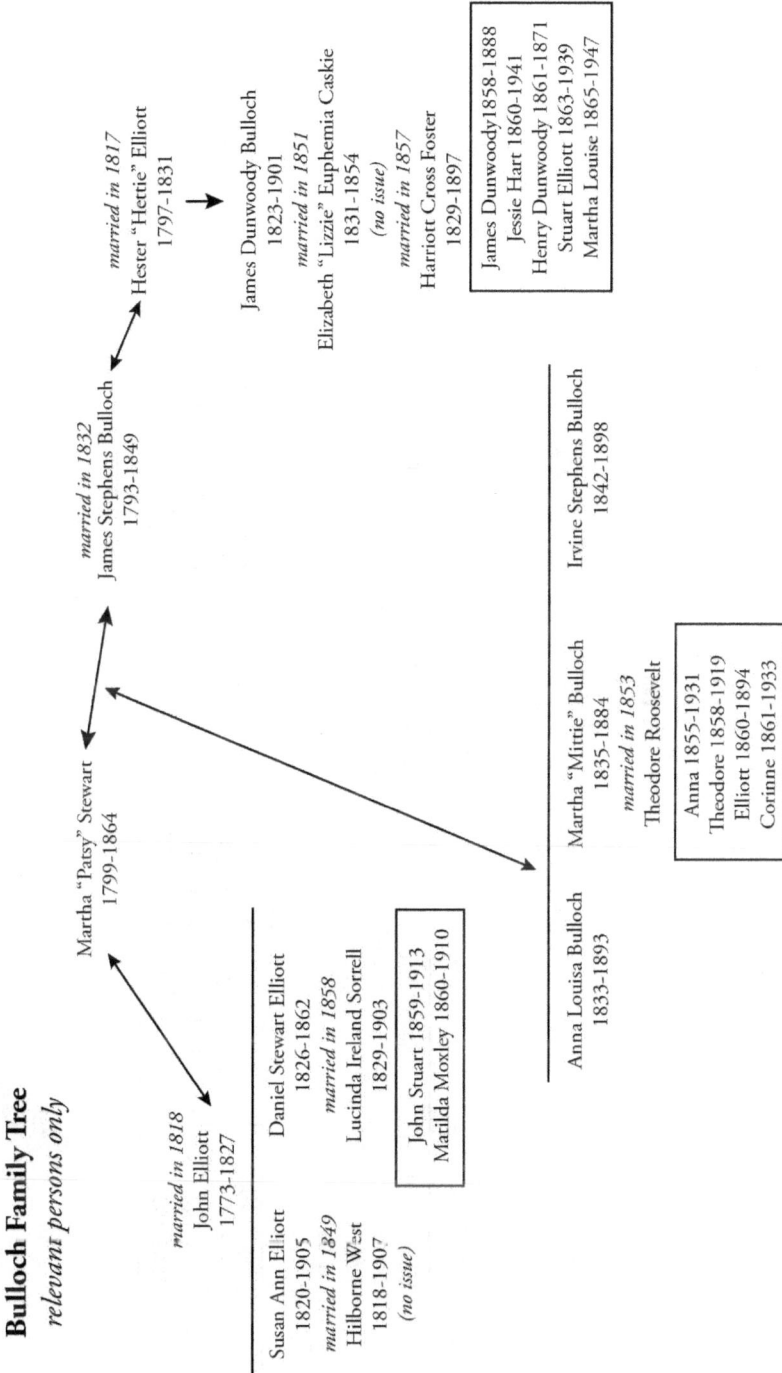

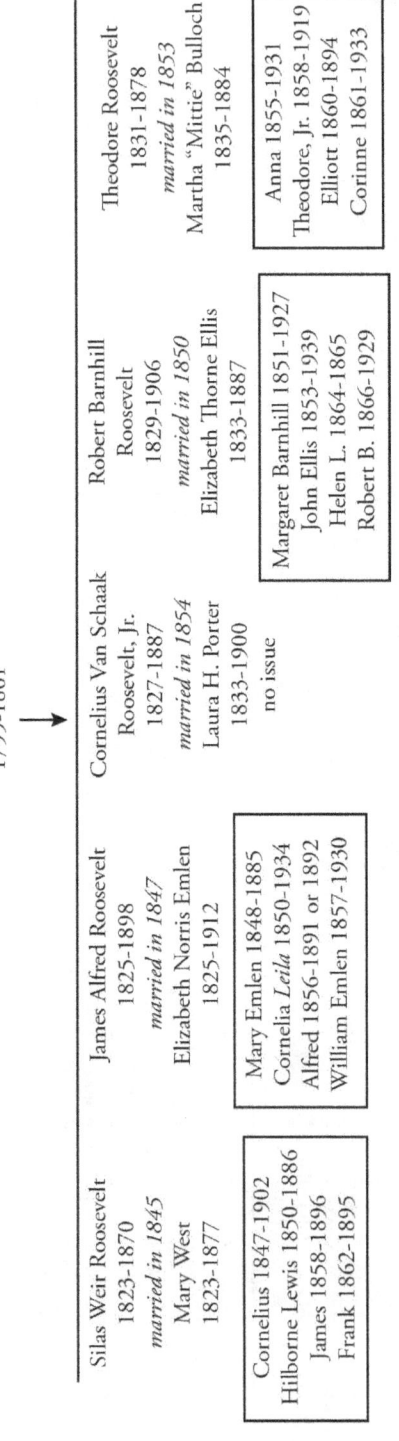

Roosevelt Family
relevant persons only

Cornelius Van Schaak Roosevelt
1794-1871
married
Margaret Barnhill
1799-1861

Silas Weir Roosevelt
1823-1870
married in 1845
Mary West
1823-1877

- Cornelius 1847-1902
- Hilborne Lewis 1850-1886
- James 1858-1896
- Frank 1862-1895

James Alfred Roosevelt
1825-1898
married in 1847
Elizabeth Norris Emlen
1825-1912

- Mary Emlen 1848-1885
- Cornelia *Leila* 1850-1934
- Alfred 1856-1891 or 1892
- William Emlen 1857-1930

Cornelius Van Schaak Roosevelt, Jr.
1827-1887
married in 1854
Laura H. Porter
1833-1900
no issue

Robert Barnhill Roosevelt
1829-1906
married in 1850
Elizabeth Thorne Ellis
1833-1887

- Margaret Barnhill 1851-1927
- John Ellis 1853-1939
- Helen L. 1864-1865
- Robert B. 1866-1929

Theodore Roosevelt
1831-1878
married in 1853
Martha "Mittie" Bulloch
1835-1884

- Anna 1855-1931
- Theodore, Jr. 1858-1919
- Elliott 1860-1894
- Corinne 1861-1933

The Roosevelt Family

Now that we have set the scene in Roswell, the much less confusing New York side of this story needs to be told. Wealthy New York businessman, Cornelius Van Schaak Roosevelt (1794-1871) and his wife Margaret Barnhill (1790-1861) raised five sons: Silas Weir (1823-1870), James Alfred (1825-1898), Cornelius Van Schaak, Jr. (1827-1887), Robert Barnhill (1829-1906), and Theodore (1831-1878).[26]

The Roosevelts lived on the corner of 14th Street and Broadway in Manhattan. Theodore's father, Cornelius, was a glass merchant, an ultraconservative abolitionist, and a Quaker by birth. Cornelius' forefather, Claes Martenszen van Rosenvelt, had arrived in the New York area in 1644. Claes' son Nicholas' two sons established the two branches of the family. Johannes (1689-1750) established the Oyster Bay Roosevelts, while Jacobus (1692-1776) established the line known as the Hyde Park Roosevelts. Each line would later produce an American president. During the intervening years, family members married into Welsh, English, Scottish, Irish, and German families, creating an all-American blood line by the time of the American Revolution.

Cornelius' business at 94 Maiden Lane started in hardware, and by the 1850s, specialized in plate glass. Cornelius also held positions in banking and invested heavily in real estate, often buying low during economic recessions and selling for profit once the market returned. The family held a great deal of wealth in New York and surrounding areas.

Theodore's 1851 passport application gave an accurate description of him as a 19-year-old man. The description states he stood six feet tall, had a high forehead, blue eyes, and a thick nose on a long face. His mouth and chin are listed as large, with lighter hair and a light complexion.[27]

Theodore *Thee* Roosevelt, age 31,
Courtesy of the Theodore Roosevelt Collection,
Houghton Library, Harvard University

The Beginnings of the Romance

How Mittie and Thee, two such different people, from so very disparate backgrounds came to meet, is an intriguing story of nineteenth-century connections. Two early-twentieth-century books give us what may be conflicting stories. Yet, like many oft repeated tales, they may just be variations of one story. Corinne Roosevelt, their daughter wrote:

> [speaking of Roswell] . . . There the beautiful half-sister of my mother, Susan Elliott, brought her Northern lover, Hilborne West, of Philadelphia, whose sister, Mary West, had shortly before married Weir Roosevelt, of New York, the older brother of my father, Theodore Roosevelt. This same Hilborne West, a young physician, of brilliant promise, adored the informal, fascinating plantation life, and loved the companionship of the two dainty, pretty girls of fourteen and sixteen, Martha and Anna Bulloch, his fiancée's young half-sisters.[28]
> Many were the private theatricals and riding-parties, and during that first gay visit Doctor West constantly spoke of his young connection by marriage, Theodore Roosevelt, who he felt would love Roswell as he did.
> A year afterward, inspired by the stories of Doctor West, my father, a young man of nineteen, asked if he might pay a visit at the old plantation, and there began the love-affair with a black-haired girl of fifteen which later was to develop into so deep a devotion that when the young Roosevelt, two years later, returned from a trip abroad and found this same young girl visiting her sister in Philadelphia, he succumbed at once to the fascination from which he had never fully recovered, and later travelled [sp] once more to the old pillared house on the

sandhills of Georgia to carry Martha Bulloch away from her Southern-home forever.[29]

Silas Weir Roosevelt and Mary West married in 1845. Susan Elliott and Hilborne West married in January of 1849. If as Corinne stated, Theodore was 19 when he met Mittie, then this would have been in 1850. Historic records show that Theodore visited Roswell in February of 1851 and was introduced as a friend of Mr. West.[30] Yet in *The Boys' Life of Theodore Roosevelt*, Hermann Hagedorn stated that Mittie and Theodore met at the wedding of Susan and Hilborne.[31] Despite this discrepancy over their initial meeting, it seems that Mittie and Thee met several times between their first encounter and the winter of 1852 in Philadelphia. The story continued in early 1853 with Anna Bulloch returning South while Mittie visited Thee's family in New York.

In the spring of 1853, Mittie and Thee began eight months of courtship correspondence interrupted by Thee's visit to Roswell in July. They married on 22 December 1853 in Bulloch Hall. The couple then moved north to New York City and took up residence with Thee's parents.[32]

The second book in this series, *Between the Wedding & the War*, presents the family correspondence beginning in the year 1854 and ending in December of 1860. Numerous events took place during these six years. Mittie and Thee produced three children, the first arriving in 1855. Anna, known as *Bamie*, arrived on 7 January of that year. Theodore, most often called *Teedie*, followed on 27 October 1858. They added a second son with the birth of Elliott, shortened to *Ellie*, on 28 February 1860.

Thee and Mittie moved into a home of their own at 33 East 20th Street by 1855. Robert, called *Rob*, and Elizabeth *Lizzie* Ellis Roosevelt lived in the adjoining home, 31 East 20th. As each of his sons married, C.V. Roosevelt purchased the new couple a home. Robert and Theodore married in 1850 and 1853 respectively, so their homes adjoined. Rob and Lizzie had two children, Margaret and John Ellis, known as *Johnnie*. Rob worked as a lawyer; his office was at 76 William Street.³³

As for the other Roosevelt sons, Silas Weir and Mary had three children: Cornelius, born in 1847, Hilborne *Hilly* born in 1850, and James born in 1858. A Columbia University graduate, Silas also practiced law at 76 William Street with his brother Robert, who had attended Harvard Law in 1848. Silas and Mary lived at 1 East 20ᵗʰ Street in 1859, next door to James and his family. However, by 1863, they had moved to 39 East 12ᵗʰ Street.³⁴

James, called *Jim*, and Elizabeth *Lizzie* (Emlen) had four children: Mary, born in 1848, Cornelia, born in 1850, Alfred, born in 1856, and William born in 1857. In the late 1850s, James' family lived next door to Silas at 3 East 20ᵗʰ Street. After the death of Margaret Roosevelt, James moved his family to 849 Broadway, his father's home. James worked with Theodore in the family glass/hardware business located at 94 Maiden Lane.³⁵

Cornelius Van Schaak Roosevelt, Jr., married Laura H. Porter in 1854. Instead of a house in the city, Cornelius Senior purchased several acres in 1855 in Maplewood, New Jersey, and sold the land to his middle son Cornelius for one dollar. More land was purchased over time, and the whole estate consisted of more than 100 acres during their residence. Cornelius and Laura built a large rambling house called *The Hickories* in the mid-1860s. They lived there until Cornelius' death in 1887. Cornelius developed his property into a park-like setting with trees, gardens, ponds, and orchards connected by trails. The Roosevelt brothers often brought their families to *The Hickories* for outings and overnight visits. Cornelius and Laura had no children of their own.³⁶

Before their home was completed, U.S. Census records for 1860 show Cornelius and Laura living in Milburn, New Jersey, with three female Irish servants. The 1870 census shows them in South Orange (now Maplewood) with three different female Irish servants and two Black male servants. By the 1880 census, Cornelius and Laura had another set of three Irish servants.

1- Cornelius, Sr. & James
2- Silas by 1863
3- Robert
4- Theodore
5- Maiden Line
6- Law offices

In January of 1856, Thee traveled to New Orleans for the wedding of James Dunwoody Bulloch. This was James' second marriage. His first ended in 1854 with the death of his wife Elizabeth Euphemia Caskie. James also resigned from the U.S. Navy in October of 1854 and now captained a steamship for the U.S. Mail service. His second wife, a widow, Harriott Cross Foster, lived near New Orleans. Their marriage had by 1860 produced two children; James Dunwoody, born in 1858 and Jessie Hart, a girl born in 1860. The family resided in New York City.

With two of her daughters and her first grandchild living in the North, Martha Bulloch packed up two of her remaining unmarried children, son Irvine, and daughter Anna, and moved to Philadelphia in the late fall of 1855. Irvine would attend preparatory school and then college. The family resided with Susan and Hilborne, who now studied medicine at Jefferson Medical College in that city. Anna soon began to split her time between New York and Philadelphia, with frequent trips to Richmond to visit the Caskie family.

Daniel Stuart [previously Stewart] Elliott, Martha's oldest son, resided in Savannah and traveled to Europe several times before settling down and marrying Lucinda Ireland Sorrel in 1858. After a lengthy honeymoon trip to the North, the couple lived in Marietta, Roswell, and Savannah in the coming years. Their first child, John Stuart was born in 1859, followed by Matilda Moxley in 1860.

The end of 1860, a time of great political turmoil and unrest, found the close-knit family *divided* only by *distance*—Philadelphia to New York to Savannah—and *allegiance*. Martha still owned Bulloch Hall and at least two slaves in Roswell. Irvine attended the University of Pennsylvania. Hilborne practiced medicine, and Thee continued in the family business. In Savannah, Stuart worked in banking. Brother Jimmie served as a steamship captain. However, the two families, deeply committed to each other, held opposite political views. The Bulloch women, Martha, Susan, Mittie, and Anna, and men, James, Daniel Stuart, and Irvine, stood with the South. Hilborne's family and the Roosevelts believed in the Union of States. Martha, Susan and Hilborne had expressed views of desiring and expecting the end of slavery. Yet, Martha and Susan held with the idea of the State's right to decide.[37]

Chapter 2: January through June of 1861

The World in 1861

In the last months of 1860, the world watched as Kentucky-born Abraham Lincoln, running on an anti-slavery platform, defeated three opponents for the U.S. presidency. Lincoln's election instigated cries of rebellion in the nation's slave states. South Carolina led the revolt and, became on 20 December 1860, became the first southern state to secede from the Union. On 4 February 1861, at a convention in Montgomery, Alabama, seven southern states formed the Confederate States of America electing Jefferson Davis of Kentucky as their president. On 4 March, Lincoln took the oath of office as President of the United States.

In January, Congress established three new territories, Colorado, Nevada, and Dakota. On 29 January, Kansas joined the Union as the 34th State. However, Congress' focus centered on developments in the southern states, where hostility, debate, and rhetoric ran rampant. On 12 April 1861, fighting broke out in Charleston, South Carolina's harbor when Confederate forces bombarded Fort Sumter for 34 hours after the U.S. Army commander failed to evacuate the Union-held fort. Union Major Robert Anderson surrendered the fort on the 14th and turned it over to the Confederacy. Taking immediate action, President Lincoln called for 75,000 volunteers to fight the secessionist Confederate States of America. By May, eleven states had joined the Confederacy.

On 19 April, Lincoln initiated a naval blockade of the Confederate States and in early May requested an addition of 42,000 men for the U.S. Army and the addition of 18,000 seamen. This blockade had the immediate effect of limiting the South's ability to import weapons and ammunition from Europe and to transfer funds from the North to the South.

In the previous year, Benjamin Henry had perfected his Henry Repeating Rifle, manufactured by the New Haven Arms Company of New Haven, Connecticut. The first of its kind, Henry's rifle could be loaded once, with self-contained metal cartridges, and fired multiple times. This development in firearms production would greatly influence the outcome of the coming war.

Around the world, events occurred that would also have long-lasting effects. Tsar Alexander II proclaimed the emancipation of all Russia's serfs. On 18 February, King Victor Emmanuel II of Sardinia became the first king of Italy. After a unification campaign led by Giuseppe Garibaldi, Italy united under Emmanuel's reign. In response to developments in the United States, Queen Victoria announced Britain's neutrality on 13 May.

On 1 March, the Pony Express stopped service. The company's huge losses and failure to continue to hold the contract for western mail delivery led to its demise. Additionally, telegraphic service inched its way across the continent and connected the eastern states and west coast territories before the year's end.[38] On 1 June, the United States and the Confederate States halted mail service to each other. This would severely limit the Bulloch ladies' communications with various relatives and friends in the South.

The Letters

Phil[a] Jan 18th 1861

My own dear Susy,
This morning directly after breakfast your dear letter was handed in by Hannah together with one to Anna from darling Mittie - Your letters are even like cold water to a

thirsty soul. My darling blessed child how I do wish that your time <u>was</u> over with the D^r that you could leave your "little Hospital bed," and occupy your own nice high level bed- but we must have patience darling - I am so glad the D^r thinks you are better - What a subject for gratitude is this - I am glad little Mittie goes to see you often and that you can sometimes see the dear children - what a companionable little thing Bamie [Anna Roosevelt] is - I know exactly how she will look when she dines with you - She will put on what Mittie calls the rag - baby look - This is her birth day, little darling! We do enjoy our nice beds very much in order not to make our beds sink in the middle Anna and I sleep first on one side of the bed and then on the other. Anna says she calculates the exact spot on which she sleeps every night so as never to sleep on the same spot two nights in succession - We went last night to a party at Mrs Pattersons - I sat on one of the sofas with old Mrs Baud all of the evening, so I enjoyed the evening - I do not think Anna and Hill were as comfortable as I was - However we all liked the supper which was a very nice one - Hill says the chicken salad was splendid - I think he must have done justice to the good things, as he confessed this morning that he had a night mare in the night - Anna says she does not know who heard him when he talked like forty doll [forty dollars] The house keeping all goes on very well - today we have a piece of roast mutton & Hill said he would rather go without currant jelly than to trouble his head about getting any - Anna says she could only make your Tiny last night wear one glove and carry the other in his hand. And this one glove was worn merely to enter the room - I am glad Mrs Roosevelt is better - I hope she may get on quite well - I have not heard lately from Stuart [Daniel Stuart Elliott] - Anna has written Lucy - We will attend to the settlement with the 16 St man today - Irvine is much more at home than formerly, and I think studies better also - I will not send Lucy, things for a long time to come as I have to have her dress dyed - The three dollars which you are to hand to Mittie I wish you to tell her are from me, and that I will write her very shortly what to

do with it - With much love to Mitty and yourself in which Anna - joins I am your most
affec Mother M Bulloch

Beginning in October 1860, Martha wrote from Philadelphia to Susan, a patient at the Hospital for Women in New York City, where she received treatment for an unspecified illness. Dr. J. Marion Semmes ran the hospital and specialized in gynecology, leading to the belief Susan's illness was most likely related to his specialty.[39] This letter coming in January, some four months later, finds Susan still in New York. Martha and Anna lived with Dr. Hilborne West, Susan's *Tiny*. This nickname first appeared in the October 1860 letters and can now be attributed to Hilborne.

Despite all the happenings in the South, Irvine still studied at the University of Pennsylvania. In the following letter, Martha continued to write of daily events, housekeeping, and minutia, first mentioning the growing tension between the North and the South.

Phil Jan 24, 1861

My very dear daughter,
Hill requested me this morning to write you a few lines as he thought it probable he would not be able to write at all today - We are all well darling but very gloomy on account of the extreme illness of Mr Lewis, and the intelligence received in a letter to Mrs West from Mary [West Roosevelt] that Mrs Roosevelt was very sick - Last night Hill staid all night at the Lewis' and came home this morning just to bathe and change his linen - He then went back saying he probably would not be back home at all today. He said he persuaded the young ladies to take a little rest last night and that he and Dr Lewis remained all night with the old gentleman - I think they entertain no hope of his life - He is at present in a stupor - I believe he cannot swallow at all - Oh Suzy dear we felt so dreadfully last evening - Just before tea time Mr Platt

rung the bell and asked for you - when he was told that Hill was out, and you were not at home he asked to see Anna if she was in - He told Anna then that Dr Lewis had requested him to call and ask Hill to go the Lewis' as Mr Lewis was very sick indeed - Hill went directly, and Anna Irvine and I went to lecture - Soon after we returned home Hill came in and said we might fasten the port door as he would not return before morning - At the same time he told us of the illness of Mrs Roosevelt - Just as I got this far in my letter Hill has come in to let us know that our beloved friend Mrs Roosevelt was dead - Oh Suzy dear what a terrible affliction is this - Poor Thee I do pity him from the very bottom of my heart - I am sorry for all of the family - but I know how Thee loved her - I know you and Mittie will try to comfort him - I have heard lately from Stuart - His cough is no better - He says he thinks he is upon the whole rather worse than when I was in Sav - He is unwilling to make the least exertion - feels no energy, and has a let-everything-go-to-the-dogs kind of general feeling that is equally distressing and alarming - Those are his words - Anna sends much love to you - we all long for you here but we must be patient - Anna says she showed her Album to Miss Lily Lewis and that she admired it very much - Mr Lewis is no better. The weather has been very has been very bad - Yesterday was the first good day we have had - We went to see Mrs West in the morning, but found her from home - late in the afternoon she came to see us - As usual she was very entertaining - She does not approve of the course of South Carolina, but in other respects she is entirely Southern in her views - She regrets that Penn gave the Republican vote and says it was owing entirely to their desires for a high tariff on iron - but I must close Goodbye for the present dear darling Suzy.

Your affec Mother
M Bulloch

You must not trouble yourself to write me darling - I hear through Hill's letter and that will answer - I think "house"

is going on very well - Goodbye darling - May God bless you
Your affec Mother
M Bulloch

With Susan still in New York, Martha wrote of bad tidings in Philadelphia. Hilborne and Dr. Frances West Lewis (1825-1902) had been attending Mordecai D. Lewis, "an old and respected merchant."[40] Mordecai's son Dr. Lewis was Hilborne's first cousin, through Mordecai's wife Sarah Francis West Lewis. She was the sister of Hilborne's father, James West. Their mother was Elizabeth Hilborne (1763-1825), explaining Hilborne's unusual first name. The Lewis family were Quakers. Mordecai passed late on the 24th, the same day Martha wrote Susan.

Bad tidings also arrived from New York as Martha and Hilborne received news of the passing of Thee's mother Margaret Roosevelt on 23 January. Margaret was 61 years old, according to the *New York Times*.[41]

A letter from Stuart Elliott told his mother about his continuing battle with tuberculosis. Stuart's condition had been worsening for several years. This letter also revealed that Martha had visited Stuart in Savannah sometime during the recent past. Stuart lived in Savannah during the mid-1850s, but by 1859 appears to have returned to the Marietta/Roswell area of Georgia.

At the end of the letter, Martha turned to the politics of the time. Martha mentioned Rebecca Coe West (1791-1882), Hilborne's mother; however, why she held Southern sympathies is not known. Little is known of Rebecca Coe, except she was a Quaker and married James West on 3 October 1816. A Quaker marriage record annotation showed this was James second marriage.

No family letters can be found for the next few months. The next letter in the collection, dated 31 May, was from Colonel William Hardee, now in the Confederate States Army. The Confederate States formed in February of 1861 and quickly started recruiting for their army.[42] Many Southern-born, U.S. Army officers resigned their commissions and immediately applied to the Confederacy for commissions.

Captain James Dunwoody Bulloch, Martha's stepson and captain of the Steamship *Bienville*, had resigned and turned his ship over to its owners on 23 April directly after arriving in New York. James, once a commissioned U. S Navy officer, had already written to Confederate Attorney General Benjamin offering his services for the Confederate Navy. On the next morning, 24 April, James received a letter from Secretary of the Confederate Sates Navy Stephen Mallory accepting his offer and posting him to Liverpool, England. James first traveled South to Birmingham, Alabama, to meet with Mallory. James greatly desired an appointment as a ship of war's captain.[43]

In early May, as James journeyed South, so did his half-brother Irvine. It is possible they traveled together. By the end of May, Irvine had applied for a position on the C.S.S. *Savannah* under the command of John Newland Maffitt. As Maffitt and James had both arrived in Montgomery on 7 May, it is very likely James persuaded Maffitt, with whom he had served in the U.S. Navy, to add Irvine to his crew and helped him obtain a commission as a midshipman.[44] It appears that Irvine or some member of his family also "arranged" for Irvine to receive a commission—this time in the Confederate States Army.

> Hd Quarters, Fort Morgan
> May 31 1861
> Honb L.P. Walker
> Sec of War,
>
> Sir,
> I take pleasure in recommending Mr. Irvine Bulloch of Geo for an appointment as cadet. He was at school at the North, but feeling it was his duty to serve his country he left school and returned home to seek employment in the Confederate States Services. I have recommended him, as he but nineteen years old to apply for a cadet's appointment which you will give him. He is a young man of fine talents,

manly in his bearing, of robust constitution, and an earnest advocate of the rights of the South. If appointed, I should esteem it a personal favor if you would attach him to a company stationed at this fort as I would like to have charge of his military education.

      With { } respect
      Yr 'ob' servant
      WJ Hardee.
      Col. C.S.A.

    Head Ins. Military District
    Savannah Geo — 18<u>th</u> June 1861

I take great pleasure in adding my testimony to that of Col. Hardee the appointment of Mr. Bulloch as a cadet would secure the services of an ardent & capable youth to the Confederate States, and gratify a large circle of friends, all of whom are true friends of our cause

      With much rgard
      Yr. obt servant
      AR Lawton
      Brig. Genl. {B_____}[45]

Either Irvine, or his family, had no doubt applied to Colonel William Hardee on the young man's behalf. Letters from mid-to-late 1860 indicate Hardee and Anna Bulloch had courted. Hardee wrote to Confederate Secretary of War LeRoy Pope Walker (1817-1884) at Fort Morgan, Alabama, to ask for the appointment for Irvine. Alexander Lawton (1818-1896), of Beaufort County, South Carolina, added his endorsement of Irvine. Lawton was a long time family friend and a distant relative by marriage.

      June 1st 1861
My dear Thee
  We feel very anxious about dear little Tedie - this cough has been of such long continuance that fever would

seem like inflammation or some change for the worse in his condition - You say the D^r does not think him seriously sick but has he been roused up fairly to the length of time the dear little boy has had the cough! I can not bear to think of his breathing rapidly and being nervous - at night sometimes lightheaded I am afraid he is sicker than the D^r thinks - Do let us know soon how he is - Mother says if he should get any sicker and you or Mittie would like to have her there she could go on at a very short notice to him as we here all packed to go on last wednesday south - She would not go unless it became <u>necessary</u> which we do hope and trust may not be the case, as if no change takes place in our affairs we will be with you all at Long branch for the summer. So Sister has begged her unless dear little Tedie should be much sicker than your letter now indicates to stay where she can have Mother until you go to Long branch - Do tell us exactly when you expect to go there as we will go at the same time would it be a good plan for us to meet you in New York and go down all together or would it be more convenient to you for Mother and I to meet you the first day you are up in the city after having deposited your family quietly there - I ask these questions as Irvine is not here to take care of us Hill says he will see that we get off safely for New York, if you plan it so that you could meet us there and let us go from that place with you - Now I suppose you are wondering how we are so sanguine as to hope again that we need not go way off all those thousands of miles from all of you whom we love <u>so</u> much - Well I "first and foremost" as Bamie asked to say Mr Brantly the gentlemen who so kindly promised to take charge of us is not going for sometime yet, indeed he has postponed his departure almost indefinitely for the same reasons that we so much dreaded the journey for Mother its length and the very great fatigue attending it. This left us without any available escort, and besides Thee on Wednesday morning I received a letter from Cousin William G Bulloch of Savannah inclosing Mothers June dividend from the central RR Bank nearly three weeks before it was due and at five percent as usual - The letter must have {been} brought on here by private opportunity as it came to me by the city penny post. It was very kind and thoughtful in him as he did not even have Mothers order to draw it - he is in the C.R.R bank [Central Rail Road and Banking Company of Georgia] and they must have unlimited confidence in him to permit him to have done so - Long ago just as Gov Browns [Joseph M. Brown of Georgia] proclamation came out I wrote to him to know how it could affect us thinking he would know just what was thought of it there but that was so long ago and the mails being entirely stopped I had no idea we could ever hear from him, and as I had only asked his opinion as a lawyer on the proclamation you can not think how his letter has relieved and astonished us - Mother has sent on to him to draw and keep for her all that becomes due until October of course if he <u>can</u> he will send it on to her possibly as he did this sum. I forgot to mention there was no exchange sum on this! If he can not get it on to her it is perfectly safe in his hands and Mother would not mind if it became necessary taking some of her beaver-meadow [Beaver Meadow Rail Road] now that she feels so sure of that being so well attended to out there - This great cause of anxiety being in a great measure removed sister and I have influenced her to wait about brother [Stuart Elliott] until the fall he may be benefited by the change up to Marietta and by that time some way may be opened more safe at least not so expensive and being for one of her age as the only one now open through the first - I hope I have not wearied you by this long account but you have been so kind and shown yourself such a dependable friend all through our troubles that in thought you would be glad to know things here looking a little brighter for us - Mother did not think it would be safe for her to make her property over to the English house as you suggest on account of her uncertainty about brother if she goes out to him it would be very bad not to be able to get her money out there - I can not tell you how very grateful I am that we can stay for it was so dreary to go off only two of us in time of war and not ever hear from you all and the blessed little children - and tho I did not like not to follow your advice and the advice of all of our friends here which was to stay quietly for the present - Thee we all think it is <u>too</u> <u>much</u> of a <u>risk</u> for Bamie to sit in the seat by you driving unless she is <u>fastened</u> to you in some way - She is so very light and her feet not touching she has no way of bracing herself and even if she <u>holds</u> on a sudden start of the horses or a very trifling elevation or stone in the road would certainly throw her out - I was thrown out once driving with my Father when I was much larger and stronger than Bamie and the wheel ran over my legs I was not hurt because the sand road was so soft that I sank down and escaped the weight of the waggon but it was a great jar one poor little Bamie could not stand afflicted as she is - I know the dear little girl is delighted with the importance of her position and enjoys it intensely but we feel so <u>afraid</u> Best Love from all to Mittie and yourself do let us hear very soon how dear precious little Tedie is -

      Your aff sister -
       Anna

  Anna's letter to Thee gave our first reference to Teedie's asthma, an affliction that continued throughout his childhood. Anna and Martha, currently living in Philadelphia with Susan and Hilborne, had packed their belongings and prepared to go South to Roswell to be with Stuart and his family. Amidst their disrupted travel plans, Teedie's illness, Mittie's fourth pregnancy, and all the political turmoil, Martha and Anna prepared instead to join the Roosevelt families at Long Branch, New Jersey, for the summer.

          Roswell June 17th
My Dear Mother
  I received a few days ago your letter of May 14th and to day I received your letter dated May 29th sent by Mr Brantly We were delighted to hear from you - It was our unexpected pleasure as we had no hope of hearing anything

of you now- I have just heard of Mr Adones expected departure tomorrow for the North to see his dying brother - and take that occasion as a God send to write you -

Stuart is better, altho he depends much upon Morphine which he takes daily to ease his pain - Oh I would give anything to see him again in the enjoyment of good health. He so often wishes for it - We are very comfortable here - and I am perfectly satisfied. My baby has been very sick - fever and sick stomach with four teeth coming through. She has two now - I felt so uneasy about her- especially as there was no Alapothic [allopathic] Physician here - and having no faith in Homeopathy I felt in dispair - but she is now better altho so debilitative and very weak - Johnnie is very well - says everything now - he is very stout and browner than ever - I wish you could see how deferential Daddy Luke is to him - I intend to make Johnnie present him with a nice pair of pants or coat of Stuarts that he no longer uses. Mom Charlotte sent him a half dozen eggs as soon as he arrived. I took him to their cottage to see them - and found the old pair very comfortable

We often speak of you dear Mother - and I feel deeply for you, for you occupy a trying position - with your heart in the South- you have those so dear to you at the North - We were speaking of it this morning - and among our measured acquaintence I do not <u>know</u> of even one in <u>so</u> unfortunate a position

I am afraid that it may be some time too before things are settled. Do give my warmest love to Tudie [Susan] Anna Hill and Mittie when you see her - I hope her little ones are well. What little sweeties they are

I have scarcly been out since my arrival here - for I was indisposed at first and then Mattie's sickness together with Stuart daily febleness rendered me miserable to go out. I can not therefore tell you much about Roswell. I like all the Kings extremely. We went over to your house [Bulloch Hall, Roswell, Georgia] and it looks a little better than I expected - altho much out of order - I fancied you all about those rooms in times past - It made Stuart so sad too to go over there

I imagined you bustling in your pantry and arranging the closets - and then in your room. We went in the summer house now overgrown with thornberry -

You allude to Mr Hutchisons death - I can scarcely realize it - indeed we have lost a friend - one I can never find again I am sure on Earth - Do you know that he has left Irvine Bulloch[46] from 25 to 30,000 - $5,000 to Stuart - $5,000 to you - and $1,000 to each of your other children from Susie down to Irvine - $1000 to each and every child named after his first wife - all these legacies except the first paid in cash poor man in our drives he would tell me of his success in speculatines and often would complain of sitting up late at night to make out his accounts etc I commeserated with him and begged him not to do so It was so useless and so injurious to him and then when I saw him reposed in his coffin to to {___} to return - I felt so awfully the perfect uselessness of everything but enough for the necessities of life - He with everything to make life pleasant - died without a white person or friend or relative to smooth his dying pillow - He expressed a great hope in the mercies of a dying Savior - and passed away without a struggle -

Irvine is here now with Stuart. He is very well but has no idea of school - as he talks of fighting - He is in a company now drilling - I made a flannel shirt for him the other day to drill in - He is a good deal with Stuart - and is much company for him - They went out to shoot terripins to day succeeded in shooting one but could not get him. With much love dear mother from both Stuart and myself to each and all of the family believe me your attached daughter -

Lucy Elliott

By June of 1860, Lucy and Stuart had settled once again in Roswell. They now had two children, John Stuart and Matilda Moxley. Enslaved *Daddy* Luke and *Maum* Charlotte, husband and wife, lived in a slave cabin next door to Bulloch

Hall, now rented by Tom King and his wife. It is not clear where Lucy and Stuart resided.

Daddy Luke and *Maum* Grace
on the porch at Bulloch Hall,
Courtesy of the Theodore Roosevelt Collection,
Houghton Library, Harvard University

The family lost a dear friend on 13 May 1861 when Robert Hutchison of Savannah passed. Robert, three times a widower, was survived only by two daughters Nannie C. and Ellen L. He left $30,000, most of his household goods, and the portraits of Senator John Elliott and Corinne Elliott

(Robert's first wife) to James Dunwoody Bulloch. Martha received $5,000 while her daughters, Susan, Anna, and Mittie, each received $1,000, as did many other friends and relatives. Robert left $5000 to Daniel Stuart Elliott and provided $1,000 to Lucy and each of her children in the event Stuart did not survive him. Irvine and four other male Bulloch relatives received $1,000 each. Several other bequests went to charities and churches.[47]

Nannie, age 10, and Ellen, age 3, who lived with their mothers' family, the Caskies of Richmond, Virginia, received the bulk of his massive estate. James D. Bulloch, Daniel Stuart Elliott, and Alexander Lawton served along with three others as executors. This was the same Alexander Lawton who provided Irvine with a recommendation. James D. Bulloch and Alexander Lawton, along with Martha Bulloch, Susan West, Mr. and Mrs. James Caskie, James K. Caskie, Mrs. Louisa Porter, and Mrs. Louisa Gilmer were appointed guardians of his daughters.[48]

Nannie, in particular, would often be mentioned in Bulloch/Roosevelt family letters. However, due to the War, James D. Bulloch and many others never received their entire inheritance. Irvine worked while in Savannah to obtain his mother and sisters' money and to find a way to ensure the funds reached them in the North. However, even at this early stage of the war, it was difficult to transfer funds from the South to the North.

Mid-June found the Bullochs relegated to various parts of the country with James now working for the Confederacy in Liverpool, England. Martha and Anna seemed committed to staying in the North and spending the summer with the Roosevelts in Long Branch, New Jersey, at Laird's Mansion House Resort. *Frank Leslie's Illustrated Newspaper* reported on 15 July 1865 that Mansion House was one of the United States' fashionable summer houses. The description read:

> . . . occupies a prominent position, not only on account of the spaciousness of the building, the airiness and comfort of the rooms,

the healthfulness of the spot and the beauty of the location, but for that genial air of home which the proprietor, Mr. Laird, throws over it. Our engraving is so accurate, that it relieves us from the trouble of describing the exterior of the building. We shall, therefore, confine our remarks to the dining-room, which is one of the most spacious in this country.

Our readers may get some idea of its size, when we state that its dimensions are 120 feet by 80, and that is will seat over 550 persons. This model dining-room has also the unspeakable advantage of being so situated that the sun cannot reach it, a fact which can be fully appreciated in summer. It is also most admirably ventilated from the roof, with Miller's patent ventilator. All these advantages make it indisputably one of the coolest and pleasantest dining-rooms in the United States. . .

Long Branch is so easy of access, and the trip there and back is so pleasant and invigorating, that we know of no other sea resort so admirably adapted for our citizens, as Laird's Mansion House.[49]

Irvine, while awaiting a possible commission as a midshipman,[50] Irvine continued to seek a place in the Confederate Army as seen in the following letter written from Roswell on 21 June. It was possible Irvine, like many young men of the age, was anxious to get into the thick of things and was not willing to wait upon active sea duty. Already he had drilled with Stuart in Roswell and knew that many men and boys among Roswell's King, Dunwoody, Pratt, and Smith families had signed up with the Confederate Army.

Laird's Mansion House at Long Branch,
Frank Leslie's Illustrated Newspaper, 15 July 1865

Laird's Dining Room,

Roswell Cobb Co. Geo Jne 21, 1861

Hon. L.P. Walker
　　　Dear Sir,
　　　　　I send you enclos ed a letter of recommendation from Colonel WJ Hardee, applying for a position in the Confederate Army for me. Hoping that I may meet with your approbation. Will anxiously await the issue of your considerations.
　　　　　　　With Much Resp to I remain
　　　　　　　Your obt Sert
　　　　　　　Irvine S. Bulloch

To
　　Hon. L.P. Walker
　　　　Sec. of War[51]

Chapter 3: July through October of 1861

Events in the War

On Independence Day, Lincoln spoke of war as "a People's contest . . . a struggle for maintaining in the world, that form, and substance of government, whose leading object is, to elevate the condition of men." Congress authorized a call for 500,000 men for the U.S. Army. To cover the cost of war, the first U.S. income tax was imposed at 3% of all incomes over 800 dollars.

On 21 July, the first Battle of Bull Run at Manassas, Virginia, occurred. Generals Joseph E. Johnston and P. G. T. Beauregard led the Confederate forces, who overwhelmingly defeated the Union forces under General Irvin McDowell. Thousands of civilian onlookers, many of them residents of Washington, D.C., viewed the battle believing it would be the one and only of the War. Most citizens, Northern and Southern alike, thought the Civil War would end quickly with little cost of life. Of approximately 18,000 combatants on each side, the Union had 481 killed, 1,011 wounded, and 1,216 missing. The Confederacy suffered 387 killed, 1,582 wounded, and 13 missing. The Union Army fled back to Washington, D.C. Lincoln commented, "It's damned bad."

Taking immediate action, Lincoln replaced McDowell with General George B. McClellan as Commander of the Army's Department of the Potomac. In November, Lincoln elevated McClellan to general-in-chief, replacing Winfield Scott who had recently retired.

The Letters

Long Branch July 20th - 1861

My dearest Susy,
    I received your dear letter from "Fly-Cottage" yesterday very late in the afternoon and was very glad to get it my darling daughter Two things in that letter made me feel sad almost created a "<u>melt.</u>" One was to hear you had to sell some shares of Beaver Meadow, and the other was that simple uncomplaining expression, "I am not strong this spring & I like to lie down by the hour on the Sofa & listen to the sweet country sounds" - Darling Susy, I do love you so much I can hardly bear the disappointed feeling I have in your not being better I do hope when you come here the sea air may invigorate you - Susy dear I am so thankful that you are a christian and that you have laid up in store for you a happy home when there shall be "no more sickness." I am glad you went to see Harriott - Anna received a letter from James last evening - He sent a great deal of love to you. He does not mention when he will return - Mittie and the children are quite well, so is Anna - {Shortness} is still quite short, and I never look at that place on her cheek which you used to kiss, but I think of you Mitties company left yesterday - She and Anna seemed to miss them very much - They are nice sprightly girls, but they sit up too late at night for my taste - "Every one to their notion" but I never could see the pleasure or advantage of turning night into day and day into night - I wrote you a few days since, but fear the letter will not reach you There was a note in it from Mittie also It was directed to Flushing to Mr Weir Roosevelts care - I have heard nothing from Stuart lately or Irvine This is a pleasant place, but there is no Church near but a small Episcopal Chapel which I have attended twice - I am going tomorrow {up} to Church some distance from this with a Mrs Solters from N York The old lady has a nice plain carriage with a good broad step that I can get into with ease - She seems to have taken a great fancy to me I don't know why - except that I sympathize with her for having lost by death all of her daughters - She is very rich, & very lonely

- She has out lived not only her daughters - but the éclat which her wealth and talents I suppose formerly gave her - She is a well educated and intelligent lady - When I think of her bereavement, I wonder that I have so little gratitude to God for my three darling daughters I am so miserable about this war - Oh Susy dear how many are hurried into eternity almost daily - When will it cease - Good bye my own dear daughter - With much love to Hill & Mrs Roosevelt I am
Your affectionate mother
M Bulloch

Harriott Bulloch had remained behind in New York when James left for Liverpool. She was expecting their third child and delivered Henry on 17 May while James traveled from Montreal, Canada, to Liverpool after meeting with Confederate officials. By the date of this letter, James had arrived and was settled in Liverpool, but Harriott still lived in New York and was busy settling affairs and arranging for her family's departure for England.

S Laird,
Mansion House,

Long Branch, N.J. July 25-1861

Dearest Susy
I fear I have not directed my letters properly and therefore that you have not received them - I write this just to say darling that we are quite well, and to repeat to you what I mentioned in some of my letters that Mittie is to leave this place on the 26th of August - Cant you come here earlier than you mentioned and afterwards finish up your visit to Flushing? If you do not you will see very little of Mittie -Tell Hill I received his little memorandum and give my love to him - I write but a short note as I have just written a long letter to Stuart, and this afternoon intend writing to James to go in the Steamer of Saturday - I see in the papers

43

that Frank Bartow of Sav was killed in the battle of Bull's Run on Sunday - You know he married Lou Berrien I saw her last winter - Oh how I do pity her and her little children - I have begged Stuart to write me immediately the number killed on the Confederate side and whether any of the Kings or Dunwodys are amongst the number - <u>Horrible war</u>! Write me darling if you are well enough and let us know when you think you will come - Direct to this place and not to 94th Lane as Thee does not go every day I hope darling you are better Give my kind regards to Mary and Mrs West if with you

Your truly loving mother
M Bulloch

NB   I enclose a piece I clipped out of a paper - It pleases me as it is for peace - I know the Republican Journals would scoff at it - But God himself says, "Blessed are the peace makers"

The War reached the family with word of the death of personal friend, Confederate Francis Stebbins Bartow (1816-1861), at First Bull Run. Francis, son of Dr. Theodosius Bartow and Frances Lloyd Stebbins of Savannah, graduated first in his class from Franklin College and served as an attorney in Savannah. He served both as a representative and a senator in the Georgia legislature and was an elected member of the Confederate Congress. After a dispute with Georgia Governor Joseph Brown, Bartow resigned. On 21 May 1861, he left for Virginia as a captain in the Oglethorpe (Georgia) Light Infantry, Company B, 8th Regiment. Upon arrival in Richmond, Bartow received a promotion to colonel. After his death at Bull Run the Confederate Congress confirmed Bartow's posthumous rank of acting brigadier general. According to some sources, his last words were "They have killed me boys, but I never gave up." His words led to the common expresssion "They have killed me boys, but never give up."[52]

Charles C. Jones, Jr. of Liberty County wrote, "We

have been in the midst of the greatest excitement consequent upon this glorious victory at Manassas,[53] and last night we received the body of General Bartow. It now lies in the exchange long room under a guard of honor; will be buried tomorrow afternoon."[54]

Like Martha, Jones had placed in his letter to his parents word of family and friends involved in the fighting and worries of others not yet accounted for. Martha worried about the sons of Barrington King and of her late sister-in-law Jane Dunwoody. Tom King of Roswell, Mittie's neighbor and former beau, received two wounds at Bull Run, called Manassas by the Confederates. His brother Joseph Henry also suffered severe wounds during the battle. Both men returned home to recuperate. Martha's nephew Charlie Dunwoody also received a wound at First Manassas. (See Appendix A)

The article Martha included for Susan was entitled *Our Voice is Still for Peace*. It read:

> At a time like this, when civil war is threatening to spread over those unhappy States, tearing men from their homes, leaving thousands of widows and fatherless children, invoking bitter and demoniac passions, laying shackles on commerce, embittering life in many thousand quiet and industrious families—a struggle, the sorrowful effects of which possibly maybe felt for centuries—at such a time we do not regret that this journal opposed the war, and used all its efforts to restore peace, love and well-being to an unhappy country. "Our conscience is void of offense toward God and toward man" in what we have done, and will be in what we shall continue to do until this fearful war shall have an end. We have no personal ambition to gratify, no unholy object to attain. We believe in those noble words of John Milton, that "Peace hath her victories no less renowned than war;" and so believing we shall struggle

on, through good report and through evil, to bring our distracted and bleeding country once more beneath her mild, benignant sway. It is no hostility to Government that actuates us, but a patriotic desire to save that Government, and all that men hold most sacred and dear, from certain destruction. At the sacrifice of personal popularity and pecuniary benefit, we honestly took our stand, and when the whirlwind of popular madness was at its hight, [sp] and we are not to be moved from our position now, when the signs of returning reason are on every side, and popular excitement has been subdued by the fearful anxieties for what the future has in store, making the most excited sober-minded and thoughtful.

We shall continue our opposition to the war, undeterred by the oft repeated threats and menaces that are hurled at us, and unmoved by the vulgar vituperation that is daily lavished upon us by the more rabid of the War journals. We look for our reward in the approving smiles of a clear conscience, the commendation of the humane, the honest, and the good: and in the gratitude of those genuine patriots who will ere long take the place of the madmen and corrupt huckstering politicians who, unfortunately for the country, have their incompetent hands upon the helm of the State.[55]

On 28 August 1861, James' wife, Harriott Bulloch, three children, two maids, and one manservant boarded the S.S. *Persia* in New York City and set sail for Liverpool, England. Harriott's party arrived on 6 September. They took up residence in Mrs. Danley's boarding house on Oxford Street.[56]

S. Laird,

Mansion House,

Long Branch, NJ Sept 7th 1861

My dearest Susy

I received your welcome and delightful letter last evening I need not say how glad I was to get it - The day you left oh how I missed you, and how low-spirited I felt - everything reminded me so much of you, particularly little Elliott - we asked him where aunt Susy was, and he said up tase [upstairs?] - I think I felt even more tenderly towards him than I did when his mother left - I have been very much devoted to him this past week - The day you left I commenced the office of detective Police - and you may rely on it I have made very many salutary reforms (as the newspapers say) He now has good nights, and eats (I think) only what I give him - but only to think the day you left I staid from dinner until Dora brought his and Tedies, dinner to them to see that his rice had salt in it and whether his mashed potato had lumps in it - Dora had told me she never gave him lumpy potatoes, and always made his rice palatable - When she brought the dinner and gave it to Annie up stairs - she had no idea I was down stairs and would examine it - I found the potato full of hard uncooked lumps and the rice perfectly {p__h} - I quietly fixed the dinner properly, and the little fellow ate very heartily - that night however to my astonishment he was restless again and in the morning when he was placed on his chair I found his bowels very bad - I felt really discouraged - When he was taken from his chair I made an examination and what do you suppose I found? pieces of peach skin nearly an inch in length which he had picked up some where 'round the house and swallowed - I showed them to Annie who declared she had never suffered him to touch any Such thing - Now you see dear Susy how impossible it is with such a nurse as Annie to keep the child well - as I have said I have redoubled my vigilance but one single ten minutes carelessness on her part will undo all of the carefulness on mine I tried him with arrow root but he will not eat it-I now prepare his breakfast and dinner myself at the table this morning he took a soft boiled egg with much relish - his dinners are soft rice and red gravy - Tedie & Bamie are quite well & Elliott much better than he has been for days - I find my whole sheet nearly has been about Elliott, but I know his loving aunt wants to hear all about him - A great many persons have left but still the house is tolerably full - Mr. & Mrs. {Cress} have gone we miss them & the little girls very much - I received a long interesting letter from James last night - he sends love to all - I hope he will soon have his family dear fellow - The weather is delightful and nothing can surpass the loveliness of old Ocean at present except the sunsets - If I only could hear from Stuart and Irvine I should feel comparitively happy but when I think of them I always try to think prayerfully - dear little Mittie too, I am anxious about her - I hope she may soon be over her trouble I send enclosed a small ~~piece~~ article which I cut out of the "Times" of yesterday - No doubt but Stuart is in one of those companies under Dubignon Anna sends a great deal of love to you and says I must tell you that your letter was delightful to her as well to me -

It is now after dinner Tedie & Ellie are at the old occupation with the blocks - Anna & Bamie are playing with them while I write Teedie is making a stable & the three legged wooden horse is lying near him - More persons are going this afternoon - It makes us feel lonely to have them go although strangers.

    Darling Susy - I love you painfully. Give our love to Mary & Hill - Good bye darling child - May God bless you dear one -

                    your loving Mother
                      M Bulloch

[Attached to Martha's letter with glue is a clipping which reads: "A Richmond letter to the Memphis *Appeal* reports the arrival of two cavalry companies from Georgia said to be the finest and most efficient troops and with the finest horses ever seen."]

    The *Memphis Daily Appeal* (Tennessee), often called

the *Moving Appeal*, was dedicated to the Southern Cause. They continued publication in that city until the Battle of Memphis on 6 June 1862, when the Union took the city. On that date, the *Daily Appeal* loaded their presses and plates on boxcars and moved to Grenada, Mississippi. In November of 1862, they moved to Jackson, Mississippi, where they stayed until May 1863. Many moves later they arrived in Atlanta, Georgia, where publication continued until July of 1864 when Atlanta fell. The paper returned to Montgomery from September 1864 to April 1865, before one final move to Columbus, Georgia, where Federal forces shut down publication. After publishing in nine different cities over a four year period, the newspaper resumed publication in Memphis on 5 November 1865.[57]

The *New York Times* article Martha included and alluded to in her letter refers to cavalry in Phillips' Legion under the command of Henry Charles DuBignon (1826-1885).[58] DuBignon was a planter in Milledgeville, Baldwin County, Georgia. Martha must have known Stuart had joined Phillips' Legion and served in the cavalry. Stuart enlisted on 4 July in Georgia and began active service as a private. Organized in the summer of 1861, Phillips' Georgia Legion mustered into Confederate service that fall. The unit contained infantry companies, cavalry companies, and a battery of light artillery. Stuart Elliott joined Phillips' Georgia Legion as a cavalry man, bringing with him a horse and horse equipment. As the son of a once wealthy landowner and prominent Georgia family, Stuart could well afford the cost of joining a cavalry unit. Although Stuart had legally changed his name from *Stewart* to *Stuart* in December of 1853, his enrollment card shows his name as *Stewart Elliott*.[59]

The next two letters written from Martha to Susan showed that Martha remained in Long Branch after Mittie and Thee and Susan and Hill had returned to their respective homes. Martha and Anna remained with Mittie's three children. There is no mention in this letter of the birth of Mittie's fourth child on 27 September 1861. Mittie named her second daughter for her deceased stepsister Corinne

Elliott Hutchison, Robert Hutchison's first wife, and Susan Elliott West's and Daniel Stuart Elliott's half sister.

Long Branch Oct 2nd /61

My darling Susy,

  I will not attempt to describe the tender homesick melancholy feeling I had yesterday after you left - I tried to be busy but even employment failed to comfort - I went into your room and thought of the bonnets until I felt like crying - then I looked out through the rain at some of the summer houses on the bluff in which we used to sit and talk and look at the waves - This of course only increased the intense tenderness I felt for you - I thought how often your dear little feet had trudged along on those cliffs alone - how often I had watched your receding figure from our piazza until I saw you returning - with all these recollections the beloved departed one was constantly associated - But darling you must not think I am going to be melancholy and unhappy - After a few days I mean to be very busy The little children too occupy and amuse me - We felt uneasy about Bamie yesterday She complained very much of a pain on the right side of her chest, just after dinner it increased so much that we took off her apparatus & laid her in bed - Anna then rubbed her and I made a mustard plaster and placed it directly over the pain - It made her more easy, and she had a pretty good night - She had fever however nearly all night which went off with perspiration - today she is better, but complains of feeling still very unwell - I think it is a bilious attack and am sure if Hill had been here he would have given her a dose of magnesia or oil, but I was afraid to insist on so doing as Bamie is such a delicate child - You know she has been complaining for some time past - I was really afraid from the symptoms yesterday that it was a slight congestion of the liver - I think tonight I will give her some magnesia - were she my own child it should be blue pill - I will write you tomorrow again if she is not better, so if you do not hear from me you may conclude she is - You had hardly left yesterday when our constant visitor <u>Minny Halsey</u> came over she staid the entire morning - several times during the morning the rain stopped, but she never hinted at going home until long after the first gong sounded and after it commenced raining furiously - then she asked Anna if it was raining and if she did not think she could get home - The result was she staid until dinner was over and until about 4 oclock in the afternoon all the time begging Anna not to let her interfere with any work she had to do in her room - Anna was completely incensed - The Halseys could not go yesterday on account of the weather, nor have they gone today - I am pretty sure we shall have Miss Minny all the afternoon & evening - To say she lacks delicacy, does not express the state of the case She is a positive bore - After dinner -

 Bamie seems better the Halseys are gone except the mother, she goes early in the morning - Minny took a farewell dinner with the Lairds [owners of the Mansion House resort]- when we went in to dinner we found her at Mrs Lairds table -The fog continues dense but I have been to walk a little way on the cliff - I thought of you all the time - Every thing makes me think of you the pebbles make me think of your love-stone hunts - The surf is grand this afternoon No body here now but ourselves - I am going to commence my dress tomorrow - The children are longing for good weather- Good bye darling Susy - Anna sends <u>much much</u> love & says oh! how she misses you - Love to all friends - If you see old Mrs. {Bond} give my love to her I hope darling you accomplished all you wished yesterday - It was a dreadful day to shop - I fear you fatigued yourself very much - My Bible darling reminds me of you as much as any thing else - I mean to read over the passage in 2nd Cor [Corinthians] about light every day - Sweet daughter! how thankful I ought to be that you are still spared me - and how thankful how inexpressibly thankful I ought to be for

the precious hope I have of dear Stuart - Bamie sends much

love you -

>Your affect Mother
>M Bulloch

I have had a search for your stud but could not find it -

> Martha considered giving Bamie a *blue pill*. Called thus because of its color, the pill was one of the most common remedies of the 1860s and 1870s. Advertisements claimed it could cure most anything from "giddiness to syphilis." Actually, the blue pill was mercury, a very poisonous element. Many cases of mercury poisoning occurred due to overuse of the *blue pill*, yet it remained popular for over 20 years.[60]

>Long Branch, Oct 9th 1861

My own dear darling daughter
I received a few days since your little note giving the account of the ink accident - poor darling! how sorry I felt about it - Anna & I wondered whether you knew milk would take it out. If put into it before it is washed - Yesterday, (tuesday) I received your sweet letter of the 7th. It reached here in the afternoon & as Thee was here I determined to write you this morning we are all quite well - The children were delighted to see their Father - He came on monday -arrived here after tea in the evening - We had the three children all waiting for him in the little parlor Every little noise we heard, we would hold up our fingers & say, hush hush! Elliott holding up his little chubby fore finger and joining in the general hush until he really became alarmed, thinking I suppose that such stillness argued impending danger - We are all busy today packing up - Thee will be here on friday evening, and, {___}, take us to town on saturday morning [12 October] - Tomorrow morning, the childrens cribs bedding, and every thing except one or two trunks are to go - But the greatest trouble is yet to come - Annie the nurse is to go tomorrow morning also - This night will be the

last for poor little Elliott to have his "<u>numinums</u>" Tomorrow morning I commence to wean him - I know he will cry very much the first night or two - Ellie is very healthy now, and I think will bear the weaning very well - I do not intend that he shall have any thing but water until morning - when I shall have something provided for him quite early - I am not going to let Dora coddle him up & stuff him with all sorts of unwholesome things - He has just been in his bath and is now asleep on my bed, and I am sitting close by his bedside. The weather has of late been very warm here also, but it rained a little yesterday and today it is quite cool. I know darling you were glad, and grateful to our good Father in Heaven when you heard that Mittie was over her trouble. Thee says she seems to have a plenty of milk - I hope this may continue - I was glad she named it Corinne - Poor Mr Hutchinson how it would have gratified him! Now Susy darling I am going to talk about the house - ("<u>Bully for house</u>") Our sweet home where we have so many delightful associations clustered - I have spent nearly six happy years there with you & Hill dear good daughter and good son, I never for a moment felt that I was not in my own house - had all of the comfort & freedom of my own house without the trouble - Experienced kindness and sympathy from Hill and you that I shall never forget - Kindness to myself from Hill and kindness to Irvine & Anna that has gone down to the very bottom of my heart. But Susy darling how <u>true it is</u> that every thing in this world is transitory -The time has come I think when duty bids us shut up dear house for the present - In the Providence of God we are at present so situated as not to be able without borrowing, (which we both dislike in our inmost souls) to return to our happy home - Let us meekly bow to - circumstances darling, and try to be grateful for the many blessings which we still enjoy - How much worse it might have been - I hope Hill may be able to rent - If not, try to keep it in repair and try to pay the $500 for taxes etc and be thankful that you have such a good home offered you, in which to wait for better times - My present plan is to stay with Mittie about four weeks, then to go to Phil to board where ever you & your good mother can get me a place for Anna & myself - In Dec sometime I think of going South - I think I am required there - I became acquainted here with a lady a Mrs M^{c}dougall - She is the wife of a member of Congress (Senator) from California - She had a very sick baby, which was sick nearly all the summer and I felt sorry for her and used to express my sympathy - Finally when the house was nearly empty she was taken sick herself with bowel complaint - I used to advise her about his diet, and made arrow-root for her - She seemed more grateful than the small services demanded. Hearing me speak of the probability of my going south she interested her husband, when he came for her, on the subject. He gave me his card that I might write him if I concluded to go, and promised to do any thing he could to obtain pasports etc Thee told me yesterday however that he could himself take me to Fortress Monroe, and make all the necessary arrangements for our getting to Richmond - Thee told me also that instead of selling any of my Beaver Meadows Stock - He will, if I desire it, borrow any amount I may require, and give my stock, or a part of it, as security- Whether I stay or go, I shall have to borrow this money - Even if I get those Bonds from James the interest from those & from Beaver M would not be over $850, which would not be enough to board a {___} Anna and Myself. This is as far as I can see into the future then is my present plan - I will write you again shortly from New York - Excuse this paper darling it is the best Lairds can afford - Good bye for the present my dear blessed daughter -

                    Your affectionate
                    Mother
                    M Bulloch

    Martha again wrote of financial matters. It seems during the previous years, Martha had contributed to Susan and Hill's household maintenance. With all of the turmoil of the War, Martha could no longer do so and needed money for a trip South to be with her son Stuart, or at least with his family, while he continued to serve in the Confederate Army. Martha considered selling her Beaver Meadow stock. Pennsylvania's Beaver Meadow Railroad, whose sole purpose was to transport anthracite coal from the mines near Beaver Meadow to the Lehigh Canal, began construction in 1830 and went into service in 1836.

A Union Democrat, Senator James Alexander McDougall (1817-1867) offered assistance to Martha. McDougall was elected in 1861 and served only one term. He never returned to California during his six-year term and was considered ineffectual due to his alcoholism.[61] The Senator retired to New York after his term ended and died in September of 1867. James McDougall was married to Marilla McConnell, and their first child Lillia (c.1848-1910) would have been about 13-years-old at this time. A second child, named for his father, was born in 1853 and died in 1855. A second daughter, May, is listed on many family trees, but no additional information about her could be recovered. However, Martha speaks of a *male* child, of which no mention could be found in any other historic record.[62]

New York Oct. 19th - 1861

My darling Susy
    I received your letter this forenoon, and determined to write you immediately - I am sorry my dear daughter that you should have felt so badly at the possibility of my going south - I should be too sorry to leave you - and the probability of my not being able to come back for an indefinite time, and not even to hear from you & Mittie is too painful to think of - I should not, I think mind the journey, but I could not bear to be separated from you & Mittie - But we may make ourselves quite easy at present I think on the subject as the Government has determined no longer to give any passes - I have been feeling very uneasy about Irvine - but I believe I mentioned to you that I have been some what relieved by having an opportunity of sending him some orders for

money - There was a Mr Shear a few days since just from Augusta Georgia who saw Thee at his store - He said he could carry any open letters. Thee thought I had better not write a letter so I simply sent an order to Mr Thomas King who owes me eighty dollars to pay Mrs Campbell $60 and Irvine $20 - I sent him ^{Irvine} an order too on Mr Barrington King who in Jan will owe me $75 for Lukes wages, to pay that sum to Irvine - In addition to these I sent an order on Wm James Bulloch to pay Irvine if he had funds of mine in his hands, the sum of $100, making in all $195 - Now I do not know if Mr Shear will ever get back to the South, but if he does Irvine will have money enough for some time to come - Thee wrote him a few lines telling him we were all well and that Mittie had a little daughter named Corinne - What makes me particularly anxious to go south is that I may be in Richmond if Stuart or Irvine should be wounded - I view it in this way; if I leave dear Susy and Mittie, they are not in danger and besides have friends to take care of them But poor young friendless Irvine has no person if he is sick except Stuart to care for him - At such times I feel that I must brave every danger and inconvenience to go to him ^{at times} - I do not think Irvine has gone to Richmond, but to ^{help} guard the coast - Oh if I could only hear from him - But darling as you say, we must leave it all in the hands of God - My faith is very weak, but I try to take courage and keep from desponding - As you say our Heavenly Father is a Refuge which never has, and never will fail — I received a very pleasant letter from Mrs Hodge lately — I will enclose it — do not send it back but destroy it - Mittie says darling she wishes you could have come - she asks if you could not come shortly & take part of my bed, and that Hill could sleep at Mary's [Mary West Roosevelt] - She says she is so much obliged to you about the servant - that she will be glad if you keep your eye on her a few days longer as her house-hold is not settled yet - Dora is going next week - Annie is already gone -Hariots [Harriott Elliott] woman has returned and she will see her on Monday - I find I have written a long letter without saying any thing about you keeping house -

Hill & I had a long talk about it, and I repeat dear Susy that I do not think you had better try to keep house -Your affec Mother

      M Bulloch

Excuse haste - I have written Mrs. Hodge We are all quite well - This is a very incoherent letter - I have written almost in the dark - Do not write darling only when you are well - Love to Mrs West & Hill & kind regards from us all to Miss Lilly and the other young ladies - Tell Hill Anna did not get the likeness - the baby is the best little thing I ever knew except Bamie at her age - Teedie & Ellie are dear little fellows. Elliott is really pretty, and as smart as he can be - Mittie wants to know if the woman you speak of can sew and do little handy things - If Elisa comes, she is to take care of Elliott - this woman would be to attend to Teedies little wants, wash & dress him & walk with him. As this would leave a great deal of time unoccupied, she wishes one for Teedie who can sew - As to the baby Tudy [Susan's nickname], I think ^{for her} she will have to get a wet nurse, as she has the same pain in her chest & arm which she had with Elliott At times she has very little milk and then it gives her pain to nurse But I must close - Good bye darling

      M Bulloch

  Martha's letter to Susan described her reasons for wanting to go south. Believing Stuart was in or near Richmond, Martha planned to go only that far south. She, at that point, was not sure where Irvine was. Historic documents provide the answer. Recently commissioned a midshipman, Irvine had briefly served aboard the C.S.S. *Savannah*, a converted 1856-built, side-wheel steamer with only a single thirty-two-pounder cannon. The *Savannah* was tasked with the naval defense of South Carolina and Georgia. By 19 October, Irvine was in Charleston on board the C.S.S. *Nashville* preparing to run the blockade to Southhampton, England.[63]

  Martha devoted much of her letter to the hiring of

nurses for Mittie's children and financial matters. Martha desired to send money to Irvine and was allotting money owed her by Tom and Barrington King to her son. *Daddy* Luke Moumar, Martha's slave who still lived in one of Martha's slave cottages, worked for Barrington King and his wages were owed to Martha. Tom King owed money for rent on Bulloch Hall.

The following is possibly a post script to the previous letter.

New York Oct 23rd/61

All well dearest Susy - I write only a line to say that Elisa has just been to say that she cannot come therefore Mittie wishes you to send on the nurse you spoke of, (if you think she will answer) as soon as possible, - Dora goes away on friday morning - Her business will be to take care of Elliott and have some supervision of Teedie also - In my letter I asked you if she would sew etc - from the change of plan this is not now necessary - All she wants is a good attentive efficient nurse - She will give seven or if necessary eight dollars per month - She telegraphs to you about this matter this afternoon, and hopes very soon to hear from you -

Yours very affectionately

M Bulloch

Over

I hope darling you are well Love to Hill -

Chapter 4: November of 1861

The Letters

New York Nov 4th 1861

My own darling Susie,
    I hope you have not fatigued in mind and body about the room for me - Oh my precious Susy what a good child you ever have been to me - I feel your kind affectionate conduct darling, and it will be a comfort to you to think, how you have always even from the time you were a little child tried to make me happy - I have telegraphed to you as soon as I received your letter of saturday this morning not to take the room I have not fully determined yet on my future movements - Little Elliot although much better is still too weak and sick for me to think of ^{my} leaving Mittie for some time to come. He is not satisfied at present with any person to take care of him but myself - For a wonder he has permitted me to come up stairs to write this note - After he gets better I suppose Bridget, who I think is to be his nurse and who arrived this morning, will by degrees be enabled to ingraciate herself with him - At present he will have nothing to say to her - Mittie has her hands full and has had several cries at the mention of my leaving her - Today after I received your letter, I told Mittie I wished to be very candid with her - that I would stay with her until Elliott was well - but that I would not consent to remain another day afterwards unless she & Thee would let me assist in house expenses to the amount which I would have to pay at a boarding house, say, $16 per week She has consented and we are to talk it over tonight - If we make this arrangement

I will remain here Nov & Dec then, if I do not go south, I will probably go to Phil. (if I can get a room) for the rest of the winter. Do not make yourself uneasy about me dearest - I could not bear to hear about that feeling in your chest, I know it is produced by distress of mind. I remember you had that feeling when Daisy [Georgia Amanda Elliott] died - I will try to be content and trust in God - It is a subject for constant gratitude that I have such good daughters & Mittie is as considerate about me as you are - little Ellie sleeps by me in his crib and she is all the time anxious for fear he may disturb me - He disturbs me very little, as he now sleeps very quietly - All he requires is something to drink and I keep a little cup of barley gruel where I can get it handily for him - He has been quite ill, but I hope now he is entirely out of danger - His nurse sleeps in an adjoining room so if I require her in the night I rap on the wall - I will write you again shortly I hear Elliot crying so must close - Anna is spending a few days with the Hyatts
                    Your affec Mother
                            MB
I am glad you have a prospect of renting rooms

   If Susan rented rooms in their Pine Street home, it might have provided them with enough money to continue to live there. Martha mentioned their paying taxes on the home, indicating they legally owned it. However, renting rooms would also make more work for Susan; for as custom dictated, she would need to provide fresh linens weekly and usually two meals a day for any boarders.

         New York Nov 7$\underline{\text{th}}$, 1861
  I received your dear letter yesterday at noon darling daughter, and intended answering it immediately, but as Ellie had been wakeful the night before I felt tired so laid down on the sofa in my room and took a long sleep instead - Today he is so much better that, if I only keep out of sight

he permits his Phil[a] nurse to take care of him and amuse him all of the time - Last night he rested perfectly well and did not wake up until twenty minutes of seven this morning - Of course I had a good night also and in consequence am quite well this morning - You have no idea what a sick child Elliott has been - I have for nearly a week past had him in my arms or on a pillow in my lap - yesterday for the first time in that period he was satisfied for a short time from me - This must account for my apparent remissness in not signing and sending to Hill the papers signifying the transfer of my Bonds to Jimmie [James Dunwoody Bulloch] for his - I have signed them this morning & Thee says he will send them this afternoon - I thank you my dearest Susy for all the care and trouble you have taken about my boarding place and more especially for the motive which led to the exertion of my poor little weak Teedie - Write me what you think of my present arrangement - Susy dearest you can't think how much obliged I feel to Mrs West for what you wrote in your letter - It is indeed very kind in her - But I could not, even on those times invade that peaceful house hold - I have not seen Mary [Roosevelt] or any of the family lately - I saw little Hill [Roosevelt] the other night - He has grown very stout and is quite a pretty boy - I have been told that Mr Roosevelt Senior is very low-spirited at times - Sometimes he stays at home all day on sunday, and generally goes to his room at eight in the evening - I think it is a great pity some of his children did not remain in the Dutch Church - Mittie says she thinks she will like the nurse you sent her very much - she tries very hard to amuse and take care of Ellie - It seems she has two names Bridget & Delia - we call her by the latter - Anna is still at the Hyatt's. She was at home so much last week on account of Elliotts sickness that they insist on her remaining with them this week to make it up - The baby is very thriving and is just as good as a baby can be - Mittie has enough milk at present and she begins to think that if her milk fails she will resort to the bottle - She has not made up her mind on that subject yet however - She has an attentive middle-aged woman as a

nurse for Corinne at present - Little Teedie has no nurse but is such a mischiefous little rogue that he requires as much watching as any of them - It is amusing when they are all around her in the nursery to see Mittie's perplexed look - Some days when Elliott was so sick and before she had her nurses, neither she nor I had time to dress ourselves - I wore my flannel gown all of the time & she her calico wrapper – We hope now for better times - Ah how I wish we could have better times in the country - that this dreadful war was over - Mittie sends much love to Mrs West & yourself - If you see Mrs Boynton & Miss Sessions do give a great deal of love to them for me - If in your walks you go by their house observe the number and write it to me - Give much love to Hill for me & remember me affectionately to Mrs West - Tell old Sam and Delia Anna & I have not forgotten them - Good bye dearest for the present - Your truly loving mother
M Bulloch
NB I am so surprised that my Dispatch did not reach you - I Telegraphed to you immediately as I received your letter and have written you twice besides this letter since.

Martha's letter mentions Mrs. Boynton and Miss Sessions. Martha's placement of the two names together enabled us to identify Mrs. Cornelia Sessions Boynton and her sister Eliza Ann Sessions of Natches, Adams County, Mississippi, by using U. S. Census records. Further research uncovered that Cornelia Sessions (1803-1892) married John Boynton in 1829. Eliza Ann Sessions (1806-1878) never married. John Boynton died sometime between 1856 and 1860.[64] Cornelia and Eliza Ann continued to live in the Philadelphia area after the War and appeared in the 1870 U.S. Census. Cornelia and John Boynton were two of the 34 original members of the West Spruce Street Presbyterian Church in 1856, along with Martha, Anna, Susan, and Hilborne.[65]

In September, Thee, Robert, and James joined a group of men to form the Union Gray Cavalry Troop. The text of the *New York Times* advertisement read:

Under this organization a number of gentlemen of his City have associated for the purpose of learning the United States drill of Cavalry Tactics, and of fitting themselves generally for the position of officers in the Army or on the Staff. They have obtained the voluntary services of officers of superior ability, and intend to perfect themselves in all the details of the service. They would be pleased to have unite with them other men of this City who take interest in the subject, and for such purpose they will meet at the office of S.W. & R. B. Roosevelt. No 76 William St. On FRIDAY, Sept. 27, inst. At 3 1/2 P.M., where any gentleman desirous of joining them may see the uniform and equipments, and learn all further particulars.

The following are some of the members

Lorillard Spencer,	Theodore Roosevelt
P.M. Lydig, Jr.,	Lewis LaFarge,
Washington Murray,	Temple Prime
David Lydig,	Henry Claus
Leonard W. Jerome,	James A. Roosevelt
A.D. LeFevre,	Craig W. Wadsworth,
John Martin, Jr.,	George G. Kellog
J. A. McVicar,	W.E. Dodge, Jr.
Edward King,	Frederick Wood
Cambridge Livingston,	Morris K. Jessup,
Henry W. Cooper,	J. Cooper Lord,
Jeremiah Loder,	Robert B. Roosevelt[66]

Despite this action, none of the Roosevelt brothers joined the Union Army. When conscription began in 1863, each paid for a substitute, as was common among the wealthy of New York and much of the North. However, Thee and his brothers heartily supported the Union and were charter members of the Union League Club. The Union Leagues, established by groups of upper middle-class men, promoted loyalty to the Union, the Republican Party, and the policies of Abraham Lincoln. They were also known as Loyal Leagues. They contributed financial support for organizations such as the United States Sanitary Commission, which provided medical supplies to treat wounded soldiers after battle, and the Allotment Commission. These clubs supported the Republican Party with funding and active participation.

Thee, along with several others, lobbied Congress, the military, and President Lincoln for a bill to strengthen and standardize a standing army regulation that allowed those men enlisted in the Union Army's volunteer forces to send a portion of their pay to their wives and families at no further cost to themselves. The U.S. Army regulation read:

> *And be it further enacted*, That the Secretary of War be, and he is hereby, authorized and directed to introduce among the volunteer forces in the service of the United States, the system of allotment tickets now used in the navy or some equivalent system, by which the family of the volunteer may draw such portions of his pay as he may request [Approved July 22, 1861.][67]

At this time, allotments could be issued, but the family often had trouble cashing the allotment certificate. Secretary of War Stanton or President Lincoln appointed commissioners for each state with voluntary forces at some time before the Autumn of 1861. Thee, William Dodge, and others from New York's Union League made it their mission to put into place a regulated way for this allotment to be processed and paid using the State of New York as a clearing house or "bank" for the payments. While no record of appointment has been found, Thee's letters and journal make it clear that he and Dodge began working as Allotment Commissioners in early November of 1861.

When the South declared independence, the Union Army did not have enough soldiers to carry on a full-scale war, so with patriotic enthusiasm, each northern state raised volunteer regiments. Prominent men in an area would raise a regiment often composed of men who had lived in the same neighborhoods and had known each other before the War. The men then elected officers and sergeants. A full-strength regiment consisted of 10 companies, each of 97 men and three officers, usually a captain and two lieutenants. A colonel commanded a regiment, assisted by a lieutenant colonel and a major. Each volunteer regiment provided their own uniforms and weapons. New York rallied more than 180 infantry regiments, and approximately 25 cavalry regiments and 40 artillery regiments. Skilled men raised at least four engineering regiments. It was the men of these New York regiments that Thee and his fellow New York allotment commissioners would be approaching.

In the command structure, regiments were grouped into brigades (usually four each) and brigades into divisions (three or four brigades). The next level was the corps, which consisted of two or more divisions, and then the army, involving one or more corps. Men, usually those with some military experience, were appointed brigade commanders and as generals at the corps level.

To document his daily work, Thee began a journal or diary when he took up his Allotment Commissioner duties in Washington, D.C. Occasionally he sent home journal pages enclosed in letters to Mittie and asked her to share them with family members and to preserve them. These journal pages are presented in this volume following the dates on which Thee wrote them.[68] Thee wrote about various individuals he met in the government and military. To clarify, first names are added in brackets where the individuals are identified and each individual is listed in Appendix B: Military & Government.

Nov 7th 61 Journal

Left New York in the evening train and after a miserable night with no accommodations for sleeping except one car, filled in Phil[a] before we arrived, reached washington

Nov. 8th 7 A.M. The soldiers who had been increasing rapidly over swarmed. Immense wagons carrying military stores pervaded every street, six, eight and ten horses or mules attached to each. Groups of very determined looking men moved quietly round and occasionaly would stop a soldier question him and then either allow him to pass on or take him with them. These are the provost guard.

I obtained a room at Willards dressed myself and immediately called upon [John] Hay, explained my object in a few words and was immediately shown into the next room where the president sat. He listened attentively read over my documents vouching for my responsibility and then at my request endorsed them.

He also gave me a card of introduction to Genl [George] McClelland requesting him to forward my plans and one to the pay master general. His little boy came in for his ball to his father and the presidents expression of face then for the first time softened into a very pleasant smile.

Armed with my cards and accompanied by Hay – I started for Gen McClelland. He had just left for a review but his father in law Genl [Randolph Barnes] Marcy gave me a letter to Genl [Thomas] Williams. Colonel [James Allen] Hardie was in charge of Genl William's office during his absence and immediately ordered a list of the New York regiments furnished me and advised me first to visit the brigade of Genl [John J.] Peck to whom he gave me a letter of introduction, ordering an orderly to accompany me.

It was five o'clock before I reached Genl Peck's camp when I found that the brigade had not yet returned from the river. After a pleasant talk with him I rode over to Col [Régis] De Trobriands' camp into which I was riding when the sentry suddenly brought me from a canter to a stand by crying "halt" and in one second bringing the musket to a "receive cavalry" immediately in front of my horse. He came into position again when I stopped and called to the corporal. When the corporal answered he said something in Dutch french which I suppose meant to go on, but the moment I tried to do so he brought his musket down again as quick as thought. The next moment as the corporal came up he apologized and said I must excuse him it was his duty.

Lieut Arnold was officer of the day and treated me with the most distinguished consideration. He took me into his tent and gave me a first rate bottle of claret and then would have me drink some horrible abysenthe [absinthe]. We afterwards went all round the camp and fort together; on this latter are four or five large guns mounted in barbette which would make it disagreeable for an enemy to come up the hill.- They make five places of brick in the bottom of the tents which Arnold ^{showed me} together with a picture of his wife and child. He said if I described my visit to him in the papers I must mention his name as his wife would like to hear of him. I offered to call and tell his wife who he said lived at 47 Grand St. He suddenly looked round with a thoroughly french expression of face and said you would not win her affections away from me?

Col De Trobriand soon arrived and, after explaining my plan to him, I returned by moon-light. He requested to be remembered to the judge. I spent the evening; by request of Mr [Ezekiel Brown] Elliott Sec^y, with the sanitory committee. Dr [John Foster] Jenkins the head man promised me their cooperation which may be of more value but I don't anticipate it. Mr Elliott talks with volubility around a subject until he has forgotten what he originally intended to say and I have no doubt has assisted materially in fixing the name of "insanitary" to the committee, which title they are often called by.

Dr Jenkins is a very lively little man somewhat on the pattern of Mr Pyore.

I met Mr Pyore at the hotel who invited me "sans ceremoni" to call on his wife, which I had to decline.

I called on Col Hardie who left his office with his clerks at eleven o'clock.

Nov 9th Col Hardie gave me the use of his horse and sent an orderly with me to Col Pecks division again whose brigade was just being reviewed.

Col Ryker [J. Lafayette Riker] of the Anderson Zouaves 42 N.Y. was mounted on a beautiful white stallion in the midst of a hollow square. After the violent use of my spurs I atlast forced my horse up to the soldiers who were firing blank cartridges which had a disagreeable resemblance to real ones as the muskets were aimed at me, and sounded still more so. The Col. broke the square for me and I entered it, he appointed an hour to see me and I retired to the seargeant's tent where I was given a little medicine to prevent my catching cold from the rain which began to fall in torrents.

At the hour appointed I called upon the Colonel who suggested to me the addition of drafts to be given to the soldiers which simplifies our system materially.

He knew the trustees had sold father notes and promised to see that his name had the opportunity of taking advantage of it. He thought all would do so.

We had curried chicken for dinner salt bacon and well cooked vegetables prepared by a colored boy. The sugar for the coffee was whit, the milk bowl was a preserve jar and there were other small incongruities about the service that added to our zest.

The colonel proposed to have my orderly sit down with us, but did not do so for fear he might feel under constraint.

While at dinner an officer put his head in the tent to borrow a flag to bury a man. The colonel inquired who was dead. "Oh! only one of Company K" was the answer. "He pretended he had typhoid fever but it looked more like laziness."

The Colonel explained to me that this was a specimen of humanity who were of no good when here and never missed when dead.

I filled up an allotment roll and then left with a borrowed cloak of the colonel's which I afterwards left at Genl William's office as I promised him.

Returning I called on Col De Trobriand of the 55th Regt who said that he had given the rolls to the captains and they were being generally signed.

Passing through Washington I arrived at Anacostia bridge near the navy yard where the 15th Col [Charles B.] Stuart was encamped.

The Col [Clinton G.] Colgate a cousin of Wm E. Dodge Jr was in command. He said a son of Morris Ketchum was captain of one of their companies [Capt. William A. Ketchum] and that he only wished I had come before.

They had just been paid off; and then he said, showing me his hand all cut and washed, is one of the effects. The men will spend the money, that they would willingly assign to their families, in drink if they have it. We punish the people that smuggle it in severely enough too he said; I caught two women and one man at it and put the women washing clothes and the man cutting wood putting them every night in irons for two weeks.

Next his regiment was the 50th Lieut Col Pittus [William H. Pettus]. He had in all his captains, explained our system to them, and promised immediately to introduce it, expressing great gratification.

It was too late for us to accept his pressing invitation to tea, especially as I had been whet through some six hours.

Pat Halsted of Newark insisted that I should be introduced to the mayor of Boston Jos. M Wightman and Marcus L Ward of Newark who represented their respective states and were here on the same subject, and desired to consult with me. Both had invented system without any regard to the law instead of adapting the system to the law.

I left them disgusted at half past nine, and took supper with Capt Kirkland, cousin of Thomas Kirkland, and Capt Mason of Boston and [John] Hay.

Washington Nov 10th 61

Dear Mittie

I will write you a letter individually and then enclose a short journal which is intended for the family also. Please have it kept as I will require it for future reference. Direct your letters and tell the others in case they write to direct to the care of John Hay Executive Mansion. I have taken a room for the sake of economy and although Willard [Hotel] professes willingness in taking charge of my letters they might be mislaid.

I have just returned from Dr. Gurleys Church where a chaplain officiated. I have no doubt a great many expectant individuals took me for the president who did not occupy his pew with us. Miss Thompson sat just in front of me in church, presumptive evidence that she is not an infidel.

Tell Bammie that the streets are all lined with wagons with eight and ten horses or mules to each, that I have a soldier who always rides behind me to show me the way and hold my horse and that several times soldiers have pointed their guns at me to make me stop when I was riding through their lines. They always send for their officer immediately and he lets me pass.

Tell Tedie that yesterday I saw a stable made of a tent with bushes at the side of it and that the poor horses had to stand in the cold all the time. The men all live in just the same kind of tents without the bushes but they have warm blankets and sometimes they dig holes in the earth and make fire places with bricks. Yesterday a man on a beautiful white horse stood in the middle of some soldiers who were firing all round and as I wanted to see him I had to put the spurs into my poor horse very hard until he bled so as to force him up to the square of men while they were firing towards me.

Kiss all the little children for me, I hope little Ellie is better and write me if it is only a few lines to tell me how you all get on. Give much love to Annie and your Mother from me.

I have not seen Mr Hyatt here, please remember me to the young ladies and tell them I did not know where he was and that every moment of my time is occupied with my mission here. You will be easily able to vouch for this when you read the sketch which I enclose of my first two days work.

I remain ever your affectionate husband
Thee. Roosevelt

Remember my special request that you should keep the house lively and not allow your mother to be melancholy. I am too late and must enclose journal in my next.

For having been in Washington for only four days, Thee had experienced a variety of situations. He had met with military leaders and the President's private secretary, been introduced to other Allotment commissioners and members of the Sanitary Commission, and toured military battlements. Thee had attended church at the New York Avenue Presbyterian Church where President Lincoln worshiped regularly, occupying the President's pew in his absence. The Reverend Dr. Phineas D. Gurley (1816-1868) ministered to this church and was a spiritual advisor to the President. The church, built in 1860, sat only a few blocks from the White House.

New York Avenue Presbyterian Church, Washington, D.C.

Thee met with John Hay (1838-1905), Lincoln's personal secretary and assistant as noted in his agreement to forward Thee's letters from home. Imagine how curious it must have been for Mittie and the rest of the family to address their letters to the Executive Mansion! Thee also mentions Williard's Hotel where he had stayed in 1855 on his trip back from Roswell.[69]

Thee's Journal

Nov 10th, Sunday. Went to Dr. Gurley's church but heard a chaplain who filled his pulpit.
Nov 11th Moved to a little room 207 P^a Av as I may be absent frequently.
 Visited 36 NY Col Innis [Charles H. Innes] north of the city several miles.
 He gave one of his captains a roll to test it which was signed in my presence by twenty men charging about ten dolls a month a piece.
 I took dinner with him in an old fashioned Virginia house belonging to loyal people. The little blackies wandering round had a very natural look.
 Three miles off were the 1st Long Island Col [Julius W.] Adams.
 The Lieut Col said he would sign it himself and was sure his men would. Capt [George] Foster took it in hand in this regiment.
 Near here were Col [John Cochrane] Cochran's Chasseurs where I met Leut Col Schailler. The Colonel had just been making an address to his men and then gone to Washington.
 It was amusing to see the blackey run and get a comb to give the last touch to Col Schailler's hair after he had his hat on. The Colonel seemed utterly oblivious of the operation.
 My horse, which I keep myself now, is a plough horse which stumbles a little and shies violently. With a very new

pair of spurs that I obtained from Newbould (late Captain) I get over the ground somehow.

Newbould is still looking for a position as officer.

Another evening spent partly in consultation with Mr [Marcus L.] Ward who expects to adopt our plan.

Dr [William M.] Chamberlain of the Sanitory Committee proposes tomorrow trying to introduce our system in New York regiment he will visit.

Theo. Roosevelt

I have no time to read this over.

New York Nov 12th 1861

My own darling Susy,

I received your sweet affectionate of the 9th yesterday morning - my first impulse was to write you immediately but I had commenced a letter to dear James & thought I had better finish that first - and write you today - The fine weather however tempted me out, and some how or other it is a peculiarity of N York that if you go out at all it consumes the day - It is now five oclock and I will not be able to mail this today -Susy darling I know from the way you write that you were dreadfully disappointed at my remaining in New York - I know you are lonely darling one and I am almost sorry that I have made the arrangement - I long to see you and when Elliott (who mends very slowly) is much better, I will leave him to sleep in his crib near Annas bed, and go on to Phil^a to see you, and if it does not inconvenience Mrs West will avail myself of her kind invitation and spend a few days with you all - My heart feels so tenderly towards you my precious child that I have frequent melts about you - In the midst of my anxiety and distress I feel that I have cause for much gratitude to God for giving me such good affectionate daughters Let me know if you do not think of visiting N York, and if you do, when. All well but Elliott & he is much better - Thee is absent, gone to Washington to try to get money from the Government for the soldiers wives

- I will write you again soon darling but feel that I must send this hasty scrawl this evening - Oh susy how awfully I feel about this Naval Expedition - I almost know that Irvine is amongst those who are on the Coast Defense I know my dearest daughter we do pray for him & dear Stuart - Oh continue to do so until you hear that prayer is no longer necessary - May our God shield and protect them in the midst of their peril

       Your affectionate Mother
        M Bulloch

  Martha's letter to Susan demonstrates their inability to receive news and letters from the South. On 29 September, Stuart had been dismissed from the Confederate Army for "pulmonary disease." Additionally, Martha worried over the Union Naval Expedition which occurred on 7 November at Port Royal, South Carolina as she was unaware that Irvine no longer served in the coastal defense, but was nearing Southhampton, England, on the C.S.S. *Nashville*.

       New York
       Nov 13th/61
My dearest Thee
  I have just received your letter of Nov 10th and also the Journal – as soon as I read them Wrote a note to Father and enclosed the Journal and also the note to Jim sent in the letter of Nov 10th – I was really delighted to hear from my dear warm Thee (I have been so cold every night since you left) tho he scolded and abused me so only the moment before he left – Anna made me read every word to her of both letters – we were much interested in the contents, you ought to be repaid for the trouble you are taking and I do hope you will succeed and "at least have the luxury of doing something for your country" – Thee could you possibly do something for Mother and me – manage in some way to let us hear from Irvine – Do ask Hay and the President, I wrote to you this morning directing to Willard Hotel, but fear you

will not get it — as you tell me to direct to Executive Mansion You received a letter from Miss French — which I put in your drawer of the Library table — I read it accidentally she thanks you for some skates, Bamie has been quite unwell, eyes inflamed tho no ulcers in them — Teedie has a very bad cold, Ellie is better, tho very delicate in the way of digestion etc. Teedie and Bamie Mother took to Barnums again to day. Teedie was afraid last night that there was a Bear in your Dressing room he is the most affectionate endearing little creature in his ways but begins to require his Papa's discipline sadly — he is brimming full of mischief and has to be watched all the time. Anna has gone to the Dominos Party and will remain with the Hyatts all night — I wrote you this morning that she was to attend me with the girls at the {Yhulhorns} — she went anticipating much fun. Caddie and herself going dressed exactly alike.

Miss Campbell has called a few days since splendidly dressed — Anna is going to spend Friday evening with her a "high neck party" Miss C termed it. I fear I owe you all of this devotion, what think you? Anna met Col Torre in the street, she will describe the interview, how distressed he is at having offended "Roosevelt" and his certainty that an explanation would entirely satisfy both parties, Caddie, Phanie, and Lillie Hyatt sent Gen Scott a beautiful bouquet the day of his departure in the wagon Anna has become perfectly charmed with the Hyatts cousin Reuben Morris who called last night, while he was here Mr & Mrs Hodge[70] called from Brooklyn, to night Mr Adams (Dr Adams' son) called but Anna had just gone — Dear Thee being so little in the world I know of nothing to interest you I wonder if your thoughts ever lovingly return to me, as Thee, Thee I try and fear not. Try to get through your business and come home for you are sadly missed. I must close for I am tired out always at night and I have written this at night being the only time unoccupied with the dear troublesome little children deserted by their Papa

           Lovingly
           Mittie

Mittie's news-filled letter was full of the events of her day and tales of Anna's social life. The Hyatt girls, mentioned in previous letters, could now be identified as Stephanie, age 22, Caroline, age 20, and Melissa Augusta, age 17. They were the daughters of wealthy shoe and boot manufacturer Stephen Hyatt (1814-1879) and his wife Dorinda.[71]

Journal Continued
Nov 12th Just as I was leaving Washington Newbold also on horseback joined me. The day was fine, the road good, and the scenery beautiful as we cross by the chain bridge onto the sacred soil of Virginia. There is one succession of teams along the road but only one or two carriages of private individuals, all are examined strictly on crossing the bridge and a pass is a necesity. As we enter the beautiful rolling country camps extend in every direction, soldiers drilling and bands playing brighten up the scene. But the country itself is fast becoming a wilderness, you can take a direct line across the country without fear of encountering a fence, and many of the houses are reduced to their frames only and look like huge skeletons.

On reaching the 43rd Regt found Col [Francis L.] Vinton overbearing in his manner to his inferiors but extremely polite to me. He complains that the Governor will not pay his regiment their state pay while paying regts enlisted later, also that he keeps skeleton regts in New York instead of filling those on the field.

I dined with him and found young Eggleton the quartermaster who was with us very pleasant. He is about to return home from ill health and requested me to see his family and tell them I had seen him.

Next visited the 33rd Col [Robert F.]Taylor and 49th Col [David D.] Bidwell. Lt Col WC [William C.] Alberger in command, also the 14th Col M. [James McQuady] Mcquade and the 17th Col [Henry S. Lansing] Lancing, Lt Col [Thomas F.] Morris in command.

While going through this last regiment a man dressed as Adjutant called out "halt Roosevelt is that you"? It proved to be James B Taylor from whose mother we bought 216 Pearl St. Mr Hawes the quartermaster also knew me and while Taylor furnished me with a bed or rather place to lie in his tent he saw that I had a profusion of blankets. I took supper with the Lt Col and then went the rounds with the Adjutant. We found eight lights lit after taps, six for parties playing cards after being paid off. Thirty were in the guard tent mostly drunk. One punishment is to tie them on the horse or round piece of wood supported at each end, with their hands tied. One man slipped round and hit his head against the ground three times.

    I visited Genl [John H.] Martindale in the course of the evening where I met Gen [George W.] Morrell and Capt Achmenty.

13th   Went first to the 44th called the Ellsworth Avengers where I know Lt Col [James C.] Rice, he says they continue to have nightly prayer meetings and no drunkenness or disorder.

    He was officer of the day and rode round with me, the full guard always being called out to salute him. I did not think much of Col [Stephen] Stryker who does not seem to receive sufficient respect.

The 25th Col [Charles A.] Johnson, Kingan's old regt until he was arrested, is now in fair order and improving rapidly, the men happier than when they had theirown way.

    In Keyes Brigade I met Sir John Murray an old acquaintance under another name, Weir will remember him Coppenger, hard of hearing at Jimmy O'Brian's. He was devoted to me gave me an introduction to the Colonels of the 14th [Edward B.] Fowler. Lt Col [Gordon F.] Thomas of 22nd (Col Phillips absent) Col Sullivan of the 24th and Frisby of the 30th and made me dine with him. Quail for dinner and ham. I may state that the fare is invariably first-rate.

    At Wadsworth [General James Samuel] head quarters I found Capt J Bryce Smith who gave me his bed and all he had to make himself comfortable although I don't know how he knew me.

Capt. Sanderson the great individual on cooking is here.

Young Wadsworth[72] [Craig Wharton Wadsworth] went with me after tea to see the Colonels of regiments in his father's brigade and he joined in a dance that was going on in an old Virginia farm house, one of the few not deserted by its inmates.

I found Col Pratt [George W.] my room companion very pleasant.

One of the Colonels stated that after pay day out of nine hundred and fifty men he could muster only three hundred and fifty.

14th The language of the soldiers suddenly changes as I come into Gen [Louis] Blenkers division and German only is spoken. There I met among others our old riding school teacher Dickel [Christian F.] as Colonel of his regiment, by whom I was received with distinguished consideration. Lieut Croft formerly of West Point as cadet desired to be remembered to "the belle Miss Caddie Hyatt." Dr {Romyon} now Capt under Dickel requested to be remembered to my wife.

I must again excuse myself from reading this over as it is one o'clock at night and I have been on the go since six this morning most of the time spent on horse-back. I must start early tomorrow too if I can hope to return to my wife and family.

I visited the outposts this morning and saw Falls Church.

Journal

Nov 15th Alexandria where I had left my horse the night before is much improved in its business position by the war. The stores let for double old prices and the streets have ten times the life that they never had before; this remark is equally applicable to Washington.

My first visit was to General Franklin's division now three miles out of town where at Genl Hooker I met Mr Hopkins who was very polite to me under the impression at first that I was the Po'keepsie James Roosevelt.

Young Howland was there also and at their mess with Genl [Henry W.] Slocum I dined.

Col Davis who requested to be remembered to his sporting friend Rob was specially interested in the object of my visit, although this was as usual universal.[73]

Col [Joseph J.] Bartlett of the 27th showed me his camp with much pride and mentioned that Genl McClelland had noticed it; one word from him seems to set any of them up for life. The tents all had log foundations increasing of course their size materially.

The difference in the camps is very striking some have quantities of fine trees and make barriers which surround the colonel's tent, others in the German division of Blencker [Blenker] have built little huts – much as used to grace the outskirts of New York, wretched enough.

Genl [William B.] Franklin was an old acquaintance, and appears like a soldier.

In Genl [Samuel P.] Heintzelman's division, was McCunns [Col. John H. McCunn] regiment in which Lt Col [John Timothy] Burke was very melancholy because his promotion had been overlooked. He requested my influence with Governor Morgan.

The 38th Mozart[74] is in remarkably fine discipline apparently; Lt Col Farmesworth [Addison Farnsworth] insisted on my staying to tea with him and was anxious to have me examine the camp thoroughly.

Genl Heintzelman is utterly insignificant in voice and appearance, but was thought well of in the Mexican war. He says he has not ventured out of his camp.

Moses of Sarah Willis memory and the brother of Dick Hunt are on his staff.

I paid a visit in the evening to Mrs Lincoln who received me most graciously, after which I called at the Sanitory Committee rooms and saw Mr [Frederick Law] Olmstead.

He expressed himself as perfectly delighted with what we ^{are} doing and the way in which we are doing it.

Nov 16th. Spent most of the evening in Genl [Thomas] William's office arranging my plans, and obtained more allotments rolls from the pay master general. I always go with them attached to the pommel of my saddle, and long for my heavy shawl to strap behind.

In Genl Caseys division I happened upon the 56th New York.75 There were stray men along the road, some drunk, one shouted to the orderly to ride by my side and there was every indication of utter want of discipline. This was the regiment of which Gus was Lieut Col. and whose absence the captain, the highest officer in the camp, regretted deeply.

In the 61st New York regt. I was received with unexpected warmth by [Colonel] Spencer W Cone who means to have his whole heart in his business.

I spent part of the evening with Governor [Alexander W.] Randall of Wisconsin talking over the allotment system.

With a kiss to each child and much love to yourself I remain
                    Your Husband
                        Theodore

Theodore discontinued keeping a journal after this last page or it has been lost to time. His notes about his experiences not only demonstrated the huge undertaking that was the Allotment System, but also the variety of men he met and the conditions which he encountered. After this date, Thee continued his work both for the Allotment Act and as an Allotment Commissioner. He spent much of the autumn and the following winter in the vicinity of Washington, D.C.

                    New York Nov 16th - 1861

My dearest Susy,
In my last short hurried note I promised to write you very shortly - but this week dear daughter I have had every moment of my time taken up - All of the children are

sick but Corinne - Bamie & Teedie both with severe colds - threatened with croup, and little Elliott (who has appeared to gain strength very slowly never has been altogether well in his stomach and bowels -) appears to day more unwell than usual. Teedie was quite sick last night and had to take an emetic - We gave him oil this morning but he seems quite unwell this evening - In addition to this dear Susy I cannot deny the fact that I have been very wretched this week - I feel almost heart-broken that the fleet has landed at Port Royal - For two days I could do nothing but cry -Yesterday was the day appointed by the Confederate Government as a day of fasting humiliation and prayer - God knows I tried to keep it with my whole heart - I prayed for complete submission to the will of God for I know not how soon I may hear that my dear Irvine is amongst the slain - If I may judge at all of the embittered feeling of the South against the North by myself, I would say they would rather be burried in one common grave than ever again live under the same government - I am confident I should - But I will not speak any more on this subject - Anna received a letter last evening from Hariot - She sends a great deal of love to you - Thee and the children were well Jimmie was not in Liver Pool when she wrote - She says "tell Susy her old D^r, Dr Simmes is creating quite a sensation in Paris - he has effected the most wonderful cures among persons of rank - sometime ago he received a book from a celebrated Physician in Paris one of his own works It had written- on the fly leaf "To the most illustrious Dr Marion S-" Hariot likes Liver Pool better than she did - She sees a great many southern friends there - She says I must write to Stuart and Irvine and send my letters there - She thinks She can get the letters to them - I shall do so - I will let you know if I can tomorrow how the children are - inn haste your truly affectionate Mother

    M Bulloch

I hope darling Susy you are well - I long to see you - The baby is almost a beauty Mittie still has enough milk for her.

Harriott gave no details about James, except that he was not in Liverpool. Mail from Harriott and James was most assuredly read by government officials before being forwarded to Martha, Anna, Mittie, and Susan.

James D. Bulloch's own memoirs and other historic documents fill in the details. On 14 October, the S.S. *Fingal* set sail from Great Britain; aboard were James, fellow Savannah native Andrew Low, also an experienced sea captain, and Major Edward C. Anderson of the Confederate Army. The ship's hold held a considerable amount of war munitions. The *Fingal* arrived at the neutral port of Bermuda on 2 November 1861. Also in port was the C.S.S. *Nashville*. The captain of the *Nashville* provided Bulloch with the latest news from the Confederacy and had aboard several naval men able to guide ships through the Union's naval blockade. Bulloch took aboard Capt. John Makin, also of Savannah.[76]

This meeting of the *Fingal* and the *Nashville* also reunited the half-brothers, Irvine and James. Martha's mind would have been eased by knowing Irvine was safe and with James; however, the news of their meeting would no doubt come to New York only after many months had passed.

Telling no one other than Makin (Low and Anderson were well aware of Bulloch's plans) of their final destination, the *Fingal* set sail for Nassau. On 8 November, Bulloch revealed his plans to the crew, few of whom were surprised. As the official holder of the title to the *Fingal*, Bulloch hauled two 4.5-inch guns to the deck, along with several other small naval cannons, and mounted each, thereby converting the S.S. *Fingal* into the C.S.S. *Fingal*, a ship of war. Small arms and ammunition were made ready.[77]

In the darkness of 12 November, with considerable difficulty, Bulloch successfully ran the blockade, sailing through the coast's marsh fog and directly up the Savannah River. At Fort Pulaski, now under Confederate control, James unfurled the Confederate flag and fired his signal gun to mark their approach as a friendly vessel. Hailed as hometown heroes, Bulloch, Anderson, and Low arrived in Savannah with the largest single-trip delivery of military arms of the War.[78]

The *Charlotte Democrat* listed the cargo as more than 12,000 Enfield rifles, one million cartridges, 40,000 lbs of powder, six 24-lb rifled cannon, sabers, pistols, shoes, and blankets.[79] The South had very few industries manufacturing armaments, and did not have the raw materials necessary.

The *Vicksburg Weekly Citizen* (Mississippi) reported the news, as did many other papers, and continued to follow James' travels to meet with various Confederate government officials. However, the Vicksburg paper attributed success of the *Fingal*'s blockade run to the Almighty rather than James.

> The circumstances connected with the arrival of the *Fingal* seems to have had a divine direction. The morning was one of the most beautiful of the season, clear and serene - when the *Fingal* hove in sight of the Fort. One of her officers insisted on going into Port Royal- the harbor it was first designed to enter- not knowing that Lincoln's fleet was anchored there. But another officer said, "No, he would make straight for Savannah." Finding no blockading vessels near, the *Fingal* was steered for the bar, but soon discovered the fleet in the distance, when a dense fog suddenly enveloped the whole squadron, and in the fog the *Fingal* entered safely beyond the reach of the shot and shell, when the sky and atmosphere became as suddenly clear as before it had been dark and foggy. Was not this miraculous and of Divine direction?[80]

James traveled to meet with Confederate Secretary of the Navy Stephen Mallory in Richmond where they discussed plans for additional blockade runners and naval vessels. James asked that Irvine be transferred to his command for service aboard a future warship, of which he was to have command. Back in Savannah, others began loading the *Fingal* with cotton and other materials that might be sold in Britain to fund James' ship buying ventures.

James Dunwoody Bulloch, age unknown

Washington Nov 17th 61

Myown Dearest Mittie

I must answer the affectionate part of your letter first, before I begin journalizing, as the receiving it gave me more pleasure that anything that has occurred since I left you.

Don't speak of my being a warm person please, you would not think so if you saw me sleeping in one of the tents; or indeed even in myown room which is as well adapted to keeping the wind out as most southern rooms. The weather has become much colder and you know I was not well provided even for riding on horseback in the cold. I will do all in my power for you in the way of getting news from Irvine but have not much hope of being successful.

I received your previous letter and should have acknowledged it in my answer but think I omitted to do so.

I saw the president and his wife in church this morning where by the bye I heard a very good sermon.

I am so glad to hear that Annie is enjoying herself. I liked Reuben Morris exceedingly and think he will be a very pleasant addition to our list of gentlemen acquaintances.

Give the little children each a long kiss from me, I cannot bear to tell you to be strict with them now that I am away, but for theirown good they ought to learn to obey you as implicitly as they do me.

I hope you get down to see father as often as you can; the clergyman in his sermon today spoke of those mothers who we should strive to prepare ourselves to meet in heaven, and I felt how much I owed to mine.

I long to see you all again and will neglect some of my work in order to get back but there is no prospect of my returning this week, do not forget me or let the children do so.

I start tomorrow for Poolesville some forty miles off and am fortunate enough to have two companions for the ride one of whom at least I would hardly have selected, David Bishop and Wm Gebhard. They are both intensely good natured which is an important item. I was three days without having my clothes off last week and I start off again tomorrow with a similar prospect ahead.

  A grand review is expected on wednesday which I will try to return for if possible, some sixty or eighty thousand troops.

  Do write me often just such letters as you wrote last
Yourown Husband
Thee

Thee was leaving Washington for Poolesville, Maryland, where Union forces guarded the shallow fords of the Potomac River, which would allow easy access to the capital city. Called the Corps of Observation, these units consisted of about 20,000 Union troops stationed in and about the town. No battles occurred in Poolesville that winter; however, at the nearby infamous Battle of Ball's Bluff, on 21 October 1861, hundreds of Union soldiers stationed in Poolesville lost their lives in a badly managed battle led by inexperienced Union generals.[81]

New York Nov 18th-1861

I wrote you a few lines on saturday darling Susy - but thinking as I wrote how sick the children were you would be uneasy I again send you a few lines - They are much better Bamie & Teedie are both clear of fever, and the cough very much abated -Elliott is better also but is a little cross - I am obliged to keep out of his sight when it does not suit me to hold him - The baby seemed a little unwell and we gave her a small dose of oil which I think will relieve her - Mittie & Anna are well - but the former has her hands full with the pitiful little sick things - She often says oh if sister only lived next door how often I would turn one of them over to her a few hours each day -Saturday night when Teedie had quite a warm fever - he said Ganma I want to see my aunt Tudie - At another time he said how I wish I could see my aunt Tudie he always calls Susie Tudie. He is playing about the room today, and gives little or no trouble Elliott, I think would have been much better but he has also taken the prevailing cold -Thee has not returned yet - He writes Mittie constantly but does not say when he will return. The Nurse Delia seems to be a good kind of creature but not smart and has no tact with children - Elliott is getting more reconciled to her and in time she may do very well I wish you could have seen Elliott last night during a visit from the D^r He cut all of the little monkey capers he could think of - when the D^r first came into the room pushed a chair for him to sit in then pretended he was a dog bear etc - Susy darling I received your sweet letter this morning - I will let you know some days before I go to see you - I could not do so before - the children got well, and Thee came home. dearest I am sorry I wrote you on saturday how miserable I was, because I know it made your tender heart ache to think I was unhappy - I hope dear Susy God may protect our dear ones - I know <u>you</u> pray for them constantly - Good bye darling precious child

Chapter 5: December of 1861

The Letters

Washington Dec 4th 61

Dearest Mittie

We had a very pleasant trip over, meeting some friends who helped us wile away the time.

Dodge was made very melancholy by the loss of his pocket book containing a hundred dolls and some memos but soon recovered his spirits.

We have seen several important individuals this morning, including Sec'y Cameron and succeeded in one part of our mission that I did not mention to you, securing the cooperation of government in aiding the sufferers on Hatteras Island.

Hay has been of material service again.

Yours as ever
Theo Roosevelt

Thee wrote of *Dodge* losing his wallet, which contained a substantial amount of money. This was most likely William E. Dodge, Jr. (1832-1903), a fellow businessman and Union League member from New York. Dodge, like Thee, had traveled to Washington to lobby Congress for the military allotment bill.

Thee also mentioned Simon Cameron (1799-1889), who served as Lincoln's first Secretary of War. Appointed in March of 1861, Cameron only served until January of 1862, when he was replaced by Edwin M. Stanton. Cameron resigned amidst allegations of disorganization and corruption. Additionally, Cameron's brother, Colonel James Cameron, New York Volunteer Infantry Regiment, died in action at the First Battle of Bull Run on July 21, 1861. Thee had no doubt heard of both the allegations against Cameron and the death of his brother the previous summer.

In the last words of Thee's letter, he wrote of yet another mission he and his companions had taken on the relief of the soldiers on Hatteras Island off the coast of North Carolina. When North Carolina seceded from the Union and joined the Confederacy, Confederate forces held the slave-constructed Forts Clark and Hatteras on the south end of the island to control access to Pamlico Sound. On 28 August 1861, seven Federal ships opened fire on Fort Clark. Unable to defend themselves due to the feeble range of their artillery, the Confederates abandoned Fort Clark and fled to Fort Hatteras. A small unit of Union soldiers landed and took Fort Clark. At dawn the following day, Federal ships began a bombardment of Fort Hatteras. After hours of intense shelling, the Confederates surrendered the fort, and all 700 soldiers were captured. It was said the taking of Hatteras Inlet was so important to Lincoln that when receiving the news in the middle of the night he danced a jig in his nightshirt.[82]

While the island's long-time residents had grown accustomed to a lack of drinking water, insects, sand, and volatile weather, Union forces now stationed on the island had few resources to combat its natural elements. On 13 November, the *Daily Ohio Statesman*[83] reported:

> Great Storm and Flood-The Island Submerged-Tents, Shanties, and Provisions Swept Off - Great Distress and Privation-Deplorable Condition of the Twentieth Indiana.
>
> Hatteras Islet, Nov. 9 1861
> The land forces at this point are now in the midst of another engagement which is of a more serious character than any of the conflicts

that have yet taken place on this coast. It is a contest with the elements. A great deluge is upon us. Last evening a gale sprang up, which continued to increase in fury every moment until morning, when it assumed the form of a perfect whirlwind, accompanied with rain, which at times fell in torrents. About three o'clock this morning the waves from the ocean began to sweep over the island (half a mile wide) into the Sound, and before daylight these two bodies of water were united. Not a spot of land was to be seen. All the lower portions of the island where Forts Hatteras and Clark are situated was under water, and so sudden was the upheaving and so violent the storm, that all chances of escape were cut off before the morning light came. It was utterly impossible for an assistance to reach them from our fleet, so terrible was the Hatteras storm. And it was not until a breaker swept across the island, carrying men tents, shanties and every creeping thing with it, that the soldiers were aware of the presence of a great flood. Men were suddenly washed out of their beds and found their clothes (what few had undressed) borne by the water to the sound. Live stock, such as pigs, chickens, horses, cattle, dogs, cats, and cooking utensils, lumber, driftwood boxes, barrels, trunks, shanties, were carried forward, together with men on them and in them, some jumping out of windows, some cutting their way through the roof, others jumping off into the water, which in many places as over their heads in depth, and making for a box or barrel in order to reach the roof of a shanty still standing. Officers on horses were riding or swimming through this moving mass, giving orders to this floating army of men who, with a gun in one hand and with the other hanging on to some kind of an object, kept themselves above water.

The article continued, telling the events of the day, including stories of wounded and ill men being swept to their deaths. It told of the Steamer *Spalding* arriving and off loading desperately needed supplies, only to have them washed from the pier over and over again. Not until the following day, when the water receded, were the men were able to find dry land and cook what meager provisions they had. At Camp Wool, some three miles above Fort Hatteras, the Ninth New York Volunteers saw their large hospital carried away and nearly all their provisions swept into the sea.

Newspaper articles about the storm spread across the Union and the Confederacy.[84] After the Union's jubilation following their first real victory, nature had taken so much and so many from them. Being in the capital and thereabout, Thee would have read and heard about the disaster and the extreme state of need for those men on Hatteras Island.

Washington Dec 6th 61

Dearest Mittie

    I am gaining experience daily in a political point of view. Everyone to whom we have presented our letters and their name in legion talks very favorable of our bill. Senator Wilson of Massachusetts has agreed to bring it in, lest Blair who is chairman of the military committee of the house, as Wilson is of the senate, promises his hearty cooperation, and unless Wilson plays false by trying to attach something else to it we can probably get it passed immediately. General McClellan has given an autograph note stating that in his view it is of the greatest importance.

    Senator Fessenden of Maine says he will do all in his power for us. In the meantime congress has adjourned 'till monday next and Dodge and myself are left to amuse ourselves until that time. We went yesterday to see Senator

[Ira] Harris present a flag to the Harris light cavalry. The speeches were uncommonly good and most of the principal dignitaries were present. The Misses Stephens sisters of Mrs Strong were present with Miss Cohan to whom they introduced me and whom I am going to call on at her invitation, they are staying with her.

Mrs Lincoln asked me to drive with her today but in consequence of a head ache deferred it until tomorrow.

Please tell Caddie and Phanie [Hyatt] that I have disposed of six shares in their afghan One to the president, Mrs Lincoln, Tom G Nicolay[85] Pres Sec'y, John Hay Pres Sec'y Saml Hooper member cong from Boston and one to W^m E Dodge Jr.

I will probably enclose with this a letter from Hay requesting the numbers as I requested him to write directly for them, please send me the numbers immediately.

I saw the review of General Keyes division this morning by McClellan and met there Maj Keyes and Mrs. Dr Van Buren West Point of memory.

Genl [Innis N.] Palmer who has charge of all the cavalry and with whom Mr Reamey Warren is staying took supper with me last night

Please send this to father as he might like to read it
Your Husband
Thee.

Thee continued to lobby for the allotment system, meeting with senators, representatives, and military leaders. He had obtained the approval of Senator Henry Wilson (1812-1875) of Massachusetts, who chaired the Military Affairs Committee. Wilson would become the 18th Vice President of the United States during President Grant's second term. Thee seemed to be concerned about support from Representative Francis Preston Blair, Jr. (1821-1875) of Missouri, Chairman of the Military Affairs Committee in the House of Representatives. Kentucky born Blair represented Missouri and was a personal friend and supporter of Lincoln.

Thee also had the support of Major General George B. McClellan (1826-1885). Appointed by Lincoln on 1 November as General in Chief, McClellan believed the Confederates were forming a massive army to take Washington, and therefore stationed more than 170,000 Union troops in defense of Washington. McClellan did not side with Lincoln and believed him to be "nothing more than a well-meaning baboon", a "gorilla", and "ever unworthy of ... his high position."[86] However, Thee had retained McClellan's backing for the Allotment.

In the midst of his important lobbying, Thee took time to sell shares in an afghan being made by some young ladies of his acquaintance. During the War, women, especially young unmarried women, often made items to raffle. The money would then be donated to various charitable organizations to supply comfort and supplies for the soldiers. Thee sold six shares, one each to his traveling companion William Dodge; John Nicolay and John Hays, the President's personal secretaries; Massachusetts Representative Samuel Hooper; and one each to the President and Mrs. Lincoln. Even approaching the President and Mrs. Lincoln with such a request shows a great deal of familiarity between the Roosevelts and the presidential family. (See Appendix C)

While lobbying, Thee and Dodge met a variety of personages. They attended a review of General Erasmus Darwin Keyes' regiment. Keyes (1810-1895) had seen action at Bull Run in July of 1861. Later, Thee and Dodge met New York Senator Ira Harris (1802-1875) and viewed the Harris Light Cavalry (7th United States Cavalry). They also met Major Keyes, and Reamey Warren, who have not been identified. General Innis Newton Palmer (1821-1900), who after distinguished service at the first Battle of Bull Run, was transferred to the Fifth U. S. Cavalry and promoted to brigadier general. One civilian Thee included in his letter was Mrs. Louise Van Buren, whom Thee and Anna had met at West Point the previous year. Louise was married to Philadelphia physician Dr. William Holme Van Buren.

New York
Dec 9th 1861

My dearest Thee
    I intended writing you last night and waited patiently for the Library which was occupied by Mr Thomas [Husbert] & about 9 oclock they are next into Lizzies [Roosevelt] but I was tired and determined to write this morning. Teedie was very unwell last night I was up with him six or seven times during the night if there is no improvement I intend giving magneism to night, Elliot has also had a sick turn, Yesterday evening Bamie was undressing Teedie (which she insisted upon doing) when he was seated up in a chair with his dressing gown on, Bamie taking off his shoes - he said "Mama I hab two harders (Fathers) one Papa and one harder in heaven" I said whhy how did you know that Teedie he said "Papa hay (say) in the morning our harder in heaven" So you see he is learning something by being down at prayers - Just now when I was getting my preparations made for writing he came into the Library and touched the Testament and said "I always bung (bring) dess to Papa in the morning" Did he ever? Lizzie Emlem [Roosevelt] said she had seen you named present at a Review in Washington - this with one letter from you is all I have heard from my Attentive loving Thee, I am so sorry Mr Dodge lost his Pocket book with the contents - Bamie is getting ready for school - and Anna has just called out to me that Corinne is wide awake
    Good bye my dear heartless Thee
    As ever yours
    Mittie Roosevelt

Washington Dec 10th 61

Dearest Mittie
    Your very welcome letter is just received and, as a sweet letter from you always does, inspires an immediate reply. Dear Teedie seemed brought up before my eyes by the little remark of his that you quoted, I suppose he cannot be very sick from you speaking of him as present this morning

after you spoke of him as sick, write me immediately how he is. He has brought me the testament that mother gave me several times.

How long we will be detained here it seems impossible to say, the proverbial delays of congress were besetting us although in a milder form than usual. Col [Francis Preston] Blair in whose Committee room I am writing this, says he will pass it through the House tomorrow if possible and Senator [Henry] Wilson is doing all for us in his power in the Senate.

Possibly this week may see me home but it seems probable that my visit may extend into next week. I amuse myself as you know I always try to through the different channels open to me. Yesterday I rode on horseback with Mrs Leydam, and dined with young Lydig and passed the evening at Secy Chases. This afternoon I dined with Genl Keyes and passed the evening at a bridal reception of Miss Carroll where all the noted individuals that one ought to see will be present. Mr Ames who has one of the pleasantest houses in Washington sent me the bride's cards. I had known Miss Carroll previously at West Point.

A party will be made up to visit Mount Vernon tomorrow to which I have an invitation (which our bill will probably prevent my accepting) from the Chases; in the afternoon or rather evening a concert is given in one of the regiments to which I am invited and after that Marshall of New York has asked us to supper. So that you see there is no lack of occupation.

I often long to see you all at home however and picture to myself your occupations at the different hours of the day while I am so differently employed. That first morning when I get home I look forward to an indefinite amount of affections, you must not disappoint me.

With a great deal of love and many kisses to each of the children I remain
        Your Ever loving
        Husband

Thee's social schedule remained as busy as his political one. He attended a wedding reception for a Miss Carroll, whom he had met at West Point. He also dined with Treasury Secretary Salmon P. Chase (1808-1873). Chase had been widowed three times; however, a daughter, Catherine Jane (1840-1897), from his second wife, remained at home and served as his hostess. They also invited Thee to visit Mount Vernon with them.

New York
Dec 12th 1861

My own dearest Thee I received your dear yellow letter last evening and Bamie was also delighted with her letters and pictures at the top - I think it is high time you were on your homeward trip I saw in this mornings paper (Wednesday) there had been a notion for facilitating the news of getting home the soldiers pay - this is I suppose your bill - I hope it will pass. Teedie is better tho he is not well and looks as Sister says like one of these very pale azalais [azaleas] I altho dread the care of Elliot at night next week and hope you will be here to share it with me You know Mother goes to Philadelphia on Saturday Bamie continues to like school and Miss Drummonds much - she says Miss D has promised to take them to see books printed and had today shown them a skull bone and was keeping up a leg bone for tomorrow,

Phanie wrote to you this morning - last night she, Caddie, Mr Hurlbut Mr Ulhern, & Mr Homs called just before they came Mr {Frahay} made his appearance - so you see they made quite a party - Phanie staid all night, Caddie at 12 o'clock walked up to 277 Fifth Avenue to see if her Mother would let her stay - but she did not make her appearance again, this morning a note arrived full of apologies saying her Mother was unwilling that she should return alone south with Mr H and "Papa" was in bed! Julia Elliot has just called, the children have just done their luncheon and I am going to send them for the drive down in the Omnibus and return again in the same one.

Tomorrow at 10 oclock Lizzie Ellis, Anna and I are going out in the carriage - to look for Christmas presents for the children - I wanted Lizzie to come in last night very much - but she wrote me the most affectionate note saying she would gladly come in and see us in the morning - but she had rushed over to go into company - much of this anon - Caddie & Phanie seem most delighted at you having gotten so many partys to take shares in this Afghans. Phanie had Mr Hays ticket about her all last evening of course constantly dropping it when it would be picked up by Mr Ulhern or some other of the gentlemen much to his disgust - she says she feels wretchedly about Cap Armstrong - I do hope the last of this week will see you at home, I have not yet sent your letters to 14th street but will do so if I get time to day

    Good bye my dear old warm Thee - ever yours
        Mittie Roosevelt

        Washington Dec 12th 61
Dearest Mittie

  I must write you, although this letter should be an answer to Anna. Tell her that I will write her if I stay here any longer very soon but she must not wait for this to enclose me a list of the numbers which she omitted in her last. Tell her that she or the Hyatts must put the names to the numbers and then enclose them immediately to the parties for whom they are, as well as duplicates to me.

  The presidential party had better all be enclosed to care of John Hay, Executive Mansion Washington. One to Samuel Hooper Willards Hotel Washington The other to W E Dodge Jr to his address New York City.

  I am getting very melancholy about our bill, it is very worrying to find unnecessary delays continually thrown in our way when all that we must acknowledge it to be of vital importance. This is doubly disagreeable when our best friends all advise us not to press the matter and in other words give us no opportunity of working where we could really at all events be actively engaged and would not be blue sometimes.

Governor Fish has been to see Senator Wilson. Bancroft is actively working with us, we have all but one senator on the Committee to which it was referred on our side but this one has prevented the whole machinery from working. This one man is working for Governor Morgan, for fear his plans should be interfered with.

I try to forget this whenever I can and you know my character well enough to be sure that I generally succeed.

Yours and Anna's last letters have also troubled me, do write immediately how the children are. I long to see the little things again and do hope they are well. Kiss each one for me.

The House has just adjourned until monday and Dodge is talking of going home, but I feel that is my duty to remain until this bill is settled one way or the other, I most sincerely hope favorably. Its importance strikes me more every day I remain here, and I cannot help feeling sorry that Mrs [means *messers*] Ketchum and Dodge were unwilling to act without legislation although I believe our present course if practicable is best.

We have succeeded under any circumstances in doing much good by bringing the matter so prominently forward and will eventually I believe get it into shape.

Excuse me for writing so business-like a letter but it has engrossed so much of my thoughts lately that it will come out.

       Your Loving Husband
       Theodore

Thee's letter mostly dealt with trying to get the allotment bill passed. He mentioned New York's former governor Hamilton Fish (1801-1893), who served from 1849 to 1850, and Edwin Denison Morgan, New York's serving mayor (1859-1862). Bancroft could be George Bancroft of

New York. Mr. Ketchum was Morris Ketchum, a wealthy New York banker.

Beginning in April 1861, Hamilton Fish participated in the Union Defense Committee of the State of New York. This committee worked with New York City's government in raising and equipping troops and disbursed more than one million dollars to New York volunteers and their families during their first year of operation. The committee included John A. Dix, William M. Evarts, William E. Dodge, A.T. Stewart, John Jacob Astor, and other prominent New York men. Fish chaired the committee after Dix joined the military.[87]

New York
Dec 15th/61

My dearest Thee

    I have received your last letter and Bamie was much delighted with hers - I read Teedies part over to him this morning with which he seemed much pleased I asked him what I should say to Papa he said "oh do tell Papa to come home - Teedie still does not quite seem himself his cough being quite troublesome at times - and he seems weak. I was thinking perhaps I had better give him quinine you remember he took it prepared in ginger syrup last Spring but neither you nor Mother being here I did not feel like giving it on my own responsibility - and if I sent for Dr C[88] it would take at least three visits before he would comprehend which child was sick Teedie or Ellie, then when he would decide it would be so late in the campaign, it reminds me of the official accounts of the battle of "Bull Run" coming out when you have forgotten all about it and have become interested in that of "Balls Bluff" - I believe I told you in my last letter that I had begun Bamie at dancing school - she has been but twice as yet - the first time she seemed very tired and uninterested, but I have determined to give her a fair trial - so on Friday last (the last dancing school afternoon) when she came home at 12 oclock I had her apparatus taken off and she laid down in bed - she seemed in consequence to have had a pleasant time, she watches Cherrands[89] quite carefully but I really can not judge at all yet. I got along pretty well with Elliot last night he slept till two oclock when he awoke in the brightest possible frame of mind - after getting up many times with him - letting him eat an indefinite quantity of crackers - being very much amused at his cunning ways when he saw Teedie asleep he would whisper "Teedie heep" then suddenly catching sight of Anna he cried out in the loudest possible voice "Allie" finally becoming very sleepy and tired myself I {___} tried to coax him to sleep which I accomplished first after a crying spell then he came into my bed and fell asleep while I was stroking his curls etc. Teedie was miserably jealous about his sleeping by me - I have Bamie up stairs singing in the most discordant voice some of her sunday school hymns. Anna took Bamie to church this afternoon (Dr Adams preached to the children this afternoon) when she returned she told me she had heard the most interesting sermon that {___} spoke to those who are from {"Guinea"}. Anna laughed and said from {"Havannah"} they also saw Mr Dodge who said he thought you would be back in a very short time, I do hope so Thee I do hope you {__} will {___} I look carefully through the report of the proceedings in Congress - how tantalizing it is to wait tho I know my dear old Theede finds much to amuse him still any thing undecided is trying - and you have taken so much pains about this, I cannot see undecided so many on your side The President, McCellans autograph - and so many others high in authority that when it can be possible you believed not to pass, yet I fear it will not.

Anna received your letter last night (Saturday) with which she is much pleased she seemed much distressed at your not having seen in the letter she wrote to you the list of numbers for this Afghan - she was afraid to put it inside for fear of you dropping it - so wrapped it round the letter - Phanie is to write you this evening according to your own plan. On Friday Lizzie Ellis, Anna and myself went in the morning shopping for Christmas, and finished up all of the children except Bamie (I feel determined to get her a china Tea set but Lizzie wished to get it instead) I think you will like the different things Teedies present is very nice It is a stable with four horses in their stalls, hay stack in front of them, in a carriage horse attached, a carriage and Hay cart, there is a loft for Hay. I know he can amuse himself for hours with it but you shall see them all - if you soon will come home - I am going to invite the Elliots to spend some evening with us this week (if Elliot continues {___}) they will stay all night, I think it will be Thursday night, I have promised Julia to invite Mr {Loubery} to play for us if he should be unengaged upon that evening. So please come home to this mild entertainment if possible I went down and read some of your letters to Father upon one afternoon last weekend I will tell you about this when we meet. I walked up with Rob. Rob and Corniel have gone shooting - Laura is in town at 14th street. I went there yesterday to dinner, but Thee something occurred there which made me determined not to dine there again unless my resolutions should be unaccountably changed Dont distress yourself about it for altho I felt my blood boil (particularly as it was the first time I had intruded as they evidently seem to act as tho they perhaps do so_ they protest they do not I suppose) for the I made no reply whatever but I could not touch another mouthful of dinner - I am sorry I have reason written this for I determined in my own mind even as lately as when I commenced this letter that I would not mention it - so I did not [realy] mean to mention it to you at least not in a letter and writing so much that the miserable thing is unnecesssary still, in account the subject - Thee I wish I could see you to night I really feel very impatient for your return - I hope you will write constantly while you are absent one from another good bye my dear Thee yours faithfully -

       Mittie Roosevelt

The previous letter is in poor condition and almost impossible to read. The ink has faded to not much more than a faint shadow in many places. However, the subject matter can still be determined and transcribed. Mittie's discomfort at the Roosevelt's dinner table gives our first glimpse of her unease when confronted by discussion of the War. There is no other subject that could have made her "blood boil." Mittie, Anna, Susan, and Martha throughout the letters tell of their love and affection for the entire Roosevelt family; however, here in the first year of the War, their division by allegiance created the first of many difficult situations.

Washington Dec 15<u>th</u> 1861

Myown dearest Mittie

  I received your letter which I had been expecting two days yesterday. It is delightful to hear from you all, especially when there seems to be a temporary in the family sickness.

  I am so sorry not to be on hand to share your care of Elliott next week, but even if my bill passes and I still hope it will I will only be able to get home for one day and ought not to do that as I will be obliged immediately to visit every regiment with Dodge and see each man. One has no right to look back after commencing this work but some times I am tempted to do so when so many obstacles are thrown in my way.

  Yesterday was one of entire business every one had been seen that could be of service, congress was not in session and I was on the {___}. Mr Bancroft my chum at present and myself rode down on horseback to see a pontoon bridge built in one hour.

  Miss Cohan, Mrs Conklin, Mrs Howland, and numerous other notables with protectors much more suitable, added to a large entourage of the common herd were present.

  The building of the bridge was extremely interesting and all completed in one hour, then a company was marched over it double quick with an army wagon drawn by four horses. After which Mr Bancroft and myself tried it on horse back on a hard gallop. It was the most exciting ride I've had in some time, the boards sinking several inches every time our horses' feet touched them.

Four boxes of wagons were then fastened together and a company paddled out into the river with shovels to show how much they would cross without boats.

We then visited the remains of a barbacue to which we had been invited, the whole camp had been made into a cedar grove at one day's notice and green arches with inscriptions abounded.

Today I walked out to see the service in the camp to the 9th cavalry of which Knox the cousin of the Mason's is Major.

It was very impressive to me the soldiers all gathered round in regular order in the open field and to hear them join in the hymns.

Tell Miss Phanie I have not received the letter you mention her writing, and tell Anna to hurry them in sending the numbers for the Afghan.
Give a great many kisses to the dear little children from me, it seems such a pity to be away from them so much and still I cannot help feeling that it would be my duty unless this has had turned up to be away from them altogether by joining the army.

I do so hope they are well it makes me very sad sometimes to think that their constitutions must be delicate.

But I must close or the mail goes. Your loving
Husband

Washington Dec 16th 61

Dearest Mittie

I sometimes feel half tempted to wait for answers to some of my letters; but I think of the many cares you are surrounded with at home and only wish that instead of

Pontoon Bridge, *Harper's Weekly*, 16 March 1863

writing you a letter I could put my arm round your waist and express the sympathy I feel.

I long to be home again if only for one day to see you all and still day by day passes and no progress is made in the object of my mission.

Tomorrow I should say would certainly decide our fate if I had not so frequently hoped that previous tomorrows would do the same.

I am gaining experience which will be valuable to me hereafter, but it is learnt at a very expensive rate to the volunteers and their families.

Every day parties are made up to which I am invited but frequently the doubt that I may possibly do something keeps me hanging in an unsettled way round the city.

Tomorrow a party go to Mt Vernon with an escort of cavalry, and some more acquaintances are going outside of our lines to have a bird's eye view of the enemy's pickets, while I am loafing around the capitol Macauber [Wilkins Micawber from Charles Dicken's *David Copperfield*] like.[90] This afternoon I rode over to Genl Butterfields and after taking dinner with him had a very pleasant talk with Genl Porter and Martindale. You would scarcely believe it was camp life to see the nice fire places in their tents and in Genl Butterfield's tent was a window of glass.

I enclose you a photograph of Genl Butterfield as a souvenir of my afternoon. Tell Anna I think his face will compare favorably with Genl Beauregards.

I have a dreadful cold but it is much better now than it has been since I left you, ~~and~~ should you have observed any special stupidity in my letters please place it to this a/f [affliction].

With many kisses to the children I remain as ever
your loving husband
Theodore Roosevelt

Dec 17th   I reopen this to acknowledge yours of the 15th just rec^d and very welcome.

Three Union generals dominated Thee's time. General Daniel Adam Butterfield (1831-1901) is known for writing or rewriting the bugle call *Taps* and may have been a personal friend as he was also a New York businessman before joining the Union Army. General Andrew Porter was born in 1820 in Pennsylvania and already served in the U. S. Army at the outbreak of the War. Fellow New Yorker, John H. Martindale (1815-1881), a New York lawyer, graduated from West Point in 1835. Thee compared Confederate General Pierre Gustave Toutant-Beauregard (1818-1893) to Union General Butterfield.

C.S.A. General
P. G. T. Beauregard (above)

U.S.A. General
Daniel A. Butterfield (right)

Washington Dec 17th 61

Dearest Mittie

After being requested to appear before the Military Committee this morning I am quietly requested to wait their pleasure in the next room, and as all rooms here are supplied with luxurious arrangements, for writing I take advantage of the opportunity to commence one of my many letters to you.

I had just written the above when Senator [Preston] King rushed in to apologize and, as nothing is ever quite so good or bad as we expect, so it proved in this case. The Committee had just determined upon an amendment that would have destroyed this whole law utterly but were not only willing but anxious to hear my views and act on them where they saw their propriety.

A slight change has been made in the working of the law but if the bill will only pass in its present shape immediately I will be satisfied. I was received with the utmost politeness by all the Senators and must give them credit in the committee for having merely worked for the good of the soldier.

But enough of business, my mind runs on it all the time and I expect to frequently wake you when I get home with night-mares about allotments.

The little home scenes you draw up about Bammie Tedee and Ellie are pleasanter than I feared they would be as sickness seems to have left them a temporary respite.

I must go into the Senate now and wait patiently action on my bill.

11 P.M. I am in my own quiet and, for a hotel, remarkably comfortable room; a nice fire burning in the grate; clothes on most of the chairs and that general look of comfort which is apt to grow up wherever one lives long. It seems weeks since I came here and I am thinking quite seriously of moving down here as a permanency.

Wandering round the camps thru moonlight nights is delightful, I have just returned from an expedition to them.

My spirits have had a decided rise today by the passage of my bill through the Senate and, although it may very probably be swamped in the house this is one step in the right direction.

If there is one quality we must try to cultivate in the children especially it is a hopeful disposition, it saves so much unhappiness and, never mind how dreary the present is, always gives a future to look forward to.

The note from Miss Phanie arrived this evening without the numbers I am so anxious to receive. I do hope they will come tomorrow as otherwise the people may not get them before the lottery is over which would be very disagreeable.

I wish I could have you with me here tonight, little Ellie might keep me awake as much as he chose if he would only make me of the party and I fancy I see little Tedee climbing over his crib at an incredibly early hour of the morning. One good night kiss from your
Husband

Washington Dec 19th 61

Dearest Mittie
    Your two letters both came together and very welcome they were. It is a great luxury to feel that there is one who really loves me, one centre to which I can always turn.

Sometimes I get thinking of you all in the House of Representatives while the annoyances and delays to which I am subjected sink into utter insignificance. I have just passed another day waiting anxiously for the time when men would learn to fulfill their promises. Today Col Blair promised positively to bring the bill up but did not either make or have the opportunity to introduce it, I could not quite make up my mind which. I do hope to be home to spend sunday and would give anything to be there Christmas. To be absent then seems really more than I can stand. I had counted so upon seeing the enjoyment of the children when they get their presents that I cannot bear to think of being away. Of course to be away permanently would be still worse but I never felt about any previous Christmas as I do about this one. All the past is so vividly recalled that I can hardly write my feelings and have really been obliged to lay down my pen and walk the room before going on with my letter. But I must not make you sad when we have so much for which to be thankful.

Col Hawkins with his wife and her sister are here and very kind to me. They are Providence ladies and not like we are accustomed to exactly, but seem to be remarkably smart people and I think you would like them.

That Brownell who we did not admire is here with Mrs Burnham who is coming to see you when she returns to the city. I do not fancy the crowd but of course could not say no.

Major Ranch has just made his appearance at 11 PM and I must finish this tomorrow.

Leave the front door unlocked saturday night.

Dec 20th I am just reminded by this date that it is friday and I have every reason to believe I will be with you as soon as this letter or within a few hours of it, I hope you will take a good long nap in the day time so that you will not mind being waked up early sunday morning for if unable to get off before I expect to come by the night train saturday.

Kiss all the dear little children from your loving husband

      Theo. Roosevelt

Thee made it home in time for Christmas. His allotment bill passed both the Senate and House as a voluntary program. A designated portion of a soldier's pay would be sent home to family or friends. The purpose stood as two-fold, first to provide for soldiers' families during their absence and second to prevent wasteful spending by idle, bored soldiers while in camp. On 21 December 1861, the *Brooklyn Evening Star* reported:

The House then passed the Senate bill providing for transmitting certificates of allotments of pay of the volunteers to their families and friends. Each State is to appoint three persons to visit the several departments of the army to receive the money. The provision of the former law allowing liens to Sutlers on the pay of soldiers is repealed and all regulations on the subject are abrogated beyond the rules and articles of war.

Thee enjoyed visiting with fellow New Yorker Colonel Rush Christopher Hawkins (1831-1920), organizer of Hawkins' Zouaves. He lived on Fifth Avenue, served as a lawyer, and collected rare books and art. His wife was Annmary Brown of Providence, Rhode Island.

All the time Thee remained in Washington, D.C., James D. Bulloch remained stranded in the South. Finally on 20 December, he made his first attempt on the C.S.S. *Fingal* at returning to Britain. Northern papers reported this attempt, saying "The Chances of the escape of the Fingal are evidently very small."[91] The end of 1861 found James still sidelined in Savannah.[92] His family spent their Christmas in Liverpool without him and very possibly unaware of his whereabouts.

Now that the Allotment Bill had passed, Thee needed to be appointed once again as an allotment commissioner. He went back to Washington to continue lobbying and prepare for implementation of the bill. The *Brooklyn Daily Eagle* reported on 31 December 1861 that New York's three commissioners to the Allotment Commission would be "Theodore Roosevelt, Wm. E. Dodge, Jr., and Morris Ketchum."

Washington Dec 27, 61

Dearest Mittie
I arrived here this morning feeling really rather better than when I started.

You know I had been a little out of sorts the last day or two and the petting seemed to do me good.

I had telegraphed for a place in the sleeping car, which I found ready for me in Phil^{a}; and had for my companions Genls Porter and Butterfield.

My quarters here are on the first floor and better than I have ever had before.

As I took piece after piece of brown paper from the different lairs of articles in my trunk, I could almost see you in your white dress overseeing it packed.

"Her dress was like the lilies
And her heart as pure as they".[93]

I wish you had not been so melancholy when bidding me good-bye, I hated to leave you so sad; although I suppose the children did not allow you to remain so long. Give each one of them a great many kisses from me and tell them I have bought some paper with pictures to write them letters on, and that I always expect a message in your letters from them.

I found Mr [John] Nicolay at the hotel and after some talk with him wrote a recommendation for myself and carried it to Senator [Ira] Harris to sign. This he did very willingly, the other senator Preston King never does anything willingly and of course did not do this but gave me what was equivalent to his name.

After obtaining them I had a long talk with the Pay Master General arranging for future operations, he is a very nice old gentleman but rather overcome with the amount of work we are going to throw on his shoulders. I next went to secure our horses from Genl Van Vliet which I found no difficulty in doing and, after ordering a thousand copies of our bill printed, found as you may imagine that the day was fast drawing to a close.

I had previously telegraphed Dodge to come on and hope that he will do so, although his father since tells me that he has been detained here himself longer than he expected and that his son may wait for his return before leaving. Governor Brockingham interrupted my letter at this point and I am afraid to have it longer open, lest it may miss the mail.

      Yours Ever
      Thee Roosevelt

  General Stewart Van Vliet (1815-1901) served as chief quartermaster of the Army of the Potomac and was directly responsible for suppling the Army. Connecticut's governor, William Albert Buckingham (1804-1875) served Lincoln throughout the Civil War. Personal friends since Lincoln's campaign for the presidency, Buckingham worked tirelessly to support both Lincoln and the soldiers from his state. In an official letter, he is quoted as saying, "Don't let any Connecticut man suffer for want of anything that can be done for him. If it costs money, draw on me for it."[94] Buckingham pledged $50,000 in personal credit to pay for military expenses.

      New York
      Dec 28th 1861

My dearest Thee
  I have felt and continue to feel too gloomy about your frequent and prolonged absences. Indeed I do most sincerely wish your business was all arranged and you safely at home again I would not mind it half so much if you were not that silent uncomplaining <u>untruthful</u> sick. please write me whether you are better. Yesterday I received a very polite note from Mr Dodge enclosing your Telegram and requesting me to send him the articles mentioned in the telegram revolver & saddlebags. the saddlebags were not here so I sent the messenger to 14th street with a note to Lizzie Emlin [Roosevelt] he was to call there on his way to Mr Dodge so I have not heard whether the saddlebags were found, please tell me in your letter if you get the saddlebags. Only think of my being so ignorant of Fire-arms as to send your "Parlor" Pistol, instead of the revolver. I received such a gentlemanly note from Mr D saying the pistol you have

been good enough to send is a parlor weapon and would hardly be of use on a horseback journey Anna (who had been out when I received the first note and sent the pistol) took up the returned pistol and said, "Why Mittie what a goose you are. Why I should think the very same revolver would have told you this thing was not what Thee meant I suppose Mr Dodge will "think me very foolish like" Dora, the child wife. Teedie slept in the bed with me the first night you left. last night he slept in his crib when ever he would wake he would lie quietly and call me out of my bed to ease him, but did not come in bed till morning when he and Ellie came in bed, Teedie was in the most ambient frame of mind, he would say "Ellie shall I stokes your little ears", Ellie would assent and lie perfectly quiet, then Teedie would say to me in the most hysterical manner, "oh doo look Mamma how he do obey me." I am writing immediately after breakfast Bamie & Johnnie [Roosevelt] are building a castle with the new christmas blocks. Teedie has his stable here and is allowing Ellie to play with him, the Stable as we thought it would afford intense amusement. Teedie has called two of the horses "Sopy & Jeannie". {____} spent one evening with Anna. Yesterday Anna called on Minerva {broner} (being her last Reception day) and took Bamie with her after which they went to Dancing school. I have not seen the Hyatts since you left. I have promised to go to church with {Boddie/Robbie} to their church tomorrow morning. Rob sent Anna and I some delightful Punch last night. Anna was so overcome by the attention that she wrote back a note of thanks. Anna is going out with the children to walk this morning and as she is going to drop this letter in the lamp post it is about time I should close good bye my own dear Thee.

From your own
Mittie

Washington Dec 29th 61

Myown Dearest Mittie

Your sweetly scented little note with its still sweeter contents reached me this morning. I was just about starting out with Dodge when it came; we were going to service in the 44th a regiment which used to go to church in a body but which we found had, through the influence of a bad chaplain, ~~had~~ now only about one hundred and fifty gathered around. The chaplain occupied most of his time in abusing his audience for not being larger and said that unless more came he would not preach at all. After service we began our duties feeling that not a moment was to be lost in influencing all possible to send money to their families before next pay day which will now be in very few days.

I went over to Kerrigan's old regiment composed entirely of low irish to influence them as far as possible, and was quite as successful as I had expected to be although I found it hard work to talk to them patiently.

I came home tonight with a feeling, that I have sometimes had after a long day's work at the Mission School, of dissatisfaction with having turned God's day of rest into one of labour. This is increased today because I forgot to bring my bible and delayed buying one, hoping that Dodge would get the next room to me and I could use his.

I had almost forgotten to tell you that my cold is rather better, and I am really afraid to acknowledge how I am writing this is my night shirt at twelve o'clock at night. The truth is I did not feel fresh enough to write until I had washed myself and do not feel as if I would increase my cold by this slight imprudence.

Tell Tedie I had a horse that tried to throw me by running me against the fence, or any wagon he was near, and that he would never have wherever I stopped without trying to throw me but I am learning to like him better than any of my others.

Kiss little Bammie from me and tell her that I often think how nicely she would help take care of the little children.

I am beginning to feel cold and know I am only obeying your desires when I close, remaining as ever
Your Loving Husband
Theodore Roosevelt

Thee mentioned Kerrigan's old regiment. He most likely referred to the 25th New York Volunteer Regiment organized by James Kerrigan, consisting almost entirely of Irishmen. James Kerrigan (1828-1899) was court-martialed, convicted, and cashiered out in February 1862 due to suspected Confederate sympathies.[95]

Chapter 6: January of 1862

Events of the War

In 1862, winter was a time of resupply and planning for the warring armies. January saw only a few minor engagements between Union and Confederate forces. On 19 January, the Battle of Mill Springs in eastern Kentucky was fought for the liberation of a pro-Union district. Union forces prevailed, but failed to achieve their goal.

The Letters

Washington Jan 1st 62

Dear Mittie

I write this while I imagine you all seated round our quiet little breakfast table, and just before I go down myself to try to scuffle through a meal here amid the crash of china and general confusion that pervades the dining room of this hotel. Anna I suppose is going soon up to the Hyatts to keep her tongue in perpetual motion all day long and come back reporting that she has increased her sore throat by five or six additional ulcers.

I can afford to be facetious about sore throats now as the continual exposure for the past few days has cured mine.

I have stood on the damp ground talking to the troops and taking their names for six hours at a time. One of the regiments that I visited last which is wretchedly offensive and composed of the scum of our city seemed for the first time to recall their families. We had an order from the General of

Division and the Colonel sent for his adjutant to carry out our desires.

He came dirty and so drunk that he could not speak straight and of course got the orders wrong. All the officers seemed to be in with the sutler while the privates said he was an unmitigated thief.

The delays were so great that I stood out with one of those companies after seven o'clock at night with one soldier holding a candle while I took down the names of those who desired to send home money. The men looked as hard as I have often seen before in our Mission neighborhood but after a little talk, explaining my object and reminding them of those they have left behind them, one after another put down his name and from this company alone they allotted while I was there six hundred dolls. This would be increased afterwards by the officers if they were decent ones from men about on guard and from other reasons.

I could not help thinking what a pretty subject for a painting it would make as I stood out there in the dark night surrounded by the men with one candle just showing glimpses of their faces, the tents all around us in the woods. One man after putting down five dolls a month said my old woman has always been good to me and if you please change it to ten. In a minute half a dozen others followed his example and doubled theirs.

Tell father Mittie my experience in the camps as I know he will feel interested in hearing how I succeed.

I have only time to add a few more words, I enclose a letter for Teedie as I thought the horse more appropriate for him.

Do take care of yourself and the dear little children while I am away and enjoy yourself just as much as you can. I do not want you not to miss me but remember that I would never have felt satisfied with myself after this war was over if I had done nothing and that I do feel now that I am only doing my duty.

I know you will not regret having me do what is right and I don't believe you will love me any the less for it.

Yours as ever
Theo. Roosevelt

Tonight I probably go to Annapolis. Over
I have forgotten {Touhays} direction. Please get some man to direct the enclosed put two stamps on it and drop it in the penny post.

    Thee encountered many rough soldiers while encouraging them to sign up for the allotment system. At the very end, Thee's letter stated what so often has been told about his desire to do his *duty* in the war effort. Many years later, Teedie would use these same words when talking about his father and the Civil War. It was also one of the letters Corinne Roosevelt Robinson used in her book *My Brother Theodore Roosevelt* as an example of her father's need to provide some service during the War.[96]

    Thee had taken with him sheets of paper with pictures on them to send notes to his children. Here he mentions sending a picture of a horse to Teedie. At the end of his letter, Thee told Mittie he had forgotten someone's *direction*, the mid-nineteenth century term for address.

Washington Jan 5th 62

Dearest Mittie

    It is a quiet sunday morning and the feeling of relief that the six days work is done is something I have not realized so fully for years.

    You know that my sundays are not altogether days of rest at home while on the other hand my working days have been so lately.

    I expect to be like the Lewis boys if I don't die during the training remarkably hardy by the time I return. We have the men drawn up in line by company Dodge begins at the company at one end and I at the other, having every mans name called and taking down ourselves the amount he desires to send home.

It takes from two to four hours to a regiment during which time standing out in the cold writing is no joke, we then mount our horses and take the next regiment. Our reception has been universally hospitable in the extreme and it throws us in connection with every general of division and indeed with the whole army more pleasantly and intimately than we could be otherwise. We have always so far been able to sleep at the hotel and will try to continue to have boards over our heads at night as long as possible. The weather here is extremely cold now.

We were made very uneasy the other night by a statement of a gentleman as he said on the best authority that Genl [George] McClellans health had failed, Genl Hallatt [General Henry Halleck] had been telegraphed for and Mc Dowell [Brigadier General Irvin] was in command. We walked round to the Generals head quarters and there found that he had been steadily improving for the three previous days.

Theodore Bronson has offered to join us in our work here and if possible we will get him appointed with us. He is an old boyish acquaintance of mine and would make a very agreeable addition to our party besides allowing us to hurry matters up and get home sooner, that communication so devoutly to be desired.

Yesterday I met a Mrs. Lansing wife of a Colonel [Henry S.] in camp with two children, she was almost the first lady I have spoken to in a week, I ought to make one more exception of Mrs. Burnside the wife of the General.

I spoke to her but a moment and would not have remembered it except for her beautiful eyes and teeth, doubly remarkable as she is not as young as she once was.

Although Mr Dodge has not yet made his appearance there he is knocking at the door and we will go down to breakfast together as it is bordering on ten o'clock.

Give much love to all at home, to father especially, and many kisses to the children, including Anna as one of them

Your Loving
Husband.

Please make the children obey your first order.

Theodore, now in Washington, D.C., and busy signing up men for the allotment, still had time to write Mittie about the children. Thee met with Generals George McClellan and probably Major General Henry Wagner Halleck (1815-1872), also of New York. While William Dodge was there with him, Morris Ketchum was not. Apparently, Mr. Ketchum did not accept his appointment, so Thee wished to see his old friend Theodore Bailey Bronson (1830-1881) assigned instead. Bronson had attended Columbia College where he studied law; he did not practice, but chose to go into business. During the War, he also served as Provost Marshall for New York City.

Among those Thee met in Washington was Mary Richmond Bishop Burnside (1828-1876), wife of Major General Ambrose Everett Burnside (1824-1881). Burnside, an engineer from Rhode Island, and his wife Mary had no children.

Washington Jan 8th 62

Myown Dearest Mittie

I wrote you last night but am tempted to do so again; you have yourself to blame for the frequency of my letters as you say you enjoy receiving them.

You enquire when I am coming home and I wish I could give you a satisfactory answer to your enquiry. We are continually at work now and to day saw three regiments, but even at this rate I am afraid to calculate yet the number of days that must elapse before I see you again.

They were all germans today, a motley crew who have few friends and no characters frequently. We had been told that we ran the risk of our lives in these regiments, and much more nonsense of the same kind; but the only risk of that we ran proved to be from starvation. We were out talking to the men until late and then found a german dinner which Dodge could eat nothing of but the brown bread. He wanted to be polite and I was much amused with his statement that he would ride five miles to get such bread. It was literally a fact I have no doubt in his then state of starvation.

The men as germans always do took time to consider and we left them chewing the allotment-card with every prospect however after due consideration of a fair number sending money home.

These germans were generally of the lowest class and with the exception of one regiment disappointed me, although I have no doubt they would fight well. There are some twelve thousand of them.

This morning I see that our efforts are noticed in the world and Tribune, the last notice I send you; please read it aloud to Anna as I know she would consider that her eyes had offended her if they rested on anything ever cut from such a paper. You have seen I suppose that we have been mentioned several times in the Times. This is particularly satisfactory as the papers threatened at first to be down on us which would have lost us the confidence of the soldiers.

I am delighted to hear that Anna intends to write me, and I hope to receive the letter before another New Years day has obliterated the remembrance of this one.

Give my love to the little children and tell Tedie that I will soon write him another letter for himself. I hope Bammie received my last one

Yours as ever
Theo Roosevelt

Numerous New York newspapers, including the *Tribune* and *Times* reported on the commissioners' activities.

The *Evening Courier and Republic* of Buffalo, New York, reported on 10 January the following:

> A correspondent of the New York World gives an interesting account of the labors of two New York gentleman, Messrs. Dodge and Roosevelt, in the army, the object of their effort being to induce the soldiers to avail themselves of the allotment system devised by the act of Congress. A large portion of the New York forces on the Potomac has been visited, and the gentleman have met with an encouraging degree of success in their labor of patriotism and love. Their method of procedure is to visit the camp of a regiment, obtain the approval and co-operation of the Colonel, and then make an appeal to the men as they are drawn up in line.
> In nearly every instance the eloquence of these noble men calls forth a noble response. Wives, mothers, children, oftentimes pinched with want at home, are remembered, and the average allotment of those companies which have entered into the plan amounts of near nine dollars per man from the private's monthly pay of thirteen dollars.
> The benefit of this operation is two-fold. Like many, it blesses those who received and those who give. Many of the temptation attendant on a soldier's life is removed, and the effect upon the homes which the soldiers have left may be guessed when we say, on the authority of these Commissioners, that if the mass of our eighty New York regiments respond in the same proportion as those already visited, the enormous amount of $7,000,000 or 8,000,000 will be returned to the volunteers' families of the Empire State alone.

When the Civil War began, the United States was very much a land of immigrants, many of whom lived in the heavily populated northern states. The 1860 U.S. Census placed the total population at 31 million. Of those, 18.5 lived in the states that would remain loyal to the Union.[97] Approximately eight million whites and four million enslaved persons lived in the Confederacy and the border states. The Union army of approximately two million men consisted of 23.4% born in foreign countries. Of these immigrants, approximately 216,000 were born in Germany, of which some 36,000 enlisted from New York alone. German-Americans were the largest ethnic group to fight for the Union.[98]

Washington Jan 12th 62

My own Dearest Mittie

I received your long expected letter today and although very glad to get it could not help feeling sad at its contents.

I know you have been over exerting yourself as well as suffering from a cold and I do not feel as if you can quite take care of yourself without my help.

I wish most sincerely that I could answer your question about the time at which I will come home, but it seems still a long way off.

I am working as hard as possible but am anxious to do my work thoroughly and have not yet been able to see more than two regiments a day. With Bronson's assistance I hope to accomplish more but there is still a good month's work before me.

I have not been actively engaged you know for a long time and it ought to do me good to be busy for a while.

Please mention in your next letter to Anna that I have no hope of being able to call for her in Phil[a] although it would give me so much pleasure. If possible I will write to Anna myself, but am so busy that I find but few moments that I can call myown.

Give Bammie a kiss from me and say that I received her letter and will answer it soon.

Tedie is too much sick, it worries me and, while I hope a great deal from next summer, I cannot help feeling that there must be something about the furnace or something, that prevents them all from being hardy. I cannot believe that they have not good constitutions, but we must place our trust in God and ask his aid where our own strength so utterly fails us. I am very thankful to feel that I can leave the little ones with you having that implicit confidence that you will take almost a little too good care of them.

Rob [Roosevelt] writes me that he is coming here, please send in immediately to him some of my cravats, I do not find any in my trunk. Tell him also that I did not fill up a blank in his letter stating the person to whom he should telegraph because I could not find it out. The conductor of the Balt. & Phil^a R R^d will answer. Ask Rob how long he is going to stay and see if you could not arrange it to come on with him. I do not know whether you would enjoy it very much but I would be intensely glad to see you

       Your Husband
        Thee

       Washington Jan 23 62

Myown Dearest Mittie

I received your sweet little letter tonight on my return from Genl Wadsworth's where we passed last night. It is always a great pleasure to hear from you, especially so after returning from a night on two benches covered by a blanket, followed by a day passed as usual in the mud. Genl Wadsworth himself helped make my bed, he is very cordial but there is a prevailing want of good fellowship about himself and staff, entirely in contrast with Genl [Christopher C. Augur] Auger and his staff with whom I think I wrote you I had passed the night last monday.

We took dinner yesterday with Colonel [George W.] Pratt a remarkably pleasant man; he, as many of the officers now build log cabins, has one for himself; it makes much more comfortable quarters than a tent.

Our orderly is the chief weight on our minds he never gets his food and gets the sulks; refuses food when he can get it and makes himself miserable. Two of these bipeds have caved in already, fortunately there are still some ninety left in the company before all are used up.

I will write Jim [Roosevelt] requesting him to send you up two hundred dolls, I fully agree with you that it is best as far as possible to avoid borrowing from your mother, indeed I do not approve of borrowing when we can avoid it.

Write me whenever you require money, pay Locke & Crogin again if they call for it as I do not remember whether I settled their bill or not. I know you are a great deal more economical than if I had charge of the purchases myself.

I long to write to Bammie and Tedee but feel used up by the time that I have my first quiet moment, never before midnight, and then feel that I must first write you. Stuart Brown,[99] Mr Winsted and some very important New Yorkers have been to see us tonight and it is already quarter of one o'clock. I hear the noise of ladies and gentlemen passing who have just left a hop which has been going on in the ball room of the house. It seems so absurd to see their fine dresses, I feel as if I belonged to a different species.

I will not apologize for my letters to you as they serve atleast to show that I always think of you
Your Husband

I have had an unfinished letter to Anna lying on my table for a week.

As Thee continued to meet with more and more of New York's regiments, his time away from home wore on both him and his family. He also met most of New York's volunteer officers, including Major General James Samuel Wadsworth (1807-1864) and General Christopher Columbus Augur (1821-1898). Augur, a West Point graduate and career officer, served briefly as West Point's Commandant of Cadets in 1861.

Family friend, Colonel William Joseph Hardee had resigned in late 1860 to join the Confederacy and was followed by John F. Reynolds, before Augur took over. Augur served as Commandant for only a few months. Colonel Pratt was most likely George W. Pratt (1830-1862) of the 80th New York Infantry Regiment. Pratt would die at the Second Battle of Bull Run in September of 1862.

At some point after this letter, Thee returned home ill. Letters from the South continued to be forwarded to Martha through Harriott in Liverpool.

Jan 31- 1862

My dearest Susy,

I mailed a letter to you this afternoon enclosing a letter from Lucy and one from Irvine - The letter from Lucy mentions her having written me before which letter I did not receive until after dinner this evening - I cannot tell you dear Susy how unhappy this letter (which I enclose to you) makes me - Oh how sorry I am that I did not receive this letter sooner- I could then have gone over under some of the flags of truce but now I fear it is almost impossible to go -

Thee is better & hopes to be well enough to return to Washington on Monday - He says he could take me to Fortress Monroe but doubts if I could get a pass over beside he says the proceedings are more warlike now than ever- he does not see how I could possibly travel south - If he goes to Washington, he will write me whether he thinks it is possible. What shall I do dear Susy? I am afraid my poor child [Stuart Elliott] will die before I can get to him, and then I shall always reproach myself that I did not go to him when I could have done so. Anna advised me not to send you this last letter as it would distress you, but darling I & Mittie both thought you had better know the worst In Lucy's letter which I sent you this afternoon she mentioned that he had rallied, but was made worse again by running five hundred yards to meet a train just arrived swooned and had a hemorhage - this seems to be the latest account - poor dear fellow! I fear we shall never see him again - Oh if he was only a christian - I shall certainly go south dear Susy if I possibly can, but I will let you know all of my movements - send me back this, and the other two letters also dear Susy - Mittie received the cushion by Express this evening, and says it is beautiful she will write you shortly - Good night darling

Your affec Mother MB

Located at Hampton Roads, Virginia, Fortress Monroe served as a Union military installation on the Virginia peninsula overlooking the Chesapeake Bay. It remained under United States control throughout the War. Early on, the fort served as both the headquarters of the Union Department of Virginia and North Carolina and a place of freedom where the military housed refugee slaves. By this time in 1862, Union Major General George B. McClellan used the fortress to stage his command for the year's military campaign.

Fortress Monroe, *Illustrated London News,* 25 May 1861

Chapter 7: February of 1862

Events of the War

On 6 February, Union forces under General U.S. Grant captured Fort Henry (Tennessee) on the Tennessee River. Confederates had built the fort to prevent Union forces from using the river. After the battle, much of the Confederate garrison retreated to Fort Donelson, built to protect the Cumberland River. Under extreme fire from Union gunboats and ground forces, on 16 February, Fort Donelson accepted surrender as their only course of action. The negotiations that followed solidified Grant's name in history, for when asked for terms, his reply was, "No terms except for an unconditional and immediate surrender can be accepted." *Unconditional Surrender* Grant quickly became a Union celebrity. He soon received a promotion to major general, making him second in command in the west. The Union victory at Fort Donelson led directly to the fall of Nashville on 23 February. Kentucky now sat firmly in Union hands and most of west and central Tennessee as well.

On another front, on the 7th and 8th of February, the Battle of Roanoke Island, North Carolina, occurred. The federal seizure of Roanoke Island provided the Union complete control over Ablemarle Sound. On 10 February, a naval battle off Elizabeth City, North Carolina, destroyed a small Confederate fleet.

The Letters

Washington Feby. 5.th 62

Dearest Mittie

I arrived safe and sound this morning and of course find my hands full. Bronson and Dodge insisted upon my taking a nap and evidently regard me in the light of glass that runs the risk of being broken at any moment.

We find an unexpected difficulty in our way which with their melancholy experiences since I left had made them both determine to leave for home tomorrow. I have persuaded them to try it for a while longer and will meet the secretary of War and the the Treasury tomorrow to see if we cannot persuade them to smooth our road a little.

We had an interview with Secretary Stanton today and were much pleased with his apparent decision of character.

I find that but six men under fifty are invited to the President's tonight and have determined to go for a short time at least. There will be the largest collection of notables ever gathered in this country, and it will probably be a sight worth remembering

If we arrange matters satisfactorily with the Secretaries tomorrow, Dodge and myself leave in the afternoon for Fortress Monroe while Bronson will go to Genl Hooker's Division down the Potomac.

Please direct your letters written on and after next sunday to me here Willards Hotel where I will return next monday.

The rush of the hotel seems particularly disagreeable after tasting the quiet luxury of home life to which I have lately been such a stranger; but I suppose I will break in again in a few days. A great many acquaintances have expressed much interest in my health and really seem to feel it, more than I supposed knew I was sick.

I would feel perfectly contented and happy if I only felt that you were well but Mittie you must take great care of yourself and remember that the same arguments you send to me are applicable to yourself

Your Husband

While Thee has returned to his work for the Allotment Commission, Martha and Anna still worried over whether or not to go South to be with Stuart. Complicating matters was the inability to receive and send mail directly into the Confederate States. By this time, James D. Bulloch's position with the Confederate government and his relationship to Martha and her daughters was well known to Federal officials, possibly due to James Roosevelt's alerting them to James' actions in Liverpool, where he obtained warships and armaments for the Confederacy. Therefore, their letters were not only intercepted but read.[100]

New York Feb 6 1862

I have just received your letter enclosing Lucys dearest Susy, & although I am very busy fixing to go south must write you a few lines I got Mittie immediately on the reception of your letter to write Thee to get a pass for Anna and myself immediately if it was possible to do so I believe darling that no time is to be lost, particularly as March which is a fatal month to consumptions will be here before I can probably reach Georgia I do not have the least fear of being in Sav, but if when I go to Norfolk Maj Gen [Benjamin] Huger tells us it will be unsafe to go to Sav, we will go to Richmond and remain with the Caskies until a suitable route and and place of destination are determined on If it is possible to avoid going to Richmond we will go from Welden [Virginia] to Augusta or Charleston. Then I could hear from Stuart, and go to him in Sav or perhaps have him carried up to Macon Vineville is in sight of Macon, or rather a part of the town It is situated on a more elevated part than Macon proper, and is composed of residences Do not be uneasy about me darling Susy, it is my duty to go to my poor dying child and I believe that the same good Providence you speak of in your letter will be with us, and guard us from all harm <u>You</u> could not possibly go my poor feeble one, but I know your prayers will accompany us I do feel dreadfully at the idea of leaving Mittie and yourself and the dear little children Mittie is not well she has a constant pain in her left side and I am really uneasy about her I wish you and She were together or at any rate in the same city She will be so lonely too with Thee absent could you not come darling and stay with her? I feel overwhelmed sometimes with the magnitude of the step I am taking It is so uncommon for <u>me</u> to take a firm stand about any thing, as I have always preferred having others to guide me but I do feel that if I do not go to see my poor son before he dies, I should never forgive myself I could not get ready to go in less than a week or ten days & you shall know all of my movements Lucy's Direction is, Care of I R Bloom Macon, Bibb County Georgia I wrote to her the day before yesterday I shall write Irvine by wednesdays Steamer and will send you message The children are quite well Elliott is perfectly lovely Love to Mrs West & Hill Remember me kindly to Mr West I hope he has recovered entirely Goodbye for the present darling If I go I will see you in Phil as I pass through

      Your truly affec Mother
      M Bulloch

  Martha most likely referred to Thurston Rowland Bloom (1822-1869) and his wife, Anne E. Fluker (1829-ca.1870), who appeared in the 1860 U.S. Census, in Macon, Bibb County, Georgia. Born in New York, Thurston was a wealthy commission merchant and owned a plantation in Vineville.[101] In 1859, he had served as the administrator of the estate of Sarah Q. Fluker, Anne's mother.[102] The relationship between the Elliotts and Bloom remains unknown.

      Washington ~~Dec 7th~~ Feb 7th 62

Dearest Mittie
  I have not yet left for Fortress Monroe, having spent all yesterday kicking my heels in the ante-room of the

Secy of War and in making out an order for him which he promised to sign and afterwards refused.

I was with him about two hours altogether and received any number of the highest kind of compliments but I wanted a more substantial proof of his good feeling which I did not get. I still hope that I may get it through the President.

I hope to get off to Fortress Monroe this afternoon which I anticipate seeing with pleasure.

I have done nothing but rest since I left you, although, a disagreeable kind of rest, and feel fully myself again

Theo Bronson had to take a blue pill last night and feels used up but it will be nothing serious at all I hope.

Dodge went to Baltimore this morning at which place I will take the Steam Boat with him in the afternoon, he will go home next week.

I was much pleased with Mrs. Lincoln's ball although there were an unnecessary number of policemen present, she says she gave it as a piece of economy in war times to include those diplomats senators, congressmen and others that it had previously been the habit to invite to a number of formal dinners.

No one in the army lower than a division general not even a brigadier was invited to the ball and of course there is much grumbling and a proportionate amount of envy.

Some complained of the supper but I have rarely seen a better and often a worse one. Terrapin, birds, ducks, and everything else were in great profusion when I was in the room although some complained of a delay in getting in as we went in in parties.

I must close now with much love to all at home. I asked Secy Stanton for a pass for your mother but he says none are issued except by Secy [William H.] Seward who I do not know.

If she determines to go I will get introduced to him however.

       Your Own
       Husband

On 5 February, President Lincoln and his wife, Mary Todd held a grand presidential party which Thee attended. Many newspapers of the time along with *Frank Leslie's Illustrated Weekly* reported on the event and touted the reception as a grand social triumph. This excerpt from the *New York Herald* printed in *The Liberator* (Boston) described the evening.

> The first ball ever given in the White House. . . Over 800 invitations were issued . . . Mr. and Mrs. Lincoln stationed themselves in the centre of the East Room, and received the guests. . . For one hour the throng moved in a current and when the rooms were full, the Marine Band, stationed in their usual position, began playing operatic airs of the finest description at eleven. . . A large apartment was thrown open about twelve o'clock, with an immense punch-bowl in the centre and sandwiches, &c., around it. . . .The supper was set in the dining-room, and is considered one of the finest displays of gastronomic art ever seen in this country. It cost thousands of dollars. The bill of fare was : [Here upwards of thirty dishes are described.]. . . The tables fairly bent under expensive luxuries heaped one upon another. At twelve, the dining room was thrown open for inspection, and guests passed in and viewed it, preparatory to the demolition of the artistic pile. About eleven, Gen. McClellan and lady and Gen. Marcy and daughter came in. All the border State Senators and Members were present with their ladies, and most of the Members and Senators from the Northern States. . . Nearly all of the Generals in the army were there. . . The ladies were dressed to the height of fashionable extravagance."

The *New York Herald* described lady Lincoln's dress thus, which it styles "simple and elegant":—

"A magnificent white satin robe, with a black flounce half a yard wide, looped with black and white bows, a low corsage trimmed with black lace, and a bouquet of cape [sp] myrtle on her bosom. Her head-dress was a wreath of black and white flowers, with a bunch of cape myrtle on the right side. The only ornaments were a necklace, ear rings, brooch, and bracelets, of pearl."[103]

The paper went on to highly criticize Kentucky-born, former slave-owner Mary Todd Lincoln for the expense of the ball, her gown, the refreshments, and the overage for recently completed and much needed renovations to the White House. The *Joliet Signal* posted the following:

Look on this picture
"Thousands of dollars were expended for confectionery for Mrs. Lincoln's grand ball at the White House." *Telegraph Dispatch.*
An then on this
"Sick soldiers in the Washington Hospital have been compelled by hunger to eat scraps, &c., scooped out of the slop pails."[104]

It seems none of the newspapers reported that upstairs in the White House, the Lincoln's son Willie lay resting sick in bed.

Grand Ball at the White House,
Frank Leslie's Illustrated Newspaper,
22 February 1862

At the Grand Ball, Mrs. McClellan, Mrs. Lincoln, and Mrs Crittenden, *Frank Leslie's Illustrated Newspaper*, 22 February 1862

Camp Hamilton Feby 8th 62
               Fortress Monroe

Dearest Mittie

I have received your little letter with some regret in consequence of its contents, stating your mothers firm determination.

I do not like to say anything with regard to the probability of the success of my application for fear of disappointment. An influential individual in Washington has the promise of the pass for me if one will be granted to anyone, but such promises are made of course with large mental reservations.

This promise too was made not by Seward but his son, and of course must be confirmed by his father.

I am writing this in Major [Charles C.] Dodge's quarters while he and his brother [William E.] are smoking after tea; it of course is what you would call roughing it to live as he does but he is really wonderfully comfortable.

Genl [John E.] Wool received us better than anyone we have yet seen, asked us to dine with him tomorrow and issued a very strong order commanding that our wishes should be fully carried out by the officers under his command. He furnished us with a two horse wagon to go out to Charley Dodge's camp from which place we have been furnished with horses and orderlies.

We dined with Charley Dodge saw his officers after dinner arranged with them about the allotments and then rode in to see Colonel [John E.] Bendix.

Colonel Bendix ordered his officers up to meet us, promised that he would head the list and we agreed at his request to leave it to his officers to see whether they could not induce more men to sign than we could by personal communication with the men.

We then again rode out to Charley Dodge's, took tea with him, and are passing one of those quiet cosy evenings so rare in our experience.

One half the hotel is used as the hospital, an agreeable neighborhood for us, and that portion of it which is left as hotel is kept in that good old southern Point Comfort way which we are unaccustomed to. The Contrabands look very home like and as devil may care as ever, some thirty two hundred now are congregated round the fort.

You forgot to mention the children or yourown health but I hope for the best from your silence. It would be a great pleasure to see the dear little things and a still greater to see you. Tell Bammie I will write her when I get quietly back in Washington.

Dodge requests to be remembered to you and this reminds me that I must turn round and make myself agreeable to himself and brother

Yours as Ever
TheoRoosevelt

I have forwarded safely Anna and your mother's letters

As he had promised, Thee approached Secretary of State William Henry Seward for passes to allow Martha and Anna to travel south to be with Stuart and Lucy Elliott. Thee mentioned that he spoke with and received a promise from Seward's son, most likely Frederick W. Seward (1839-1928), who served as Assistant Secretary of State. However, Thee might have spoken with Major Augustus Henry Seward (1826-1876), a career Army officer.

William E. Dodge's brother Major Charles C. Dodge (1841-1910) received his commission as a captain of the 1st New York Mounted Rifles, also known as 7th New York Volunteer Cavalry, in December 1861. His promotion to Major came quickly afterward. Charles commanded this cavalry detachment during Maj. Gen. John E. Wool's Norfolk expedition. Wool (1784–1869) had served as an officer during the War of 1812 and the Mexican-American War and was widely considered one of the most capable officers in the army and a superb organizer. Colonel John E. Bendix (1818-1877) commanded the 7th New York Infantry which he helped form.

Thee spoke of *contrabands* at Fortress Monroe. The United States military applied the term *contraband* to certain escaped African slaves or *those Negroes* who affiliated with Union forces. These men, women, and children often set up camps near Union forces. While the Army helped support and educate both the adults and children, they also used many for paid labor. Thousands of men from these camps enlisted in the United States Colored Troops beginning in 1863.

Contraband Camp at Former Female Seminary, circa 1863

New York Feb. 12th, 1862

My dearest Thee

I have received both of your letters since writing very last to you both of which were <u>very</u> much appreciated. You still do not mention what difficulties were, and I am still anxious to know both on my own account and also to be able to answer rightly when questioned by outsiders. I think you seemed rather to be enjoying your visit to Fortress Monroe and your road seemed much "smoother" than Monday. Ellie and Teedie broke out with the "Chicken Pox" and this morning Corinne, so you see our hands are full with sick children. Ellie does not seem as sick with it as Teedie does. Last night he had a very restless uncomfortable time of course I was much disturbed with him. His throat is sore as Bamie's was, the chicken pocks are all on the throat and tongue, as he is not able to gargle his throat He has to take some of the black gargle (the same as Bamie and yourself used) diluted with water. They are all asleep now and Mother says Teedie feels clear of fever. So I will hope for a better night for him. I am so sorry for the dear little boys to be kept in the house all of this time. I suppose Bamie became so reduced from the chicken Pox that her eyes have become sore, she has an ulcer on both eyes. Dr. Tim touches them with caustic every other day and besides ordered the weak solution dropped in the eye. She takes her iron and book [or bark?] after each meal. I get cream for her every day. I hope they will begin to get better soon.

  Anna and I are thinking of Anna accompanied by Ann Butler taking Bamie out for a few days to "Long Branch" next week. The change and the salt air, we feel sure will do her good, Anna, the Scots [Scotts], Jimmie and Julia Elliott {Crishe or Cash?} are staying with the Scots & some gentlemen and Rob [Roosevelt] who Anna asked went out to "Central Park" last night to skate by moon light. Anna said they had a very jolly time.

  Rob brought them all back to his house and gave them whiskey punches, Anna says Julia was so amusing and characteristic she helped Rob make all the punches - but was so afraid all of the time that the noise was disturbing to Lizzie, at which {___} Rob was exceedingly hilarious and laughed heartily.

  Dr. Phillips called on last Monday, paid a long visit. Then called again in the evening he seemed to be rather in awe of mother who was very much reserved thinking of him in connection with the South. On Tuesday he sent Anna the most beautiful basket of flowers all sweet smelling delicate flowers on the same evening he called Home and Aston Hutton also called, the former asked most particularly after you, Anna received a long letter from Captain Armstrong yesterday which was sent Phanie to day. Anna has received an invitation to another large party at Mrs. Royal Phelps has not yet determined whether she will go.

    This morning old Mr. Scot called upon Mother to invite us all to hear Cordova read at his house on Friday evening he came particularly to insist upon Mother's going but she will not be tempted, besides feeling so miserably about Brother and her state of uncertainty regarding the "Pass" she is so distressed over the affair at Roanoke Island.

    Anna is very sad as she knows so many of the Richmond gentlemen must have been engaged in it particularly fearing some of the Caskies might have been among these engaged. With Rob and Willie Caskie having been with Wise in Western Virginia at the Gauley Bridge [pronounced "Wauley" Bridge] affair. I am so afraid Mr. Leonards son may succeed in getting the "Pass." I cannot tell you how the idea haunts me. Oh Thee dear I have a heart ache when I think Anna and Mother may get the <u>Pass</u>. I do not feel as tho I could endure the grief of parting from them for how long? Oh who can tell if she tries to get the <u>Pass</u> she will feel much more satisfied with herself but for my sake I do hope she will not get it.

    Anna went skating with Mr. Gracie this morning whom she declares teaches her better than anyone else, Mr. Gracie went and found out all about the boats leaving for Long Branch etc. When I heard Bamie say her prayers to night she asked so much after you, said "do give my love to dear Papa Mama." I have not heard from you today which I am always sorry for as I rather look forward to receiving your letters.

    Please remember me to Mr. Dodge.
    Good bye, dear Theedie so I'm yours
        Mittie Roosevelt

In the 1860s, chicken pox and other infectious diseases ran rampant across the United States and caused hundreds of deaths. Soldiers as well as children were afflicted. It seemed that Bamie, or possibly Thee, first contracted the disease and then spread it to the other three Roosevelt children. With Bamie on the mend, Mittie and Martha considered sending her with Anna and Ann Butler, Bamie's nurse, to Long Branch.

Social events continued despite the children's illnesses, with Anna's involvement in the forefront. Anna was learning to ice skate in Central Park, often accompanied by Rob, Thee's brother who lived next door with his wife Lizzie and their two children. Mittie wrote of several social visits including the John D. Scott family, the Huttons, and a letter from Captain Armstrong. Dr. William Wurt Phillips (1796-1865), minister of the First Presbyterian Church at the corner of 5th and 12th Avenues, came for a long visit. Martha attended this church when in New York.

John Doughty Scott (1810-unknown) and his wife Nancy asked Mittie and Martha to attend a reading by Raphael J. DeCordova (1822-1901). DeCordova, born in Jamaica, had achieved success as a *Sephardic*[105] humorist in 1857. In 1862, announcements of his lectures included one at Clinton Hall on "Fun Seriously Considered" which was hailed, by his critics, as "such a topic, handled by a master of the art, cannot fail to be mirth-provoking in the highest degree."[106] On February 18th, De Cordova spoke again at Clinton Hall with a "new humorous lecture, with an introduction in verse." His lecture entitled "Ball is Up" dealt with a party determined to learn to ice skate late in life.[107] Surely Anna would have enjoyed this one! He continued his lectures in New York and surrounding cities until May of 1864. De Cordova was one of several New York Jews who worked to promote literary and philanthropic efforts on behalf of a Jewish return to Zion.[108] It is too bad that Martha's desire to obtain a pass to go South to be with Stuart weighed so heavily on her thoughts that she refused to attend.

Raphael J. DeCordova

Anna received an invitation to a large party at the home of Royal (1809-1884) and Anita Phelps (d.1872). The couple had one daughter, also named Anita (1832-1873), who was about Anna's age and also unmarried. Phelps, a wealthy businessman, ran for the Assembly in 1861 and served on many charitable boards. That same year, Phelps, John D. Scott,

Thee, and his brother Silas all supported George Opdyke for the office of Mayor of New York. A wealthy clothier, John Doughty Scott was married to Nancy Opdyke, one of George's sisters. They had three children in 1855.

Mittie told Thee about her and her mother's concerns over Robert and William Caskie, sons of John Caskie (1790-1867). The men were brothers to Mittie's half-brother Jimmie's first wife Elizabeth Euphemia (1831-1854) and to Robert Hutchison's second wife Mary Edmonia Caskie (1822-1855). In previous years, Anna had often spent time visiting the Caskie family in Richmond, Virginia. Robert Alexander Caskie (1830-1928) enlisted and was commissioned as a captain on 9 June 1861 with Company A, Virginia 10th Cavalry Regiment. William *Willie* Henderson Caskie (1834-1900) enlisted and was commissioned as a 2nd lieutenant on 11 May 1861. Willie served in Company C, Virginia 38th Light Artillery Battalion, also known as *Read's*. (See Appendix A)

West Virginia's Gauley's Bridge battle, mentioned by Mittie, took place on 1 September 1861, and occurred simply to hold an important bridge where the Gauley River and the New River form the Kanawha River. The battle consisted of a ragtag assortment of Confederate troops under the command of Brigadier General Henry Wise. They abandoned and burned the bridge during their retreat.

An important person in Anna's life makes his first appearance in this letter. James King Gracie (1840-1903) began teaching her to ice skate. A wealthy New Yorker, James worked as an investment banker.

Head-quarters, Department of Va.
FORT MONROE, VA. Feb 12th 1862.

Dearest Mittie
      I have neither a plan nor a moment in which to write you although so much to say.

At New Port News Gen Mansfield received us as his guests and had everything that we could suggest done for us.

All the officers received us in the same spirit, the weather was united to make our stay agreeable and we passed there two of the pleasantest days that I have enjoyed when away from home.

The Gen¹ suggested some practice with the parrott gun to show us how far it would throw and, after two shots, while we were standing within five feet ~~feet~~ of it one of those unfortunate accidents happened that seem here regarded as merely the incidents of war. I had suggested to Isaac Bronson laughing that he had better move for fear it should burst although I was standing nearer the gun than he was, when suddenly my words uttered in jest were verified.

The gun burst and two men, ~~who~~ standing one on each side of it were killed, while two others were very severely injured. One of the men killed had been married just before leaving home and for the first time had obtained a furlough on which he expected to return and see his wife.

While returning in the steam boat this morning we picked up a man in a small boat who had escaped from Norfolk, he had been out two days but seemed well and reported that among the workmen there was much unwillingness to do anything there for the present pay there. He then took out of his pocket a bank note which I bought from him and enclose you; please keep it as a curiosity.

We have been treated like princes here, the steam boat was put at our disposal and when through a misunderstanding it left before we were on board, another one was immediately sent with us. This afternoon the mail boat was ordered to wait for us and now I am trying to scribble these few lines on board of it.

Your Ever Loving Husband
Theo. Roosevelt

Thee's travels for the Allotment Commission continued. At Fortress Monroe, Virginia, he visited the command of General Joseph King Fenno Mansfield (1803-1862). Mansfield, a West Point graduate, from New Haven, Connecticut, served as a brigade commander with the Army of Virginia. He would die later in the year at Antietam after heroically leading his soldiers into combat. Mansfield demonstrated the firing of Parrott guns for Thee and Isaac Bronson, a cousin of Allotment Commission member Theodore Bronson.

The Parrott rifle was a muzzle-loaded, rifled artillery weapon used extensively during the War. West Point graduate Robert Parker Parrott invented the weapon in 1860, and it had just come into service in 1861. Parrott guns ranged in size from 10-pounders up to 300-pounders.

Washington Feb 14th 62

Dearest Mittie

I am once more what I almost consider now as at home again. I occupy my old room and am made just as comfortable as the people here can make me, but I miss the home faces around me painfully. I feel more lonely than usual this evening because Dodge has just left and I am without any companion; but Bronson [Theo] will soon be back again to keep up my spirits. Under any circumstances I have so many acquaintances here now that I can easily find a temporary companion.

Hay is going with me to Sewards tonight who on your mother's account I would prefer meeting first on a friendly footing.

It seems very doubtful whether I can attain the pass in consequence of her connection with Captain Bulloch who is reported to have made a fortune by running in one cargo of contraband goods and to be now in Bermuda preparing to run in another.

I have not given up all hope yet but will keep you informed of my prospects.

In Baltimore I saw or fancied I saw on the faces of one class of the inhabitants their feelings in consequence of the news just received of the taking of Roanoke Island, they looked very blue.

I enclose you an extract from the Albany Evening Journal which you will read with interest. It is with the exceptions of the clause in case of loss a correct description of the law. Father might feel interested in looking over it, as it is an answer to a piece I think he saw in the Evening Post. Show it to Rob and see if he feels disposed to have this inserted in the Post as they copied into their paper the original article.

The sutlers are our main obstacle in getting allotments, as soon as we see a regiment and persuade the men to allot they send around an agent to dissuade them from signing their names and convince them that it is a swindle, so that the money may be spent in camp and go into their pockets instead of being sent home to those who are in want.

I enclosed you a flower in my last growing in the open air at Fortress Monroe, tonight I enclose one from a boquet on the table of the Executive Mansion; also a piece of silk from an old fashioned piano in Arlington House.

I have received but two letters from you since I left and am hoping to get one tonight, you must not begin to forget me yet.

Kiss the dear little children from me, I would give anything to see you and them tonight

Your Own
Husband

Thee's letter left little doubt about the family's friendship and connections with the Lincolns. Lincoln's personal secretary John Hay planned to join Thee to visit William Henry Seward (1801-1892), Lincoln's Secretary of State. Despite Mittie's misgivings about the journey, Thee still sought a pass for Martha to go south. Additionally, he enclosed a flower from the table arrangement at the White House (Executive Mansion). Thee also sent Mittie a silk piano scarf from General Robert E. Lee's home, Arlington House.

During this early period after the passage of the Allotment Act, newspapers printed articles almost continually about the Act, how it would be implemented, and how the family back home would receive the money. Sutlers, civilian merchants who sell provisions to an army in the field, in camp, or in quarters, had previously been allowed to place a lien on a soldier's future pay in exchange for goods. The Allotment Act repealed this provision of a previous law. No longer able to sell goods to the soldiers in exchange for their next pay check and having many soldiers reduce their pay by a significant amount (their allotment), sutlers saw a dramatic decrease in their profits. For example, most privates made $13 per month during this period, newspaper articles stated most soldiers allotted four-fifths of their pay to their family, leaving them only $4 per month to spend in camp.[109]

Some confusion about how the family would collect the money came about due to the involvement of the various Union state treasurers. The law called for each state treasurer to receive the allotment certificate and pay the amount in gold. In other words, each state's treasurer acted as an agent of the State of New York in the distribution of the funds. As one can imagine, during this period when communication was carried out mostly by letter and telegraph, the whole process took time to set up and created nightmares and mass turmoil for many involved.

As for speculation that James Dunwoody Bulloch made a fortune on the sale of the war armaments he delivered on the *Fingal*, nothing could be less true. The Confederate government and private representatives of the Confederacy paid for those goods, and any profit went directly into additional shipments and the purchase of war ships for the Confederate Navy.[110]

Washington Feb 16th 62

Dearest Mittie
    I have just returned from Dr Gurley's church where I have enjoyed the last two hours quietly listening to a remarkably good sermon.

His text "receive not the grace of God in vain" was in itself sufficient to make one thoughtful; and as he dwelt upon the number of times that this grace was offered to us, the warnings that we received continually of its importance, of the uncertainty of our life here, and the dredful future that awaits us unless we place our trust in Christ all the little annoyances and troubles to which I have been subjected here sank into insignificance and I felt that, while I would try to do my duty as fully as ever, I would leave the rest in God's hands.

You ask me what the troubles I am subjected to are.

1st   The officers who while we are present are polite and promise everything, frequently neglect to fill up the rolls with the names we have taken down and the fruits of days of work is lost.

2nd   The sutlers have formed a league and hired men who follow us in the guise of good fellows, friends of the soldier, and persuade many not to sign their names after having agreed with us to do so.

3rd   The City of New York is anxious to make some offices and swindle the soldier; in order to do so it has appointed agents who try to persuade the men to change their allotments from our rolls to theirs and this impairs their confidence in our system while they get no more money for the families of the men.

A general order from Secy Stanton would remedy a large portion of these difficulties. He wrote one for me and it was his refusal afterwards to sign this that disappointed Dodge and Bronson as I wrote you in one of my previous letters.

It snowed here so hard that yesterday there was some sleighing, indeed I saw one or two sleighs out today and crowds of boys have their sleds out.

I was on horseback riding through the snow all the morning and took down the names in an independent cavalry company of some fifty men out of sixty five present who wanted to send money home.

Some of these were always in the habit of spending their money for liquor and now agree to send it to a Savings Bank.

Tell little Bammie I was very glad to receive her valentine and would have sent her some had I thought it was valentine's day. I will write to her instead however and think just as "fondly" of her as if I had written it in a valentine.

I am so glad to be spared seeing little Tedee Ellie and Corinne with such an unbecoming complaint, although sorry not to be on hand to assist you in taking care of them.

Do not lose too much rest or let them over fatigue you, but remember that you owe a duty to all of us as well as to yourself.

Does that pain in the side continue?
              Your Own Husband
              Theo. Roosevelt

              Hall's Hill Feb 18th 62
              H^{d} Quarters Genl Butterfield

Dearest Mittie

I have the prospect of another night under canvas.

Genl Butterfield came in last night to see me and found me with what would have taken me several days to accomplish, interrupted as I am in the Hotel; putting the allotment rolls in shape.

It is merely clerical work and he offered me three clerks if I would come over here, and his own quarters if I would stay all night.

This accounts for my being here where I feel at home as I have frequently been a visitor in the same quarters before.

Today I for the first really had occasion to regret that I undertook this work.

Secr^{y} Stanton had refused me a general order which he had originally written requiring the officers to give me their cooperation.

I got all the members of the Military Comm[ts] of the Senate to sign a request that he would issue such an order which I presented to him. He treated me with so much rudeness as to border on insolence and what I principally regret is that I took it without showing half the anger that I felt and of course felt twice as angry as if I had shown it.

Just as I was coming from the War Department I met Mr. Goelet who joined me in a ride out to this place where I have since been very hard at work.

He was delighted with everything although the roads were so deep with mud that we were covered from head to foot. Even his horse which was a walking skeleton he praised, and if it had not been for the everlasting chatter that he kept up I had no reason to complain of him as a companion. I rode ahead of him a little when you may imagine my feelings at seeing him fall back by the side of the orderly, who is not too respectful at the best of times, and draw him into conversation.

We parted at the 44th Regt. to the Colonel of which I introduced him.[111] I received an invitation to dine with General Porter which I accepted and once more experienced that hospitality which it has been my good fortune almost always to receive from the officers of the army. Indeed I can think of no exception to this rule.

I wrote Bammie last night and steal this opportunity to write a few lines while the two clerks are doing my work, or rather closing it up as it is now ten o' clock at night. Robbins the brother of your friend is making us sherry cobblers, while a beautiful band is playing outside

Yours Ever
Theo. Roosevelt

Feb 19th

My dear Thee

Mother and I were taking care of the little children just after dinner when Rob sent in Nora to say if I were

going to be home he would come in to see us, as I was decidedly <u>at</u> <u>home</u> a heavy snow storm going on out side and no inducement whatever to leave Mother Mittie and the children I answered him in the affirmative shortly after he arrived with some lobster salad and a bottle of such punch as only a genius could make – Mittie took two glasses and has slept on the sofa ever since, I would give anything I possess almost to have you here to talk with for as soon as Rob had made his court like entrance he was obliged to brave having another engagement I feel so alone! The children are very nearly well – And long to see you I romp with them and try to fill your place as well as I can but feel conscious of my short comings – Mother has just roused Mittie and said "do come to bed you will get to be a drunkard I am afraid" Mittie sends her love to you and says she is "perfectly miserable". Mittie suffers so much from the pain Mother and I are very anxious about her – she trys so hard to attend to all of her duties and has had so much sickness to battle with in the children – As they are all better now I hope she may get stronger – Thee I have just heard there is a letter for me detained in the Baltimore post office for want of a stamp – as I send on the needful stamp will you get it out for me I should not give you so much trouble but I do not know how to get it out myself – Will you please attend to this at once as it may contain news of poor brother Stuarts health – Bamie always sends love and Tedie and Elliot in a heartless kind of way – The babie has grown so pretty you ought to love her – Phanie and Caddie always send love and enquire most affectionately about you – Goodbye dear Thee your sister
Anna Bulloch
Mr Doge [Dodge] called last night and gave us most satisfactory accounts of you – Take care of yourself -

Washington Feb 21ˢᵗ 62

Dearest Mittie

   I have received once more an affectionate letter from you, (especially drawn out apparently by the Times letter) which I prized highly.

  Tonight I received one from Anna to which as I have written so many more letters than you have answered I ought ~~myself~~ by good rights to have given my first attention. Please tell Anna I will answer hers soon and meanwhile have written for her letter to be forwarded to her from Baltᵃ.

  She wrote about that pain in your side which I do not like at all and really think you ought to take care of. If there was no better reason to urge than saving me uneasiness you might rest and if it possibly comes from nursing Corinne give up that luxury. Anything of that kind may become chronic and one ounce of prevention is vastly better than a pound of cure.

  I have been awaiting that miserable letter to the Tribune which, added to my many other occupations, has already brought it as usual into the small hours. The man who wrote the Times letter is named Mitchell, he seems devoted to us does he not.

  I enclose you a few words which appeared in the Tribune and also a piece which probably Mr. Dodge has sent you a copy of from the Commercial Advertiser, I suspect Dodge had a hand in it although some parts of it remind me a little of Rob.

  Today I visited two regiments with about the usual success, the mud is drying up a little once more and the riding was not quite so dreadful. Last night I was introduced to Genl Banks and Mrs McClellan both of whom made a very pleasant impression upon me, the latter especially she so hearty and unaffected in her manners. I generally go into the hops at the house here just to keep up my acquaintances and I have of course formed many here. This is almost a necessity as I never get time to pay those many calls that I owe.

Genl Ripley, an old gentleman of over sixty, called on me the other day; Genl Van Vleit has asked me frequently to his house and dozens of others have equally good claims on me.

I have felt so sorry for the President in loosing his child, I hope the other will recover, Mrs. Lincoln too whatever her faults must have been a devoted mother and is entitled to our sympathy.

Do dearest Mittie remember my request and remember that you will gratify me more than by anything else in taking care of yourself. I could not bear for you to be sick

Your Own
Husband

Thee met Mary Ellen *Nelly* Marcy McClellan (1836-1915). Nelly had married George in 1860, four years after his first proposal, one which she had rejected. Her father was McClellan's former commander, Capt. Randolph B. Marcy, now a brigadier general. She received eight other proposals that year from Federal army officers and had accepted one from Ambrose Powell Hill of Virginia. However, her family did not approve, and Hill withdrew. In 1862, he served in the Confederate Army as a general.

Massachusetts native, Major General Nathaniel Banks (1816-1894) served under McClellan. Brigadier General James Wolfe Ripley (1794-1870) of Connecticut occupied the post of Chief of Ordnance.

Thee commented on the sad news of William Wallace *Willie* Lincoln's passing, who had 15 days earlier been restricted to bed during Mrs. Lincoln's Ball. Willie (1850-1862), the third son of Abraham and Mary, was named for Mary's brother-in-law Dr. William Wallace. Ill with what most historians believe was typhoid fever, Willie and his brother Thomas *Tad* (1853-1871) had been bedridden for several weeks. Typhoid fever is usually contracted by consumption of contaminated food or water. The White House drew water from the Potomac River, where thousands of soldiers and horses were camped.

General George and Mary McClellan

Willie gradually grew weaker as Tad began to recover. Abraham and Mary spent much of their time at little Willie's bedside until he passed on Thursday, 20 February 1862, at 5:00 p.m. Abraham said, "My poor boy. He was too good for this earth. God has called him home. I know that he is much better off in heaven, but then we loved him so much. It is hard, hard to have him die!"[112]

Willie (center) and Tad (right) Lincoln with their cousin
Lockwood Todd (left)
Photograph by Matthew Brady

Washington Feb 24th 62

Dearest Mittie

I received Bammie's note today. Tell her it was all my news from home and that I was very glad to hear through her of you all.

I went to the funeral of the President's child today and paid quite a long visit in the afternoon to [John] Hay who is on the sick list. The President's other little child [Tad] is fortunately better and there is every probability that it will recover.

The Captain of the Company from which our orderly comes has just lost two of his little children and will probably loose the remaining two this week. The climate here is bad enough for grown people but for children seems particularly unhealthy.

It has been so windy today that we were almost blown from our horses and found when we reached the regiment all the men so occupied in holding fast to their tents which were blown down that they could not attend to us if we could make ourselves heard which was impossible. We were obliged to return therefore splashed with mud from head to foot after a bootless errand. The roads are drying up rapidly and three days of this weather will see an advance and, to speak of it merely in a selfish point of view, probably relieve me for sometime of my duties as Allotment Commissioner. It will be a great relief to finish it all but this I can hardly consider that I will have done until the war is over. I will feel that this will be half accomplished if we meet with a great success here on the Potomac and that will be decided in a few days now.

How pleasant if we could only once more sit in peace under ourown vine and fig tree and enjoy home; and still while anticipating this I feel almost oppressed by the prospect of the responsibility of four little children of whose bodies and souls we are to share the care. I must try to find some business where there will be a better prospect for the future and where there will be a better opportunity for work. But this of course will be a matter of very serious consideration.

Why did not Bammie go to the sea shore as you proposed?

Tell me any speeches the little children make, it brings them up more vividly before me.

No letters except Bammie's was received today and I have not heard from you in a long time

Your Ever Loving
Husband

Send copy of enclosed to Rob and keep the other.

From late 1861 and into 1862, General George McClellan, Lincoln's secretary John Hay, and thousands of others fell ill in and around Washington, D.C. Most had contracted typhoid fever. Some recovered. However, children succumbed more often as did soldiers in the many camp hospitals. Civil War records show death after death caused by this and other infectious diseases.

New York Feb 26th -1862

It is a long time my darling Susy since I have written you - but I have been very busy and very anxious of late - I have had Hannah working for me for the last week and worked with her to shorten the time - We are nearly done now - I had my rep silk turned, and made up very plainly with full long sleeves- a grenadine barege & a nice foulard silk made I have also fixed up my common merino wool very nicely - All nearly now completed - I wrote Mrs Boynton on saturday and asked her to show you my letter and one I received from Susan Winston which I suppose she has shown you I have written to Mrs Stiles to know whether she has received her passport and when she is going- will let you know her answer when I receive it - I think I will be guided very much by her movements- most of my friends here think this would be a better time to go south than later- Oh Susy my dear dear child you know by your own heart what a trial it will be to me to leave you & Mittie There is so much uncertainty too attends the whole affair - I do not know when I will return for this reason - While Stuart is so low I cannot leave him, and he may, (poor dear fellow!) linger on many many months - You will see by Lucys letter which I enclose that I shall probably be in Macon and not Sav- On our way south I think we will stop some time in Richmond and will Telegraph to know how and where Stuart is - If I do, I will write from Richmond to you - I will write again as soon as I get to Macon or where ever Stuart is - We heard this morning from Irvine - He was on the point of Sailing - Hariot [Harriott] wrote a short letter also in which she mentioned the death of her mother - poor Hariot seems deeply afflicted - Mr Charles Green paid us a visit this morning - You know he has just been released from Fort Warren - His head has whitened very much since his troubles - He offered, in case he can get a pass to escort us south, but I would prefer going with Mrs Stiles - several ladies have left N York very lately for the south - Darling you must not be anxious about me - I do not dread the journey, only as it separates me from you and Mittie- she has been taking quinine & iron and appears stronger - Bamies eyes have been inflamed but we think are better - the baby has the thrush but not badly - Elliott and Teedie are well but Ellie is about to lose his nurse - She is going to leave of her own accord - We had all begun to like her very much for although not perfection she was a kind attentive nurse - she complains of pain in her side and says she would rather be sick amongst her friends. Mittie has engaged another nurse but I know we shall have trouble at first as Elliott had become fond of Delia I hope my darling daughter you are well - I thank you my blessed child for your offer to have more plain caps made for me - but I have to economize soon so have bought some materials and will try to hatch up some for my self - I will carry some of the pretty ones you gave me - perhaps one of them - I have not worn them since I saw you at all - Anna & Mittie send much love to Mrs West & yourself - Good bye for the present dear dear

Susy - That our own precious Redeemer may ever be near you is the constant prayer of your
affectionate Mother
M Bulloch

Martha's letter was addressed to Mrs Hilborne West, 1316 Walnut Street, Phil^a Pa. At some point in the previous year or early 1862, Hilborne and Susan had moved from their Pine Street home to the home of Hill's parents. Martha discussed several types of fabric including merino wool and barege, a sheer fabric constructed in a leno or gauze weave of silk warp and cotton or worsted filling, often used to make veils and dresses. Foulard silk is a soft, lightweight fabric, either plain or twill weave with printed design.

Ladies' Caps
Peterson's Magazine, April 1861

Martha's letter proved she was not the only Southern lady stranded in the North. Susan Winston (abt. 1832-unknown) was the orphaned niece of Barrington and Catherine King of Roswell. Susan and the Kings had family in New Haven, Connecticut. A close friend of her late father, the Reverend Joseph Clay Stiles led the South Congregational Church in New Haven from 1853 to 1860. His wife and Susan's grandmother were half-sisters. Susan also had an uncle in New York City, Frederick Seymour Winston, a wealthy merchant and president of the Mutual Life Insurance Company.[113] Mrs. Stiles could be any of the extended Stiles family of Liberty County, Georgia.

Charles Green who had recently been released from Fort Warren's prisoner of war camp for Confederate officers was an old family friend from Savannah. Born in Liverpool, England, in 1809, Charles immigrated in October of 1833 to Savannah and began working for Andrew Low's mercantile and importing business. He rose quickly in Savannah business and became, by 1861, a very wealthy man with homes and businesses in Georgia and Virginia. He married three times and had at least eight children. Charles also had become a true Southerner in spirit. In the autumn of 1861, various sources reported Charles to have sailed for England to purchase guns and other supplies for the South. There he was followed by Union detectives back across the Atlantic to Windsor, Canada, and on to Detroit, Michigan, where he was arrested and imprisoned at Fort Warren, near Boston. After three months, Charles was released.[114] Officials also arrested, on suspicion of carrying secret dispatches for Confederate President Davis, his sister, Mrs. Mary Elizabeth (John) Low, who had accompanied him. Despite the fact that no dispatches were found, she was imprisoned briefly at the Old Capitol Prison in Washington, D.C., before being released. She immediately traveled to Richmond and met with President Davis. Some sources indicate she hid the dispatches in her hair.[115]

Additional sources indicate Andrew Low and Charles Green worked with James Dunwoody Bulloch in the autumn of 1861 to purchase a fast steamship for the purpose of running the blockade and bringing in war munitions. John Low, Charles' brother-in-law, sailed with James on the C.S.S. *Fingal*.[116] Charles' visit to Martha, Mittie, and Anna would have brought recent news of their Liverpool family and perhaps James' activities for the Confederacy.

Harriott's mother Julia Louise Duvall von Schaumburg Cross (b. 1810) died on 11 January 1862. She married Osborne Cross, an Army officer in 1827, in New Orleans, and had three children still living. Her son Edwin Bathurst Cross served as a lieutenant in the United States Army. Harriott like many Americans had family on both sides of the War. Colonel Osborne Cross served in the Army's Quartermaster Corps. He would remarry only six months later on 8 July 1862, the widow of Lt. Colonel Roger Sherman Dix.[117]

Washington Feb 27th 62

Dearest Mittie

I have entirely lost count of my letters and as I do not know that it is of much consequence if you loose a few I will stop numbering them. The balance is certainly very much in my favor and you show no disposition to turn the scale.

The morning is once more lovely although a hard rain yesterday afternoon and evening gave us all the blues.

For the first time I am obliged to keep quiet about military affairs although I suppose you know as much in New York as we do here.

As my stay in Washington is drawing to a close I regret very much not keeping a little diary. All those whom I have seen in social intercourse day by day will be characters in history and it would be pleasant to look over hereafter myown impressions of them and recall their utterly different views upon the policy which should be pursued by the government.

I but rarely have been able to leave my room in the evening it has been so filled with visitors, but I have not felt the loss of liberty from the fact that those who were my

163

guests I would have taken a great deal of trouble to see and never could have seen so informally and pleasantly.

It has been of course more my duty to entertain those whose hospitality I was daily receiving in the camps; but the civilians who drop in during the evening are all striving to make their mark as statesmen and some we will hear from hereafter.

Senator [Ira] Harris has impressed me more favorably than anyone I have met, both as a man of a high class of mind, and, as a still greater wonder here, an honest man. He has a remarkably sweet expression of face and is one of the few who from the first moment I came here believed that I had no ulterior object in view, and was my friend.

Bronson has just arrived to go with me to breakfast and I must close what I fear you will consider rather a dry letter. It is a simple expression of my thoughts induced by the prospect of leaving those whom I have learned to regard in some cases as friends and who are about to go from here in a few days possibly not to return.

                    Your Husband
                    Theo. Roosevelt

Chapter 8: March through July of 1862

Events of the War

March began with the Battle of Hampton Roads, better known as the Battle of the *Merrimac* (C.S.S. *Virginia*, its Confederate name) and the *Monitor*. On 8 March, the *Virginia* destroyed two wooden Federal ships, the U.S.S. *Congress* and U.S.S. *Cumberland,* and was preparing to attack the U.S.S. *Minnesota* when darkness fell. All of this took place off Hampton Roads, Virginia. During the night, the Federal ironclad *Monitor* arrived and took up position to defend the *Minnesota,* which had run aground. On the morning of the ninth, the battle resumed and three hours of intense naval warfare took place without any significant damage to either ironclad. The *Virginia* returned to Gosport Navy Yard for repairs and strengthening, while the *Monitor* remained to guard the *Minnesota* until it could be moved.

On 11 March, Lincoln relieved McClellan of his command as General-in-Chief and took on the role himself. His reasoning was McClellan needed to devote all of his time and energy toward victory in his coming campaign.

On 17 March, McClellan's army finally began an active campaign. McClellan sailed his army from Alexandria, Virginia, in an armada transporting 121,500 men, 44 artillery batteries, 1,150 wagons, over 15,000 horses, and tons of equipment and supplies.[118] After landing on the Virginia peninsula, south of the Confederate capital of Richmond, on 4 April, they began their advance.

On the western front on 6 and 7 April, at Shiloh Church (Pittsburg Landing), Tennessee, Confederates under the command of General Albert Sydney Johnston carried out a surprise attack on the Union forces of General Ulysses S. Grant. During the battle, Gen. Johnston fell to a mortal wound, and General P. G. T. Beauregard replaced him. Union reinforcements arrived overnight, and the Federals held their positions. They now outnumbered the Confederate force of less than 30,000. Grant's counteroffensive forced the Confederates to withdraw. Over 24,000 men died or were wounded in those two days of fighting.

On 24 April, 17 Federal ships sailed up the Mississippi River and took New Orleans, capturing the Confederates' greatest seaport. Back in Virginia, small battles between the two opposing armies continued until 31 May, when the Battle of Seven Pines occurred outside Richmond. Confederate forces under General Joseph E. Johnston attacked and almost defeated McClellan's forces. Johnston, badly wounded during the battle, was replaced by Robert E. Lee the following day.

From 25 June until 1 July, the Seven Days Battles occurred near Richmond as Lee's Army of Northern Virginia, in defense of the Confederate capital, attacked McClellan's forces. Despite very heavy losses on both sides, neither proved victorious, but McClellan began to withdraw back toward Washington, D.C.

Lincoln appointed General Henry W. Halleck as General-in-Chief on 11 July, once again putting a military man in charge. Lincoln himself had held the position since 11 March.

The Letters

Baltimore March 1st 62

Dearest Mittie

I received your letter stating your mother's final determination yesterday and came immediately over here for her pass.

Genl Dix says that she can go with Anna but it must be on condition that they will not return, he also states that he has information that the Rail R^d is out at Weldon by our troops and would very decidedly advise them not to attempt it. He gives no passes now except when the people are ready to start but will not allow any detention to occur here. I will meet your mother and Anna at Barnums here next friday afternoon if they determine to start by the first flag of truce and accompany them to Fortress Monroe and see them off, we must leave in the boat from here saturday.

Before that time a battle will have been fought or Manassas [Virginia] evacuated and your mother will be better able to judge if it is advisable to go while matters are so unsettled.

Write and telegraph me if she will be here next friday, of course not unless she will. I will want to make my arrangements so as to meet her, write me what you think will be her determination even if she is doubtful. I am very confident that Chatanooga [Tennessee] is the point about to be taken by the Western army and I really doubt very much if your mother could under any circumstances reach Georgia while she will be unable to return here to you.

I write this in Charley Dix's room as I wish to relieve your anxiety and this must be the excuse for even a worse scrawl than usual.

It is thoroughly bachelor quarters, the table moves with the pen while the pen is execrable. Dix himself is lying on the bed rather under the weather; only excited occasionally by the passing of troops under the window. The late movements among the troops is drawing our work to a close and the early part of the week after next will probably see me home. I do not like to state the time certainly for fear of disappointing you and myself.

I leave here again for Washington this afternoon.
Kiss the children from me.

                    Yours Ever
                    Theo. Roosevelt

Your mother of course can leave here any saturday and I will go with her if she prefers waiting until I return, which would be my advice.

Thee wrote from the room of Charles Temple Dix (1838-1873), son of Major General John Adams Dix, former New York governor and former chairman of the Union Defense Committee of the State of New York. John and Catherine Dix had seven children, however, only four lived to maturity.

Charles and Thee resided at Barnum's City Hotel in Baltimore. Built in 1825, the hotel sat on the corner of North Calvert Street at Fayette. Its four stories held 172 bedrooms and suites, an enormous dining room, another for private parties, and a public reading room. The entire structure contained gas lighting by the 1860s.[119]

Barnum's City Hotel, Baltimore,
The Book of the Great Railway Celebrations of 1857

Thee wrote a second letter dated 1 March; however, he meant 2 March, as he states in the letter that the day was Sunday.

Willard's Hotel
Washington DC
Mar 1st 1862

Dearest Mittie

I wrote you yesterday from Baltimore stating that your mother could go south on condition that she would not return, also that the R R^d near Weldon was out by our troops, that it was probable the one from Norfolk would be before she reaches there, Chatanooga would probably be taken in a few days and that it seems possible she may find herself unable to go in either direction.

If she still determines to go I will meet her as I proposed on friday at Baltimore.

I want to know her decision immediately as my plans depend on it.

I promised Anna long ago a photograph and have with difficulty procured one worthy of her acceptance, I enclose it. It is Col. Van Allens body servant. She met the Colonel as a civilian at West Point.

All here have been in a state of excitement for some days past caused by movements in the army foreshadowing a general battle; the snow which is now falling fast is casting a damper over all our spirits.

The movement almost breaks up our plans for seeing the men and our work is now principally putting in order the rolls, and persuading those regiments visited previously to send them in. It is a great relief to feel that it is not one's duty to work as we have done during the last two months, although it of course will give us more trouble hereafter to see the regiments we miss. Several of the Generals have stated to me their belief that the war so far as there was any necessity for so large an army would be closed by sometime in May, probably the 1st; if so my work will be all over when I return to New York and I can once more feel that I have a wife and children and enjoy them. It is sunday afternoon and I have a peculiar longing to see you all again, the quiet snow falling outside, myown feelings being very sad and that of those around being in the same condition makes me turn to myown quiet fireside for comfort. I wish we sympathized together on this question of so vital moment to our country, I know you cannot understand my feelings and of course do not expect it -

But I must close this as Bronson has just come in and insists upon my going immediately to dinner

Your Loving Husband who wants very much to see you
Theo. Roosevelt

Thee sent Anna a photograph of Colonel James H. Van Allen's body servant, or a photograph belonging to him. Colonel Van Allen led the 3rd New York Volunteer Cavalry, known as Van Allen's Cavalry. During the Civil War photographers captured likenesses of a large percentage of the soldiers on both sides. This War was the first to be extensively documented with photography.

New York March 12 ? 1862

My dearest Susy,

I wrote you on the 8th, (saturday) & hope the letter did not take as long to reach you as the one I wrote the saturday previously - I gave that letter to Hannah {____} to drop into the Lamp Post on her way home. When I questioned her I found she forgot to do so until monday or tuesday afterwards - Mittie seems a little better of her pains & I think is better of her sore nipples also - The baby is better of the sore mouth - She eats now barley gruel with her cream Bamies eyes are somewhat better - Tedie & Elliott are well Elliott is becoming quite reconciled to his nurse for which I am quite glad as Ganma consequently does not have him clinging to her so constantly - He is a sweet little fellow & grows prettier & prettier - he is a great talker and speaks more distinctly than Tedie does - He and Tedie live in an imaginary world, and the greatest compliment you can pay either of them is to call them bears, or tame cats - Elliott is decidedly the prettiest of the family, and Mittie says the name I have given him is very appropriate "apple blossom" I am quite well darling - Anna and I spent last evening with Mrs Henop I wore one of the very pretty caps you gave me. Mittie & Mrs Henop admired it very much indeed - I told Mrs Henop it was a present from my dear Susy - Mittie has been very busy for a day or two getting the spring and summer out-fit for the children - It has tired her very much but still I think being out has benefitted her - While I think of it darling I want you to ask Hill what he could sell a few shares of Beaver Meadow Stock for - I shall not have enough money for house expenses and to get what is necessary for the summer - I could borrow very easily, but I dont wish to do it - I have thought it best although the times were stringent to let Anna go to Dr Ballard, and you know Dentists bills are no triffles. I am not in a hurry about this matter, as I have enough on hand <u>now</u>, but I will require about $300 more than I have to carry us through to first of July when the Hoboken interest is due - This I will require whether I go south or remain - I enclose you darling Susy a letter I received from Irvine the day before yesterday - when you have read, return it - Dear fellow! I dare not think of the perils he may yet be exposed to - I some times wish he was an infant again - & - course I have not heard lately from Stuart - Mr. Green of Sav lately from "<u>Fort Warren</u>" is going south if he possibly can and went to Baltimore yesterday to endeavor to get a pass - I sent by him a verbal message to dear Stuart, but could not write - Oh dear daughter what a comfort it would be if we could cast all of our burdens on the Lord - It is our privilege & duty to do so and yet we will not avail ourselves of this inestimable privilege I have not heard from Hariot lately - When we heard last she was in deep grief about the death of her mother - Give our love to Hill - remember me kindly to Mr & Mrs West. Goodbye for the present my blessed child - I know, and it is a great comfort

to know, that you pray for our dear ones constantly - If you could write a few lines to our poor Hariot and send them to me, I would direct them to her ?
      Your loving mother -
      M Bulloch

  While no letters exist from the period of 1 March to 12 March, it is evident from Martha's letter to Susan that they did not go South on the first Friday in March, but still considered going. However, Martha also looked to staying in the North and was setting up her money for the summer. Martha intended for Anna to see Dr. Charles W. Ballard, a dentist located at 139 Fourth Avenue.[120]
  Martha showed her new cap to Mrs. Julia Dickson Henop (1814-1887), who lived at 10 East 34th Street. Julia's husband, Frederick Lewis Henop (1805-1873) was a merchant, and their son Sidney Stewart (1842-1865), who lived with them, was a lawyer. They had at least one other son, Louis Philip Henop (d. 1918), a U.S. Navy officer prior to the War. He now served as a Confederate lieutenant with Company A of Whiteside's Naval Battalion in Georgia. All of the Henops hailed from Virginia and at some point had lived in Philadelphia. The family returned to Philadelphia after the War.[121] Martha often misspells her name as *Hinop*.
  With Thee at home, letters between family members became scarce. Thee did not travel again until mid-April, and his trip lasted only a few days.

        Washington April 16th 62
Dearest Mittie
  I am here safe and sound and find more to do than you, or I should say than I for a moment imagined when I left New York.
  A larger number of regiments are here which I had supposed were in York Town and which I must visit. The first day was occupied at the President's who behaved as well as

he always has, and in arranging my plans with the assistance of General [James S.] Wadsworth, obtaining horses and orderly. I also invited the 101st Regt Col Fardella and Sam Mitchell the same day, had the officers called together and addressed them.

Today I have seen two more regiments and am now writing this in Mrs. Odell's room; she has that pleasant way of making people at home which so few possess and which indeed must come from some peculiarity of temperament and cannot be educated into any one. A motherly manner is the only way in which I can describe it.

Our treatment has been as kind as possible from all; the President sent for the Pay Master General who agreed to issue an order which I have in vain requested before; Col Fordella has invited me to breakfast with him to meet the ambassador and Col. Havelock; Sam Mitchell and Ed Sturgiss were of course delighted to see me and invited me to dinner the afternoon that I passed with them, while Senator [Ira] Harris' family are as socially inclined as ever. The weather however is my principal pleasure as riding you know is no hardship to me.

I am about to pay my respects to Mrs. Lincoln although of course not expecting to be received.

I did not ask you to write when I left and suppose that you will not think of it, but inquire anxiously for letters, I wish the children were well. It will be too late to write when you receive this as I return saturday night, I do not like to say sunday morning although of course it will be five o'clock sunday morning really.

Excuse these few words from
Your Affectionate Husband
Theo. Roosevelt

Thee visited Washington not long after the Siege of Yorktown, Virginia. On 5 April as McClellan's forces moved toward Richmond in the Peninsular Campaign, Brigadier General Erasmus D. Keyes' IV Corps made initial contact with Confederate defensive works at Lee's Mill. Confederate leader General John B. Magruder moved troops back and forth in the area to convince the Union that the works were strongly held. An artillery duel ensued, and McClellan ordered the construction of siege fortifications and brought his heavy siege guns to the front. In the meantime, Gen. Joseph E. Johnston arrived with reinforcements for Magruder. Fighting continued on the day Thee arrived in Washington, D.C.

Thee planned to dine with Colonel Enrico Fardella of the 51st New York Regiment who would introduce him to Colonel Charles Frederick Havelock (1803-1868), aide-de-camp to Major General George B. McClellan. Commissioned in the British army in 1821, Havelock saw action with the 16th Lancers, in the Siege of Bhurtpoor, India, the Afghan War (1839), and the Sikh Wars (1845-1846) before being wounded. He received promotions to Lieutenant-Colonel in the service of the Ottoman Irregular Cavalry and, in 1856, to the rank of Major General before he came to America and volunteered at age 58. After speaking with the President in November 1861, Lincoln appointed him to the position of McClellan's aide-de-camp.[122]

New York May 5th 1862

Dearest Susy

I am sorry I could not conveniently accept Mrs West polite & kind invitation to accompany her back to Phil Perhaps I may sometime in the course of the present month go to Phil for a week, but at any rate Mittie says you will stay certainly a month at Long Branch with her, I will then darling have the pleasure of being with you. I do want to see you dreadfully but really when I come to think of it, as we expect to go to Long Branch the first of June, I do not know that it will be in my power to go to Phil at all - One important consideration is the expense. This tho' small has to be thought of these times. Little Teedie is still very unwell. The rest are well. I went with Mittie today to look at a place in the country. It is a very pretty place but it is not determined yet whether they will conclude to take it. If they do, they will not move there before the fall. I hope you will rent your house.

Ask Hill if he thinks he <u>can sell my furniture</u> to let me know as that will determine me what course to take about The Beaver Meadow? Oh Susy darling I think of you constantly, my blessed child you dont know how much I love. Nothing of late from those we love. Much love to Hill.
Your affec Mother
M Bulloch
God bless you darling Susy

A rare letter from Anna follows. Teedie, age 3, and Bamie, age 7, seem to enjoy the activity of writing. Thee, Mittie, and baby Corinne were still in New York. Anna and the three older children were at Long Branch with Martha.

June 15th

My dear Thee

Tedie and Bamie were delighted to get your very interesting letters - Tedie was going to write a note to you this afternoon I gave him a nice piece of paper and my pencil and he seemed charmed until I commenced to writing and then he insisted on having "<u>ghie</u>" too. I told him he could not write with ink (glue) until he was a bigger boy he is so displeased with me that he says when he is a big boy and has a gun he will "shoot Aunt Anna dead" - I have tried in vain to work upon his feelings but he is so much provoked that he can not forgive me. Bamie is writing but I think it is only a copy as she soon expects to see you - We will all be delighted to see you and Mittie and little Corinne on Tuesday. I hope you may have a pleasant day to come down not too violently warm in the city or the contrast here will be too great for the baby. Be sure to see Caddie and Phanie [Hyatt] before you come to let me have the latest news of them - Quite a number of people came here last night for so early in the season. We had gas for the first time. Mr Grace [Gracie] has offered to take this note tomorrow so I feel sure it will reach you before you leave I should be uncertain if it were to go by mail. My fan came in the hamper nicely mended I am much obliged to you did Mittie give you an other little commission for me I sent her the dimensions of a paper box I wanted you to get for my portfolio. The Misses Jenkins came down last night with them who is quite devoted to the largest and least interesting of the two. Mr Laird seems very anxious to "halve" you come to consult you about several little things I have been surprised at the humor of people that have sent down to engage rooms nearly all the best rooms are gone already those over the front piazza being engaged by new comers so that Mr Laird says that with his old customers he will soon have no rooms left. Mr Isaac Knox was here some night last week he mentioned having seen you last sunday what a nice pleasant visit visit you must have had at the Dodges - Corinne seems to have enjoyed it as much as any one. What a little pet Corinne has been since the other little ones left. I am sorry to write so stupid a letter but really the constant interruptions have entirely prevented me from any connection in my letter The boys and Bamie are now down on the beach and the water and sky are clear blue the air is soft and lovely so I hope they are enjoying themselves - we are going to look at them presently - Love to you and Mittie from all - The little children all send kisses to Mama and papa Goodby dear Thee I enjoyed your letter much more than you will this -

yours truly
Anna Bulloch

Isaac H. Knox (1827-1888) appeared in earlier letters as *Ike*.[123] He lived in New York and was a wealthy merchant. In 1862, Ike and wife Augusta had four children. The 1870 census also shows three domestic servants and a carriage driver, all from Ireland.

Long Branch June 15/62

My very dear daughter [Susan Elliott West],

On friday evening I received your acceptable ~~letter~~ letter of the 12th - I was truly glad to hear from you darling and was quite interested in hearing of you & Emily being busily employed about your summer work - Also about the bundle, pamphlets etc. being sent to Mrs Boynton & Harpers & being reserved for the hospitals - I know they will give much comfort to the recipients. On the same evening I received a letter from Lucy. Anna immediately wrote you a few lines enclosing it to you. I suppose you have received it by this time, and I know its contents give you much pleasure - I cannot impart to you my feelings on the occasion - First of all I was so surprised at receiving such a letter knowing that there was no mail communication. Then it struck me that Stuart was dead - Judge of my delight then on reading the letter to find not only that my poor child was ~~not only~~ alive, but that his precious soul had (as we have strong reasons to hope) received life from above - Susy darling it is what we have been longing and praying for a long time, and now we are permitted to hope that God has graciously heard and answered our prayers - Oh how good our Covenant-keeping God is - He has in his holy word promised to bless those who trusted in him - but this is a richer blessing than I could ever have had the faith to expect - I have often tried to solace myself with that precious promise in Jer 49-11 "Leave thy fatherless children, I will preserve them alive; and let thy widows trust in me." but I have felt so unworthy of such an unspeakable mercy that I could not appropriate the promise, and felt that that it was <u>too</u> good for me. But blessed be God it is not for any worthiness in me that he has done it, but from his free Sovereign infinite mercy in Christ. How wonderful is the goodness & Mercy of God! - Good & upright is the Lord; therefore will he teach sinners in the way Ps 25-8^{124} You cannot think dear Susy how anxious I am to go to him. I think from Lucy's account that he cannot live much longer, and it makes me feel dreadfully to think that he feels hurt at my not going to him - I heard a few days since that Mrs Stiles had just received a letter from her husband, in which he said the person who would deliver that letter was a Clergyman & that she might go south under his escort - the person did not deliver the letter in person, but it was put under her door. I wrote to her on saturday asking her if she had yet seen the bearer of her letter, whether she had any idea of going south, and if she had, whether she would admit me as one of the party - I have not heard from her since- I feel as tho' I would be almost willing to go in some of the vessels which attempt to Run the Blockage I have just heard of an opportunity to write to my dear Stuart and Lucy - A vessel sails for Nasau New Providence from New York on the 20th of this month - Mr Cress is here at this time looking for rooms - He says he will send my letter with the outer envelope directed to a certain house there, which will forward it to the Confederate States - I will write at any rate whether it reaches them or not - We have had some very uncomfortable weather since we have been here, but this afternoon is delightful. The children are quite well, and have gone down to the beach each with a little pail & shovel to play in the sand with - They are delighted here & play out the whole day when it does not rain - Ellie has grown very stout and is still a great grandma boy - All the morning they were busy raking up the grass which had just been mown in front of the cottage - It was a pretty sight to see the three on the green so busy and Bamies kitten playing about with them - The house is gradually filling and Mr Laird has a great many rooms engaged - I think this a very pleasant place - I wish you were here with us - Hilly's field of action seems to be farther from Phil[a] than I expected, but I think he will be very much interested in his work, and the daily exercise will do him good - Give our love to him and remember me affectionately to Mr & Mrs West - With much love Your loving mother

M Bulloch

NB We expect Mittie and Thee tomorrow afternoon - Love to Mrs Boynton & Miss Session

MB

In several letters, Martha named various family servants such as Emily in Philadelphia and Hannah in New York. During this period, both households employed a number of Irish women as maids, cooks, and nursemaids. Emily worked for Susan and Hill when they lived on Pine Street, and according to this letter continued to do so when they moved in with Hill's parents. Hannah does not appear in either the 1860 or 1870 U.S. Census as part of the Roosevelt family.

Long Branch June 22

My dearest Susy,

Mittie arrived here on saturday evening with the intention of remaining - she had sent Teedie back on the previous Thursday as the physician thought his attack of asthma was over - The Doctors were mistaken or, if the attack was over he had the same symptoms of difficult breathing etc. as soon almost as he returned to Long Branch - Therefore this morning at an early hour Mittie & Thee left taking the little boy with them - I think they left with the intention of going for ten or fifteen days to Saratoga in hopes that the dry warm air of that place may benefit the dear child. So you see darling we are again left with Bamie Ellie & Corinne. Bamie today has complained of a cold - the two little ones are quite well - The weather is uncomfortably cold - indeed a good fire would all of the time be pleasant.

June 23 - afternoon

Dearest daughter I did not finish my letter yesterday - Today we have had some sunshine and moderately warm weather - Bamie is better, the other children quite well - have not heard from Mittie since she left except that a gentleman who went in the car with her yesterday told me Teedie appeared pretty well & that Thee and Mittie had abandoned the idea of going to Saratoga and would go instead to West Point. The house here is filling up by degrees - Mr and Mrs Laird are very busy fixing the different rooms - Every thing looking quite green and fresh - Anna & I walk when ever

the weather permits - After each meal we take care of the children some little time, then sew read or walk as it suits us - My principal comfort during the past cold weather has been in the thought that you were not suffering with heat in Phil[a]. I suppose the worms are over - Susy darling Mittie told me when she was here about her taking the ether I do really think it is wrong for her to take it - just to think of her taking no breakfast or dinner fatiguing herself all the morning and then inhaling ether!! I think it was really running the risk of losing her life, or her reason. Bamie wrote you a few days since and enclosed a letter from Lucy - I am sorry to hear of that enlargment of the neck which Lucy speaks of and hope it may be temporary - I am quite well - I long to have you come darling, as I feel confident the change will improve you - I wish so much that dear Hill could come and remain here with you - I wish also that Mrs West could come to Long Branch I know she would like it - I think it would do Mr West good also - Do give my love to them all - If you see Mrs Boynton & Miss Session give my love to them Goodbye for the present darling - Anna sends much love & says she will write you very shortly ?
      Your ever affectionate mother
      M Bulloch

  Ether, either by mouth or inhaling, was popular during the mid-nineteenth century, especially in Ireland. Most takers diluted ether by using boiled water with a pinch of sugar or honey and added cinnamon or cloves. Many believed it a miracle cure for almost any ailment.

      Long Branch June 29 62
My dearest Susy,
  I have been feeling a little uneasy for fear you are sick - Last saturday or friday was a week ago when Anna wrote you a few lines enclosing a letter from our dear Lucy giving an account of Stuarts extremely weak state of body, but mentioning that she had good reasons to believe

that our dear invalid rested his hopes of salvation on our precious Redeemer - This letter gave me much satisfaction, and knowing how very anxious you felt also about the poor fellow we enclosed it immediately to you - I wrote you also about the middle of last week - I hope darling you are not sick - I know it is sometimes so warm in June in Phil[a], that I have feared you were - We are all well. Mittie with little Corinne came to Long Branch this day last week - The children were very much delighted to see her. Thee went back to New York on wednesday morning & went that night to Washington where he has been ever since. His business there was that same allotment concern, in which he has been so much interested for the last six months - It remains so cold that but few persons have come to L B as yet - It looks very sweetly here now - every thing so fresh and green - Little Teedie and Ellie seem very happy - They play out all day unless it rains, then they play in the piazza's - I suppose Hill has commenced fairly at his new vocation by this time - Give my love to him - I need not say how sincerely I wish him success - Remember me affectionately to Mr & Mrs West

Susy darling I <u>hope</u> you are well - I <u>long</u> to see you dear dear daughter - I think you will be more comfortable in your little room this summer than you were last - The bed is better & there is a bureau in the room we all anticipate your coming so much - in fixing the furniture Mittie always says it shall be fixed in this, or that way when sister is expected - Goodbye for the present dear darling Susy -

Your Mother
M Bulloch

Love to Mrs Boynton - Miss Session - is Miss Session better? Susy darling will it put you to inconvenience to get Mrs Tomlinson to make me another morning cap & bring it for me when you come? If you have not room darling, dont trouble yourself as I think it is probable I have enough - I enclose one dollar - if it costs more tell me when we meet

Your affec Mother
MB

Long Branch July 16 - (62

My own dear Susy -

I sincerely hope you are by this time at Flushing - I have thought of you during the hot days we have had constantly - I know you were so weak after your sickness and so little able to bear the heat of Phil^a The long letters I sent by the hamper to meet you in New York were returned last saturday enclosing the one from Irvine and one from Mrs Stiles - I send <u>them</u> to you at this time - You need not send me back Mrs Stiles', but destroy it - We are all well darling - Mrs Mickler is spending a week with Mittie - They have just all gone down to bathe - Anna, Mittie, Bamie and Teedie bathe every day - Little Teedie was fearful at first, but now lets the bather take him in the midst of the surf without the least apprehension Ellie would not consent to bathe at all, and scarcely will consent to witness it - Little Corinne has improved very much since she has been fed - Her wet nurse became so insolent that they had to dismiss her, so although this week Thee remains on Long Branch he had to go yesterday to New York to procure another nurse - He brought a little demure looking woman in the afternoon and Mrs Riley was sent off this morning -

July 17 - morning   I was interrupted yesterday afternoon, so finish my letter this morning - Anna, Mittie, Mrs Mickler & the children went in *bathing this morning at ten oclock Anna was knocked down by the waves and says she will not go in again except at very low tide. Mittie & Julia did not go in as they were frightened by Annas fall. The baby takes to the new nurse very kindly and nurses without any difficulty - The nurse seems to be a very well-bred nice woman and I think Mittie will like her very much - I hope my darling Susy you are much better - As you perceive they or rather two of them did not bathe

How kind the old {Sise} was - I am sorry Marys baby is a boy - but these matters are not in our hands, and I know it is for the best, for God does all things right - I hope she is recovering rapidly, and that the last little man may be as smart and interesting as Jimmie is - Ellie has been suffering of late from cutting his back jaw teeth, and from the consequent petting from Granma The other night he cut great capers and would not go to sleep. After a while he called to Dona Dola! call Mrs Bulloch to my - he calls himself 'my' - He is now knocking at my door and thinks it very hard that I will not open it - Sometimes when he is offended with me he threatens to tell my papa about me - says Ganma is a naughty gool & 'my' dont love ganma a bit - I dont know who he thinks is my papa. The house is full - Mr Laird says there are about four hundred persons here, I believe not counting servants and children - Anna received a letter two days since from Hariot - She says the children are all well, Jimmie goes to school and had just brought home a prize of which he was very proud She and James sent much love to you - Nothing more of course from dear Stuart - If I had wings I would soon be with him, poor fellow! but I trust darling it is <u>well</u> with him - I fear I shall never again see him - but I can feel resigned to this as I have such a sweet consoling hope that he is a child of God - You see by Irvines letter that work seems to agree with him - dear fellow how I long to see him with much love from Anna, Mittie and oceans from myself I am your
affec mother
M B

Martha's letter conveyed all the family gossip including the birth of Mary and Silas' fourth son, Frank. This was the couple's last child.

MANSION HOUSE,
S. Laird, Proprietor.

Long Branch, N.J. July 24- 1862

My dearest Susy,

Your dear letter of the 21st I received two days since and I am truly glad that you are out of Phil^a, and with such a good kind friend and sister. I hope sincerely dear precious child that you may now improve daily in health and strength - I think of you constantly, and although anxious and uneasy about your health my thoughts generally lead to a feeling of gratitude to our good God that through his almighty power and pure sovereign grace you have been led to trust in our blessed Redeemer and to give your heart with its best affections to him - we cannot now whilst in this world have a just estimate of this great blessing, but darling we shall yet (I trust) praise our Triune God for this, and all of his other mercies throughout eternity - I have often thought that our good God gave you twice to me - first as a sweet little infant, (which my beloved sister used to warn me not to idolise -) and then my covenant-keeping God gave you to me in a higher nobler sense when he changed your heart and made you his own child - I have not the power to give expression to my feelings on this subject when I think of you, and I am still less able to comprehend the goodness of God when I contemplate his dealings with dear Stuart - Susy, darling, what a struggle that poor fellow has had before he would submit - but oh I trust now that he has yielded - How kind, how merciful! When the poor body is withering, that he who said "arise take up thy bed and walk" has infused new life into that immortal soul - what troubles me is, that I cannot realise and feel corresponding gratitude for this stupendous mercy - But this is only a part of my short comings - Oh whose could we stand darling daughter, if our own right feelings, and right actions were to be the ground of acceptance - I desire to be washed in that blessed fountain opened for sinners, and to be clothed with that perfect robe of righteousness wrought out by our glorious

High Priest - I did not intend when I sat down to write to be so solemn - but some how I had to write what I this morning felt uppermost - We are well Mrs Mickler spent last week with Mittie - this week the Elliotts are here - They all appear to enjoy themselves very much - Mrs Mickler is a very amiable fine woman, and appears to refuse Mrs Roosevelts memory - her children who are delicate improved whilst here - The Misses Elliott are fine girls - very lady-like & well bred - The Hyatts are to be here on the 31st and after this visit is over then the room is to be fixed for dear Susy

Bammie is uncommonly well - so are Tedie & Ellie - the latter is so sunburnt that he has lost some of his good looks - There is a great deal of hopping & frolicking here, which I am surprised at, but I suppose it is difficult to realise the amount of suffering at present - One of our gay young ladies is the wife of an officer in McClellans army who in the battle before Richmond had his horse shot under him. She does not seem to think that the next time it may be the man and not the horse - Thee sleeps less than usual - and very frequently there are egg-nogs, or some little jolity going on - last sunday afternoon he came into my room and said it was more easy to keep the sabbath in New York than here - I told him my room was in such a quiet corner that I was not disturbed He then read by my request that chapter in Cor [Corinthians] which you admired so much when I was in Phil - "Though I speak with the tongues etc" Then he read several of Bonars poems, and said afterwards that it was the pleasantest hour he had spent that day - Little Cona [Corinne] has had a bad cold but is better - She is a sweet little thing, but I think her aunts without intending it have over-rated her beauty. Even partial grandma does not think her a beauty Anna is quite resigned to Irvine's predilection - We do not think he will have the time to make love for a great while - By that time the young lady will be memories probably - Mittie & Anna send much love - with much love to Mary and to Hill when you write, I am lovingly
                                     your M Bulloch

Do remember me kindly to Susan Newberry - Mittie says she knows her daughters were delighted to spend the day at Flushing -We have had a great deal of damp cold weather - In consequence of the damp my caps have suffered very much - I covet Mrs Wests power of keeping her caps and every thing else so nicely - As soon as my caps find out that they belong to me they get crushed soft and crooked - I have two demure caps very fresh and nice as yet, but the reason is, they are but seldom taken out of the bandboxes - My caps behave well tho' in comparison with undersleeves -these are absolutely unbearable. If I take little Con - for five minutes they are done for - This is altogether a bad place for dresses caps etc, and I sometimes feel tired of thinking and contriving so much about appearance - Mr Laird too has put something to fasten back the windows which keep us all busy mending rents - I wish you could have seen Anna this morning, soon after such a catastrophe you would have supposed that she had nothing in the shape of happiness to look forward to - There is to be a Fair here which I will write you about in my next

    Thee read the poems of Horatius Bonar (1808-1889), a Scottish minister, hymn writer, and poet. His most famous poem/hymn was "I heard the voice of Jesus say."
    The following partial letter appears to fall at the end of July or early August based on Martha's previous comments about the upcoming church fair.

The proceeds of this fair are to be given to the two Churches - the Episcopal and the Dutch Reformed - They are both struggling churches & deserve aid - Thee is quite interested, and I believe is expected to bring some of the materials for the work today I will make some pincushions and knit some reins, if nothing more - Give my love to Mr & Mrs West when you see them

Your affec Mother
MB -
We are reading a delightful book - "Recreations of a Country Parson" - Thee has received the check for my Dir - I am sorry it

Church of England minister Andrew Kennedy Hutchison Boyd (1825-1899) published *The Recreations of a Country Parson* in 1860 or 1861.[125] In all he wrote four books about his life as a minister.

A Churchyard Gate, *The Recreations of a Country Parson*

Irvine Bulloch in his Confederate Navy uniform

Chapter 9: August through October of 1862

Events of the War

Fighting intensified in late August as 55,000 Confederate soldiers defeated 75,000 Union soldiers under General John Pope, at the Second Battle of Bull Run (Manassas). Led by Generals Stonewall Jackson and James Longstreet, Confederate forces pushed the Union forces back toward Washington, D.C. Lincoln relieved General Pope. Only one week later, Confederate General Robert E. Lee pushed his 50,000-strong Confederate army toward Harpers Ferry, only 50 miles northwest of Washington. McClellan pursued Lee into Maryland.

On 17 September 1862, the Battle of Antietam became the bloodiest day in U.S. military history as McClellan stopped Lee's forces from moving further north. Some 26,000 men lay dead, wounded, or were missing. Lee withdrew back to Virginia.

The Letters

Long Branch Aug 13

My dearest Susy

I received your letter of the 9th the day before yesterday, and would have written you yesterday but really there was so much confusion I could not write - The expected Fair took place, and all was uproar the whole day - It is over and I am very glad of it, for if there is any thing I long for it is peace and quiet - I assisted all I could in preparing for it, and I think it would have been a very successful effort, but just as the tables were all arranged there came up a sudden storm of rain and wind which nearly ruined half of the expensive and beautiful articles. I should have told you that the tables were under a tent - Instead of $1000 dollars clear which Thee expected, ($500 for each of the churches), there will not be more to give them than $200 each - I was very much surprised darling to find that you were in Phil[a] - Thee did not tell me one word about your intention. The weather has been intensely hot, and I know you must have suffered, and do still suffer very much from the heat - Let me know dear daughter when you expect to be in New York on your way here, as I will meet you there and stay that night with you at Mittie's - If the weather is at all bearable I think of going to N York to do some shopping, for darling I feel that I must make the effort to see poor Stuart before he dies -

Mittie wrote you on sunday telling you that she expected you on monday next - I hope you got the letter - I long to see you my own darling daughter Thee says have your trunk directed to Mr Samuel Laird Mansion House Long Branch - Wercots Express Little Corinne has been very unwell but is better - Teedie also is not strong - The rest of us are well - Be sure and let me know when you expect to be in N York - Give our love to Mr & Mrs West and dear Hill - I received a letter last evening from dear Irvine which I will show you when you come - Your affec Mother M Bulloch

Oh darling how sad it is to think of dear Stuart - I am so much afraid from Mr Caskies letter that he will not live until I can see him - It is really very trying -

---

Long Branch Aug 15th

My dearest Susy

I received your sweet letter yesterday, also one came to you directed to this place which I enclose I am glad darling

your letter speaks of having a little cooler atmosphere, for if I may judge by weather we have had here I know you have suffered most dreadfully with heat. some days the thermometer stood at 96 all day - I thought of the poor horses much at the time and do not wonder that men and horses died from the extreme heat - Mitties children have not been very well of late - Little Cona in addition to cutting a new tooth has had a rising on one of her fingers which has given her a great deal of pain - it is better now, but she will lose the nail - I told you in my letter which I wrote the day before yesterday how you were to direct your trunks here but will repeat for fear you may not have received my letter - Direct to Theodore Roosevelt to the care of Sam Laird Mansion House Long Branch by Westcotts Express. The reason why I did not write you last week was because I was so busy with the work of the Fair - I wrote you about the fair in my last letter - I wrote you also that I wished to meet you in N York as I wanted to so some shopping in anticipation of going South - I long to see you to consult about it - I feel as though I must try to see dear Stuart before he dies. I have not spent a pleasant summer - there is too much company and frollicking for my feelings - A young man who died a few days since and was buried yesterday danced with Anna about a fortnight since at a hop at the US Hotel - He had bathed with her also, and was amongst the most pleasant and gay of the party - "What phantoms we are, and what phantoms, we pursue" he was the son of President King of Columbia College NY - was a few months older than Irvine- I hope you received Mitties letter, telling you she was ready and expected you on monday next - this is friday - The Miss Hyatts will leave on monday morning - they would have left this week but the elder of the two has been a little unwell - with much love to your household I am your
affectionate mother
M Bulloch

Anna danced with Augustus Fleming King (1841-1862), the youngest child of Charles King (1789-1867) and his second wife Henrietta Liston Low (1799–1882). This second union produced six children. Charles had eight with his first wife. Augustus died of a fever while in camp on 11 August 1862.

As most of her family was now ensconced at Long Branch for the summer, Martha's letter writing dropped off. Letters to those in Britain and the South are not present in the archives. For the next letter, Anna used Mansion House stationery.

S. Laird,
MANSION HOUSE,

Long Branch, N. J. Sep 9th 186[2]

My dearest Mittie
        I write only a few lines to let Thee and yourself know the dear little children are well - Elliot is still a little out of order in his stomach but notwithstanding it is lively and well in other respects - Mother and I tried to the best of our abilities about the zouave shirt but I assure you Mittie it is almost impossible to fit Tedie - I think it is all right now with the alterations Mother wrote you about yesterday - Tedie was really excited when I said to him darling I must fit this zouave or Mama cannot have it made his little face flushed up and he said "are me a soldier laddie" - I immediately took his own suggestion and told him he was and that I was the Captain and that I would fit his soldiers clothes for him - This kept him still a minute or two! These two last days the bathing has been at five o'clock in the afternoon and as it has been a little cool I have had Bamies bath in the house - Mr Van Brant told Mother that a lady had just gone away for whom he had brought salt water all summer without paying him a cent - How can people be so mean, she is quite wealthy lives in the fifth Avenue. David has gone his wife was sick and in his place we have a waiter I have noticed all during the summer with aversion he is really very obliging

devoted to Bamie - I wonder if you can remember him at all very short and fat the image of Count Fosco in the Woman in White David seems to have impressed our horror of flies upon him - for when we come to table everything is so served up that the dishes appear as great a mystery as the Sphinx - no one could imagine that it only bread under the close secret folds of the napkins, or butter (not so good either) hidden away under the big deep plate that covers the small one that covers the butter. While we eat he takes one of the long lilly shaped napkins out of the tumbler and brushes flies all the time greatly to Bamies amusement for he stands just at her elbow and leans close to her and asks her in the most cautious whisper "is there anything you'll be helped to Miss" - Bamies reply is so very polite and snotty as to be scarcely audible - And now you must wonder why I dont like him such a treasure about flies and I can only say it is really principally because he is so fat that his white apron stands off straight more like a standing up collar than anything else - Mother gave to day for Ellies dinner some well boiled rice with the red gravy poured on it and a small piece of rare beef she minced up for him herself at the table - She sends Ellies little meals to him by Count Fosco - Mother does not think Dora shows the least judgement in selecting their meals so she fixes Ellie herself poor Tedie will have to get on until he sits at the table by his Father which I do hope he will do when he gets home - It is only necessary for Mother to ask the simplest question relative to his food or clothes indeed I might say anything for the Dragon that harnessed them together and drove them as a pair of ponies - It would have amused you to see Ellie doing everything Tedie did - I only walked near but Bamie had entire charge - They all had an enchanting time - now they are down on the beach it is a most lovely afternoon - Love to dear Thee tell him to write to me soon - Mother sends love to you both - Goodby my darling please remember me very kindly to Mrs Newbury [Newberry]-

      Yours aff^{ly}
      Anna B -

Civil War Zouave uniforms were based on those of the French Army's light infantry regiments that served in North Africa. Several Northern and Southern units copied this unique uniform style. It became quite popular to wear Zouave shirts and jackets and to dress young boys in this style. Many young unmarried women also adopted the style for everyday wear.

Unidentified Union Drummer Boy in Zouave Uniform, Library of Congress

Fashionable Gown based on Zouave Uniform,
Godey's Lady's Book, September 1865

Considered one of the top 100 novels of all time, *The Woman in White* by Wilkie Collins was printed in 1859 in England. In the book, Count Fosco, who's full name is Isidor Ottavio Baldassare Fosco, is described as a "grossly obese Italian with a mysterious past: eccentric, bombastic, urbane but intelligent and menacing. He keeps canaries and mice as pets."[126]

Long Branch Sept 28

My own dear daughter, I received your letter from New York dated thursday afternoon yesterday. I was very glad to hear from you and glad too to find that you could spend an evening & night with poor little Mittie before you left for Phil[a]. It is just like you darling to feel as you do with respect to keeping house and just like that truly good woman Mary to sympathise with you with respect to this matter - I always have, and always shall, like Mary Roosevelt She has a large and warm heart - But still darling I do not see that you can without great loss keep house this winter. If you staid at Mrs West's you might save what you have now in hand - But if you keep house darling (if with the strictest economy) you know how money will go - I shall feel all the time too as though you made this arrangement on my account, and that you know would not be a pleasant feeling - I should be all of the time anxious for fear that you are injuring yourselves - Borrowing money is a ticklish business, for you shurely incur debt - Now darling although it would please me above all things still for us to be together again, I do not think upon the whole it is best for you to try to keep house at present - I suppose I could get good and moderate board somewhere near you. and then I could see you almost every day - Anna and I would both be delighted if we could again settle down at the dear home and with those we so much love as Hill and yourself, but indeed I think it would be an imprudent step on your part - The weather is generally very fine, but sometimes we have it rainy and tempestuous Yesterday afternoon & last night was of this character - today is lovely - The children are quite well - Elliott looks chubby & robust. After you left Long Branch I devoted myself to the little fellow - at first he did not appear to improve, but for some time past he has been like another child - They all live out of doors & I shall be sorry when they have to go back to New York - Poor little Mittie must be tired waiting - I wish it was well over with her - There are not over four boarders here now except ourselves - It looks lonely to see the long piazza's empty, and the rooms shut up - The country tho' is delightful - the grass is so green, and the sun shines with such a mild radiance on it - Please give my love to Mr & Mrs West & Hill - Anna sends much love also - Good bye dearest until we meet

      Your loving Mother
      M Bulloch

  This letter presents us with a mystery in the line "Poor little Mittie must be tired waiting - I wish it was well over with her." No additional reference to Mittie's health concerns in 1862 has been found; however Mittie could have just been waiting for Thee to return home. Susan and Hill must have still owned the house on Pine Street, once occupied by them, as Susan once again considered keeping house. No doubt, her desire stemmed from wishing to have her mother in Philadelphia.

      Baltimore Oct 14th 62
Dearest Mittie
  I received your letter dated the 10th and post marked the 9th today on my arrival here. Write me to Willard's Hotel Washington hereafter as I leave for that place tomorrow morning.
  Since I last wrote you I have enjoyed my pleasantest experiences as Allotment Commissioner. The weather was lovely our horses good and Major Dix accompanied us from the Fortress to Yorktown. It was about twenty five miles of historic ground passing over the same country that General Mc Clellan had taken his army along last spring.
  First come the ruins of the little town of Hampton burnt by [General John B.] Mc Gruder, then through Big Bethel where Schanck was whipped to the approaches to Yorktown. Here ravines have been cut through miles of roads made and immense breast works thrown up by our army.
  Leydam was away but the rest of Genl Keyes staff received us most hospitably and after dinner furnished us

with fresh horses to visit the regiments, one of their numbers accompanying us.

I had practice for both my french and German in the Enfans Perdus Colonel Confort's regiment and it was quite late before our return. As I had broken my eyeglasses I had to trust entirely to my horse who jumped over the ditches in a most independent manner. We all sat up together until about twelve except Bronson who had seemed used up all day and had not accompanied me to the regiments. He seemed to feel the shock of the fall when the car ran off the track, and not to recover from it so easily as myself.

Next morning we rode another twenty five miles to Newports News to see the Irish Brigade Genl Corcoran was there and accompanied us to the regiments first suggesting Irish whiskey to strengthen us. At dinner also was the beverage and after dinner each Colonel seemed to have his own particular tope.[127] On our return they made an irish drink called "scal thun" and at about one o'clock gave us "devilled bones." The servant was invited in to sing for us and furnished with drinks at odd times by the General who never indulged however himself to excess. We then went the grand rounds with the General at two in the morning, arrested two officers for not being at their posts and returned at half past three well prepared to rest quietly after a very fatiguing day, and one of the most thoroughly Irish nights that I ever passed.

Next morning (yesterday) we had a delightful ride over to Fortress Monroe and had lunch at Genl [John A.] Dix's before leaving in the boat.

A dozen of the officers were down at the boat and we felt as we bid good bye to some of them like leaving old friends.

Charley Dix [Major Charles T.] and Lord really seemed sorry to part with us.

Major General [John J.] Peck came on with us in the boat and takes the same view about the course of the Government in sending off Genl [Nathaniel] Banks that all seem to have, as in New York.

I arrived quite early this morning and am writing this before breakfast, which important meal I will now take before closing. -

Dearest a few words more and I must close.

Bronson has a very bad cold and decides that he will leave me tomorrow. If well enough he will undoubtedly call on you. Of course this makes me doubly home sick but I must see it through.

                Good bye
                Yours as Ever
                Theodore Roosevelt

    Thee visited the camp of Les Enfants Perdus, the Lost Children, organized by Lt. Colonel Felix Confort. Frenchman Colonel Confort had once served in the French Army as a captain and spoke not a word of English. This lack of English proved detrimental as a mutiny of sorts took place, and by the time of Thee's visit, Confort was in the stockade at Fortress Monroe.

    Recently released from a Confederate prisoner of war camp, Brigadier General Michael Corcoran, a New York Irishman, led the 69th New York Regiment. A close confidant of Lincoln's, Corcoran became known before the War for refusing to parade his militia regiment in salute to the Prince of Wales in protest of the British's lack of response to the Irish Potato Famine. After his capture in late 1861, Corcoran's name appeared on a list of officers to be executed by the Confederates in retaliation for the Federal court's sentence of death placed on the officers and crew of the *Enchantress*, a Confederate privateer.[128] A colorful leader, Corcoran was immortalized in many songs and poems of the day. He died on 22 December 1863 when thrown from his horse.

                New York Oct 17

    I had just come upstairs my dearest Susy to write you a few lines when I received your letter of the 16 - Thank you darling for the caps etc I am sure such a supply ought to last me until the winter and spring are over - I know they would last neat, clean, nice Mrs West - Darling you are a kind good daughter to me - No body knows how much I appreciate you, and all that you do - But I must tell you about Mittie & the children - I wrote you how very unwell Bamie was when we were at Long Branch - she was nearly a week sick - soon after she recovered Teedie was taken nearly with the same symptoms only not as severe - He very soon recovered The weather how ever which during part of the time which we remained at the Branch was remarkably fine, changed during the last week of our stay and we had a cold rainy northeast storm which lasted four or five days - All of these days poor little Teedie had to be kept a close prisoner for fear he might renew his cold - But on tuesday the 14 the clouds appeared to become somewhat lighter so we made a very early start bag & baggage for New York - It did not rain that day and we arrived safely here at half past eleven AM - It was tolerably rough in the boat and little Teedie & Elliott were both sea-sick - Teedie threw up, Elliot did not but turned very pale and said he hoped he would not be sick - We found Mittie & Cony quite well - Thee was at home but was making preparations to leave, which he did the next evening at ten o clock - The very afternoon after we arrived here Elliott was taken with the most violent colic I have ever witnessed - We put him in a warm bath and I made use of all the remedies I could think of We then sent for Dr Metcalf who gave him 3 grains of blue pill and followed it with castor oil - He is better but does not seem perfectly well - Mittie yesterday was very unwell with a violent cold - She is better today but is still in bed - She and Anna both send love - She desired me to enclose two bills which she says are both paid - I had my bombazine made by Miss Lane at L Branch she made it very nicely - Mr Cress came over last evening and told me if I could write a letter he had an opportunity to send it south - I consequently wrote a long letter to Lucy and sent it to him this morning early-

Love to Mrs West & Hill & very kind regards to Mr West & Mr Lew West - Remember me also to Mr {Baud/Bond} & Mrs Boynton & Miss Session
Your ever loving Mother
MB -

Bombazine was a fabric woven of silk or silk and wool. Quality twilled or corded bombazine was made with a silk warp and a worsted weft and used primarily for mourning wear.

Lewis West (1829-1867) was Hilborne and Mary Roosevelt's younger brother. He served as a master in the U.S. Navy, commanding the U.S.S. *Fernandina*, having enlisted in April of 1861.

Niagara Oct. 18<u>th</u> 62

Dearest Mittie
    I have often thought of you since I left you so lonely and used up on the 2nd story landing; I hope your aches did not prove the forerunner of one of your old fashioned colds which I particularly dislike to see you have. Did you offer Gracie a bed, I left him at our house although astonished that Anna allowed him to be out so late.

Reaching the cars I found Bronson waiting for me and we both obtained top berths tucked ourselves in in and retired for the thirty first time in two months to spend the night on the Rail R^d.

Three nights at home had accustomed me to a bed, not to speak of the companion who I missed from my side, and my night was rather a restless one.

At the Delaware House Albany we met Bliss and took one of those breakfasts that I have described to you which appear however better to me returning than when starting on a trip.

All our party started, five in number, to Fonda and I had a hard day's work.

The men had many of them been deceived about the bounty and were suspicious about everything including the Allotment Commission.

The officers' dinner was a good deal like pigs eating at a trough. ~~and~~ When at night three companies had not yet been visited, I determined to do it whole-sale. I had two tents pitched, and occupied one already prepared; placing a table candles and an Allotment Roll in each.

I then had the three companies formed into three sides of a square and used all my eloquence. When I had finished they cheered me vociferously. I told them I would be better able to judge who meant the cheers by seeing which company made most allotments, and raised a spirit of competition in this way that made these rolls the best that we had taken during the day. The sargeants of the companies took the names of the men in each tent at the same time and by eight o'clock we found our work done, dark as pitch and the rain descending in torrents.

They had sent down for a carriage for us but could find none and with a soldier to carry our carpet bags, lantern in hand, we had to walk over a mile to town.

Bronson discovered that his sheets were not clean and with much difficulty had them changed, after all in the house had gone to bed but the unfortunate proprietor himself.

Yesterday going from Herkimer to a regiment, about twenty in a wagon, we were about to cross a covered bridge when one of the party discovered printed in very large letters "This bridge is condemned".

A proposal was made to walk over but as the driver said twenty two had crossed safely the week before in a wagon and that by keeping on the right hand side he could do it again all kept their seats to try.

Was it not a thoroughly American operation?

The work yesterday was much more pleasant although our success has not been as great in any of the new as in former regiments.

Finding that Lockport was our next place we came on here to pass sunday at Niagara.

After Lockport will come Elmira and then home again for the rest of the week at all events.

I am sorry I did not have a play with the children that last afternoon, instead of the drive that I have no doubt increased your cold. There is no hope of my receiving a letter from you so do not write

Your Loving Husband
TheodoreRoosevelt

Visiting more regiments in upstate New York, Thee went to the towns of Fonda, Herkimer (Camp Schuyler), Elmira, Lockport, and Niagara. Some of these small towns had armories; others held training camps, while a few later in the War, like Elmira's Camp Rathbun, included prisoner of war camps.

Niagara Oct 19th 62

Dearest Mittie

I devoted the first hour of my arrival here to writing you before visiting the Falls.

Everything looked just as natural as when we last saw it here together and I could not help regretting your absence now.

If all goes well at home you must try to come to Auburn with me next week when I visit the Regt there. McMillan has brought his wife here last night and they both dined with us today.

Tomorrow for Lockport then Elmira and home. I know you would like me to tell you the exact hour of my arrival but as usual it is impossible for me to be so accurate.

Mr Siddons and family are here, fortunately staying at the Cataract House while I am at the Continental, the Monteagle where we stayed looks more dreary than ever.

The Falls are glorious, looking through the mist and rainbow at the beautiful hues of the changing leaves as a background.

The sun was bright and warm and nothing took away from the pleasure of the scene but the want of a companion with whom to appreciate it, as I am sorry to say that Bronson was asleep on the bench by my side.

I will soon be home and look forward to having you in my arms again and making one more effort to carry out our good resolution. With one God to look up to for help, and one Heaven to look forward to; we must be entirely united here on earth feeling that we are only here as a preparation for eternity. Let us try.

Your Devoted Husband
Theodore Roosevelt

Niagara Falls,
from Picturesque America[129]

New York Oct 22nd 1862

My very dear daughter,
The box arrived last evening, so after dinner Mittie had it opened. Susy darling we were all astonished at the beauty of the caps - those with the tarlton frill around

the crown particularly. they are perfectly beautiful - I will try to take good care of them and will never wear them without thinking of the darling child who so lovingly and with so much taste directed the work. How beautifully too they were packed - But there was one thing which caused a melt - that <u>you</u> should have given me two of those six caps - Darling I do not think you ought to have done it - It gave me pain to think it would cost you some self denial - It is not exactly the widows mite, but it was instigated by the same self denying love - Mittie is delighted with the little spoons & forks - she will not let the children use them until Teedie's birth day which occurs in a few days - She told me to thank you over and over. She would have written to you today, but her eyes are in such a condition that Dr Metcalf has forbidden her to use them at all - She cant read or write or sew - I believe I wrote you what a dreadful cold she had taken - She kept her bed two days, but is a little better and is up again - Since I wrote you too little Elliot's sickness has developed itself into ventilate intermittent - It (the fever) came on with cold hands and nose about six oclock every other evening and lasted all night - Dr Metcalf gives him a preparation of iron after each meal, he also gave me two powders (quinine) about five grains each to be given him at 4 oclock of the days I expect chill & fever - I gave him the first one yesterday at 4 - he had no chill and no fever last night at all - still, I am to give him the other powder tomorrow at 4 oclock again - Teedie & Bamie are quite well - Cony has a bad cold - Mittie expects Thee hourly Anna got another letter this morning from Mr Caskie. He has lost his little infant Fanny. Mittie will carefully send your little package to Mrs. Weir Roosevelt [Mary West Roosevelt]. Bamie is going to visit her aunt Mary and her new little cousin I believe this afternoon - She has commenced school with Miss Doremus - Mittie & Anna send much love - with many thanks my darling daughter for the pretty caps, and much love and kind regards to all of the family

                              I am lovingly your
                              Mother M Bulloch

Mrs [Susan] Newberry told me she was delighted with Mrs Weir Roosevelt That she was indeed a fine woman.

I could respond with all my trust to the opinion - Excuse the soiled postage stamps, as I have at present no other

How did you manage to get four caps and five papers of needles with so little money?

Martha described the fringe around her caps as *tarlton*. Again her spelling was not quite right, as she meant *tarlatan*, a sheer, open-weave cotton fabric usually heavily sized or starched for stiffness.

Although the next letter has an incomplete date, it referenced Claude Brownrigg's illness. Martha did put *Saturday*, in the heading, making the date 25 October.

Paper Needle Folder

New York Oct 1862
saturday afternoon

My dearest Susy,
I have been trying to write you a few lines all day but have been interrupted - I know you must feel anxious to know how Mittie and the children are - Mittie is much better of her cold, but is obliged to be careful still of her eyes - Elliott has missed his fever and the rest are well - We received a letter from Hariot this morning She asks very affectionately after you - says how is "Susys health I hope better." and says tell her her old Dr Semmes is now living

in London - She says when Irvine was with her in Aug she was very much pleased with him - She says he had when he arrived there every thing to make him comfortable and he had not drawn his pay for two months - he receives 55 dollars per month - He desired her to "say to Mother he had never drawn the money which she desired him to, that it is still in Bank." - From all this I infer he is no spend thrift - I am glad of this for his own sake and I am gratified to think that he remembers my advice to him - Hariot speaks sweetly and affectionately of dear Stuart. She says "the death of poor brother is an event we all have been led to look forward to for weeks past. still ones heart will endeavor to cheat itself with the hope of its not coming just yet" - She (Hariot) sent us the likeness of little Jimmie I will send it for you to see when Anna can spare it - She says James has written me a letter nine pages long, which I hope will come in the next Steamer - I will send you extracts when it comes - Darling daughter I hope you are well. I spent yesterday by the bedside of Claude Brownrigg - She is extremely ill - her disease is typhoid Pneumonia, I do not think she will live - I called this morning to enquire but she was no better. She is a dear little girl & I have always felt an interest in her I believe she is a professer of religion and those who know her best think highly of her as a christian - she is very useful in the Sunday school - But dear Susy how sad it is to think of one so young passing away - I will write again on monday and let you know how she is - Her mother and Mr Shelton are very much distressed - Mr Shelton is devoted to her, gives her her stimulants and medicines himself, and will scarcely ever leave her bedside - I shall always like him - Good bye darling daughter - I peep at my caps now and then but have not worn any of them yet - Mr or rather Dr Rice begins his lectures on the new testament characters tomorrow after noon John the Baptist he communes with. I anticipate hearing him, and think it a great privilege to attend his preaching - Love to dear Hill - kind regards to all from your loving Mother
            M Bulloch

Dr. Nathan L. Rice (1807-1877) replaced Dr. James Alexander at New York's Fifth Avenue Presbyterian Church on 26 April 1861. Alexander, their beloved pastor of many years, had passed away and several calls to the pulpit were turned down before Rice accepted. The 700-plus strong congregation offered the post to an unlikely man. Rice, born in rural Garrard County, Kentucky, studied first at Centre College in Danville, Kentucky, before entering Princeton Seminary, where one of his classmates was Charles Colcock Jones, a Bulloch family friend from Liberty County. Rice was pastor to several churches before bringing his family to New York. As a Southerner in a New York church, Rice accepted a very delicate position. One biographer stated that, "by a discreet avoidance of all political topics, he maintained the affection and esteem of his people."[130]

New York Oct 28 1862

I promised in my letter of saturday dearest Susy, to write you a few lines on monday but it was cleaning day in my room - , so that I could not write in the morning, and in the afternoon I was interrupted. We are all quite well - Thee's off again - I say quite well, but Mittie complains of pains in her bones - she complained last winter in the same way - Claude Brownrigg the D^r pronounces a little better, but to me she appears the same, only weaker - Instead of going to church on sunday I sat by her bedside all day - In the evening Mr Shelton brought me home in a carriage, and took Anna back with him - she sat up sunday night - Yesterday she (Claude) was thought better - have not heard from her today yet - Today Teedie had his little cousins Alfred Emlin and Jimmie to dine with him in celebration of his birth day which was yesterday - The little fellows enjoyed themselves very much - now they are having a play on the piazza - Jimmie was very quiet himself, but appeared to have a keen appreciation of Emlins wit - Teedie, (the host, was too busy during dinner with his chicken & potato to converse much, but as soon as he finished he made this sage remark,

"that he loved chicken, roast beef and every thing that was good better than salt water - This speech occasioned a roar of laughter - and was evidently thought very witty - Teedie too appeared to be under the false impression that it was smart - He seemed to be inflated with vanity for some time after wards - Little Coney was highly delighted too at seeing the children and wanted to join in the plays - I got a long letter yesterday from Jimmie [James D. Bulloch] - It was mostly on my business - He had to employ a Lawyer and himself make, or rather sign affidavits to prove that I was not an alien he says the affidavit made by him was to this effect - "Mrs Martha Bulloch is my mother - She is a native of Georgia and is still a citizen - of that state her domicil being in Roswell - She was detained at the North wholly by domestic necessities - etc etc etc, I can not write it all - he thinks it is all safe now he says the $5000 left me by Mr Hutchinson was placed by Maj Porter in the State Bank that he Maj Porter made no return of it to the Officers under the Sequestration act and that money would be available to me at once if I were south - I am in hopes that Maj Porter did the same with yours Mitties and Annas money - After speaking very affectionately of dear Stuart - he ends his letter by saying give my dear sisters Nancey [Anna?] Mittie & Susy my undying love - I must close darling as it is late and Hannah will put this in the lamp post - Love to dear Hill from Your affectionate Mother
                    M Bulloch

Teedie entertained two cousins for his fourth birthday celebration. Alfred, son of James and Lizzie Roosevelt, was two and a half years older, having been born in April 1856. Jimmie, son of Silas and Mary Roosevelt, was also four, like Teedie, and born in July 1858.

James' letter from Liverpool discussed the monetary settlement of Robert Hutchison's will. Robert left money to every senior member of the Bulloch family. However, his death in 1861 came right as the War began, making it difficult to transfer the money and other items to those living in the North.

While the family still worried about *poor* Stuart in Georgia, in August in Liverpool, Irvine appeared well just before sailing under Captain Semmes on the S.S. *Bahama*.[131] The *Bahama*, built for the Confederate Navy, was a tender.

Martha and Anna sat at the bedside of Claude S. Brownrigg, born in 1839 in Mississippi. She was the daughter of the late Dr. John Henry Brownrigg (1807-1840) and Elizabeth Martha Haskins Brownrigg Shelton (1819-1903). Elizabeth had remarried and had a daughter from this marriage, Adelle, born in 1848.

Chapter 10: November & December of 1862

Events of the War

    Not happy with General McClellan's failure to pursue Lee's forces as they fled south after Antietam, President Lincoln visited the battlefield in October and met with McClellan. On 7 November, Lincoln replaced him with General Ambrose E. Burnside. Once in command of the Army of the Potomac, Burnside pursued the Confederate Army into Virginia. On 13 December, Federal forces suffered a costly defeat with the loss of over 12,500 men at Fredericksburg in more than 14 frontal assaults on well-entrenched Confederates on Mayre's Heights. It is said that one Union soldier expressed, "We might as well have tried to take Hell." Confederate General Robert E. Lee exclaimed, "It is well that war is so terrible - we should grow too fond of it."

The Letters

New York Nov 10th - 1862

    This is cleaning day in my room my dearest Susy and I can only write a hurried note. We all continue well, and are going at one oclock in a carriage to Green-wood to visit Mrs Roosevelts grave - yesterday morning was so stormy I did not go to Church, but went in the afternoon - It was communion we had a delightful address from Dr Rice before the communion on the love of Christ - It was an interesting sermon - Susy darling Anna and I went on

211

saturday afternoon as sloppy as it was to see Mr Douglass - It was not Mr D who was expected to go south, but a Dr Moxley who is another uncle of Lucys - we found that Dr Moxley had left New York for Baltimore three weeks since - So darling there is no hope of sending any bundle from that quarter - I shall write to Hariot and send Lucys letter to her as soon as I can - I am sorry Hipman will not give the measure - I would tell him that it is to have shoes made for Mrs Elliott, in England as they cannot be conveyed to her from this country - I do not think you need send your boots, as there is no way of getting them to her I know she would be glad of them if she could get them If you write to Lucy direct to Mrs Leonard Mackall Saratoga Street Baltimore I will enquire of Anna & send you Mr Caskies address We all want to see you dreadfully darling - Mittie says when Thee goes to Washington again which will be in about two or three weeks, (he is to stay there about three weeks -) she intends fixing up his dressing-room in a cunning little way for you, and beg you to come -Anna says she is so sorry she did not know the Lewis' were here, that they left the very day your letter got here -Thee got your letter this morning from Washington, says he will write you. I did not finish this note yesterday It is now tuesday morning - we went yesterday to Green Wood & I picked two rose buds off the grave of dear Mrs. Roosevelt. If you send a letter to Mr Caskie direct the inner envelope to Lucy and the outer to Ge^{nl} Dix Comandant of Fortress Monroe Love to all - what do the Philadelphians think of the displacement of Ge^{nl} Mcclellan. although I have read so much about him I have forgotten how to spell his name - Darling I long to see you-good bye for the present   Your ever loving mother
                                   M Bulloch
The letter to Lucy sent to Mr Caskie will require to be sent to Mr James Caskies care
Richmond Va

    Letters sent to relatives and friends within the Confederate States could be and often were read by Federal officers looking for information that could be considered traitorous. Martha and her daughters had to be very circumspect in their communications, even with James and Harriott in Liverpool. Dr. Moxley, mentioned by Martha, appears to have been Dr. Benjamin Gustavus Moxley (1809-1899). Dr. Leonard Mackall of Baltimore was a dentist. Why his wife would have been able to ship letters south remains unknown.

Anna's reference to the Lewis family most likely referred to Robert Adams Lewis and his wife Catherine, formerly of Roswell, who, by 1862, lived in Castleton, Richmond County, New York (Staten Island). Robert and Catherine's household included Robert, age 17, Isabel, age 15, Anna, age 12, William, age 9, and Francis, age 6. Also living in the home were Eliza King and her husband, James Audley Maxwell King. Eliza was Robert and Catherine's oldest daughter.[132]

New York Nov 15^{enth} 1862

My dearest Susy

We received your sweet letter to Anna - I called on Mrs Shelton this morning and told her of your letter and of the expression of yours & Hill's sympathy - She seemed touched at your kindly remembering her, and said she had had all the comfort that human sympathy could give - She seems very lonely without Claude, and says she thinks of giving up house keeping - This afternoon darling I am all alone - Mittie & Anna have taken the two children Bamie and Teedie to see the performances of the {Barels}, & Ellie and Corinne have gone to take a short walk - Susy darling there is a young lady here (in New York) who came to pay Claude a visit - She had been with Claude about two weeks when poor Claude was taken sick - She has had a most melancholy visit of course - She wishes to return to Baltimore sometime next week - She has kindly offered to take a package for me to Baltimore, and says she is almost sure she can get it safely to Richmond - If it could be conveyed to Richmond I know Mr Caskie could get it to

Lucy - I do not know whether I have done right, but I have accepted this young ladies offer and purchased the following articles for Lucy - nine yds of bombazine for a dress with linings for the body & lower part of the skirt - cord, hooks & eyes skirt braid etc - I have also purchased spool cotton black & white - pins black and white & needles - also eight shims of black sewing silk - The above is my purchase. then I got as yours and Mittie's contribution, two pairs of shoes for Johnie & two pairs of shoes for Mattie - 6 pairs of stockings for Johnie, 6 pairs for Mattie & one pair of gloves for Lucy - the whole costing nine dollars & sixteen cts - $4.58 cts each ? I am at a loss whether to get Miss Tiernan the young lady I spoke of to send the package to Richmond, or to send it to Mrs Leonard Mackall. A week before dear Claude died Miss Tiernan told me that she had an aunt in Richmond who had just written to her mother in Baltimore to send her some articles of clothing - I asked her how she could get them to her? she said it could be done - three or four days afterwards she read me a part of a letter acknowledging the receipt of the articles - I then told her of my desire to send this package to Lucy, and asked her if perfectly convenient whether she would take it for me - She very kindly offered to do so - I think it is a risk, but if dear Lucy does get it, what a boon it will be to her - As I have already said I am at a loss whether to get Miss Tiernan to undertake sending the package to Richmond, or to get her to deliver it to Mrs. Leonard Mackall I wish you were here to consult. I gave for Lucys bombazine $1.30 cts per yd, it is a rather lighter article than ours but will suit a warm climate and is a very pretty black - We have not written to Hariot yet because we have heard that the House to which we direct is in bad repute here, consequently our letters would not leave N York - Mittie seems much better - she has been taking whiskey and I think it benefits her - she does not use her eyes yet by reading or sewing however - She is a dear good daughter and so is Anna - Thee is still at home, but I rather think the trunk will be packed before long - Thee is a good young man - I really think if any one ever tried to do their duty he does - Darling you must always remember our dear Irvine in your prayers - I do feel so anxious about him, and such a yearning to see him - But when I think of how good God has been to me, I feel that I can trust my dearest interests in his hands - Truly I have much to grateful for - Love to Mr & Mrs West & dear Hill - By the way do ask Hill what price Beaver Meadows commands now. I shall have to sell four or five Shares - Good bye for the present my own precious daughter -

Your loving Mother
M Bulloch-

Martha had recently visited with the mother of Claude Brownrigg, who died on 1 November 1862. By omission and description, Martha alluded to another death in her letter, as she sent black bombazine to Lucy along with gifts of clothing for her and the children, but not one item for her beloved son Stuart. Stuart Elliott passed away on 3 August 1862 after a very long battle with tuberculosis, leaving Lucy a widow and in dire need of mourning clothing. Lucy buried Stuart in Roswell's Presbyterian Cemetery. His stone reads, "Leaving this last

Stuart Elliott's Tombstone, Roswell Presbyterian Church Cemetery

testimony I die in Christ." Where Lucy and the children resided at this time is unknown. Although Martha would never obtain any possession of Stuart's, he left his mother and sister, Susan West, an item of their choice in his will, written just three days before his death. The rest was left to Lucy and his children, with the exception of fifty dollars to *Daddy* Luke Monroe, the beloved family slave (Appendix D).

    To pay for her expenditures, Martha once again considered selling Beaver Meadow stock. On 17 November, Beaver Meadow was valued at $57.50 per share, but in December rose to $64.625.[133]

New York Nov 20th

My dearest Susy
    Your dear letter written on monday last, I received on tuesday - I intended writing you yesterday, but after writing Lucy a long letter I was tired and put off writing until today - We have fixed the bundle up as compactly and nicely as we could - Anna and Mittie did it - Anna has just directed it and written a note to Miss Tiernan which with the bundle will be sent to Miss T this evening - I saw her this, or rather yesterday morning and she promises to leave no stone unturned to get it to Lucy - I told Lucy you had lately written her and directed your letter to the care of Mrs Mackall I told her also how much you had felt for herself & the children, and that you and Mittie both wished to get other articles for the package but that I objected as it would make the package too large for Miss Tiernan to carry - I feel so glad that it is all fixed - My letter to Lucy was not sent in the bundle but in an outer envelope to a Mr _____ of Baltimore a friend of poor Claude, who was at Long Branch last summer & who promised to send letters south for Claude Anna or my self - this is the first letter I have sent by this opportunity - but others sent by it have reached their destination and been answered - You sent me too much money darling so I return 50 cts - you and Mittie each gave $4.50 for the little shoes & stockings - I did not

add anything to the package after I wrote you but some writing paper, envelopes and toilet soap - we are all well. little Corinne is very cunning and smart - Bamie is taking French lessons (oral) she improves astonishingly - A french teacher gives her an hours lesson every day - the same person who teaches Lizzie Emlins children - Thee gave a party to some Federal officers & their wives on tuesday night - Of course I made myself scarce - Grandma came up to bed at the same time Bamie did - At twelve o clock they, or rather Mittie sent me up some nice things - but I was afraid to indulge at that unreasonable hour. I enclose dear Susy what I know will interest you, and what you may have over looked in the papers - It is Mr Stiles account of a wonderful work of grace in the Southern army. Poor fellows! I hope they may by the grace of God be prepared for whatever awaits them - I have no doubt but that that was Irvine who was the classmate - I had read the letter - Good bye for the present my blessed daughter - Please ask Hill to enclose me in your next letter the form of an order to sell five shares of Beaver Meadow- I do dislike very much to sell but think I shall be obliged to do so. I will sign the form & send it back to him- Love to dear Hill-
      Your affectionate
      Mother M Bulloch
Please send back the account given by Mr Stiles - Darling I cannot let you give any thing towards the dress etc etc - I have just had a very pleasant visit now and conversation with Dr Adams more of this anon ?

  Martha's vigilant reading of New York's papers probably found the following article containing a letter from the Rev. Dr. Stiles about witnessing and preaching to the Confederate Army. Stiles wrote of ministering to armies assigned to Generals Lee, Early, Jackson, and Trimble. Stiles' letter went on to tell of the numbers brought to Christ and those who asked for prayers, etc.[134] However, not all Northerners rejoiced in this news. The

217

Liberator (Boston, Massachusetts) printed Stiles' letter and then added the following:

> Alas! How horrible it seems, in the light of His Gospel who came to "preach deliverance to the captives," to hear this professed *Evangelical* preacher talk about men coming forward to "solicit an interest in prayers"! What can pray mean in the estimation of those who are hurling destruction around, and fighting like tigers to eternize a system of piracy and robbery, the blackest upon which the sun ever shone! God forgive them, and save us from the blasphemy of naming the Christian religion in such a connection![135]

However, the part Martha mentioned as referring to Irvine was not specifically found in the newspaper article and must have referred to something else she sent Susan.

New York Nov 29-1862

My dearest Susy   This is a dark dull afternoon - the dear little children have been in the house all day - Elliott has been in my room all the morning - I love to have the dear little fellow, but this morning I had determined as soon as I darned two prs of stockings to write to you - At one o clock the lunch bell rang - after the little things had taken their dinner they were wrapped up and carried into the piazza where they are now playing - Elliott asked me this morning if I was not lonetum (lonesome) without him - I told him yes - last sunday morning I was going down stairs on my way to church - he met me and said do ganma dont go to tutch, (church) if you do go, I will be lonetum for you - I told him you dreamed of kissing him, all he said was "aunt tudie". Little Cona is a great dancer holds her dress in a most affected way. Thursday Mittie & Thee and the children went to take Thanksgiving lunch at 14 Street - Cony was dressed up & carried with the rest - Mittie said they all behaved remarkably well - She said she was a little scandalized by Teedie & Ellie both asking for icecream the moment they got in the house. This exhibition of the want of good manners appeared to please their grandfather and he helped them to icecream before he helped the grown people - I had a very quiet day on thursday to my self - I did not go to church but tried in my own room to recall gratefully I trust Gods great mercies to me during the past year, and oh how numerous and how great they were - It has been a year of signal mercy to us darling Susy - A year in which our dearly beloved one was brought out of darkness into Gods marvelous light, and safely removed from all of his trials and sufferings to his eternal rest - truly we can say "Bless the Lord oh my soul and all that is within me bless his holy name." May we have grace ever to trust him - ever unto death - Your last sweet letter of the 25 inst. I received including the form from Hill - tell dear Hill I send him my love & thanks I will enclose the order and certificate with this letter - Thee is now preparing to leave for Washington on monday - I think his throat is a little weak and Mittie is uneasy about him such constant talking to the regiments is not good for him - He promises Mittie however to be careful of himself - Susy darling Mittie cant help giving those little suppers to Thees friends - He wishes it and you know he does not feel as we do, and it is his own house - It jars upon my feelings, but of course I keep my room - Mittie cant do this, and it is to please her that Anna does not absent herself we will talk this matter over when we meet - My own darling Susy I long to see you. Miss Tiernan before she left promised to do all in her power to get the package to Mr Caskie safely - I hope she may succeed - I did not think about its being put up on the birth day until you mentioned it - dear child! it would have been his thirty-sixth birth day what a brief and troubled life his was - ah but it is all over now - as you say "in the past only joy and rest in the future!" - Bamie sends much love to dear aunt Susy -

Remember me very affectionately to Mrs West -
                    Your loving Mother
                    M Bulloch-over

New York Dec 2nd
    I wrote you a long letter on saturday afternoon darling daughter so now will only add a few lines, as my principal object is to inclose a letter which I received last evening from Lucy - you will perceive the date is nearly a month previous to the one I sent you not long since that is dated {12} of Oct the one I now send is 14 Sept - Had I received this letter previously to sending the package I would have sent 8 yds more of bombazine but it is too late now - I will write to Hariot request her to send it She mentions the number she wears of shoes, I will mention that to Hariot also, and if I hear of any opportunity to send them I will try to do so myself. At any rate I think I will keep a pair of boots in readiness <u>to</u> send if opportunity offers - Thee goes to Washington this afternoon - I do not think he is well enough to do so, but Mittie cant persuade him to wait any longer - Bamie is a little unwell with sore mouth, (nothing serious) This morning Mittie had the carriage so she took the children & granma to Central Park, It looked very beautifully, but was too cold to be pleasant - Bamie is busy in my room sewing she says give my love to aunt Susy - Mittie is gone to Arnolds & Anna to walk -Good bye darling Susy Love to all -
                    Your affectionate Mother
                    M Bulloch
send Lucys letter back when you have done with it-

    Martha's letter refers to Stuart Elliott's birthday, 20 November 1826. Also, she planned to send the information about Lucy's shoe size and other needs to Harriott in Liverpool, in hopes that Harriott could send the items directly to Lucy in the South. By late 1862, the blockade had halted almost all shipments of everyday goods into the Confederacy. Shortages occurred, and with the lack of factories, raw materials, and trained manpower, the South had minimal ability to produce such goods for themselves.

Baltimore Dec 3rd 62

Dearest Mittie
    I had a very quiet time in the cars last night, feeling the importance of following the Doctor's advise I did not even look for an acquaintance.
    At four this morning a man shook me and said as I understood him "Alderman" being so accustomed to the grads {grades?} from General to Capt this did not strike me as a peculiar address and I inquired what he wanted. He repeated "Baltimore" arousing me to an appreciation of my position immediately.
    Four o'clock never seemed so cold to me before and I was generally miserable when I reached the Eutaw House.
    I laid down for a few hours and then had breakfast and paid my respects to Genl. Wool. He shows his age very sensibly, but was as polite as he has always shown himself to me, ordered my horse and orderly and any information I desired given me.
    I rode all day around to the different regiments mostly stationed in the forts and cut out my work with Bronson for tomorrow.
    I paid a very pleasant visit this evening to the Morris.[136] The old lady sent a great many messages of love to you and said she would like very much a long talk with you such as she had once. If you hear of any reason why Mr Tracy[137] was taken up and imprisoned she wants to know it.
    I know you will expect me to tell you how well I am and then insist upon disbelieving it, but I really am much better tonight and with the exception of that weakness of the throat perfectly sound.
    My room is wonderfully little and very cold so that it is not much to offer you, but I would very much like to have you here to share it with me

Kiss all the dear little children for
Your Loving
Husband

The large and fashionable Eutaw House sat on the northwest corner of Eutaw and Baltimore streets. Built between 1832 and 1835 by William Hussey, Eutaw House was a rival of Barnum's Hotel where Thee had stayed previously.

New York ~~Nov~~ Dec 5th /62

My dearest Susy
I received your letter the day before yesterday and would have answered it yesterday but was anxious to finish a piece of work in the morning, and in the afternoon had to take a long walk up to 36 St to see a lady there who could give me another address to Hariot. I got the address and am going to write H immediately. My principle object in writing her is to get her to send some articles of clothing to Lucy - I shall write to Lucy today also, as the lady above mentioned sends a trunk tomorrow or monday to Nassau NP by a gentleman who promises that it shall (if possible) get to Charleston SC - My letter to Lucy will be sent in this trunk. I shall write Hariot to get a mourning cloak for Lucy or bombazine enough to make one - Also shoes for the children and boots for Lucy - Also needles sewing silk writing paper etc etc etc - I write for these things to Hariot for fear the bundle we have sent by Miss Tiernan may not reach her - even if it does reach her there was nothing in it to make a cloak - Darling Susy I cant tell you how much I am touched with yours and dear Hills interest in my pecuniary matters - How pleased you both were in my good fortune - How much that sum in Arithmatic sounded like Hill! thank you dear ones - I am so thankful that I can as Hill says "be able to get along these trying times without lessening my profits - If the Beaver Meadow does declare this ten percent for Stock Div, it will be nineteen Shares of Stock Div, I

have received from it - I shall write Hariot that Lucy will refund her for any sum she may spend for her - Love to all
Your affectionate Mother
M Bulloch-

Martha previously requested Hill sell some of her shares of Beaver Meadow Railroad stock. However, it seems Hill instead suggested a coming dividend would make that unnecessary. Martha held 19 shares. On 4 December, the *Philadelphia Inquirer* listed Beaver Meadow at $64.625 per share. So Martha's dividend would equal about $122.79, about $2,980.00 in purchasing power in 2015.[138]

Baltimore Dec 6th 62

Dearest Mittie

I received your letter here today having been detained, and finished work here which we intended to do on our return.

You will be perfectly safe in asking Susan to spend a week or two with you. I hope she will extend her visit so that I will be home part of it, I could sleep on the sofa in the parlor if Rob has not a room to spare.

Tell Bammie that I have made great use of my needle book already I have sewed two buttons on my red flannel shirt of which I am more proud than of all the rest of the shirt put together. My pins I am afraid will be scarce before my return, I purchased myself a thimble for four cents today.

I met Charley Leydan the other night at a place that I know Mrs Bulloch will be troubled to hear that I was to be found. We enjoyed some steamed oysters together, which you have heard me speak of ordering by the bushel.

He took Bronson's horse the next day while Bronson drove with Dr Wainright[139] and we visited some of the forts together.

It snowed and sleeted all day long and there was a general care about the party before we returned.

Leydan expects to go on with us to Fortress Monroe to night.

My tongue, which you know is my barometer, is perfectly natural and you know even to deceive you I would not tell a direct untruth; I really feel perfectly well.

Write to me here at the Eutaw House until I tell you to the contrary, it is a great luxury to hear from home and I often think of you all.

Tedee's speech portrayed the great benefits of early religious training, although I fear it was natural devilment.

I saw Lord Cavendish and Hartington for a moment this morning and did a little more politeness on your account.

Kiss little Cony Ellie and Tedee for me, a kiss was indeed in my message to Bammie

      Your Ever Loving Husband
      Theodore Roosevelt

      Camp Dodge Dec 8th 62

Dearest Mittie

  Before going to sleep in Colonel [Charles C.] Dodge's bed I must write you a few lines. He has just finished a log cabin of the original kind used by all of our fore fathers but just before our arrival has been sent out with his regiment. Fortunately being acquainted with the Major of his regiment I am ensconced in his quarters.

  The trip from Baltimore was quite pleasant although a gale came on in the night and broke a good - deal of the glass in the Steamboat, exciting the nerves of some of the passengers to a very high pitch and the stomachs of others still more. Early in the morning we arrived and as Allotment Commissioners landed while poor civilians had to remain on board.

  Major [Charles T.] Dix, Caddie's friend, received us most hospitably and sent to the hotel for our trunks so that we were the General's guests during our stay. Captain Lord and Barstow, also on the General's Staff, were equally polite and rendered our stay a very great pleasure. The General is thoroughly a gentleman and gains the affection as well as respect of all around him.

We received orders to have Steamboats RR^d trains and horses put at our disposal by Colonel Ludlow the Chief of Staff, Bronson says entirely in consequence of that cravat which he wears to remember you by.

This morning General Veilé [Egbert L. Viele] came up with us in the Boat and, having seen us so frequently mentioned in the papers, fell in with the fashion and was very devoted. We are to telegraph him when we want a train to return in, and take dinner with himself and wife in Norfolk. I hope for your sake his wife does not "make eyes" at me.

We had the train from Norfolk to Suffolk all to ourselves, everyone else being turned and kept out, and found General [John J.] Peck even more complimentary and ready to do anything for us than the others.

Tomorrow we hope to finish the regiments here and next day return to Norfolk where the ship is to be launched which was on the ways almost complete when the city was retaken.

A magnificent old Virginia wood fire is in the grate and I must go to bed while it lasts. Give much love to all and keep most for yourself Yours Ever Theodore Roosevelt

---

Love to father.

Fortress Monroe Dec 10th 62

Dearest Mittie

Over a week has passed since I left you and my work seems just begun. It is very different in its character now however from what it was before the Doctor prescribed no more talking to the men much to Bronson's gratification. I am once more the guest of General [John A.] Dix sitting in a delightful room surrounded by all the luxuries we do not expect in a soldier's life.

No more log cabins at present, but I will not scorn what has been really delightful the sojourn of two days in Dodge's cabin. He has won my heart entirely, whole-souled and utterly forgetful of self, I hope to introduce him to you one of these days.

We visited all the regiments in General [John J.] Peck's brigade, among them those miserable specimens who gave so much trouble while near New York City, and sent up this morning to have the train stop at Dodge's camp for us.

The orderly unfortunately did not reach the depot in time and we missed the train. They offered to send for an extra train or furnish a small car with four blacks to work the cranks. The last we accepted sitting on a kind of railing with our feet out urging the _free_ colored gentlemen to make time. They worked with a will and just as we were making fifteen miles an hour we came to a switch turned wrong and in half a second the party were flying over the country generally without any very accurate impression of where they would land. The contrabands were all on top of Dodge & Bronson was examining one leg under the impression that it was off when I rose to my feet. It was one of those scenes where the ludicrous predominates over the serious while there is strong tincture of both. An immense rent in my pantaloons about the knees was serious as I was to dine with General Viele, the scratches and bruises were the "Gook". The car fortunately was not broken as soon replaced on the track off we started. But the negroes' nerves were shocked and our time was not as good, so that we proposed a mile to work the car ourselves against their time. This put them on their notch again, but the race proved a failure on our side. General and Mrs Viele[140] received and welcomed us warmly after we arrived at Norfolk, the dinner was informal but very pleasant.

After it was finished the General ordered an extra steamboat and here we are once more at Fortress Monroe.

The evening was beautiful crossing the bay and now the water here seems historical, so that we could enjoy all the poetry of the scene doubly. There was the buoy by which the Merrimac lay when she was blown up while the masts of the Cumberland were just visible in the distance.

But Good-bye I must say farewell for the present with much love to all

Yours Ever
Theodore Roosevelt

Thee referred to the U.S.S. *Merrimack*, burned to prevent her capture on 20 April 1861 at the Gosport Navy Yard in Portsmouth, Virginia, to prevent her capture. The Confederates then raised the remains of the *Merrimack* and used the hull and engines to build the ironclad they called the C.S.S. *Virginia*. On 8 March 1862, during the Battle of Hampton Roads (also known as the Battle of the Ironclads), the C.S.S. *Virginia* sank the U.S.S. *Cumberland* and the U.S.S. *Congress*. Thee saw the buoy marking where the U.S.S. *Merrimack* sank, and the remains of the U.S.S. *Cumberland*.

Washington Dec 17th 62

Dearest Mittie

I have been waiting to hear from you, as your last letter was dated Dec 9th, but at last despair.

My trip has been very quiet since my last. Bronson staid one day in Baltimore after I left and then followed me here but found himself unable to do anything and returned today. I expect to return myself if possible saturday night or sunday morning so do not write me again. Everyone here has been as polite to me as I have always found them and I have now quite a variety from my former visits. Mrs. Vcile has bored me to death, but you know my misfortune of taking a violent like or dislike, and either feeling becomes stronger when thrown much in contact with the object.

First at half past six I had to leave the hotel in Baltimore to meet her at the boat and accompany her to the cars.

Then the numerous grass hoppers- in the way of going in to breakfast dinner and tea with her became burdens.

I met Mr Lane of our church here with a party and found them very pleasant, he always was a favorite of mine and I went up with them to see the President and madame much to the enjoyment of the ladies.

I have ridden all day with Parmley visiting the different forts through the wind until my face has assumed that hue that brother Alex's has as a permanency. Tell Anna I expect to be a great favorite with her in consequence of the resemblance. Captain Montgomery has been sitting reading the newspaper while I have written the first part of this letter, and now as it is drawing towards midnight has left me. He is recovering from his wounds and weakness makes him resemble his brother Phil much more than he used to.

My room is on the fifth floor and I have been fortunate in securing that as the hotel is more crowded than it was even last winter.

I am anticipating my return home and Christmas with all of you, although I have really been made so low spirited by the late news that I feel that it will require a great deal of affection on your part to make me enjoy myself. Kiss the dear little children from me and say I hope to do it for myself next sunday

Your Ever Devoted Husband
Theodore

Thee's late news may have been the Union defeat and high number of dead and wounded on the Fredericksburg battlefield. Thee's constant immersion with Union forces afforded him many friends and acquaintances among the Army. No doubt, he, like all Americans, worried over those who served.

New York Dec 18th 1862

My dearest Susy,

    I have not written to you for some time past, nor have we heard from you - I hope you are not sick darling - I always try not to be uneasy about you but I cannot prevent anxious thoughts sometimes - Mittie is out today in the carriage. I believe getting christmas things for the different little nests of Roosevelts - Our share of the little ones are on the tiptoe of expectation, even little Corinne seems to know that something unusual is going on - Mittie has a very pretty little ba lamb for her which bleats most unnaturally - Teedie & Ellie each have a horse large enough for them to ride on, with saddles which can be taken off and on, and with hair & flowing mane and tail which can be curried and combed -
I believe she has purchased curry-combs and brushes for the steeds already - Great secrecy is preserved, so that the joy on christmas morning will be complete - Dear little things! I am glad they *can* enjoy it - You told me in one of your former letters to give you a hint on the subject of toys I heard Bamie say she wished aunt Susy would get her a globe with the countrys on it, or an Atlas - I think the Globe would be best - Bamie has taken such a turn for study, that she does not seem to care much for toys - I have purchased her a few little things for her dolls house Her French teacher says she improves rapidly - Thee is still in Washington, but I suppose will be at home about christmas times - I have heard nothing from Lucy lately - In my last letter to you I enclose one from her which I had just received - did you get it? I have not heard a word of the fate of the package - I have been very busy of late assisting in making up shirts etc for the Confederate sick prisoners in Fridrich Md - The box I believe is gone & another will soon be prepared - I have not been out today, as I took a little medicine - The warm weather of last week made me feel a little unwell and yesterday afternoon as I felt the want of exercise I took a walk - Just as I was near Dr Emmets in Mad St on a part of the pavement which was rough I fell down flat - It stunned

me a little at first but I soon recovered - However as I had a head ache last night I thought I would take a cooling draught - It has quite restored me, and I am quite well again - Since my fall I have thought so much of Mr West what a dreadful fall his was.
[Incomplete, no signature]

Mittie shopped for Christmas presents for the many Roosevelt children. Including her four, fifteen children would carry on the Roosevelt name. Silas and Mary West had four boys, Jim and Lizzie Emlen had two girls and two boys, and Rob and Lizzie Ellis had two girls and one boy. Mittie's own included Bamie, who would be eight on 7 January, Teedie, just now four, Ellie, almost three, and the baby Corinne, just over a year.

Martha mentioned Dr. Thomas Emmet, located at 79 Madison Avenue, who had provided care for the Roosevelt family since Thee met him on the train in 1855. Dr. Emmet was called for when Mittie began labor for little Thee, but could not be located.[141] Dr. Emmet was born in Virginia in 1828 and studied at Jefferson Medical College (Philadelphia), graduating in 1850. Emmet married Catherine Rebecca Duncan (1825-1905) in 1854, in Montgomery, Alabama, her hometown. Catherine had borne four children: John (1857), Anne (1859), Mary (1860), and Thomas (1863).

Martha sewed shirts for ill or wounded Confederate soldiers currently housed in various makeshift hospitals in and around Frederick, Maryland. These soldiers probably fought either in the Battle of Antietam (Maryland, 17 September) or Fredericksburg (Virginia, 13 December). When well enough to travel, officials shipped the Confederate prisoners to Fort McHenry and then Fortress Monroe for exchange. At this point in the War, neither the Union nor the Confederates had enough prisoner of war camps to hold all those captured. Therefore, both sides often exchanged or paroled prisoners. Paroled prisoners promised that they would not again take up arms.[142]

New York Dec 23rd-1862

My dearest Susy,
    Thee brought me your dear little note, and the bad thing never gave it to me until sunday evening - I was so surprised darling to find that you had not only sent back my letter from Lucy, but had sent me the one she wrote you also - I have never received either of them - Mary Ann is so careful that I know they have not been mislaid here, and think it must have been done at the {Sub} Post Office - Mittie is going to write you today, to tell you what a success the Globe is - It is a perfect beauty. Mittie is delighted with it and we know Bamie will be for it is what she has been wanting - I give her a copy of "Swiss Family Robertson" and Anna a small fingering [finger ring] and a Copy of "Aunt Kitty's Tales," by Min M^{c}intosh - To the little boys I have each a ball & Anna a small whip - Where did you get such beautiful candy? I would have written you yesterday but it was cleaning day, besides that the rooms were in cleaning disorder we had charge of the little boys up stairs, that Corinne might have the nursery to herself. She has been very unwell of late has been threatened with lung fever - Dr Metcallfe has been attending her & she is now much better - not well enough yet however to be dressed and play around - Mittie & Anna have been up a good deal at nights with her - Thee said he did not think you looked well (darling Susy I wish you could be quite well) - said he had a delightful dinner, and a friendly welcome - Mittie says why is it that no body keeps house so nicely as Mrs West?
    Give my love to Mr West & herself and of course to Hill - Mittie is now getting ready to go somewhere in the carriage and asks me to go with her ~~so~~ I must close - So for the present my darling precious daughter I must say Good bye
                    Your loving Mother
                    M Bulloch

The family used more than one physician, as can be seen in these last few letters. Most recently, Dr. John T. Metcalfe had been called to look in on baby Corinne. Dr. Metcalfe's practice was listed at 34 East 14th Street in *1862 Trow's New York City Directory*.

Martha purchased Bamie a copy of *Swiss Family Robinson*, by Johann David Wyss, first published in 1812. Anna purchased *Aunt Kitty's Tales* by Maria Jane McIntosh (1803-1878), a fellow resident of Liberty County, whom Martha calls *Min* in her letter. The Elliott/Bulloch families could claim kin to almost all of the plantation-owning families of Liberty County.

New York Dec. 26nd 1862

My darling Susy,

    I thought I would write you a few lines yesterday afternoon, but as christmas duties did not cease until late in the afternoon found I could not - On wednesday evening after the little ones had all gone to bed Mittie had a white table cloth spread on the Library table - we then waited a while for the presents to come in very soon the bell rung & the mysterious paper packages were sent by the different kind aunties - first a dray & horse from Aunt Lizzie Emlin for Teedie & a car with two horses for Ellie, from the same also a doll for little Cona and a broach for Bamie - Then came Aunte Mary's presents - A box for Bamie with two dolls with a bathing apparatus for them - a cradle for Corinnes doll - a pretty little arrangement with four bells which if struck skilfully would play a little tune, a race course & several little horses on it, this last was for Teedie, the bells for Ellie - Lissie [Lizzie] Ellis sent Corinne a little doll in a cradle Ellie a box of blocks for building Bamie a pack of visiting cards with her name engraved on them and an accompanying plate. I forgot what Teedie got - Altogether the table was pretty full - Corinne's things were on a small table to themselves - Bamie's things were on one end of the table, Teedie & Elliotts on the other - There were a great many little things in stockings for the three older children - those they were allowed to take out before breakfast, to keep curiosity a little at bay - After breakfast Thee opened the folding doors and the happiness was too great. It really seemed to bewilder the poor little things - They would pitch first at one thing then at another as if they were half crazed by the excitement. I took the first opportunity I could to abstract some of Elliotts things. I have put away four of his presents - the bells amongst them. The embarrassment of riches is so great that he does not miss them at all - Bamie is delighted with her globe and has twice asked me to thank dear aunt Susy for it. Teedie says he wishes Christmas would come every day - (I am glad it does not -) The day was concluded by their going to dinner at five at 14 St

There every thing was done to make all the juveniles happy - they had all sorts of company and exciting games - Mitty says Mary was devoted to them all - Teedie & Ellie were brought home at eight o clock, tired & ready for bed - Bamie staid later - thus ended Christmas day of 1862 - The impression I have is, that pleasure is less fatiguing to the young than to the old. I do like these festivals for the dear children tho' - In after years they look back upon them with real delight - I have written this to amuse you my darling Susy - Often yesterday we would say oh if sister, or if Susy were here - Nothing yet of the letters dearest I fear they are lost - Love to all, God bless you my own precious child.
                              Your affec Mother
                              M Bulloch
Conas ba lamb has already lost one leg and one horn - her rabbit has one ear nearly off

"Preparing for the Christmas Party"
Godey's Lady's Book, December 1862

Chapter 11: January through April 1863

Events of the War

On 1 January 1863, President Lincoln issued his Emancipation Proclamation. In so doing, he not only freed all slaves within the Confederacy, which considered itself a separate nation, but also encouraged free Negro men in the North to join the Union Army. Lincoln's act now focused a war, once fought to preserve the union of states, into a war for the abolition of slavery.

Lincoln quickly followed with changes in command of the various Federal armies, first with the appointment of General Joseph Hooker on 25 January to head the Army of the Potomac. Four days later, he appointed General Ulysses S. Grant to head the Army of the West and ordered him to capture Vicksburg, Mississippi. Dwindling enlistments forced Lincoln to institute a draft of all male citizens between the ages of 20 and 45, on 3 March. Men could avoid the draft by paying $300 or purchasing a substitute.

The Letters

New York Jan 2nd 1863

My darling daughter,

I received your sweet letter written on monday, the next day, but was prevented [writing you that day] and thought I would write on wednesday morning - On that morning I stooped to get something out of a trunk, and was seized with such a sharp pain in my back that I could hardly get back into my seat on the lounge - I thought it would soon pass off, but it did not, so I had to go to bed All day yesterday, and from about two o clock on wednesday I kept my bed, and was not able without assistance even to turn myself in bed - today I am much better, but still have to remain on the bed. I am now this afternoon so much better that I am seated in a rocking chair with a pillow to my back to write these few lines - Dr Metcalfe was here yesterday to see little Corinne, and Mittie would have him to see me - He said it was the sudden snapping of a small muscle in the lower part of the back which gives a great deal of pain but is not dangerous - Advised being very quiet in, or on the bed - I am a great deal better today indeed when I remain in a recumbent position & can still feel no pain at all Little Corinne is getting quite well - Anna & Mittie have been excellent nurses and so has dear little Bamie. They are now all downstairs arranging Bamies birthday party - Mittie anticipated the day as she thought it best to have it during the Holidays - Darling I am so sorry to hear you have been- sick - Thee told us you did not look very well - Do write me what it is particularly - I felt as you did darling about our dear little absent children, but if God gives them health & strength they can be very happy without fine clothes or toys - My precious daughter we have commenced another year - God grant that we may so live as to be ready whenever he calls us home May he "so teach us to number our days that we may apply our hearts unto wisdom -" I sent you Bamie's first composition - or rather something read to her which she wrote from memory As it regards hoops Mittie & Anna say they are just the same - no smaller - {Dresden/Driden} is the authority - All that I have observed look just the same - Tell dear Hill I thank him for his kind offer, but shall so soon be in funds that it is not necessary - send back the composition whenever you write - I do not send you the compliments of the sermon precious child but my heart is full of love for you. May God Almighty bless you my own darling Susy -

Your loving mother
M Bulloch

New York Jan 9th—1863

My dearest Susy,
  Mittie & Thee arrived safely night before last at or near eleven o clock - we were so glad to see them and to hear from you darling - Mittie said she had a very pleasant visit, but that it seems as though she had seen you only a few minutes - She said you and dear Hill were <u>so</u> <u>affectionate</u>. The day after she arrived at home she spent pretty much in the kitchen - The day before every thing in the closets of the kitchen had been taken out and scrubbed and cleaned until they shone - The whole kitchen had been white washed and cleaned until there could not have been detected an atom of dirt - But yesterday she was having every thing put back she said "<u>in order</u>." Well by six o clock in the evening "all was right" but poor Mittie had to take her bed she was so very unwell. She looks better to day, but is still quite unwell I am quite well again darling The children are well - Anna and Thee are gone this afternoon to learn to skate, and I am going to read to Mittie as soon as I finish this note -
How stupid it was in me to forget to sign the order - I suppose what made me forget was I had Dated it Dec instead of January, and had to alter it.
  Darling how thankful I am that the Beaver Meadow has done so well. I wish I could have done without selling those six shares, but I could not - When I see you I will tell you all about it - Mittie is very anxious for you to pay her a visit - but she will write you herself as soon as she is able - She and Anna do not know I am writing or would send love - I know you must have enjoyed the week of prayer - I do not know darling that I should have done so I have to pray myself and try to exercise all the christian charity I possess to enable me to listen & bear meekly the morning prayers of the sabbath day - I still go to Dr Rice, church - next

sabbath will be communion sabbath there I have prayed for guidance & direction, and can (I think) go conscientiously go with christians there to the table of the Lord - I have done so all of the winter & fall, and will continue to do so my life is spared - The children of God ought to be able to meet on the broad platform of true religion - I try to forget conflicting opinions and feelings and endeavor to obey my Blessed Redeemer, command - "Do this in Remembrance of me" - If we can't meet around his table, I do not know how we can meet around his throne in glory - Dr Rice has the sacrament of the Lord's supper every two months I believe Susy darling I hope you are really better, I have been fearing that you were suffering as you did the summer you went to Coopers. I know you are so uncomplaining that I constantly fear I do not know the truth about you - You are very precious to me my darling Susy, and I never can bear to think of you suffering in any way - I often think of you and fear you are lonely - I wish we could be in the same city - good by for the present darling daughter.
       Your loving mother
       M Bulloch

      New York Jan 30th 1863
My Dearest Susy,
  This morning just as I had placed my writing materials on the table to write you Mrs Shelton and Mr Shelton called to get us to go with them to see the dwarf girl Lorina Warren - Mittie and Anna went, but as I did not wish to go, I determined to take a walk and afterwards write you -
I took my walk - delightful overhead but sloppy and very watery under foot - Lunch is over and the girls have not returned yet - Your letter of the 24 darling was a sweet affectionate letter and I felt like writing you as soon as I received it - But I have been very busy with sewing work, and could not conveniently do so - This morning before I

went to walk, - Hill's kind note enclosing Mr Alex Benson & Co's Check on Cammam & Co New York for four hundred and seventeen 75/000, dollars, and also bill of sale of the six shares of Beaver Meadow Stock was handed me. Please give my best love to Hill, & tell him that I thank him sincerely for all that he has done - Susy darling I hope I feel grateful too, to a kind Providence for thus providing for me - You remember last year the sale of furniture presented my spending capital, now this year from an unexpected source I am again saved from resorting to that expedient Truly he has born to me the wisdom God - Oh that through his grace I may feel corresponding love and gratitude for all his mercies. How many and how stupendous have been his mercies to me the past year - I know that I fall infinitely short of realizing for a single moment the length breadth and depth of his goodness in saving the soul of our dear Stuart - I trust, we shall yet join our dear one in praising God throughout eternity for this unspeakably great mercy - I send you a little tract. Perhaps you have seen it, but it struck me as being very good - Bamie got your letter today - when I handed it to her the little thing flushed with pleasure - I hope your letter may reach our dear Lucy - Anna received a letter two or three days since [from Mr Caskie] in which he says he has lately sent two letters of different dates - both sent from Lucy to me. I have not received either of them yet. Mr Caskie mentions also that Mrs Caskie has lately received a package from Hariot by the Giraffe which ran the blockade - It contained gloves needles thread etc etc. I feel very hopeful that she, (Hariot) sent Lucy a package by the same opportunity - I wrote Hariot about two months ago, and begged her to do so - Mr Caskie when he wrote had not received our package to Lucy - I hope he has it by this time - Darling I long for your visit to us - Elliott told me yesterday he loved aunt Susy - Mittie says you must let her know a day or two before you come We all look forward to the time eagerly -

                            Your loving mother M B.

Ask Hill if I must send him a formal receipt for the check and bill of sale.

M Bulloch

I am so sorry the Photographs failed - Love to Mr & Mrs West

The *Brooklyn Daily Eagle* reported on 26 January 1863 the upcoming wedding of General Tom Thumb and Miss Lavinia Warren. Both diminutive persons performed in various shows staged by P.T. Barnum. He planned to hold the marriage in one of New York's prominent churches and to sell tickets, to which one newspaper exclaimed, "It is bad enough to turn the solemn rites of marriage into a public entertainment for the gaping crowd of morbid curiosity hunters, without profaning the house of God with such an exhibition."[143]

Despite the paper's objections, Tom Thumb and Lavinia Warren married in Grace Episcopal Church on 10 February. Barnum held a wedding reception for the couple at New York's Metropolitan Hotel, where they stood on the grand piano to greet their guests. President and Mrs. Lincoln held a reception in their honor at the White House before the newlyweds began their European tour.

General Tom Thumb's Wedding
Harper's Weekly, 21 February 1863

The named James Caskie, who successfully managed on several occasions to send messages to Martha and Anna in New York, could be James Caskie (1792-1866) or his nephew James Kerr Caskie (1818-1868). His most recent letter alluded to the S.S. *Giraffe*, a Clyde (Scotland)-built, iron side-wheel steamer of light draft and considerable speed, which had previously been used as a packet between Glasgow, Scotland, and Belfast, Ireland. Now wholly owned by the Confederate States, under the direct supervision of James Bulloch, and renamed the *R. E. Lee*, she ran the blockade fourteen times in ten months, beginning in December 1862 and ending in November 1863. She carried out of the South some six thousand bales of cotton, sold to supply the Confederacy with funds for more ships and military armaments.

Martha made an excellent profit on her sale of stock. For six shares she made $417.75, approximately $69.63 per share. This letter confirms Martha sold some of her furniture the previous year. While no historical record has been found, it appears Martha, while keeping house in Philadelphia with Hill and Susan, either brought with her some furniture from Bulloch Hall or purchased furniture in Pennsylvania.

New York Feb 10th 1863

My dearest Susy,
   I received your dear letter several days ago and afterwards a short letter enclosed with two from Lucy the short one I sent you, & one dated 7th of Dec - Since the reception of these letters I have received another from dear Lucy dated the 7th of January - this last I will enclose you - I perceive she did not receive the letter I wrote her in Nov - in that letter I mentioned to her that you & Mittie sent the shoes etc - This letter in Nov I sent by the way of Baltimore the letter she mentioned having received was sent by Miss Welsman {here?} to Nassau in a package of letters which she sent to her sister in Charleston - in my letter to Nassau I only recapitulated the list of articles without mentioning the particulars - I am writing to Lucy today by

another opportunity to Nassau through Miss Welsman - A friend of hers will take my letter with another package from her - Beside this opportunity to write now, in about ten days Miss Welsman's nephew a very obliging young man is going himself to Nassau on account of his health - he says he will take letters or a package or both for me - this same young man is gone to day to Baltimore, so last evening I got Anna to write Miss Tiernan and request if she has not already sent our package, to give it to young Mr Brown, who will take it to Nassau when he goes on the 20th inst - Anna is to day writing to Jimmie B & I have sent a memorandum for Lucy - we are all well dear Susy and expect to see you before long - with much love to Hill & kind regards to Mr & Mrs West, I remain
     Your truly affectionate Mother
     M Bulloch

Several months passed in which Martha visited Susan and Hilborne in Philadelphia. She wrote this letter upon her return to New York.

     New York April 3 - 1863
My own blessed Susy -
  I intended to write you a few lines yesterday to tell you of our safe arrival on wednesday afternoon, and how well Mrs West and I got through that "slough Despond" which reaches from the Ferry Boat to Broadway when we took one of those high, disagreeable things called Omnibuses - things which old ladies can with difficulty climb into - Particularly when dear little Susy was not near to encourage our efforts in the ascent - We however surmounted the difficulty in despite of hoops, crowds of dirty men with dirty boots etc,etc, and yet to 12th St. in safety - I then got out with Mrs West and bade her adieu at the corner of 12th & Broadway, and walked to 33 E 20th St. Here I found all sick with colds except Anna - The children had been quite

sick, but were better - They are now much better - I found here two letters from Lucy which I enclose you. You need not send them back - But I have digressed so much that I have not yet told you why I did not write you yesterday. I thought I would first call on Miss Welsman and find out whether she had heard any thing of the packages we sent Lucy. I found she had received letters which said the trunks containing them where shipped in a small vessel on the 16 of March - This vessel she thought was the Omega - In the morning papers she had seen that the Omega had arrived in Charleston - So in this information there was nothing sure, but while we were talking a letter was handed her from young Mr Brown saying the trunks had been shipped in the Omega - This vessel has arrived in Charleston, so dear Lucy is now in possession of the package. Now I must tell you that I have heard from Irvine - you recollect at Tuckers there was a man named David Harvey - this man - was at the head of the Mill Run - Irvine used to be very fond of him, & he of Irvine - well when the Alabama took the Hatteras off Galveston - David who was Sailing Master of the Hatteras says he saw a tall, large fine looking young man whose countenance he thought he recognized - Irvine on the other hand kept gazing at David - presently David said to him I have certainly seen you before and he said to David is not your name Simpson? David said no, but I think I saw you at the Naval School - No said Irvine but perhaps you saw my brother - Capt James D Bulloch there - Then David said is your name Bulloch - Yes - Not little Irvine Bulloch I knew at Tuckers - With that there was mutual recognition - & much rejoicing on both sides - Irvine then went to Lewis Kell and asked permission - - to have David in his mess which was freely granted. David says not only was he, himself, but his entire party treated most kindly owing in part to this circumstance - He says Irvine looks the picture of health & is of a truth the smartest of all the young Officers - Irvine told him he was engaged to be married to a young lady in Richmond, but that he (David) could not remember the name - I should like to but tell you of a promise Irvine made him, but must do that another time - Mittie and Anna and myself are going to see Mrs West this morning -

> Your own
> mother M B -

Martha arrived back in New York by train and then ferry. She traveled with Mrs. Rebecca West, Hilborne and Mary West Roosevelt's mother. No doubt Rebecca stayed at Mary's during her visit. Once in New York, they first traveled through Martha's "slough Despond" or swamp of despair, a fictional, deep bog in John Bunyan's allegory *The Pilgrim's Progress,* where the protagonist Christian sinks under the weight of his sins and his sense of guilt for them. This took the two ladies from the ferry boat to Broadway. They continued their journey by omnibus. One of the first forms of public transportation, it consisted of a large bus-like conveyance

Omnibus,
L'Illustrations Journal Universel, 26 September 1863

usually pulled by large draft horses. Some types had seating on the upper deck or roof. They departed the omnibus at Broadway and 12th Street where Mrs. West continued on to Silas and Mary's home at 39 E. 12th Street. Martha then walked on to 33 E. 20th Street to Mittie's home. Martha's trip across New York City can be traced on the map on page 20 She would have most likely arrived on the Philadelphia Rail Road Line ferry at the base of Liberty Street on the west side of the peninsula.

Imagine Martha, Susan, and Mittie scouring the daily newspapers for information about son and brother Irvine in the Confederate Navy. Obviously from the information in this letter, they were aware he was aboard the C.S.S. *Alabama*. Not long after the *Alabama* sailed from Liverpool in late August 1862, Northern papers took notice of her exploits and her colorful captain, Raphael Semmes. By late October, tales of the *Alabama*'s numerous prizes could frequently be found, and the papers called Semmes a pirate, buccaneer, and brigand. On 31 December 1862, a letter from one of the *Alabama*'s officers appeared in various newspapers, including the *Buffalo Commercial*. The author stated that he boarded the *Alabama* in Liverpool. The following is a brief excerpt from the letter:

> Since we have come into these waters we have got some splendid guns additional, all mounted; and, what with our own crew and the brave volunteers who have since joined us, we are now able to fight was well as run, and both at the same time if need be so. We have also plenty of news about ourselves on board in the *New York Times* and *Herald*, the *Shipping Gazette*, Liverpool *Mercury*, and *Gore's Advertiser*, &c. some of the New York papers, illustrated, give frightful pictures of the engagements their vessels have had with us, making them all surrounded with smoke, and firing into us, all of which we heartily enjoy.

> One thing is certain - they never will take the *Alabama*, nor a man of us alive. Captain, officers and men know their duty, and are quite aware of the doom which would befal [sp] them if taken, for there are no croakers or skulkers here; but if so unlikely a thing should take place, the hair of one of our heads be injured, our commander assures us that the government of Richmond will hang a regiment of Yankee officers in retaliation.
>
> Captain Semmes (or the admiral, as we call him among ourselves both fore and aft) is of opinion that the war will be settled in the beginning of the year, and in that case we shall all be provided for for life. No more sea for me after that. Previous to the 20th of this month our prize money alone was worth from £400 to £500 a man. So I am looking forward to the day when I shall return to Liverpool, and, relieved from the drudgery of a sea life, spend my remaining years in peace and contentment.[144]

Since U.S. papers did not provide the original introduction about the letter being written by a petty officer, did Martha and her daughters wonder if Irvine had written it? No doubt each time the *Alabama's* name appeared in a newspaper they were relieved to read that no one aboard had died during the latest engagement.

Just the day before this newspaper article was printed, the same paper reported from Captain Jones of the U.S.S. *Ariel*, a U.S. Mail steamer, taken off the east end of Cuba on 7 December. A portion of the article read:

> Capt. Jones says that the Alabama deserves all her previous reputation for speed. She can steam 14 knots with 17 pounds of steam, and is allowed to carry 25 pounds of steam. . . . Capt. Jones further says that the

Alabama has a fine crew, and that they are well - disciplined, that the ship is in fine order, and that the deck is arranged for two additional pivot guns, which he was informed were 100 - pounder rifles, and in the Alabama's hold, ready to be mounted should they be required. Capt. Jones says that the rebel Captain treated him remarkably well. He was not confined, had the privilege of the deck, and messed in the wardroom.

Martha had recently heard of Irvine from a personal contact - David Harvey, sailing master on the U.S.S. *Hatteras*. He had his encounter with the C.S.S. *Alabama* off the coast of Texas. From July to early December of 1862, the U.S.S. *Hatteras* was on blockade duty between Pensacola and Mobile. On 6 January, the *Hatteras* had moved to take up blockade duties off Galveston, Texas. The story of the sinking of the U.S.S. *Hatteras* appeared in Northern newspapers in mid-February after a letter arrived from Kingston, Jamaica, from her former commander. The letter tells of being ordered to pursue a strange sail which was quickly approached and hailed. After hailing the ship and being informed it was British, he had lowered a boat and sent a crew to investigate, at which time the *Alabama* correctly identified herself and ran up the Stars and Bars. The ensuing battle, won by the *Alabama*, ended with the sinking of the *Hatteras* with "every living being" rescued by the *Alabama*.[145] Five men aboard the *Hatteras* were wounded and two killed. The men launched in the small boat managed to be safely rescued and returned to shore. Semmes released the crew and officers in Kingston.

David Harvey (1838-1898) of New York City continued to serve in the U.S. Navy, reaching the rank of captain according to his obituary. He married, but had no children. Harvey died in New York at the age of 60.[146]

Martha mentioned *Lewis* Kell (why she called him Lewis is unknown). This would be John McIntosh Kell (1823-1900) of Darien, McIntosh County, Georgia. A family friend, Kell had previously toured some of north Georgia with Daniel Stuart Elliott.[147] Like James Bulloch, Kell had served in the U.S. Navy during Mexican-American War. He sailed with Commodore Matthew Perry's expedition to Japan. In 1861, Lt. Kell resigned from the U.S. Navy and received a commission as a first lieutenant in the Confederate Navy. He served under Raphael Semmes on the C.S.S. *Sumpter* before sailing with Semmes on the *Alabama*, where he served as Executive Officer. After the Civil War, Kell returned to Georgia and became a farmer. In later years, he served as Adjutant General of Georgia.

New York April 8 - /63

My dearest Susy

I believe Mrs West leaves this morning, and I am so sorry we have seen so little of her - I found Mittie very unwell indeed as I told you in my last letter - then the weather, except one day, has been uncertain and very bad. In addition to this Mittie has been completely upset by the want of a cook - The day before yesterday I was nearly all day out hunting for that necessary evil, and late in the afternoon found one with good recommendations, and as Mittie had no one at all in the kitchen she has taken her. whether she will prove good remains to be proved - Mittie is a little better, but on sunday evening had one of her old palpitations - Teedie too has one of those ulcers on the eye which Bamie used to have - Night before last dear Susy an Englishman who had just arrived called on me, and brought a letter from Harriet to Anna, a short letter from Jimmie to me, and a long, affectionate and interesting letter from Irvine to me - Of an old date was Irvines but I wish you could see it - I cannot send it to you darling for reasons which I will tell you when I see you - Indeed when you go to Long Branch and read the letter you will perceive them yourself - The letter was nine pages long and dated new years day - He sends a great deal of love to his three dear sisters, but I will write again darling and make some extracts - Hariot sends

a great deal of love to you also - says she received Lucys letter & has sent her a package of goods - Although I have been writing constantly to J [James Dunwoody Bulloch] and herself they did not received any letters from us - They had been writing to us constantly also Harriot has another baby - which she has named Stuart Elliott she says after "poor brother" the prettiest baby she says she ever had -
      Good bye darling -
      Your affec Mother
      M Bulloch

        New York, April 8 /63
My dearest Susy,
  I wrote you a hurried note this morning, and thinking that Mrs West was going by some early train, Anna and I went to tell her goodbye soon after breakfast and I took the note with me for her to take to you. When we got to Marys I found Mrs West had put off returning until tomorrow, but I still left the note with her - I hope you will receive that note before you get this, as it is somewhat of a preface to this - Mrs West will tell you all about our arrangements about Long Branch & so I need not repeat - I begged her to tell <u>you</u> all about their housekeeping &c &c The note this morning told you of letters I had received from James & Irvine, and one Hariot had written to Anna. Now as I cannot send the letters to you I will give you a few extracts - First Irvines letter to me - After the date January 1st and some account of his cruise, he goes on to say, "so you see your son is perfectly safe except in fact from the dangers which must accompany every one who goes to sea such as storms gales &, of which I have seen some more dreadful than I ever thought there could be, especially when we were cruising on the Bank of New Foundland, and off New York however we have weathered them all, and so fine a Ship as I am in bids fair never to be overcome by any thing. The amount of it is that Providence is on the side of the right

&c &c &c." He goes on after much which I leave out to say, "Though the life is as hard as it is exciting as painful to be away from home and family it is pleasant to think I am doing my all for my oppressed country, still these are times, (although I am happy and merry as a lark) when I feel sad dear Mother. It is when I think of you and my dear sisters - when I remember that it has been nearly <u>two years</u> since I have seen you knowing that you think of me often and feel so anxious and even distressed at the state of affairs - it is then that I long to see and pray for the day to come soon when there shall be peace, and when we shall all meet again a happy family. Oh my sweet mother do take care of yourself, and do not be worried and petted about me, or any of your children, or the country, (as I fear you are) but keep a bright cheerful heart knowing that we are doing well, that this war mus[t] end at some time, and end to the advantage of our glorious side. Let these things cheer you and not do as sisters for you must take for you must take care of your health, and some day your Irvine who is learning Seamanship both as it regards books and hard study, will be the commander of some fine Steamer in the Merchant service. (for like bro Jim I like that better than the Navy) and then I want to have you and Annie live with me in whatever Port my vessel shall sail from - You perhaps will laugh at this, but I am in earnest, more in earnest than I have ever been in My life - Shortly after this war is over I intend to be fit for, and will try and get a trans Atlantic steamer, for of course there will be a line from some of our Ports. So keep yourself carefully, and I pray God dear Mother we may live to see each other again - Don't let dear little Annie or Mittie, nor dear sister Susy worry themselves or feel anxious either. Give my love to all three of them, and kiss Nancy[148] almost doubly affectionately for me, for unlike the other two she has no husband to love her, only you dear Mother" - Then a good deal which I omit mostly about the time when he came very near seeing John Ellis and his bride {Julia?} Then he goes on to say "Tell Anna if she writes to the Caskies to give my love particularly to one, for you know Ive an interest there in a sweet little lady, nothing like what Nancy used to think she was - kiss Mittie's dear little children for me, and make those that can remember me do so, and teach those that of course do not that there is such an one as uncle Irvine" Then he sends a reminder to Mittie that the two last* new years days were spent at her house so happily - then says" I have your likeness Blessed which I had taken from Sister Hatties at Liverpool - It is a fine one and I often look at your sweet face - I believe you are an angel darling, when I look at it and remember how good you are - it is a great comfort to me - do take care of your sweet self, and caution my dear little sisters to take care of you too, with devoted love to all three of them and my greatest love for yourself dear darling Mother I ever am your loving and ever affectionate Son "Irvine S Bulloch" *the two before the last two -

Harriot in her letter dear Susy sends to you a great deal of love - says she and Jimmie have written to us very frequently and never get any letters from us - That she received a letter from Lucy and hopes (poor girl) she will receive safely the articles she has sent her I have written you in this mornings note that Harriot has another son and has named him Stuart Elliott - Dear darling I hope you are much better your little funny note I tore up as you requested Grandma to do - When you write let me know how the owners of the Noah's Ark are and how the poor crying child is - I can't describe how tenderly I feel towards you my blessed child -
    your affect Mother
    M Bulloch

Dr Metcalffe has been to see the children today and says Teedie has Streumas Opthalmia - I don't know how to spell the words, but Hill will know what it means - love to dear Hill - How is the pencil?

  Finally, Martha shared part of Irvine's letter. He told her of his great plans for the future, including marrying a girl from Richmond. If she was a Caskie, then her identity is unknown as all of the Caskie girls were ten or more years older than Irvine. She may have been a cousin or simply a young woman known by Anna based on her many visits to the family before the War.

Dr. Metcalfe had visited Teedie once again and identified his eye ailment. Strumous ophthalmia, also known as conjunctivitis of the cornea, was a serious, but treatable condition.

Only one reference to Noah's Ark could be found; however it came from Annapolis, Maryland, rather than Philadelphia. In February of 1864, a large three-story, brick structure burned and was completely gutted. The newspaper article mentioned "the fire originated from the chimney in 'Noah's Ark,' where there were some twelve families living, of all colors and complexions." This suggest that homeless shelters existed in several cities under the name Noah's Ark.[149]

Chapter 12: May through August of 1863

Events of the War

The next great battle of the War began on 1 May at Chancellorsville, Virginia. Four days of fighting ended with Union forces, numbering some 130,000 under General Hooker, being defeated by General Robert E. Lee's daring and a force of only 60,000. Unfortunately, Confederate General Stonewall Jackson fell to friendly fire. Again, the large number of losses staggered the nation. The Union suffered 17,000 killed, wounded, or missing. Confederate casualities were recorded at 13,000. On 10 May, Stonewall Jackson died of his wounds, his death a massive blow to the Confederacy.

Upon his victory, Lee took the initiative and once again invaded the North by heading into Maryland and then Pennsylvania. Lincoln, who had lost all confidence in Hooker, replaced him with General George G. Meade in late June. The Army of the Potomac had now seen five commanders in less than one year.

The Battle of Gettysburg began on 1 July, and the South suffered a massive loss and would never again invade the North. More than 160,000 Americans participated in the battle fought on three hot July days across the hillsides and cornfields of Pennsylvania. The dead, wounded, and missing from each army numbered over 23,000. The Confederates loaded their wounded on wagons and headed South, abandoning their dead. Once again a Union commander failed to pursue a weakened foe. Lincoln wrote of his extreme frustration with

Meade saying he missed a "golden opportunity" to end the War right there.

Independence Day also saw the surrender of Vicksburg, the last Confederate stronghold on the Mississippi River, ending a six-week long siege. Union forces now commanded the Mississippi River, splitting the Confederacy.

Not quite two weeks later, anti-draft rioting broke out, primarily in New York City. After the deaths of more than 120 people, Union forces from Gettysburg arrived to restore order. Poor immigrant whites, who could not avoid the draft, focused most of the violence against free Negroes.

In late August, pro-Confederate William C. Quantrill led 450 followers in a raid on Lawrence, Kansas. Quantrill's Raid, or the Lawrence Massacre, came in retribution for free-state militia or vigilante groups, known as Jayhawkers, raiding into Missouri's pro-slavery western counties. Quantrill's raiders pillaged and set fire to the town, killing about 200 men and boys, many of them specifically targeted. They burned to the ground a quarter of the buildings in Lawrence, including all but two businesses, and looted most of the banks and stores.

Closer to Martha's ancestral home, the 54th Massachusetts Infantry Regiment, comprised of Negro soldiers under the command of Col. Robert G. Shaw, attacked Darien, Georgia, on 11 June, destroying the mostly deserted town. On 18 July, Shaw lead his troops against Fort Wagner in South Carolina. Over half of his regiment died on the battlefield.

The Letters

New York May 18 -1863

It is a long time since I have written you my dearest Susy - and I know my darling daughter you have frequently felt like hearing from us, but really since I returned from Tuckers which is three weeks this very day I have been so busy that I have scarcely given myself time for exercise - you will wonder what I have been so engaged about, well I have been helping Anna the first two weeks after my return and last week I undertook to rip up my old foulard silk dress sponge, ~~and~~ renovate it, and make it up anew - I have not yet finished it but hope to do so tomorrow - The woman who was to assist Anna with her work has been prevented from doing so by having a very sick husband, so that more {____} on us than we expected - Teedie was very much benefitted by his trip in the in the country, but Bamie has suffered with her eyes for the last three weeks very much - Elliott & Cona are well - The Hyatts, Cady [Caddie/Caroline] & Phany sail this morning for Europe - Mittie and Anna have been kept in a state of confusion by this circumstance, as they have gone to the Pier from which they embark several times to bid them farewell - As they went in a sailing vessel they could not go until the wind and weather permitted - This morning however they have gone - Anna with several other ladies and a few gentlemen have gone with them as far as Sandy Hook - Perhaps not to be back before ten o clock tonight and to be <u>sea - sick all day</u> - <u>This is pleasure!!!</u> Anna received your amusing letter, and will write as soon as she gets back as she will them have the Hyatts off her mind - Anna and I will go to Long Branch by the first of June, Mittie will stay a week or two days later in New York - I have not yet received Lucy's promised letter - Anna received one last week from Mr Caskie in which he says he had just sent me a letter from Mrs Elliott. Strange that we should have received his letter and not hers - Susy darling I hope you are better during that warm spell of weather I thought of you a great deal - I fear you will try to remain in Phil too long and get sick - I hope my blessed child that our kind Heavenly Father may restore you to health - It is my constant prayer that if it accords with his blessed will you may yet enjoy that blessing - You are very dear to me precious Susy - I do feel grateful to God that I have a dear christian child and I hope never to be unmindful of this great thing - I have I think good reason to hope that I have five children in Heaven - What an unspeakable blessing - Four others are still on earth - but I try to commit them to the same covenant keeping God - This is Irvine's birth day - <u>twenty one years old today</u> - dear boy!!! I have been feeling very low spirited for the last four or five days on account of the death of Stonewall Jackson - only 37 years old! just the age of dear Stuart - <u>he</u> was 36 when he died last summer. Oh what a great and good man has come to an untimely end - But he has gone to that Savior whom he served so faithfully on earth - I have heard that Mr Jackson once prayed for his death. I cannot think this is true - If it is, I do not envy him his feelings - I heard this morning that Marys [West Roosevelt] two little boys Jimmie & Frank have the measles, but that they are not very ill - I would go to see them but Mittie would fear the infection - I hope the dear little fellows may soon get well Mr Roosevelt they think much better - Give my best love to Mrs West and kind regards to Mr West - Much love to dear Hill -

Your loving mother
M Bulloch

Martha had been to Tuckers resort in New Jersey. Before the family began going to Long Branch, Tuckers had been their summering place. Located on Long Island near New Rochelle, the area is today known as Tucker's Point or Tucker's Beach.[150]

Martha sorrowed over the loss of General Stonewall Jackson at Chancellorsville, Virginia, just as his loss plagued all the South, as Jackson was considered one of their most promising leaders. Martha associated his death and Stuart's due to their relatively young age. She mentioned to Susan having five children in heaven. Martha lost four children from her marriage to Senator John Elliott: John Whitehead (1818-1820), Charles William (1824-1827), Georgia Amanda (1822-1848), and most recently Stuart. From her marriage to James Stephens Bulloch, son Charles Irvine (1838/9-1841) died not long after their move to Roswell, Georgia.

The letters tell us nothing more about Anna's work. Memoirs written by Mittie's children, in particular Bamie and Theodore, mention only that she was their nanny and conducted their lessons. The following letter indicated Anna was engaged with several sewing projects.

New York May 29 [63]
I really do feel badly my own dear daughter at not having written you for such a long time - You know blessed child, it is not because I do not think of you for you are always uppermost in my thoughts - But you can scarcely realize how very busy I have been - Anna has had a great deal of work - She had four white dresses to make - we have just finished three of them and am on the fourth - You know we have not had any assistance whatever Besides these white dresses we have assisted Mary Ann
[Missing Text]
D^r does not wish him to walk for some time to come I wonder what can be the matter with him - she says Stuart is a very promising child - Jimmie & Jessie also are very fine children - Mittie & children are pretty well - Bamie's eye is better - Lelia told me yesterday that Mary's children had recovered & that she was going in the country today - I hope Mr & Mrs West are well please give my love to them - With much love to dear Hill and yourself
Your affec Mother
M Bulloch

This partial letter described their sewing activities and of a bit of news from Harriott in Liverpool, who told of her and James's four children, Jimmie, Jessie, Henry, and Stuart. Henry suffered from rickets. "Mary's children" refers to Cornelius *Connie*, Hilborne *Hilly*, and James, the children of Silas Weir and Mary West Roosevelt.

Long Branch Jun/26/63
My Dearest Susy,
Bamie received your letter yesterday, which quite delighted the little thing - indeed Grandma was

equally delighted to hear from you darling one - - I wrote you a few days since a long uninteresting letter - in it wrote you Mittie had gone to West Point - Thee came to Long Branch last night and the night before - he had staid with Mittie monday - - tuesday nights - said Teedie was much better - He gets to West Point tonight - Mittie expects to be back here on tuesday of next week, but it seems to be clouding up again & I seriously fear we are going to have another northeast Storm - If so I hope she will not bring Teedie here until it is over - The rest of us are all well - The {____} {____} him {____} to fill up {____}- Miss Lily Hyatt is here by invitation from Thee and Mittie - she will return on monday - We have some interesting books, and I have ample time now to read - I am now reading Miss Mintons last work "Two Pictures." It is very interesting - I hope darling the Raid into Pennsylvania will not frighten or annoy you in any way - The Confederates are now trying to make the federals feel a little what poor desolate Virginia has been suffering - but they will never do what has done to them - burn and ruin villages inhabited only by helpless women and children - Darien for instance - Poor little {____} I hope she was in the up - country - I have just been bathing little Cona she is very interesting, can speak distinctly has all of her teeth through except her two stomach teeth - they {____} quite new - While I was in the nursery I found Elliott had red spots on his neck and {____} - {____} with {____} {____} he was {____} - he seems well today - If you do not hear from me in a day or two you may conclude nothing of consequence is the matter with him - I do hope dear dear Susy that you may not be made sick by the warm weather in Phil[a] - I shall count every week now until you come - love to all - I suppose Mrs Boynton is quite {____} - She is such a great coward - I must say good bye for the present darling Susy May our constant God ever grant you his presence & blessings -

your affect Mother MB

When war comes near, or into our homes, we feel it more intensely. Martha worried about Susan and several friends in Pennsylvania when Confederate troops began marching into that state in the month before Gettysburg. Martha's other concern centered on the total destruction of Darien, Georgia, so near her former home in Liberty County. Newspapers of the day published the following story:

> From the Savannah News, June 17
> Destruction of Darien
> Our readers have been informed that the city of Darien, one of the oldest towns in the State, the New Inverness of Oglethorpe's time, has been totally destroyed by Yankee negro forces. A citizen of Darien writing from "Dunwoody's Plantation, near where Darien stood," under date of June 12th says:
> "What has been so long threatened has at length come to pass. Darien is now one plain of ashes and blackened chimneys. The accursed Yankee negroe vandals came up yesterday with three gunboats and tow transports and laid the city in ruins. There are but three small houses left in the place The Methodist church was set on fire but it did not burn. All the other churches, the market house, court house, jail, and clerk's office, are all gone. The villains broke open all the houses and stores and took what they wanted, and then poured spirits of turpentine over the floors and applied the torch. It is a sad sight to see the smoking ruins now. The wretches shot the milch cows and calves down in the streets, took some of them on board their vessels and left the rest lying in the streets, where they still lie.
> They carried off every negro that was in the place, except one old African woman, named Nancy, who told them she was from Africa, and that

she would not again go on the big water. After destroying the town, on their way to Doby they burnt Mr. Morris' plantation buildings. For myself I feel this calamity severely. You know I have lost heavily since the war commenced but I had still a good home left. This is now almost gone. The value in money I would not have thought so much of, as I am getting used to it; but there is something in the word home that puts money out of the question. One of the boats started "to come up Cathead creek to this place, but the sneaking rascals changed their minds, and contented themselves with sending us a few compliments in the shape of shells." The town was destroyed by a negro regiment, officered by white men - - the 54th Massachusetts Volunteers, Colonel Shaw.

The destruction of Darien was a cowardly, wanton outrage, for which the Yankee vandals have not even the excuse of love of plunder. The town had for a long time been nearly deserted, and there was nothing left in the place to excite even Yankee cupidity. It afforded a safe opportunity to inflict injury upon unarmed and defenceless [sp] private citizens, and it is in such enterprises that Yankee negro valor displays itself. [151]

While Martha anguished over the destruction of Darien and her late brother-in-law's family plantation, Northerners took a totally different view of the actions of the 54th Massachusetts. While some praised the bravery and actions of those Negro soldiers,[152] others compared the destruction of Darien to the C.S.S. *Alabama's* actions on the high seas.

The houses of Darien were private property. So was the good ship Jacob Bell. So were the little fishing schooners which were seen in flames yesterday off the Massachusetts coast, with a rebel ship lying near to insure their destruction, and chasing still others of the fleet.

No doubt the rebels will cry out against the destruction of Darien as a barbarous act. So it is; but in what way does it differ from the burning of helpless merchant ships and fishing schooners, which has been practised [sp] so long by the rebels? Except in this, perhaps, that Capt. Semmes risks nothing when he attacks one of our fishermen. While Col. Montgomery at any rate takes the chance of blows when he marches into the enemy's country to burn and destroy. Otherwise the two acts are precisely parallel. Now it may be said that a rebel atrocity does not excuse a like act on our part. Certainly not - but unfortunately the only way to keep a barbarous enemy within the limits of lawful warfare is to retaliate upon him the cruelties he commits upon us. This is a recognized custom of war; it has been practised, and sternly practised by the most civilized nations.[153]

Martha no doubt worried about Irvine, so close just off the Massachusetts' coast, yet so far from her loving embrace. While being on aboard the *Alabama* kept her son out of land warfare, his position on aboard a ship of war was just as precarious.

July 14th 1863

We are quite well - Teedie very much better - He still sleeps from the sea shore at first they took him to Edenton a village over five miles from Long Branch, now his sleeping abode is at Mrs Tabors in Long Branch village about one and a fourth mile from Mr Lairds - Mittie begins to feel a little more settled & has at length unpacked her trunks - Today however we are all a little unsettled by the news from

New York (I suppose you you have seen in the papers the account of the riot there yesterday) Thee went to town this morning, and we have some fears that the citizens may be called upon to assist in putting down the mob - It is to be hoped that order will soon be restored, but really I do not wonder that the poor mechanics oppose the conscription - it certainly favors the rich at the expense of the poor - And they all know that it <u>is</u> unconstitutional - The times appear very gloomy - may our good God have mercy upon us all - He <u>can</u> as you say bring order out of confusion - May all of our sufferings work out for us real good - His loving kindness has never failed me individually, for which I desire to be truly grateful - I feel that it is not presumption in appropriating the 31st ch of Jeremiah 3 verse to myself - Humbly I would say - that this portion of scripture gives me much comfort. I have been much struck lately too with the 381 hymn of our collection.

We are really delightfully situated here - the cottage is very pleasant indeed - the weather has been very unfavorable, but I think we shall have summer before long - I have a full view of the sea from one of my bedroom windows. It looks magnificent today from the storm of last night - there is a little piazza upstairs in the front of the house - I anticipate sitting out there some sweet mild evenings with my darling Susy - If you get tired sitting our rooms are only a step from the piazza where you can lie down and rest, as much from obseration as you would be in Roswell. Mrs Blatchford is our nearest neighbor - she occupies the room I had last summer, indeed she has those four corner rooms - one of the front rooms she has made a little parlor. They are very pleasant people - I wish Mrs West could come to L Branch a little while, tell her she would not know {Howlands?} it is so much improved - Mittie & Anna send much love - Little Corinne speaks distinctly she has lately cut her eye & stomach teeth - she is now quite well again - Love to all

                Your affectionate Mother
                      MB -

Martha referenced Jeremiah 31:3 which reads " The Lord hath appeared of old unto me, saying, Yea, I have loved thee with an everlasting love: therefore with loving kindness have I drawn thee."

Long Branch July 22

My dearest Susy,

Although I have had several letters to write lately, I must send you a few lines - You know I told you I had written to Miss Knop to send to Mrs Boynton (giving her address) an inquiry whose to send certain boxes & hospital stores which I thought she (Miss Knop) had in hand I received an answer from her yesterday in which she said those boxes have been sent to the Gettysburg battle field - Many sufferers are there still being nursed in the open air No shelter being yet provided for them - In connection with this I will tell you about a a copy of a letter which she sent me in the same envelop with hers to me but it will take me too long to write - I will only tell its destination It is a letter from Emmetsburg Md - I showed it to several ladies, one a Virginian gave me $500 another this morning came to me while I was at the breakfast table and asked me if I would give her that letter - that she was writing to her friends in California, and she wished to enclose it to them She lives in Washington City is a North Carolinian and loves the south - her husband is minister to Portugal, and of course in the Federal service - She says last winter she received $1200 dollars in gold to be used for the confederate prisoners from California - That she has used it all and was writing for more, and would send that letter to show the great need of money - I, of course, gave her the letter Miss Knop writes me that since the ninth of this month she has received from southerners and southern sympathizers $900 (nine hundred dollars) - Of this money she has sent to Mrs Bulloch of Baltimore three hundred dollars and two large boxes containing hospital stores, for prisoners in or around Baltimore – To Mrs Dickson of Phil[a] two hundred & fifty dollars and 4 large boxes of clothing for

Fort Delaware prisoners - A gentle man made her a present of 64 hats which she also sent to Mrs Dickson for the same prisoners - She has heard from those ladies that the money and boxes had been received and that the poor fellows were very grateful for them - But although this is cheering yet it is but as a drop in the bucket - I sent her this morning twenty dollars from ladies here - Susy darling I was thinking that if you could get a good price for my silver bowl I would like you to sell it and give the money for some comforting things for the poor fellows in Fort Del - the original price was 90 or 95 dollars, even half of that would help somewhat - When you sell it let it be known that the money is for the sick & suffering and I think they will be willing to give a good price - We all are well darling Susy - I have just written a long letter to dear Lucy and told her how you had been employed -

Your loving Mother - MB

Martha, and others in her social circle, collected money to buy care package items for prisoners of war held at Fort Delaware on Pea Patch Island in the Delaware River. Once a harbor defense facility, the fort now held Confederate prisoners of war, political prisoners, federal convicts, and privateer officers. The first detainees occupied sealed off casemates,[154] empty powder magazines, and two small rooms inside the sally port of the fort.

The first Confederate general to be housed at the fort was Brigadier General Johnston Pettigrew.[155] During the War, about a dozen generals were held within the fort as prisoners-of-war. By August 1863, the island held more than 11,000 men, and by the War's end, about 33,000. Compared to many Civil War-era prisons, historians consider the conditions to have been decent; however, about 2,500 men died while held there. Half of those deaths occurred during a smallpox epidemic in 1863. According to National Archives records, about 215 prisoners died as a result of typhoid and/or malaria. During the War, death also took 109 Union soldiers and about 40 civilians employed at the prison camp.[156]

By July of 1863, imprisoned enlisted men and junior officers lived in wooden barracks on the northwest side of the island. In 1864, the War Department ordered the prisoners' rations to be cut in retaliation for the treatment of northern soldiers held in southern prisoner of war camps such as Andersonville. Fort Delaware's prisoners received only two small meals a day; however, officials allowed them to purchase extra food from the sutler and to fish in the waterways on the island and the Delaware River.[157] Private Henry Berkeley wrote:

> Things here are not quite as bad as I expected to find them. They are, however, bad, hopeless and gloomy enough without any exaggeration. We went into dinner about three o'clock, which consisted of three hardtack, a small piece of meat (about three bites) and a pint tin cup of bean soup. We only get two light meals a day.[158]

Federal records show that prisoners at Fort Delaware received more care packages than any other such camp in the country.

Martha collected and knew of collected sums for such care packages. The $500 from Virginia and $1200 in gold from California equaled about $9,740 and $23,400 respectively in purchasing power. Mrs. Knop's $900 had a value of $17,500, while Martha's silver bowl, if sold for $92.50, would bring in about $1,800![159] None of these were paltry sums, and each provided for a large number of properly-selected care items.

Martha's letters to Susan do not disclose the news about the death of their relative and Roswell neighbor Major Henry Macon Dunwoody at Gettysburg (See Appendix A). While some Southern newspapers carried lists of wounded and dead after various battles, most lists arrived by teletype. Northern papers generally carried only Federal dead, wounded, and missing. The following letter may have been Martha, Mittie, and Anna's first news of cousin Henry's death.

265

Unionville August 10th

My Dearest Mother

    I am so much discouraged on hearing anything from you - that I feel it almost useless to write - knowing that my letters cannot reach you who - but I will try and get this to Havana I have not heard one word from you since Mrs Brown came from Nassau with letters - with letters - and two small packages previous to that. I heard from you frequently - all your letters coming through safely -

    Today dear Mother is just one year and one week - since dear Stuart's death how many sad recollections does this day bring with it - Every expression - word and look - seems to come back to me so vividly - How much I wish that we could have a long talk - but I fear this cruel war will prevent it for some time yet - It seems indeterminable - but we must be patient - God alone rules - and He only will put an end to it when he sees proper -

    I suppose you are at some summer place for the season - but I will direct my letter as usual - It will be forwarded to you - I was quite disappointed the other day - in the arrival of a Dr Roosevelt here from NY - with letters to many friends - He says he is a connection of Thee's - and I was so in hopes he could bring me some news of you - I suppose he is not intimately connected with the family - He has resided here for years - but had gone North to bring his wife out - who had been detained there - on some account or other - The children are very well - Mattie suffers very much from heat - but I keep her very cool - Her entire apparel being at this moment - but a chemise - and paddies - from the latter I would dispense with but for there being so many boys in the house - She informed me this morning that she liked boys better than girls - She is such a little scamp - both of the children have a great idea of singing - such as it is - They are singing now at the Highest pitch of their voices - much to my annoyance while I am writing - The weather is perfectly intense here - never having experienced such heat in my life - The Andersons are all up - and are our neighbors we see them every day - It is pleasant to know some Savannah friends here poor Georgia Nicoll is dead - died of Consumption - I wrote you in one of my previous letters of the death of Mary Low - Mary Cowper Stiles - She left several children - we have had so many sad deaths in Savannah - some killed in battle others by disease

    I hope that you all continue well - I am very anxious to hear - I hope dear Susie has received some of my letters at any rate - and Bamie the one I wrote her by way of {___} - You must excuse the want of interest in my letters but I am compelled to be so cramped and circumscribed - that I must be stupid - Do manage to write me a few lines to say you are well etc - Many of your friends enquire for you - someone asked the other day if Susie was not against us - I was so indignant - at the idea - and denied it positively -

    I hope you have received the children's likenesses by this time - when we return to Sav - I intend to have their "Cartes de visités" taken for you - I hope we will be able to go back to S [Savannah] - this fall - as father finds it very expensive to keep up two establishments these times - If we go down - I will have to find a place to board - as Sister's whole family - (she expects an increase too) will be here - and the house in S - will not accommodate all of us - therefor if any body leaves I think I should - I will try to get with some of my friends if possible - and induce them to let me pay a share in the expenses - One can however make no plans for the future now - every thing is so unsettled and uncertain - "We know not what a day may bring forth" - we have much to be thankful for - having plenty to eat and to wear, such as it is - and our brave men to defend us - They are happy hopeful, - and contented, - Therefore we ought to be so -

    I wrote to Harriot Bulloch by Charley L [Low]- of S - [Savannah] to send me a Bombazine and some crepe I hope she will do it - The package entrusted to miss {frenow} never came - my disappointment is great - as I am sadly in need of the contents it contained - Mrs Glenn is much distressed at the death of her brother Henry - He was killed at the Battle of Gettysburg - and her grief is much increased at the fact of his body resting on Yankee soil - They are all living in Yorkingston Wilkes Co - M⁻Adam Alexander - (Felix Alexander's father) is said to have addressed Lillie Dunwoody several times - but she does not consent - I am told she is a lovely attractive young girl - she would say she shows more taste than wisdom -

Give my best love to all - and hoping to hear from you soon - from your affectionate daughter Lucy Elliott - Johnnie and Mattie send kisses to Grandmama and aunts - They are growing so rapidly that you would scarcely recognise them now - and so mischievous - that sometimes I dont know what to do with them - I am so afraid of their teasing {fact__} altho he pets them a great deal -

I hope you have heard from Irvine I have heard not one word M⁻ˢ Kell has not received letters from her husband for months - but she is not at all uneasy about it as he told her it would be so -

Lucy and her two children had taken refuge in Unionville, South Carolina (now called Union). Her letter suggested her father, Frances Sorrel (1793- 1870), also resided there at that time. Her mother Matilda Aminta Douglass Moxley had died in 1860 when she plunged to her death from their home's second or third floor balcony.[160]

Lucy mentioned a visit from Dr. Cornelius J. Roosevelt (1820-1880), one of Thee's many distant cousins who resided in Macon, Georgia, with his wife Margaret Pruyn of Albany, New York. He was a physician. Her letter told of the death of Georgia Clifford Nicoll (1828-1863) of Savannah, the widow of James Skelton Gilliam (1828-1860). Georgia also died of tuberculosis.

Mary Cowper Stiles Low (1832-1863) was the second wife of merchant and businessman Andrew Low (1818-1886) of Savannah, and mother of five children, four of whom lived to maturity. Both Mittie and Anna considered Mary a personal friend. She served as a bridesmaid in Mittie's wedding. The following year, Anna attended Mary's wedding to Andrew Low in upcountry Georgia.[161] The lack of letters from the South meant Martha and her daughters did not learn of deaths among their friends for months or even years.

Lucy mentioned her desire to return to Savannah to the family home. She wrote of a sister who was "increasing." Lucy had three sisters: Amnita Elizabeth Douglas (1823-1904), Agnes Eugenie (1844-1898), approximately 19, and Annie M. Sorrel (1849-1934) only 14 years old. Most records show that Agnes never married. In 1844, Amnita married Brigadier General William Whann Mackall, a career U.S. Army officer and graduate of West Point before he resigned and joined the Confederacy. Mackall served as chief of staff to General Braxton Bragg and then General Joseph E. Johnston. By this time, Amnita and William had four children. This evidence suggests it was likely Amnita who would need the Sorrel home in Savannah. No record has been found of a birth to Amnita in 1863 or 1864.

Sorrel-Weed House, Savannah, Georgia,
Historic American Buildings Survey, circa 1936

Lucy not only informed Martha of Henry Dunwoody's death, but also that his wife and children and other members of the family resided in Wilkes County at that time. Henry and his wife Matilda's father both owned plantations in Early County, Georgia in 1860. Henry and Matilda (1829-1902) had three children at the time of his death: Althea (1853-1866), Edward Maxwell (1856-1873), and Corinne Elliott (1860-1875). According to Lucy, family members staying with the Alexander family included Jane Marion Dunwoody Stanhope Glen (1821-1885, twice widowed), who would marry Adam Leopold Alexander (1803-1882) in 1865. Adam owned Hopewell Plantation in Liberty County, along with a plantation in Wilkes County.

Laleah "Lillie" Dunwoody (1844-1919), daughter of the Reverend James Bulloch Dunwoody and his first wife, Laleah Georgiana Wood Pratt, would have been about 19 years old. William Felix Alexander (1832 - 1907) was Adam Alexander's fifth child and first son. In total, Adam had ten children, all of whom outlived him. Felix, a widower, served as a major in the Confederate Army. In 1863, he served on the staff of General Alexander R. Lawton (his former brother-in-law and Bulloch family friend), Quartermaster General for the Confederate Army.[162] Felix did marry before the War's end, but did not marry Lillie Dunwoody.

Lucy mentioned Julia Blanche Munroe Kell (1836-1917), the wife of Captain John McIntosh Kell, the C.S.S. *Alabama's* executive officer. The 1860 U.S. Census shows the Kell family living at The Navy Yard, Escambia, Florida, with two children, Nathan Munroe (1857-1863) and John McIntosh (1859-1881). At that time, Kell served in the U.S. Navy. Other records show an additional child born in 1860, Blanche McIntosh (1860-1863). The first and third child both died in 1863, as did so many Southern children during the War due to disease and malnutrition. Even among the previous plantation class, death became a much too common occurrence.

Chapter 13: October of 1863

Events of the War

  The Confederate defeat, at the Battle of Gettysburg, in early July, forced the Rebels back into the Southern states. On 19 September, Confederate General Braxton Bragg's Army of Tennessee defeated General William S. Rosecrans' Army of the Cumberland at Chickamauga, located on the border of Tennessee and Georgia. In mid-October, again disenchanted with his leaders, Lincoln appointed General Ulysses S. Grant as commander of all the western theater.

The Letters

  No September letters exist in the collection. It is not until 1 October that a short note indicated that the Bulloch women continued their humanitarian efforts. In this case, the package appeared to cross into the South destined for Lucy Elliott. The letter after it, written to Susan, may have contained this note.

Mr Jackson in reply to Mrs Roosevelts enquiries of this morning is glad to be able to say that he can forward the articles she names as his friend will take a box as part of his baggage, but he will require a list of the articles to save trouble at Custom house-- any time before friday next will answer

     New York October 1st 1863--
she (Mittie) got the note last evening -
       MB

New York Oct 2/nd 1863

My dearest Susy,
    I promised to write you a line as soon as I got here - We arrived yesterday safe & sound & all well - The children were delighted with the change, but towards evening Cony wanted to go home and go back into Grandma's room - that this was not gronding oom [Martha's version of Cony's babble] - I think Teedie looks badly, and his appetite is poor - The house & Mittie look well - every thing is so clean and nice and the food so plentiful and inviting - But we miss the sweet invigorating sea-breeze and the extensive piazza, and yard for the children - The cats were kept in a basket by Mrs Tabor who on the next visit said they were quite at home so happy - Bamie gave Mrs T a half dollar in advance for their board - I must not forget to tell you that the day you left Long Branch Frank got so drunk that he had to go to bed - that day we came very near not getting any dinner - in the evening Frank made his appearance, and said he had been suffering all day with <u>violent cramps</u>. There was great economy practiced in food the last three or four days we remained at Long branch.

Susy darling since I returned to New York, I find we have an opportunity to send letters and a bundle to Lucy by the way of …… - Mittie wrote Mr Jackson to know when the bundle must be ready - his note which I enclose answers - he must have the bundle between this and next friday - we think he must mean this day (friday) week - I shall send either Mitties or Annas, cloak - whichever looks best - Mittie will send a nice new delane[163] dress, which she wore only a few times last summer—We will give Mr Jackson a list of the articles as he requests. While I think of it dear Suzy do let me know if you have Irvine's likeness - I think perhaps I may have given it to you when I gave you the childrens - If you have it not some body has taken out of my drawer at Long Branch. Please darling let me know.
    Mittie is going to send all of Ellie's little stockings to Mattie She is going to put long stockings on <u>her</u> two

little boys - I do not know yet what I will send—but I know nothing will be amiss - I enclose you a letter which I received from Lucy after you left L.B. —You will see then that dear Henry Dunwody is no more—killed at the battle of Gettysburg - Oh how sad! I am quite well darling and will be very busy getting Lucy's bundle ready -
   Kind regards to Mr & Mrs West and love to Hill -
       Your loving mother
       M Bulloch
Excuse blots & blunders

Mittie has just been up in my room. she thinks in addition to the dress and cloak which she sends that we had better send a new bombazine dividing the expense between us - The dress will cost about $13 - (thirteen dollars) what do you think of this plan - it will cost each of us. (Mittie yourself and myself) about four dollars and a half -
       MB

The following letter and note were dated 5 October, but with no year denoted. However, they belong in 1863 as each refers both to the list of items for Lucy and the death of Major Henry Dunwoody.

     New York Oct 5th
My dearest Susie,
 Mittie has just received your letter and we were glad darling to hear from you - Before I write another word I must say that your breast pin my dear daughter was not left in the drawer - Oh how sorry I am that it is lost - I am sorry too that I did not write you about it in my last letter - I shall write Lucy tomorrow -- we will send the bundle to Mr Jackson on wednesday - Mittie has sent her a dress & cloak a pair of congress boots of Jeffers make which were only worn I believe once - They were too small for her - she has also sent her a little marino jacket of Teedie, (made up) &

273

Susys and some soap - I send her also 2 cakes of soap and about 2.50^{cts} worth of spools of cotton black white and slate colored - six papers of nice needles one box of black pins & one paper of white skirt braid bombazine buttons etc etc - I send her also the linen I showed you at Long Branch & a nice crape veil - (Mittie also a veil) tomorrow I am going to Arnolds to get a little plaid woolen dress for each of the children - Mittie & I have been talking about the bombazine dress - we think it is best to send it, as it will be the only entirely new thing we send Lucy - The sacks you mention would be very nice, but they would take up more room than the dress - I wish darling you were here to help us make up the bundle you do it so nicely - and I know you take so much interest in it - Anna will send something also if the bundle is not too large - I send Johnny a little whip and some marbles Mattie a small doll - Bamie sends the children some toys also. The warm weather has made me feel a little weak - but this delightful change I think will do us all good - Little Cony has a cold but is better - Susy darling I have so many clothes that I think I will not have to get any thing for myself for a long time, so can afford to send Lucy these things - I thought I would get a new marino, but my old one is so nice that I think I will not want the new one for some time to come - Dearest Susy you can't think how I enjoy the quiet of home - Anna Mittie & Thee seem to have settled down into very quiet habits - I think Thee & Mittie have both resolved to have no sunday evening visitors except Mr Gracie, the family & Fred Elliott - Yesterday I went to church both morning and evening to Dr Adam's - (I mean afternoon) In the afternoon there was communion and it was very solemn & interesting - The subject of the morning sermon was Justification through faith in Christ - It was a most delightful sermon on this most comforting doctrine - I have paid up to Thee all of my summer expenses and had a little over $50 left - of this I gave $30 to Anna - Good bye my precious child - love to all -

Your affectionate Mother
M Bulloch

New York Oct 5
Your list will be a great help to us in making out ours - If you can hear any thing about poor dear Henry D do let us know--

MB--

Mittie purchased her boots at William H. Jeffers, who sold ladies' French shoes at 573 Broadway, New York. Congress boots rose to ankle height and had elastic gussets on each side to facilitate putting them on. Englishman Thomas Hancock (1786-1865) invented what we now know as elastic in 1820. It was first used on shoes, suspenders, stockings, and gloves. In 1863, retailers advertised Congress boots of kid leather and with cloth uppers. They came in black, brown, and white. William H. Jeffers ran text advertisements throughout the 1860s in both the *New York Times* and the *New York Tribune*.

New York Oct 12th 1863

My dearest Susy,
I received yours & Hills last letters on saturday - I intended writing you this morning, but was prevented this afternoon I must write if only a few lines - Hills letter I was delighted to get - of course the well-known hand I knew immediately - Tell him I thank him for the kind letter and of course I was highly pleased to find the Beaver Meadow Stock stood so high - Paying the Div quarterly suits me just as well - Mary your good sister has just been here - Mittie & Anna were out so I was the only one of the family who saw her - she looks very well, but complains of a pain in her knee - I told her I was just going to see her, but that today I was suffering with pain in my back - (lumbago) Not as severe an attack as I had last winter - She says she is going to Phil on saturday - Susy darling we have sent the package to Lucy - It would take a foolscap[164] sheet to tell you all the trouble we had with it - I hope the dear child may get it - At first I rolled it up as compactly as I possibly could, (I mean

the different small packages which composed the large one - then I made one package of all of them, sewed them up in coarse cloth and directed the bundle to Mrs Stuart Elliott care of Francis Sorrel Esq Savannah Georgia - Mittie then sent the package according to instructions to Mr Jacksons house by their coachman John - scarcely had John returned, when some good Fairy sent me a nice bottle of quinine - Mittie then posted John back for the bundle, and after a great deal of trouble we got in the quinine and sent it back to Mr Jacksons - I thought then surely my trouble is over with "<u>the bundle</u>" But no - no such good luck - in the evening Mr Jackson sent us a note saying he could not get it in the trunk - that by opening it and putting the small packages about he might get half of them in - Mittie immediately sent again for the package with a note to Mr J saying if all the things could not go we would like to select the articles of most value to send - Presently in came John with the bundle again - We felt despairing - but we set to work trying to get the most important and portable things in a small bundle to do this we had to open all of the small packages - We took the gloves, shoes & soap out of yours - the new bombazine dress with the lining trimmings etc all of the threads pins needles etc, soap, in all seven cakes - all of these things we made into one bundle - when we had gotten thus far, Mr Jackson came in himself and said all could go if we would make them into separate small packages - We then reconstructed all of the packages and directed them each to Lucy & to Mr. Sorrel's care - Late friday night we finished them all, and sent them again to Mr Jackson - That is the last of the bundle I do not think I shall ever to send another - the cloak we determined not to send at all as it was so bulky - Everything else went except darling your pieces of crape which when we took out the gloves we must have miss placed - I thought as you would not again require crape I would keep it - I will send you the list of things sent - I wrote Lucy a long letter, Marion [Jane Marion Dunwoody] a letter and Anna and Mittie wrote Marion & Mittie wrote

Lucy - Your two letters with all of these others we sent in one of the packages -

We got Lucy a very nice English bombazine - your proportion of the expense dearest is five dollars twenty five cents - I am going to write Lucy also by Flag of truce but shall only mention then we have sent to her by way Nassau a package of letters - I send you a list of things sent - except, - like Mr Lairds bill of fare some things stratched out - On the blank side of the list is the direction by Flag of truce - Love to all dear Sudie

Your affectionate Mother
M Bulloch

Do tear up all of this miserably written trash darling - I wrote it because I know how much interested you are -

MB

List of Articles in package

Three papers pins
one small box of black pins
Six papers needles 10 spools cotton
Six skeins black sewing silk
One piece of black shirt braid
One doz buttons
2 skeins darning cotton
two pairs of boots
two dresses made up
~~one cloak made~~
a small package of toys
One spelling book
A black bombazine dress not made
two crape veils made
One yd linen
2 ½ yds black cambric muslin
Two pair of leggins
two pairs small silk gloves &
Seven Cakes of soap

One pair ladies silk gloves
A few sheets of paper & envelopes
Black cashmere shawl & Talmen
One Yd of slate col (—) muslin ?
~~2 yds cotton flannel~~
1 bottle Quinine &
Bamie sent to the children package of small stockings

Mr. Jackson regrets that he cannot take all the articles in the list but can send about one half of them if she returns the whole & marks the articles she particularly desires to send he will send them on along if possible.

Directions by Flag of Truce
General Foster,
Commanding General
Department of Virginia & North Carolina
Fortress Monroe

A letter just from Norval Caskie says that Capn King of Roswell was killed at the battle of Chickamauga - we do not know whether this is Tom, or Joe, or Cliff - Miss [Susan] Winston thinks it is Cliff -

John Norvell Caskie (1844-1900) served as a private in Company D, 3rd Virginia Regiment, Confederate Army. His information about a Captain King of Roswell being killed at Chickamauga proved correct. Miss Winston's guess as to which King brother was entirely wrong. Clifford King served in Savannah at this time. Joe King and Tom King, both wounded at First Manassas (Bull Run) had been convalescing at home since that battle. (See Appendix A). However, Tom King, anxious to do his duty, had returned to action just before Chickamauga. Tom's death came on the day of his return to service.[165]

On 14 September 1863, Tom hopped a train north, determined to rejoin the War in any capacity, although he still hobbled with a cane. Arriving on the morning of 19 September, Tom joined the staff of Brigadier General Preston Smith at Chickamauga as an aide-de-camp. That night, General Smith and several aides accidently crossed enemy lines and were fired upon by members of the 77th Pennsylvania. General Smith and Captains Tom King and John Donelson died during the ambush.[166]

New York Oct 20eth 63

My dearest Susie,

I was waiting to hear of Thee's success in his enquiries about the breast pin before I wrote you. He told me last evening he had been entirely unsuccessful in all of his endeavors to find it. I am so sorry darling Susie for I knew how much you valued it from association - While I think of it too, I must tell you the Expsenage of the bundle you sent was fifty cents - This is all of business of which I have to write - The family are well, the children never tiring of play - Corinne of course becoming more and more of a tom-boy - Mittie now quite busy with her fall shopping - There is also on the tapis a ball to be given to the Russians. As this is a political affair, Thee is very anxious for Mittie to attend. She is therefore now engaged in ordering the dress for the occasion. Anna is unwilling to go for many reasons, but perhaps as Mittie is very anxious to have her go she may yet consent to do so - If she does her dress will be a plain tarlton etc - I am glad darling that you have had a visit from Mary - I know it will cheer you - How are you dear daughter - I fear this continued warm weather has made you weak - I wrote Lucy by Flag of Truce a few days since. I told her of our having written to her by way of Nassau, and of our having sent a package by the same opportunity - I told her also that you had written her very often - I hope she may get the letter - I am going to write Hariot today or tomorrow - I have not been very well since I returned to New York - All of last week I had a pain in my back, but I am quite well again - It is such a comfort to me that I can go to Church

without any trouble. Indeed dear Susie I feel that I have great cause for gratitude I have every thing that heart can wish in this world, with an humble hope that God will be with me even unto death - I know that if I do not forsake him, he will never forsake me - Love to all - with much love my dear child I am your
affectionate Mother
MB -

Mittie and Thee planned to attend the *Soirée Russe,* or the Russian Ball, which would take place on 5 November at New York's Academy of Music. This ball would honor Russian naval officers visiting the city.

The following note was found alone in the collection. The letter from Lucy was returned and later sent to Harriott.

Oct 25

My dearest Susy I received this letter from Lucy last evening - will you please send it back to me when you have read it as, I intend sending it on to Hariot - Perhaps it would be as well to read the most of Lucy's letter to yourself - Susy darling I am quite well this week - The rest of the family are well also.

I have just written a long letter to Hariot - so will say good bye for the present- your truly
affectionate mother
MB -

New York Oct 28th 1863

My dearest Susy,

Your letter of the 24th I received on monday morning, & I ought to have answered it immediately as it contained money ($5,75) - I went that morning with Mittie on one of her shopping expeditions, resolving to write you next day, but next day which was yesterday, (tuesday) I went to see Miss Netty McIntosh who had a few days previously fallen in comming out of Dr Adams' Church and broken her arm - It is a compound fracture, and dislocation of her wrist - She is quite an elderly lady, between seventy & eighty - I have been twice to see her & she appears to be doing well - to-day I resolved that I would let nothing prevent my writing - I have not received that letter you speak of at all dear Susy - I am very sorry, and cannot imagine what has become of it - perhaps you had better in future just throw your letters in the lamp post - I have always observed that those which are lost were put into the Sub-post Office - Lucy's letter was just in time to be enclosed to Hariot, but I am so provoked with myself for neglecting to copy that address to Baltimore through which I could write her - If you copied it dear Susy will you please send it to me in your next letter - I have not seen Mary since her return - This is Teedie's birth day and Mittie invited little Jimmie to meet some other little children here this afternoon to celebrate the anniversary - Mary wrote his acceptance at the same time sending me some maple sugar candy which you had asked her to purchase for me on her way back - Thank you darling how well you always remember my predilictions. Susy darling how good Mary is! I shall always feel grateful to her for her kindness to you - Indeed I have always remembered with gratitude how kindly she nursed Mittie when Bamie was born - She is just like Hill - It is really refreshing to see any one so unselfish - I did not enquire, but I believe dearest there was no expense incurred about your lost breast pin - I have heard of the arrival of our package to Lucy at Nassau, and that it was sent by some of the blockade runners, but did not hear the name of the vessel - If Lucy only gets this package she will be quite made up, will she not? We are quite well. I am well and strong again.

You wish to know how Mittie's plan about the children works. It appears to do very well - Little Cony seems very fond of Dora and having the care of Cony, keeps her from killing Teedie with her kind of kindness - Mittie has to be again in search of a cook, as the present incumbent thinks the work too hard for her; besides she has been seen not

herself, & as Mr Weir Roosevelt said about a drunken man he encountered "<u>not any other person either</u>."
I am anxious to hear what Mrs Parsons said about Hariot, I fear from what I have heard that little Dunwoody, Hariot's third child has the rickets

Love to all - Good bye for the present dearest Susy - affectionately yours etc
M Bulloch

Please dear Susy look through the two books I had of yours last summer "Prize Essays & Keith on the Prophecies." It is possible I may have put Irvine's likeness in one of them -
MB

Henry Dunwoody Bulloch, James and Harriott's son, may have suffered from rickets, a defective mineralization or calcification of bones due to deficiency or impaired metabolism of vitamin D. In children, it causes bowing of the legs. At this time, Henry was only 2 years old.

On 30 October, the *New York Times* printed the following:

THE RUSSIAN BALL
The Preparations on an Unprecedented Scale
The Academy of Music to be Made a Fairy Palace
THE BANQUETING IN IRVING HALL

The grand Russian Ball, the anticipated splendors of which agitate the dreams of all Japonicadom, is close at band, the date having been fixed for Friday, November 5. The banquets, junketing, speech-making and excursions that have preceded it ring through the length and breadth, not only of America, but even of Europe; and the Cossack sentry, far away on the borders of Caucasia, has by this time caught the rumor of the wonderful friendship displayed by the people of the West for his Supreme Hetman, the Czar. It is quite in place then, that there should be a special flutter here about the crowning festival, and we are happy in being able, this morning, to communicate some highly interesting particulars on the subject.

THE ACADEMY OF MUSIC is, as all know, to be the scene of the general display, There will be transacted all the promenading, grouping, bowing and scraping, flitting and dancing. The edifice itself will, of course, do its best. Retouching, repainting, dusting, and grubbing, greatly needed will brighten its general appearance. The whole interior will be thrown as far as possible into one vast space, the scenes removed and the parquet floored substantially throughout its entire extent. The decorations on the galleries and walls will not be so crowded and overdone as upon former like occasions, but selected with special taste and an eye to rich, but simple effect. LEWIS, the scenic artist of the establishment, is preparing some splendid and altogether novel combinations, and every ornamental appliance will be freshly original. Workmen are now engaged in repapering the lobbies in imitation of maple and satin-wood. These, as well as the other portions of the interior, are also to be furnished with new crimson carpets, which, in contrast with the statuary and marble vases ladened with blooming exotics that are to stud each "coigne of vantage," will alone compose a brilliant picture. The draperies of flags, the wreaths and garlands, the thickets of evergreens and rare flowers, the lighting up a *giorne* from innumerable jets and chandeliers, and the superb grouping of fair dames and gallant gentlemen, in their freshest and brightest gala dresses, will offer a spectacle surpassing all the preceding *fetes* that gave New-York renown. The interior will afford accommodation for 3,000 persons, including the floors, corridors, side-rooms, boxes and galleries, with space to move and breathe at ease, and care will be taken that all the frightful heat, crowding and destruction of dress and decorations that marred other festivals in the same place shall be avoided. Over the stage will be stretched a superb new white canopy with golden fringes, and beneath and beyond it will be arranged the most beautiful international devices. The building will be admirably and ingeniously ventilated; the atmosphere continually renewed, yet soft and summery, with perfumes rising from groves of oranges and citrons, and bowers of myrtle and jessamine, starred with all the choicest beauties of the lands of the sun, or of "any other lands." Cloak and dressing-rooms are to be so arranged that there need be none of the old confusion. Having thus in outline foreshadowed the arrangements of the grand dancing palace, now to

THE SUPPER ROOM. Turning to the entrances of the Academy on Irving place, the distinguished visitors will be conducted, at a given hour, through a covered passage across the way to Irving Hall, now under the control of Messrs. BENEDICT & HARRISON. The assemblage, after leaving the Academy, will be in charge of LAFAYETTE HARRISON, Esq., whose taste and liberality are widely known. In the present instance his reputation is to be most worthily sustained. The passage leading to Irving Hall is an ingenious work, to be put up and removed again within twenty-four hours. It will be 125 feet long, 17 feet high, and 26 feet wide, and lead from the vestibule of one building to that of the other. It will be solidly put together, and so inclosed that neither the November air nor prying outside curiosity can invade it. It will be elegantly carpeted, draped with hangings of blue, gold and white, the Russian colors, and decorated with, international devices, Russian and American emblems, escutcheons and shields. The passageway, which will take the whole width of the Hall, at its entrance, will be Illuminated with 12 large gas-chandeliers wreathed and entwined with evergreens and flowers. After crossing the street, the guests will be dazzled by a coup d'etat inferior only to the Academy scene itself. The entrance and lobbies of Irving Hall will be freshly decorated in green and black walnut, and the grand hall, the banqueting apartment, will be adorned and dressed in crimson, with white medallions of flower-wont. The room is 100 feet in length by 71 in width, and 37 1/2 in height: it will be finely illuminated, and with its canopies of flags, its vases and groups of exotics, its display of Muscovite and American banners and emblems, and the enticing array of the tables, the Hall will well nigh eclipse the Academy. DELMONICO will, for the first time, have here a fair and open field, and intends to make the occasion his battle of the Pyramids -- (no allusion to the creams and jellies,) -- his Austerlitz. At the Prince of Wales Supper he was pinched for room, and the whole affair was in a barn -- a barrack; but here the whole basement range of Irving rooms and kitchens will be at his disposal, and he can make an effort worthy of his "genius."

THE TABLES will be arranged on each side and to the rear of the hall, the guests occupying them from the centre; the army of waiters will be ranged in the passages next the walls, and thus separated from the company, although at the most convenient points to serve them. At the banqeuting board there will be accommodation for 800 persons at one time and from 11 P.M. onward the supper will be served. The wines, viands, confectionery, fruit, etc., and ornaments will surpass any catering attempted in this country. A fine band of 40 pieces will furnish the music in the supper-room. Two celebrated bands of 50 performers each will furnish music in the Academy. Take the whole festival together and it will surpass in all its features any that have hitherto delighted the great American Metropolis.

The morning of the ball, the *New York Times* printed the rules:

> 1. The doors of the Academy of Music on Irving-place will be opened for the admittance of company at 9 o'clock on the evening of the Ball.
> 2. The entrance to the Ball-room will be from the main lobby in centre, and the exits on either side by paths distinguished by vases of flowers.
> 3. The music will be under the direction of the Floor Committee, and will commence at 10 o'clock by signal from the Chairman, at which moment the gas will be turned on in force. The music will from thenceforth play continuously, following the card prepared by the Committee on Music and Dances.
> 4. The floor will be under the control of the Floor Committee whose duties will be to provide partners for the foreign guests, prevent the crowding of any one part of the Ball-room,

and aid dances in finding sets, and in obtaining space for waltzing.

5. No lady will be admitted on the Ball-Room floor wearing a bonnet, or gentleman carrying a cane or hat. Ladies and gentlemen are required to appear in full evening dress.

6. The House Committee will see the arrangements made by them in various parts of the house for the comfort of guests are properly carried out.

7. The Supper-room will be opened at $11^{1/2}$ o'clock. Supper will be served at all times thereafter during the night. Tea and coffee will be served in the north lobby from 10 o'clock during the continuation of the Ball.

8. On entering the covered way leading to the Supper-Room, by the north door of the Academy, on Irving-place, the way will be found divided in the centre by a cord. Parties are desired to keep the division cord to their left hand, in going and returning.

9. Carriages both in setting down and taking up company, will form in line of the north side of 14th-st., trailing up 4th-av., they will enter Irving-place singly, and, keeping the west side of the street, turn and deliver their company at the Academy, with their horses' heads toward 14th-st, and go out of 14th-st. by the 3d av.

10. Parties leaving the Ball will take the first carriage in line, and will be set down at any spot on 45th-st. for $2 fare.

11. Each ticket will be numbered, registered and countersigned by the Secretary, admitting one person only lady or gentleman.

By order of the Committee of Arrangements.[167]

Mittie and Thee planned to attend the ball. Despite the War's devastating effects throughout the country and especially in the South, many northern businessmen made money during the first half of the 1860s. The opulence of their lives contrasted drastically with those of families who had husbands and sons fighting, wounded, or killed and who often lived on more limited incomes.

Chapter 14: November & December of 1863

Events of the War

On 19 November, Lincoln delivered a two-minute speech, known now as the Gettysburg Address, at the dedication of the battlefield:

> Four score and seven years ago our fathers brought forth, upon this continent, a new nation, conceived in liberty, and dedicated to the proposition that all men are created equal.
>
> Now we are engaged in a great civil war, testing whether that nation, or any nation so conceived, and so dedicated, can long endure. We are met on a great battle field of that war. We come to dedicate a portion of it, as a final resting place for those who died here, that the nation might live. This we may, in all propriety do.
>
> But, in a larger sense, we can not dedicate we can not consecrate we can not hallow, this ground The brave men, living and dead, who struggled here, have hallowed it, far above our poor power to add or detract. The world will little note, nor long remember what we say here; while it can never forget what they did here.

It is rather for us, the living, we here be dedicated to the great task remaining before us that, from these honored dead we take increased devotion to that cause for which they here, gave the last full measure of devotion that we here highly resolve these dead shall not have died in vain; that the nation, shall have a new birth of freedom, and that government of the people, by the people, for the people, shall not perish from the earth.[168]

The War continued in the South when on 25 November, the Rebel's siege of Chattanooga ended with the defeat of General Bragg's army. Spurred on by their defeat at Chickamauga, Union soldiers charged up Missionary Ridge shouting "Chickamauga! Chickamauga!" They ended the day with "My god, come and see 'em run!" as Confederate forces retreated into north Georgia.

Winter came, and the War became quiet and still.

The Letters

New York Nov 9th 1863

My dearest Susy,
  Your last dear letter received on wednesday last was dated Nov 2nd - That day (wednesday) as soon as we received the letter Anna went to see Miss Lilly and found she had left for Phil^a. Tuesday evening we heard that the ladies were at Mary's & Mittie wrote a letter to Miss Lilly telling her all about the clock etc etc. I hope darling your dear Susans head took no cold from the washing etc - who ever heard before of washing hair pins! - Yours was an interesting letter - poor Lucy to think to what straits she she has been reduced - I am glad my precious little Johnnie now has shoes - I sincerely hope our bundle may reach her - we are all well - Mittie says she will send your bombazine dress tomorrow by Express - she says also that Dr Littinger will call on you in a day or two to tell you he has seen us

all & she hopes you will see him. Mr & Mrs Jenkins came here to attend the Russian ball - Mrs Blatchford goes to Phil[a] today & I believe is going to call on you - When I see you I will tell you all I have heard of this Russian ball - Thee was anxious for Mittie to go for political reasons, and Mittie would not go without Anna so they both went - Annas tarlton dress was almost torn off her person by the crowd - Anna is thoroughly disgusted with balls and I hope may remain- so - I did all I could to discourage their going, but people prefer learning by experience - I believe that such amusements are absolutely sinful - how I wish they could think so also - Life is too precious to be squandered away by such trifles - I can only pray that Anna & Mittie may yet be taught by the Spirit of God - Then they will know how to value time, money, health & a conscience voice of offence The little children seem well & happy - Teedie is very well indeed - Cony is as smart as ever - Bamie goes to school 3 hours every day - I think she has improved since she has practice from Flory and Anne Little - She is very much interested in her sunday school, and she is now busy helping me to work for a little Fair which Miss Henop is going to have for her church - I am assisting because the Clergyman was very kind in giving testaments and prayer books to the poor Confederate soldiers - at Davids Island - Susy darling before I write you again - I hope I shall have a letter for I fear you will scarcely be able to read this scrawl - I forgot to tell you about our little Ellie - he is doing very well - Bessie takes care of him - Dora, Teedie & Cony - Corinne is devotedly attached to Dora - (no accounting for taste) Ellie sleeps in the large crib by his mothers bed - Teedie & Cony in the nursery by Dora - Darling Susy how I wish I could see you this morning - love to all from your loving Mother
      M Bulloch

Like Martha, others decried the waste and opulence of the Russian Ball. Newspapers across the North printed articles about the evening, many with detailed descriptions of the ladies dresses and the number and wealth of diamonds worn during the evening.[169] Later in the month, *Harper's Weekly* printed two Winslow Homer engravings of the evening along with the following editorial:

> THE Ball is over, the music is hushed, the dances ended, the wine drunk, the costly laces and diamonds put back into their places. And now that the sounds of the revel are dying out it recurs to us that we have a headache, and we are saying wisely to each other that the ball was not, after all, so very sensible a thing; and that, when our brothers and our sons are dying on battle-fields, and thousands of brave Union soldiers, prisoners at Richmond, are being starved to death by the Southern chivalry, it is hardly decent for us here to be dancing, and making merry, and throwing away fortunes on diamonds. There is something in the idea. Should this number of Harper's Weekly fall into the hands of some poor wounded fellow at Chattanooga, or some half-starved Union prisoner at Richmond, the contrast between his own condition and that of the scented and perfumed dancers who figure in the ball picture may not improve his temper. "They are fiddling while I am dying," is the remark which would not unnaturally occur to him, and it would leave a bitter taste behind.
>
> "What then?" says Shoddy.[170] "Are we all to put on sackcloth and ashes for the war? Are Mrs. and the Misses Shoddy not to have an opportunity of displaying their beauty - to say nothing of the splendid dresses and the magnificent diamonds which I bought them with the proceeds of paper-money - simply because we are engaged in a war? The notion is monstrous! I pay for the war: taxes on my

income, taxes on my clothing, taxes on my house, horses, carriages, silver, and every thing that I've got; I send my blood relations to the war to fight and die; I give money for bounties and money to the Sanitary Commission; I vote to support the Government. Having done all this, I submit that my duty is fulfilled, and that I may, if I choose, get up balls for Mrs. and the Misses Shoddy, and that they may enjoy them as becomes their age, their means, and their spirits. Dancing and balls are not bad things by any means. It is good that young people should enjoy themselves while they can. They will all find sorrow enough in life by-and-by. Besides, our Russian Ball had a political significance, and may render good aid to the Union cause."

Thus much Shoddy. And though his reasoning is likely to seem very shallow and very selfish to the brave suffering men on Belle Isle or in Castle Thunder, it must fairly be admitted that, in past time, balls and battles have often jostled each other, and the dying sounds of the dance have often mingled with the blast of the bugle. "There was a sound of revelry by night" within a few hours of the battle of Waterloo, and the dance was never more popular in Europe than during the Napoleonic wars. The Preacher gives the key to the apparent paradox when he says, "Let us eat, drink, and be merry; for to-morrow we die."

And now - good Shoddy, fair Mrs. Shoddy, and sweet daughters of the Shoddy house - that you have had your dance, and flirted with your Cossack, and flashed your diamonds in a thousand envious eyes; now that you have spent - so they say - over a million of dollars for one night's enjoyment; have you time and do you care to think of a suggestion by which your pleasure and our suffering heroes' needs may both be satisfied?"

There was a time, not many years ago, when a commercial crisis precipitated the poor of New York into great suffering. At that time large-minded men and women gave their thoughts to the subject, and while soup-kitchens were established by A. T. Stewart and others, fashionable ladies gave a series of calico balls, the rule of which was that every lady present donated the dress she wore to the poor. By this means thousands of poor girls and women, who would otherwise have gone half clad that bitter winter, were furnished with clothing. What say you now, ladies, to a DIAMOND BALL, the jewels worn to be given after the ball to the Sanitary Commission, which has our wounded soldiers in charge?

If, as is stated, a million of dollars' worth of diamonds were worn at the Russian Ball, a million of dollars might be procured by such a Diamond Ball as we suggest - enough money to secure every comfort required by our wounded soldiers, and probably to save hundreds of lives which are now sacrificed for want of suitable attendance, clothing, and food. Could the jewels be put to a nobler use? Would not their radiance, in such a case, flash not only from wall to wall of the ball-room, but down through the vale of time to the most distant age, lighting the fame of New York women, and proving that they were worthy wives and daughters of the brave men who are dying for their country?[171]

Winslow Homer engraving of the Russian Ball
Harper's Weekly Magazine, 5 November 1863

Winslow Homer engraving of "Dancing at the Russian Ball"
Harper's Weekly Magazine, 5 November 1863

Martha wrote of Davids' Island, located off New Rochelle, New York. DeCamp General Hospital on the island had become the Army's largest, and by late 1862, housed more than 2,100 Union soldiers. Following the Battle of Gettysburg, the War Department opened the hospital to care for hundreds of wounded Confederate soldiers. Soon Davids' Island held more than 2,500 Confederate prisoners. As they recovered, these Confederate soldiers were moved to various prisoner of war camps.

Nov 21st (saturday)

My dearest Susy,

    I received your sweet welcome letter of Nov 13 a week since, and ought to have written you directly afterwards, but I was so busy with working for a fair & so much taken up with the children, that I put it off from day to day until today. The Fair I was working for is to assist a small struggling Episcopal Church - You know I never was a sectarian, but love all christians - But in this instance I must confess another feeling beside a desire to assist the Church impelled me - I felt that I owed the Clergyman a debt of gratitude for his christian kindness to the Confederate prisoners at David's Island last summer - He visited & comforted the sick and dying and out of his own slender means gave them prayer books and testaments - God will reward all such, but I felt a desire to give him my mite also - Mittie and Anna gave me pieces of silk white crape etc. etc, so I sat to work and made (at moderate charges) about $20 worth of articles. Now I have undertaken to do some work for another Fair, the proceeds of which are to be appropriated to the "Home for old & indigent females" This work however shall not prevent my sometimes writing to my beloved Susy - I consider this employment a blessing to me in as much as it keeps me from reading the news papers - We are all well at present but since I wrote last Mittie has been very unwell About a week since she had one of her palpitations of the heart - I think it lasted over an hour - I applied mustard over the region of the heart and put her feet into a warm bath with mustard in it--Thee then sent for Dr Metcalfe and in case he was out, for Dr Markoe - Dr Markoe came and said what had been done was right except that the mustard plaister was just too low and had it put six or eight inches higher - This all took place a little after our late dinner time. As soon as the attack was over the D^r said she must go directly to bed - she did so and remained all the next day in bed - Dr Metcalfe came the next day, examined her heart thoroughly and said there was nothing in the world the matter <u>with</u> her heart - that the palpitation was owing to poverty of blood. He is now giving her Cod liver oil with iron and whiskey in it - she is much better now - Mittie has just received your letter - She sends you darling the following message - The little collar and sleeves were sent to dear Susy from Mittie intentionally - she got the collar etc from Larmande who sells them for half mourning Deider has the same kind which she also sells for half mourning - Mittie was sick when the box was packed, & she forgot to write on the collar and sleeves - The collar is the right fit, and Susy must adapt the under handkerchief to it - Mittie says if you wish to augment your "giving away fund" still more she will purchase from you, your nice pair of blankets - (that is if you wish to dispose of them) let her know whether you do wish to dispose of the blankets, when you write me again - I am glad to hear how nicely you spend your evenings - I knew you and Hill would like the book "Praying & working" - What astonished me when reading that book was the wonderful results of faithful prayer and untiring efforts - I am glad you have seen Mrs Blatchford I forgot to tell you that little Cony has been very unwell - She was feverish several days, but is better now We will let you know about the christmas presents in good time - I am sorry darling I did not write you about the detention of the box - There was some forget-fulness on the part of some body (I rather think Thee) which kept the box in the house several days after it was nailed up - Anna & Mittie send you much love. By and I will begin to work next week for the old women's fair - Bamie is busy today getting little flat pincushions cut out - the kind called bachelors pincushions - I think it does some good to keep Bamie employed - Not a word from Lucy lately - I fear she has not received our last package - Love to dear Hill & Mrs West - Good bye darling Susy

     Your loving mother - M Bulloch

  It appears the Bulloch women wore mourning for cousin Henry Dunwoody and son and brother Stuart Elliott.

The Ladies Book of Etiquette, Fashion and Manual of Politeness published in 1860 said:

> There is such a variety of opinion upon the subject of mourning, that it is extremely difficult to lay down any general rules upon the subject. Some wear very close black for a long period, for a distant relative; whilst others will wear dressy mourning for a short time in a case of death in the immediate family. There is no rule either for the depth of mourning, or the time when it may be laid aside, and I must confine my remarks to the different degrees of mourning.
> For deep mourning, the dress should be of bombazine, Parramatta cloth, delaine, barege, or merino, made up over black lining. The only appropriate trimming is a deep fold, either of the same material or of crape. The shawl or cloak must be of plain black, without border or trimming, unless the fold of crape be put on the cloak; the bonnet should be of crape, made perfectly plain, with crape facings, unless the widow's cap be worn, and a deep crape veil should be thrown over both face and bonnet. Black crape collar and sleeves, and black boots and gloves. The next degree is to wear white collar and sleeves, a bow of crape upon the bonnet, and plain white lace facings, leaving off the crape veil, and substituting one of plain black net. A little later, black silk without any gloss, trimmed with crape, may be worn, and delaine or bombazine, with a trimming of broad plain ribbon, or a bias fold of silk. The next stage admits a silk bonnet trimmed with crape, and lead color, dark purple, or white figures on the dress. From this the mourning passes into second mourning. Here a straw

bonnet, trimmed with black ribbon or crape flowers, or a silk bonnet with black flowers on the outside, and white ones in the face, a black silk dress, and gray shawl or cloak, may be worn. Lead color, purple, lavender, and white, are all admissible in second mourning, and the dress may be lightened gradually, a white bonnet, shawl, and light purple or lavender dress, being the dress usually worn last, before the mourning is thrown aside entirely, and colors resumed. It is especially to be recommended to buy always the best materials when making up mourning. Crape and woolen goods of the finest quality are very expensive, but a cheaper article will wear miserably; there is no greater error in economy than purchasing cheap mourning, for no goods are so inferior, or wear out and grow rusty so soon.[172]

Society expected widows to wear full mourning for two years, while a widower wore a black armband or black flower for only six months. Children mourned parents and parents mourned children for only one year. Siblings and grandparents were generally mourned for only six months, with all other relatives being mourned for considerably shorter periods of time. However the lengths were not universally accepted or maintained.

Martha sent the book *Praying and working; being some account of what men can do when in earnest* by the Rev. William Fleming Stevenson (1832-1886) of Dublin. Stevenson first published the work in 1862. An Irishman, Stevenson studied theology in Belfast, Edinburgh, and Germany, before returning to Ireland in 1860, where he was ordained as a Presbyterian minister in Dublin.[173]

New York Dec 3rd 1863

My own dearest Susie,

I was just going to write you when your dear interesting letter was handed me - I had just finished reading the 116 Ps - my work was on the bed in full sight, and I felt anxious to get at it, but had determined not to do any thing until I wrote my precious daughter. Darling your letter is truly interesting - My heart is sorrowful and aches when I think of the sufferings of the poor prisoners, and now when I hear that there are Pratt's Bulloch's & Lewis' among them I am still more interested - The Bullochs mentioned we think is Wm James, the Pratt either Charlie or Nat - Miss Henop is preparing boxes for Point Lookout now and I will send your message to our friends and let them know how much you are interested about them, and wish & hope to aid them
I feel with you darling Susy that what I can do is but a drop in the ocean, but, as you say when we have done what we can we must leave the rest to God - I will let Mrs Emmit know about Mr Duncan - How thoughtful you were dear Susy to enquire about those names - Now about the Christmas presents - (I can hardly bear to think of them) Mittie says get darling just what you think proper - I think it is best to get for Ellie just what you get for Teedie I think a dray-horse will suit him better than a doll - besides if a doll has to be dressed for the little silly thing I had better do that as my hand is accustomed to that kind of work - (I have just dressed five dolls for the Fair -) For Bamie & Cony any thing except dolls - I think Bamie likes Games - Oh how I dislike to think of the vast sums which will be spent for toys, when there will be such a necessity for money for the suffering - the children are all well dear little affectionate aunty - and as to our dear little fatherless ones - if they enjoy good health, they will be just as happy without play-things as with them - I can remember when a corn - stalk horse gave me as much pleasure as beautiful toys appear to give city children - Our prayers for them I trust will in much mercy be answered - I hope the precious little darlings may grow up good soldiers of Jesus Christ, for I think there will be much

need of such in those trying latter days of the Church - I will write Lucy before long - This day the Misses Hyatt are expected if they bring letters from Harriot & James I will let you know - Mittie is very much better - The Cod liver oil and iron has benefited her - she has taken one bottle of the oil, and is taking the second - Thee's throat is better also - The cold weather has made me quite strong - no symptoms whatever of chill. Susy darling I want to send five dollars to Mrs Boynton - in this letter - but I fear the letter may be lost - Mittie speaks a little of going to Phil^a after Christmas & I could send it by her or perhaps I had better - give all Shares to spare to Miss Henop - I will consult Miss Henop today - How kind in Mrs West to give those shirts - ! Please give my most affectionate regards to her - love to Hill & kind regards to Mrs Boynton & Miss Session -

Your loving Mother
M Bulloch

Anna Mittie & Bamie send much love - If you hear any thing more about our prisoners do let us know - your information about dear Henry is just what we wished to get, as Capt Rufus King told Anna if she could ascertain the Reg, he could find out where he was buried.

MB -

Mittie sends much love and says she is very contented about the blankets, as she thinks Stewart has at this time very nice ones,

MB

Martha read Psalms 116:

1. I love the Lord, because he hath heard my voice and my supplications.
2. Because he hath inclined his ear unto me, therefore will I call upon him as long as I live.
3. The sorrows of death compassed me, and the pains of hell gat hold upon me: I found trouble and sorrow.

4. Then called I upon the name of the
>   Lord; O Lord, I beseech thee,
>   deliver my soul.

5. Gracious is the Lord, and righteous; yea, our God is merciful.

6. The Lord preserveth the simple: I was brought low, and he helped me.

7. Return unto thy rest, O my soul; for the Lord hath dealt bountifully with thee.

8. For thou hast delivered my soul from death, mine eyes from tears, and my feet from falling.

9. I will walk before the Lord in the land of the living.

10. I believed, therefore have I spoken: I was greatly afflicted:

11. I said in my haste, All men are liars.

12. What shall I render unto the Lord for all his benefits toward me?

13. I will take the cup of salvation, and call upon the name of the Lord.

14. I will pay my vows unto the Lord now in the presence of all his people.

15. Precious in the sight of the Lord is the death of his saints.

16. O Lord, truly I am thy servant; I am thy servant, and the son of thine handmaid: thou hast loosed my bonds.

17. I will offer to thee the sacrifice of thanksgiving, and will call upon the name of the Lord.

18. I will pay my vows unto the Lord now in the presence of all his people.

19. In the courts of the Lord's house, in the midst of thee, O Jerusalem. Praise ye the Lord.[174]

Martha mentioned Point Lookout's prisoner of war camp on the Maryland peninsula's southern tip. Point

Lookout was the largest and worst of the northern camps. Fourteen foot high wooden walls surrounded about 40 acres where the prisoners lived all year in the tents in the open air. On top of the wall, Negro guards patrolled on a walkway day and night. Many prisoners reported brutal treatment by these guards. The Confederate soldiers were given sleeping tents until overcrowding became so bad there were not even enough tents to go around. While capacity was listed at 10,000, Point Lookout held at any given time during the War from 12,000 to 20,000 prisoners. Of the 50,000 men held at the camp between 1863 and 1865, it is believed nearly 4,000 died.

Martha's correspondence indicated her concerns that Charles and/or Nathaniel Pratt, William James Bulloch, and a Lewis boy were held at Point Lookout in late 1863. She was correct about Charles Pratt (see Appendix A); however, Nathaniel never saw active duty. William James Bulloch (1825-1865) was the son of William Bellinger and Mary Bulloch. William Bellinger Bulloch (1776-1852) was Martha's late husband's youngest uncle. No record has been found of William James Bulloch serving in the Confederate Army. There were many other Bulloch's serving in the Confederate Army, some of whom were distantly related to Martha and her daughters.

Robert Adams Lewis (1813-1906) and his family lived in Holly Hill, located near the Bulloch's Roswell home, until they relocated to New York's Staten Island in 1854. They remained in the north throughout the War. Their oldest son, Robert Adams Lewis II, served in the Union Army, and their second son was too young to serve.

However, Robert's brother John, who lived in Savannah, Georgia, had three sons who served in the Confederate Army; John Adams (b.1835), Robert H. (b.1837), and George C. (b. 1844). Records indicate his sons all joined Olmstead's 1st Georgia Regiment. Robert was captured at Fort Pulaski and spent time at Castle William and Fort Delaware. He was released in 1862, according to his request for a pension. His release came a year or so before this letter from Martha.

Captain Rufus King (1838-1900) served in the 4th U.S. Artillery and fought at Gettysburg. He won the Medal of Honor for bravery at White Oak Swamp Bridge, Virginia, on June 30, 1862. How the family knew Captain King is unknown; however, he was a New Yorker by birth and related to the Gracie family on his father's side.

The Mr. Duncan mentioned by Martha was the brother of Catherine Emmet, wife of Dr. Thomas Addis Emmet, one of the family's physicians. Catherine was from Montgomery, Alabama. Her brother has not been further identified.

New York Dec 4th 1863

I wrote you yesterday my dearest Susy acknowledging the receipt of your letter - In the afternoon I went to see Miss Hinop and found out how I could write to the Point Lookout prisoners - I also obtained fifty dollars from Miss Henop, which with five added making $55 I gave Thee this morning to have checked for me, as I was afraid to send such a sum in a letter - He promised to do it <u>this morning</u>, but you know how forgetful he is - let me know dear Susy when you receive it - It is for the Fort Delaware Prisoners - Please darling when you have made your purchases send me a list of them with your signature I mean the purchases you make with the fifty dollars - never mind the five - This money is part of an English fund which is sent to Miss Hinop from a Club of English gentlemen expressly for the Confederate prisoners - She is very liberally supplied by these gentlemen & is very particular by in remembering her account to them - She, Miss Hinop has lately sent to the Point Lookout prisoners, I think she said seven or eight hundred dollars worth of clothing - I obtained also from Miss Henop the Address to the Point Lookout Prisoners and will write to Mr Bulloch today or tomorrow - This letter to Mr. Bulloch must be enclosed to

     Major Patterson
     Commanding
     Point Lookout

St Mary's County
Maryland

a line inside of this envelope requesting Maj Patterson to hand the enclosed note to Mr Bulloch or Pratt or any other, if respectfully or politely made is always attended to - Mrs Emmet has already sent a box of Clothing to Mr Duncan which he has received - We are all well darling - Susy dear if I can get up a box of Clothing for the Delaware prisoners to whom must I direct it - Miss Henop who is good authority tells me that she never makes any difference about the color of the clothing - she says they talk a great deal about color, but really do not care however if my friends will make me up a box, I will try to have grey and blue excluded -

Your affectionate Mother
M Bulloch

Dec 4 -
I wrote you yesterday my dearest Susy - I enclose you this morning $55 (fifty five) dollars which Thee is to check for me as soon as he goes to the store - Keep an account darling of the fifty dollars - You need not mind about the five - This sum is sent for the Fort. Delaware Prisoners -

Your affec Mother
M Bulloch

not Point Lookout

New York Dec 7th 1863

My dearest Susy,
    I have just seen your last dear letter of the 5th, I was out when it first arrived. I am truly glad darling that I could send you the $55 - Now I must tell you what I have been doing since - I went round to nearly all of my southern friends, and have stated to them the situation of the Fort Del prisoners - I have now in hand $22 with the promise of about $40 more - I could send you tomorrow this $22 but think I had better wait a while as I am sure I shall have a

great deal more to send

So much for Fort Del - Now I must tell you about Point Lookout - I, or rather I got Anna to write to Mr Bulloch to request him to let us know about Messers Pratt Lewis & himself. She wrote on saturday & we await an answer - In the mean time I am collecting articles for a box which we will send them - Now too my friends are most liberal Miss Cress sent me a large bundle of very nice warm clothing which her young gentlemen friends have given her - Mrs Noys sent me some nice woolen socks. Mrs Price has promised me a new suit of very nice woolen clothes and a number of acquiskutum {acquisitions?}(I don't know how to spell it) shirts - Mrs Blatchford that dear good little soul - is the only northern lady I have spoken to. She is to send a bundle of articles over - among other things eight nice new shirts which were made for Mr Blatchford but are too small - You know M^r B is a very large man - She also gave me, with tears in her eyes $10, - ten dollars - Now let me tell you what Miss Mcintosh the authoress is going to do - She is going to give a reading! - She is a great favorite and no doubt the rooms will be crowded - She is a beautiful reader and has done the like for charitable purposes before - Mrs Patterson (Virginian)[175] who lives in 21 St. & who lives in an elegant house lets us have her two front rooms - they open by a folding door into each other like Mitties but being a corner house are lighted by side windows - The rooms are much larger than Mitties - Miss Lucy Winston (Susan's sister) called also to tell me that if I find out that Mr Pratt is our old Ministers son she will send some things in the box also - when I hear from the young man dear Susy I will let you know - but do not send money in a letter - I shall be sending money on to you, and can keep back your contribution and let you pay the same amount for the Fort Del prisoners - my five dollars - keep for the Fort Del prisoners You see darling the wheels are set to work, but it may be over a week before I know the full results - I will let you know as soon as I can - Now about the hoops - The Hyatts have just returned from Paris and London and say that hoops are worn as large as ever - Madame Deider also, who is the "Glass of Fashion" in N York and who has also just returned from Paris, says hoops are as large as ever - Then on the other hand a great many ladies in New York wear them much smaller - Lissie Emlyn [Lizzie Emlin Roosevelt] wears no hoops at all, only crinoline - Mittie says "tails" are worn long, and tails are worn short - She will write you to night if she possibly can. She has not been very well had a slight palpitation last evening - The children are quite well - Little Cony is too smart for any thing - Teedie promised Bamie yesterday afternoon (sunday) to be good - at dinner he said "I have made Bamie a rash promise, but I will try to keep it" Ellie is sweet and good as ever - He is a lovely child - Teedie said today at lunch well our Santiclaus in Phil^a is aunt Susy - I said yes Teedie aunt Susy loves you all very much - Elliott said in his little people voice - she loves me -

Do not get Elliott a doll I am going to dress one for him I shall get them very simple things - money is too much wanted for the needy to be squandered - I may say, as you did, and from the same cause, "I {but} money"

A lady has just been to see me dear Susy, who says Mrs Mayo of Elizabeth (a connexion of the Gracie's) has just received a letter from - her niece. This lady Mrs Mayo's niece has just returned from Point Lookout & says that the prisoners there are in a wretched condition - They are on quarter rations and some of them almost literally naked she says she is almost sorry she went there as it was not decent to see them - It was Mrs Henop who has been here to see me I asked her whether I understood Miss Henop to say that she had sent to Point Lookout six or seven hundred dollars worth of clothing to those prisoners - that I had written you to that effect - Mrs Henop did not know but I will go in the morning & see about the matter - It is possible Mrs Egerton in Baltimore Miss Henops friend had not sent them when Mrs Mayos niece visited Point Lookout - I think Mrs Boynton if she has a box ready had better send it at once to Point Lookout -

Dearest Susy you will be surprised to see our dear Mittie, but she will tell you why and all about us all - I send you a small paper of ginger, and a great deal of love -
>Your affec Mother
>M Bulloch
>Good bye darling
>Your affec Mother
>MB -

>New York Dec 9th

Dearest Susy -
Inclosed is a check for 56 dollars - Please clearly acknowledge the receipt of the same All well - with much love your affec mother
>M Bulloch

Dear Hill
I have added twenty four dolls of myown to Mrs Bullochs with the request that it shall only be used to prevent positive suffering.

While our men are under their present course of treatment, theirs do not deserve any luxuries.
>With love to Susan I remain Yours
>Theodore Roosevelt

Dec 9th 63
Dr Hilborne West.

>New York Dec 15 / 63

My dearest Susy,
Your last dear letter I have not yet acknowledged as Anna wrote you when she sent the patterns - I cannot describe to you how disappointed I am in not being able to send the boxes - I greatly fear the poor naked fellows will perish with cold - I had been very successful in collecting funds, and have now locked up in my dressing case $230 - two hundred & thirty dollars - beside if I could get permission to send them I have been told where I could get a barrel of shoes, or

perhaps more - I will keep the money, perhaps the order may be countermanded - Oh is it not trying - I intended this $230 to be spent entirely for the Point Lookout prisoners. I meant one box to be sent exclusively to the three young men Pratt Lewis & Bulloch I wrote to the commander & enclosed a letter to Mr Bulloch. I have received no answer - Dear Susy I yesterday received a letter from dear Irvine written from Cape Town - the 23 of Sept - He says he is quite well - and sends his "devoted love to dear little Annie Mittie & Teedie tell them I often think of them, and am very anxious to see them all" - He sends his love also to Lucy and dear brother Stuart, so he had not heard of his death 13 months after it took place - I would enclose the letter but fear it may be lost - I will show it to you when we meet - I am glad you wrote dear Lucy - what a dear affection-ate child Lucy is - I am thankful to hear our little darlings are well - I will write her by Flag of Truce after christmas - I thought it was best to wait awhile as you had written - I greatly fear she has not received our package, and never will - Mittie is not well. I feel quite concerned about her - She does not have much palpitations but at times has much pain about the region of the heart - The D^r thinks it neuralgic - She is still taking the Cod liver oil and iron - She has not been regular (ciss) indeed has had none for four months past - I have dressed Elliott's doll and am now busy with Cona's - Elliott's is very complete. I wish you could see it - the clothes are all made to take off easily -

  Irvine is a sweet affectionate little darling child how I long to see him - He entreats me to be happy and take care of my self for his life almost depends on seeing me well once more - also he says my dear sisters & brothers - I know darling Susy you pray for him - Oh Susy what would we do in this dark world, if it were not for a Throne of Grace - I feel very uneasy about Mittie darling - if she was only a christian, I think I could feel more satisfied - Susy dearest this world is a great enemy to grace - I am quite well - tomorrow the Fair I have been work for comes off - I will write you about it - Good bye my own blessed daughter

- Love to all of your house hold - I suppose Hill does not require his gold-headed cane quite yet <u>dear Hill</u> - give the "brown bead" much a great deal of love from me - Love to Mrs. Boynton & Miss Session - Keep whatever money you may have in hand perhaps you may be permitted again to use it -

Your affectionate Mother
M Bulloch

MB   If you see Mrs. Boardman ask her all about Ella's symptoms when her heart was affected.

    Irvine Bulloch first set sail on the C.S.S. *Alabama* in August of 1862. For over a year, the *Alabama* stayed at sea with one mission, to wreak havoc on Union shipping vessels. During August and September, the *Alabama* sailed the shipping lanes southwest and then east of the Azores, where she captured and burned ten prizes, mostly whalers. In October and November, New England's shipping lanes provided her prey. Ranging as far south as Bermuda, Captain Semmes and crew burned ten prizes while capturing and releasing three others. In December and into January of 1863, the *Alabama* resupplied by rendezvous with the C.S.S. *Agrippina* before sailing for the Gulf of Mexico and sinking the Union side-wheeler U.S.S. *Hatteras*.

    From February until July, the *Alabama* sailed the south Atlantic, mostly off the coast of Brazil. Here she captured 29 prizes before sailing for South Africa's coast. At Cape Town, while receiving supplies and being refitted, Irvine posted his letter to Martha in early August. Following this stop, the *Alabama* worked in tandem with the C.S.S. *Tuscaloosa* during August and September. The *Tuscaloosa* was a bark captured by the *Alabama* off the coast of Brazil before being renamed and refitted as a privateer.

    The C.S.S. *Alabama* next sailed to the Indian Ocean in September and stayed there until November of 1863. She took three prizes before returning to the South Pacific in

December. However, Martha probably knew little about this latest journey.

Throughout the year, the C.S.S. *Alabama* appeared often in the newspapers. Rumors of her capture, tales of her prizes, and reports of her whereabouts could frequently be found.[176]

New York, Dec 30eth 1863

My very dear Susy,

My last letter to you was written so long ago that I really do not remember when it was - It seems to me that I have been never more constantly occupied than I have been this winter. Even now, although I have but little to do with the active operation the coming New Year confuses me - I think it ought to be a calm time - a time for reflection - a time for great thankfulness and good resolutions - But alas shines too much gaiety for any of these things - There is so "much <u>to do</u>" as to learn but little time to think - Mittie & Thee give a large party New Years evening - All <u>day</u> they will receive visitors - Just imagine how tiresome it will be - It is well that Mittie seems a little better than she was a short time since or she would break down - The children were delighted with Christmas - Mittie spread the table as usual with toys the evening before - then to keep the children from being too anxious in the morning to be admitted into the Library she had each of their stockings filled with the smaller toys candy, & etc. Teddie woke up at three o'clock in the morning, and in a very short time afterwards Bamie Ellie and Cony were also wide awake - The stockings were in Mittie's room so of course as soon as they could get any warm covering on, they all went tearing in there - As soon as the stockings were emptied and the contents examined by the dear little eager things - they were taken back in the nursery bearing their treasures with them - By the time they were all washed and dressed breakfast was ready - (I think as the Library was closed there was no family prayers that morning) It was very hard work for them to eat their breakfast - then, after hands

were washed the library door was opened. In they all rushed, so happy that they were bewildered. I have never seen such an exemplification of the "embarrassment of riches" - They played all day in the library - in the evening (five o'clock) they went to their Grandpas, to dinner - Anna, Mittie and Thee went also I remained at home. About nine o clock the three were brought home worn out and sleeping - They were soon put to bed when they forgot all of the days excitement in a sound sleep - In the meantime while they were at Grandpas the presents from Phil^a arrived - They did not see the beautiful present from the Phil^a Santaclaus, (aunt Susy) until the next morning - they were indeed very pretty dear good aunt Susy - The children were delighted with them - We were all struck with the pretty little gilt-letters on the drays and said of course that was Hill's handy work - Mittie says she will write you before long - And now darling I will tell you what I have done lately with regard to the soldiers - There is a gentleman here, Genl [Daniel] Butterfield who has for a number of years ^{been} in the Mexican service - This gentleman being in foreign service has received a permit to send a box of clothing to a relative of his wife now in Fort Del - I have a copy of the permit which is signed "by Order of Brig Genl A Schoepff [Albin F. Schoepf]" The name is pronounced Scheff - At any rate he is in supreme command at Fort Del - As soon as Genl Butterfield informed me of his permission to send this box and offered to put any thing into it which I desired, I went out and bought 12 flannel shirts 12 pr of flannel drawers 12 pr of woolen socks, 12 comforters for the neck and 12 pocket handkerchiefs - 6 combs 6 fine tooth combs, 6 tooth brushes, 12 packages of soap each package containing 3 cakes of soap, 36 cakes in all, - Besides I sent Mrs Butterfield a large bundle of clothes which had been sent me by Mrs Cress and two pairs of nice socks which Mrs Noyse had knitted and sent me - the bundle contained several nice thick almost new pantaloons, and a warm vest - I am interrupted and cannot finish my letter today.
Thursday morning Dec. 31st 1863 - the last day in the

year - Blessed Susy I have just received your dear letter written yesterday - Oh how interesting it is and how glad I am that God ever put it into the hearts of men to desire that Christian Communion - What a blessing the religion of Jesus Christ is! I will give Miss Knopf her receipt & I will also send Mrs Paddocks note to Mrs West, very shortly, I am anxious for Thee to see it first - In this list which I wrote you yesterday of shirts and drawers, which I sent Mrs Butterfield, I called them flannel but they were also the grey marino - My precious daughter I am so sorry you have been sick

Darling darling child do take care of yourself. I cannot tell you how precious you are to me. The toys arrived in perfect safety, - I think Bamie's perfect - I amuse myself with it in the evenings quite as much as Bamie does. I did not do the work of the bookmark but purchased it at Miss Hinop's Fair - By the way she told me that they made clear of all expenses $550.25 cts. beside she has a clock on hand worth $100 and a picture worth $50 which were presented to the Fair- Also a sable martin fur cape which cost $100 - The avails of this cape are to be divided between the Church & the Confederate soldiers - this cape was owned by a southern lady who says she cannot conscientiously wear any thing so extravagant while so many are naked and suffering. Goodbye darling Susy, but before I close I must tell you that Anna received a short letter from Hariot lately. In it she said James was not with her that her children were well except little Dunwody - That it was pitiful to see the poor little fellow encased in steel. She sent a great deal of love to you and said must tell you she had lately seen Mrs. Semmes who sent her [who sent also?] her love to you - with her letters she enclosed one from Irvine to James but the date was farther back than the one I received from him lately - The poor fellow appears very anxious to hear from us all - sends oceans of love to all of us by name - he then says "do give my best love to my dear bro Stuart - poor fellow! I hope he is better" Hariot sent me a Photograph of her little son <u>Stuart</u>. I think he looks very much like him. Poor Hariot is in affliction again. Her young brother (who I daresay you remember) was in the Federal army, and was killed in battle last summer.

Your affectionate mother
M Bulloch -

NB I had almost forgotten to mention a little matter of business - My Hoboken Coupons for Jan will be due first Jan. Ask Hill whether he can get a check for the amount and send it to me. It would not be safe to send the Coupon as our letters are sometimes meddled with - You ask me about Point Lookout, I have never received a word of answer from Col Patterson to whom I wrote. But Genl. Butterfield who seems to have much influence has promised me to write to Washington and get permission from headquarters to send clothing etc there - Besides, Miss Henop has a friend in Baltimore to whom she promises me to write - this person is perfectly trust-worthy and will get your money or clothes safely there. I have now in hand $192.29 cts. - this sum I was reserving for the Point Lookout prisoners. Perhaps I had better get you to give it to the Christian Commission. Let me know what you think best in your next letter - "No more last words" from your affectionate mother M B -

Julia Elizabeth Brown Butterfield (1835-1877), wife of General Daniel Adams Butterfield, was a New Yorker. Her participation in obtaining items for Confederate prisoners of war appears to have been due to compassion and not to any Southern sympathies. Julia and Daniel had only one child, Edgar Bergh Butterfield (1858-1861).

Harriott Cross Bulloch's brother, Lt. Edwin Bathurst Cross, died of typhoid fever on 8 August 1863 in New Haven, Connecticut. His obituary reported significant details about his life:

> . . .It often becomes our melancholy duty to chronicle the closing scene in life's great drama,

when the actors have been those whose career were watched with anxiety and interest. Today we are called upon to record the mortality of one whose fate seems enveloped in circumstances peculiarly sad and trying.

Lieut. E. B. Cross was the son of Lieut. Col Cross, Deputy Quartermaster General of the regular army, and at the time of the organization of the 27th regiment, C.V., was a member of the Yale Law School in this city. He was born in New Orleans, La., and reared amid the institutions peculiar to his native State, and inherited to a perceptible degree those pleasing traits that have ever been a marked feature of the highly cultivated and polished sons of the South.[177]

The article goes on to report on Edwin's service record. He enlisted as a Sergeant Major in the 27th Regiment, Connecticut Volunteers, and was commissioned a second lieutenant after the Battle of Fredericksburg. At Chancellorsville, he and most of his regiment were taken prisoner and marched south to Richmond. Edwin was exchanged at Annapolis and returned to his unit. Soon after the regiment's return to New Haven, Edwin succumbed to the fever. His obituary ended with:

It is not strange if the worldly compound in the hearts of those who loved him, should rise in rebellion against such a stern decree. They have followed him with tears and prayers through an eventful and severe campaign anxiously watching for the hour that should reunite them again, and when the hopes of weary waiting months are about to end in fruition, they are dashed to the earth in one fell swoop; but the hand that causes this affliction is the hand of Him that doeth all things well.[178]

Such emotional sentiments could have ended the obituary of so many young men during the War. Many died without anyone ever writing or printing an obituary, remembered only in the thoughts and prayers of loved ones.

Chapter 15: 1864 & 1865

Events of the War

Spring arrived and the armies of the North and the South prepared to take to the field from their winter camps. On 9 March, Lincoln once more made a change in leadership, placing General Ulysses S. Grant in command of all Union armies. May brought massive coordinated campaigns in Virginia and Georgia. In Virginia, Grant advanced toward Richmond engaging Lee's Army of Northern Virginia at the Wilderness (May 5-6), Spotsylvania (May 8-12), and Cold Harbor (June 1-3). On the western front, General William Tecumseh Sherman began his Campaign for Atlanta, captured on 2 September, followed by his march south to the sea at Savannah, which fell on 21 December.

In August, amidst the background of War, the Democrats nominated George McClellan for president, while the Republicans stayed with Lincoln. Abraham Lincoln won his second term on 8 November.

The Letters

New York January 1st 1864

A happy new year to you my own blessed daughter - May God in his infinite mercy if it be his holy will spare you this and many other years - May he restore you to perfect health - but above all things may he draw you continually nearer and nearer to himself. And dear Hill too, may he be the recipient of all heaven's choicest blessings - I wrote you yesterday & the day before - I hope darling that you are quite

restored again - Enclosed in Mr Paddock's note, and one received by Mittie from Mary in answer to an invitation to come to the party tonight - I thought it would amuse you - Thee read Mr Ps note last evening, but did not appear much impressed by it - I carried Miss Henop's receipts to her - she was not at home but I gave them to Mrs Shephard her sister who will be sure to give them to her - Let me know if I can reach the Point Lookout prisoners through the Christian Commission - Bamie and I have commenced this new year with a resolution to have a drawer of ready made clothing for the poor particularly poor little girls about her size and smaller She and I will make the clothes - I don't know where we will get the materials - Children often come to Thee very bare & cold - They are from families which he visits, and with whom he is well acquainted - he gives them shawls and shoes but cannot furnish them with clothing - indeed if he could give them clothing not made it would do them very little good, as they cannot make them We have commenced this morning with a canton flannel petticoat she has nearly finished the skirt and I am making the body - I think the arrangement will benefit dear little Bamie in two ways - it will help to teach her plain sewing, and it will make her take an interest in others, - Of course I expect her zeal to abate, but I will give her charge of the drawer, and she shall always hand out the clothes - The reception is going on bravely down stairs - Mittie & Anna are dressed beautifully and I hear the carriages constantly coming to the door I wish you could see the flowers down stairs - mostly presents - they are splendid - Annas dress is a beautiful light lilac silk - a christmas present from Mittie - Mittie's dress is white illusion - One of the baskets of flowers came from Phil[a] - Mr Dick Jenkins brought it for Mittie. Love to all -
      Your affectionate
      Mother MB

 Three years of War brought about great suffering among those at home. Thee, seeing the crippled soldiers and their families often suffering from dire want of the simple necessities of life, joined in organizing the Protective War-Claim Association. Without charge, the Association helped these families claim back pay and pensions. He also toiled for the Soldiers' Employment Bureau, which helped those who could not return to their former jobs find new positions. It was through this work and Thee's work with the orphans of New York, that he found so many wanting.[179]

In 1853, Thee and other New York philanthropists helped Charles Loring Brace establish the Children's Aid Society. Brace, often called the *pioneer social worker*, said of Thee, " Whatever he had to do, he did all out." Beginning that year, the Society sent children west on the *Orphan Trains* to find new homes in the developing parts of the nation.[180] This work often consumed Thee's time and energies.

New York Jan 6 - 1864

My dearest Susy,

I received Hill's letter yesterday & Thee received the Coupons - Tell dear Hill I thank him very much & that I was delighted to hear that the Beaver Meadow had declared a 5 pr ct Div. He threatens me with a taunt when he sends me the Check I would rejoice in such taunts every day - That is the best investment I ever had and I always feel as though I have to thank Hill for it – I did not tell you dear Susy that I have lately had a little glimmer of hope that I might sell my Roswell house - I received a letter lately from Oxford Mass. from a Mrs. Leagare saying that her son in law Mr Adams who resided in Roswell, wishes her to write me and know what I would take for my house and lot – I wrote her immediately saying I would take $3,000 that I considered it a low price, but that one condition I would insist on. That as I was Providentially here (at the north) I must be paid here, and in United States money She wrote me word back that the sum was what Mr Adams offered, and as the transaction was through her I would be paid here - but in the same letter she says if she can get her daughter

here she will not purchase - So the matter rests just there. I have not much hope as to the final issue - It really seems though as if Providence has almost wonderfully taken care of me, for which I do desire to be grateful - I am so glad Mr Paddock has received the articles for the poor prisoners - Mrs ^Dr Emmet has received a Permit to visit her brother at Fort Del and is going there this afternoon - I went to see her yesterday, and requested her to make enquiries about the trunk & valise sent by Genl Butterfield - I also gave her $18 (eighteen dollars) which D^r. Emmet was to change into 25 cts shin plasters - these 25 ct pieces she was herself to distribute amongst the prisoners - I believe I wrote you that I had sent a check to a lady in Baltimore (One known to be reliable by Miss Henop of $150 (one hundred and fifty dollars) to be expended for the Point Lookout prisoners - I have now in hand of prisoners money, only twenty three dollars! I am so sorry my fund is nearly exhausted - We are all well darling - Love to all
      Your loving Mother
      M Bulloch

NB Mrs Emmet three weeks ago received a letter from Fort Del saying her brother was dead and while she was mourning over him as dead she received a letter from said brother - She says she cannot imagine the object of the first letter -

    MB—

  Mrs. Leagare [probably Légare] has not been identified; however, her son-in-law might have been Theodore Dwight Adams who was the storekeeper for the Roswell Manufacturing Company.[181] She offered Martha $3000 in U.S. currency for Bulloch Hall. In purchasing power that amount equals approximately $46,700, and in historic income value $607,000. Either sum would have assured Martha sufficient funds for many years to come.
  Martha continued to worry about and aid the many Confederate prisoners at Fort Delaware. Mrs. Catherine

Emmet's brother was a prisoner there, as well as others known to the Bulloch family. As Southerners living in the North, Martha, Mittie, Susan, and Anna seemed connected to so many of like circumstances. One might imagine that before the War there had been little intermarriage between North and South. However, the habit of wealthier Southerners to summer in the North created numerous North/South marriages, such as Mittie and Thee's.

A *shin plaster* was a common name for paper currency of low denomination. Often banks, merchants, wealthy individuals, and associations issued these as banknotes or circulating IOUs.

The following letter is the only one in the 1861 to 1865 collection written to Hilborne West by Martha Bulloch, Martha sent Hill's note with a letter to Susan.

New York Jan 14th - 64

I received your letter inclosing Check for two hundred and sixty dollars dear funny Hill yesterday morning - I would have answered it immediately but the same mail brought me one from Mrs Boynton which required me to go out forth with to see about a poor woman who was in a very destitute condition - I will write Susy my message to Mrs Boynton, so will say no more on this subject - It is refreshing to meet with one who can amuse - Some how your kind warning instead of making me realize the awful peril I was in, only made me laugh - I am astonished at my apathy on the subject - I fear it is a bad sign - I sent the Check down town this morning - Perhaps Thee will save me all of the danger you mention by quietly letting it slip out of his vest pocket - who knows - But seriously I thank you dear Hill, and I fully appreciate the <u>sterling</u> qualities of Beaver Meadow. I hope too the Quaker behind the counter of which you speak, will fulfil all of our desires - Anna says she would be delighted to have you accompany her on the Skating Pond - you cannot think how well she skates - Since the ice will allow she has skated some part of every day except sunday Last night a party of whom she was one, skated until nearly midnight. With much love to all

      Yours with affection
       M Bulloch -

      New York Jan 14th/64

My dearest Susy,
  I have not written you for several days - I am very busy just now making up some things for myself - your letters, some of which urged me to dress warmly followed by that extreme cold weather, induced me to go out & get flannel and under vests - Now I am busy making a dress and some flannel skirts - I am either more indolent or more slow than I used to be, for I do not accomplish much in finishing off these things - darling Susy how much I love you! Are you well dearest? I hope so - Mittie seems much better and the little ones are all well - Bamie & I have only made one little canton flannel dress & one hood both of which she gave out this morning - Yesterday dear Susy I received a letter from Mrs Boynton requesting me to enquire about a former southern lady who is very destitute in this city - I wish you dearest to say to her that I went immediately to Mrs Emmets who is a Roman Catholic lady and engaged her to go with me to St Catherines Convent this morning - The Sister and Mrs Meredith who is a sister but not one of the order both confirm the report which Mrs Boynton heard - We did not see Mrs Boardman, but Sister Anne will write us when we can have an interview Mrs Emmet and I left something for Mrs Boardmans immediate necessities - and as soon as we ascertain more about her I will write Mrs Boynton - Tell Mrs Boynton that in the Car as we were going down Mrs Emmet met with a gentleman of her acquaintance who said he knew Mr Monroe the brother of this ladys father - That Mr M is living in New York, is wealthy and that he the gentleman in the Car will see to it that he Mr Monroe shall assist his niece - Tell Mrs Boynton

I do not think it will be necessary for her to distress herself or send any assistance - however I will write her -

It is getting so dark I can write no more - Good bye for the present dearest -

Your loving Mother
M Bulloch

Please dear Susy with the enclosed dollar $^{\text{and 25 cts}}$ get me 1 pkg of No 7 - two of No 8 two of 9 & one of 10 Smith's needles from Miss Rodgers - tell her to send me Smiths best - If any money is left ask her to send me one paper No 8 ground down and one paper No 9 ground down Smiths - I like the needles which I generally get from her - I do not like a slim uncertain needle

MB -

tear up this after you see Mrs. Boynton

Martha wrote about visiting the St. Catharine's Convent run by the Sisters of Mercy at 35 East Houston Street. Rushing to the aid of a Mrs. Boardman, she was attended by Mrs. Emmet, the doctor's wife.

Martha's purchase of needles probably came from either Hannah or Lydia Rogers, two dressmakers in Philadelphia. Susan, like many daughters, obviously failed to follow her mother's directions to tear up the letter.

Martha and Anna cared for Mittie's children when their parents were absent, as seen in this next letter, probably written 22 January 1864.

Thursday evening

Dearest Mittie,

Ellie and Conie are gone to bed - I have just been up to see them both sound asleep - neither of them have even whimpered since you left - I was in the nursery when they were undressed - I told Cony I was glad she was such a good girl - she said she had told her dear aunty she would be good & let Ann Butler put her to bed - The sweet little creature is asleep in your room in the crib by your bed & Ellie on the trundle bed near Bessie's bed - Bamie is writing you a few lines - It is near her bed-time and she will soon be asleep also - The children were so good that I persuaded Anna to go to dinner next door - I will not go to bed until she comes home. I am quite well tonight - I went this afternoon to see Mrs Emmet who has just returned from a visit to her brother at Fort Del - She gives a woful account of what she saw and heard there - amongst other things she says the prisoners of war are allowed a five cent loaf for two meals for each dinner besides, they have a piece of meat about the size of the palm of her hand and for each breakfast a cup of coffee - that as a general rule, they are squalid in the extremes - - The sick she did not see, but her brother and others told her that the well prisoners were made to work without remuneration Indeed the Provost Marshal (Federal) said in her hearing that the d- - -d rebels should be worked hard - She says there were small boxes of clothing or something arrived while she was there, but what was a few hundred suits of clothing when there are 3,000 prisoners there - Oh it is hopeless and disgraceful to think of. Do not let this letter be seen except by Susy, as I have mentioned Mrs Emmet's name -

 I will not send my letter tonight as I wish to let you know how the children sleep - Good night darling

Friday morning
All well this morning dear Mitty the children slept well & are well and happy - no crying at all - Thee got home at 7 o'clock this morning - with love to Susy and yourself - (Thee told me you went to see dear Susy last night) I am your affec Mother
       M Bulloch

      New York Feb 8 1864
My dearest Suzy,
 I have just received your dear letter - What a dear

good child you are. I know I shall like the room, and shall never wish to be without you - I do not care at all about boarding-house smells, but you must not be making any little sneaking plans about the board - that is all already arranged here I will tell you how when we meet. Dear Hill took tea with us last evening - His boil is very much better, but it seems to have been a very painful one He said he intended going to Morris Town today and would be back this evening - Mittie & Anna Hill Thee and the two Hyatts are going this evening to Wallacks to see "Rosedale" - They say it is a very unexceptionable little play, and very very much admired - Mittie has Thee's consent, and is going to take Bamie - Hill says he anticipates seeing Bamie's enjoyment. I am so glad darling that my boarding place is so near you - I do not think darling we shall be in Phil before thursday - Hill told me last evening that we would go by the ten o'clock train thursday morning - Poor fellow his boil has been so troublesome that I fear he has not enjoyed himself much - Engage the room dearest if you have not done so already - I would have written you several days since, but was quite busy - I long to see you, and anticipate with real pleasure so <u>soon</u> seeing you - I am much better than I was, but still my friends here think the change will be beneficial - I do thank you darling for all of your thoughtful care of me - I will close as I wish to get this letter in the Lamp Post before it is late Anna & Mittie send much love - Your loving and grateful
      Mother M Bulloch
Love to Mr & Mrs West

  Rosedale, the play, opened on 30 September 1863 at Wallack's Theatre. The advertisement in the *New York Times* stated the play was written by Lester Wallack.[182] Born in New York, but raised in London, John Lester Wallack first appeared on stage in New York in 1847. He co-owned, with his father, and operated their theater. He often starred as Elliot Grey in his own play *Rosedale*, a romantic comedy. By 1864, the theater stood at the corner of Broadway and Thirteenth.

327

New York, Monday evening

I wrote you this afternoon my dearest Suzy and told you that Hill had gone today to Morristown - He did not as he expected go today, but will go tomorrow - He is apparently quite well again and in his usual good spirits - They have all, Mittie, Anna, Cady and Phany Hyatt, Bamie, Hill & Thee gone to Wallacks to see Rosedale performed - Bamie was in extacies about it. Hill took tea with us, and I was truly glad to see him looking well again. We leave on the ten o'clock train on thursday ^{morning} - In my letter this afternoon I acknowledged the receipt of your dear letter which I received about mid day - Susy dear you are a good child to me - indeed our Heavenly Father has blessed me with very kind good children - I will tell you when I see you how very kind and attentive Mittie & Anna, and indeed Thee also have been to me - I have been very unwell but am decidedly better - I feel better tonight than I have felt for several weeks past. I will take great pleasure however in my Phil[a] trip for I long to see you darling - I will be sure to watch to see you cross broad St - The children have colds - I think Teedie does not mind {food?} The little fellow's appetite is not good and he looks pale - Little Corinne too is not well - I am writing in the Library all alone - one half hour since a merry party had just left When they return they are to have (with the exception of Bamie) a chicken salad. Grandma will be in bed & sound asleep before that time - I write you tonight because I gave my afternoons letter to Johnnie Bugs to put in the lamp post, and it struck me afterwards it was a bad plan as he seems to be such an absent minded child - Good night darling Susy

Your affec mother
M Bullloch

An attached note written by Corinne Douglas Robinson (1886 -1971) identified Johnnie Bugs, mentioned in the previous letter, as little John Elliott, whose father was in the Confederate Army. Johnnie had been brought North to stay with his cousins. Corinne wrote that her mother Corinne

Roosevelt said he was "always one of Mother's most intimate friends, most charming, delightful, intelligent and amusing companion but remained absent minded until the day of his death."[183]

Due to Martha's visit to Philadelphia, there are no letters again until June of 1864. It seems she returned to New York in time for the family's annual sojourn to Long Branch.

Long Branch June 7th

My dear daughter,

Mr Gracie came here last evening and promises to take this note to Mr. Weir Roosevelt's office himself - I was glad of this opportunity as I had entirely forgotten the direction you gave me - Do if you have time drop me a line and let me know the n<u>o.</u> in Williams St as I may write you again during your stay ~~there~~ in Flushing.
We arrived here on Thursday afternoon quite safely, bag & baggage Cat, (Coupons) and all - The children are delighted with the change - If I had ^{not} left you my own dear darling for such a long time, and if I had not left dear little Cona with such a dreadful looking eye I should feel almost happy - that is as happy as I can feel during the war - Our accommodations here are delightful - they surpass very much my anticipations - It is not at all lonely either as there are upwards of fifty persons here now - Every thing in the country looks green and beautiful and the old sea looks perfectly lovely - My appetite is already restored to its <u>Walnut St</u> proportions, and I have not had a pain or an ache since I have been breathing this pure air - Oh how I long for you to be here - You will have a charming little room opening into mine, and which opens also into an entry -
I hope you and dear Hill may keep well - I felt so melancholy at parting with you on thursday afternoon, I seem scarcely to have seen you at all - It was but a confused little glimpse which I had of you - Darling I am not going to sew so steadily now - I only have enough work to amuse me and I will take exercise when the weather is cool and take good

care of myself - I shall have some interesting books to read also - All I have to pine after now, is to have you enjoy this June air with me - I hope for all these great memories which I enjoy God may give me the assuring blessing a grateful and trusting heart - Good bye for the present dear dear child
Your loving mother M Bulloch

Not long after the family's arrival at Long Branch, news of Irvine came in the most distressing way. In the first week of July, newspapers reported the C.S.S. *Alabama* sat in Cherbourg harbor (France), having arrived on 11 June. After unloading some 40 captives, she began taking on supplies and coal. These same news articles reported the U.S.S. *Kearsarge*, a corvette tasked with hunting down and sinking the *Alabama*, was at Flushing Roads (the Netherlands), on the 14th.

Soon boxed in by the Union warship, Captain Semmes drilled his crew and prepared for battle. Through official channels, he sent Captain Ancrum Winslow of the *Kearsarge* the following message: "My intention is to fight the *Kearsarge* as soon as I can make the necessary arrangements. I hope these will not detain me more than until to-morrow or the morrow morning at farthest. I beg she will not depart until I am ready to go out. I have the honor to be, very respectfully, Your obedient servant, R. Semmes, Captain."[184]

On the morning of 19 June, the *Alabama* sailed into the harbor. Witnesses claimed the *Alabama* fired 370 rounds at her adversary, averaging one round per minute per gun, a very fast rate of fire. The *Kearsarge*'s gun crews fired less than half that number, taking more careful aim. After little more than an hour, a white flag fluttered from the *Alabama* halting the engagement.[185]

It is said that as his ship sank, the injured Semmes threw his sword into the sea, thereby depriving Captain Winslow of the traditional surrender ceremony. The *Kearsarge* rescued the majority of the survivors, but 41 of *Alabama*'s officers and crew, including Semmes, were rescued by the private British steam yacht *Deerhound*. Winslow watched helplessly as the

The Sinking of the C.S.S. Alabama
Harper's Weekly Magazine, 23 July 1864

Deerhound spirited away to England his much sought-after adversary, Captain Semmes and his surviving shipmates.

The *New York Times* reported the story, on 6 July, stating that about 14 of the *Alabama's* crew were killed or drowned, including one officer. There was no list of those rescued by the *Deerhound*, the yacht of the wealthy English businessman John Lancaster. On vacation with his family, Lancaster had offered them the choice of church or sailing out to watch the sea battle. As the *Alabama* sank, Captain Winslow hailed Lancaster and shouted "For God's sake, do what you can to save them!" Much to Winslow's dismay, Lancaster then asked Semmes where he wanted to land and Semmes replied, "I am now under English colors, and the sooner you put me with my officers and men on English soil, the better."[186]

James Bulloch, the Confederacy's naval agent, was known to be in France and is believed to have watched the battle from ashore. He traveled back to England that night and arrived in London the next day to assist the *Alabama's* crew. There he would find his brother safe. It is not known how long the news of Irvine's escape took to reach his New York family.[187]

The War progressed badly for the Confederacy during the summer of 1864. In Roswell, Georgia, the residents watched and waited as Sherman's Army marched toward Atlanta. Roswell stood in its path. Some families, like that of Barrington King, president and partial owner of the Roswell Manufacturing Company, fled south, while they still could. By the end of June, all of the founding families except Reverend Pratt's had fled. The mills still operated turning out cloth and cording. Captain James R. King prepared his woolen mill. The village waited.

On 4 July, General Sherman ordered General Kennar Garrard to move into Roswell, keep the Western and Atlantic Railroad free from attack, and assure Union communications remained open. Union soldiers arrived in the small village on 5 July. The story of what happened to Roswell's mills and homes is told in many books.[188] Bulloch Hall survived, but Martha and her daughters had no knowledge of how their home, village, family and friends fared.

It appears very few northern newspapers carried stories about the Union actions in Roswell. A search of old newspapers found only two short articles. The following came from the *Buffalo Commercial*, dated 22 July 1864.

The cotton factories destroyed by General Sherman at Roswell, on the Chattahoochee river, were very extensive, and valued at two million of dollars. Large quantities of cotton cloth were found in them, considerable of which was distributed to the destitute population of the neighborhood. Some fifty thousand dollars worth of cotton was also destroyed. Roswell is a pretty village, built up by the manufacturing interest there. The house of James King, one of the owners of the cotton factories, is a fine mansion, surrounded by beautiful grounds, and was occupied as the headquarters of one of our Generals of Division.

The home, described as belonging to James King, was Barrington Hall, the home of his mother and father. Bulloch Hall stands nearby. When Martha and her daughters read this report, and possibly more extensive ones, they must have worried over the destruction of the mills, so important to the village residents.

Finally in early October, a letter arrived from Irvine. He was in Liverpool, England, with his half brother, James.

Liverpool Oct 8th 1864

My Dear Mother
I do hope sweet Blessed[189] that the as cold wea -ther comes on your health will improve, I have been hoping that it would now since I heard that you were so sick I am perfectly well and still with Brother Jim & family who are all well and send quantities of love, but to day darling I leave if England for some time and you will not be able to write me but I can write you through brother Jim and will do so whenever an opportunity presents. I have got a very fine outfit of clothes and every thing that I needed in the way of needles pins etc etc. thanks to dear sister Hattie - As I told you in my last letter darling you need feel no anxiety on my account and sister Hattie will tell you in the course of a few weeks something of my whereabouts so make yourself perfectly at

ease Blessed. Give my love to my dear little sisters kiss them all for me & kiss sister Mittie's little children so Good bye dear dear mother, I'll write when ever able to send a letter.

Your own devoted son
Irvine

Only one day after Irvine wrote to his mother, he was once again at sea. This time he sailed under Commander James Iredell Waddell on the C.S.S. *Shenandoah* as Acting Sailing Master. Irvine sailed from Liverpool on or the day after the date of his letter. The *Shenandoah's* mission mirrored that of the *Alabama* - to disrupt Yankee commerce, in particular to destroy the Yankee whaling fleet in the Pacific Ocean.

It is doubtful Martha ever received this letter or knew of Irvine's assignment on the *Shenandoah*, for Martha Stewart Elliott Bulloch died on Sunday morning, 30 October 1864, in Madison, New Jersey,[190] after a long, painful summer and autumn. Martha was 65 years old.

The family laid her to rest, far from either of her husbands and her many lost children, including Daniel Stuart and Charles Irvine buried in Roswell. Her final resting place lay next to the Roosevelt plot at Brooklyn's Green-Wood Cemetery.

On 3 April 1856, in Philadelphia, Martha, Susan, Hilborne, and Anna had signed as four of the thirty-four founding members of the West Spruce Street Presbyterian Church. Many years later, the Reverend W. P. Breed, D.D., of the West Spruce Street Presbyterian Church, wrote about Martha's death in his history of that institution:

> A scene in the last hours of one of this cherished Thirty -four [Martha] was too remarkable and touchingly suggestive to be omitted in this record. The end was drawing near. Night came, and often during the night the daughter [Anna], watching by her side, noticed her arm extended and her hand lying

open on the pillow, and once or twice drew the arm gently beneath the cover, only to see it soon replaced in its former position. In the morning, when questioned for the reason of this, she replied that she had wished to pray, but feeling too feeble to control her thoughts, she held out her open hand to her Heavenly Father, well assured that he would know her meaning.[191]

In Liverpool, James learned of her death in early November. Irvine, somewhere at sea, very likely did not learn of his mother's passing until his return to Liverpool in early November of 1865.

Although the family had written to Lucy, it's doubtful Martha's southern family and friends learned of her passing until the spring of 1865. In January of 1865, Anna wrote to her aunt and cousin in Savannah. With that city now firmly in Yankee control, letters passed more easily.

New York Jan 23d 1865

My dear Cousin,
    So long a time has passed and we have suffered so much, that I am too bewildered to write anything connectedly out of the chaos of thoughts that chase each other in and out of my mind Now that I have once again the way open to tell you that all these long years I have faithfully remembered and loved you and my dear Aunt and Cousin William. I have written to you and also Cousin William during the war but as few letters reach their destinations mine have been most probably lost. You have I suppose heard through Lucy Elliott of our great affliction. Our beloved Mother was ill nine long months and after <u>such</u> suffering that we call last summer her passing summer, she died on Sunday morning Oct 30th at Madison, N.J. from the sixth of May until she died my sisters and I nursed her they assisting me in the day and I alone at night - You can get some idea of her intense

suffering when I tell you that from May sixth until she died neither she nor I ever slept one night through, being up most nights every half (and sometimes oftener) hour by this watch. I believe it would have killed us to see her die if her great agonies had not made us thank "God for his saint departed this life" when he took her home. All these long months of sickness she never uttered one impatient word and only groaned when no human being could have endured what she suffered. One thing that overcomes me entirely is the remembrance of the longing to see poor Irvine that never left her night nor day - One night when she was extremely ill, she called me to her bedside and said "Anna if I should get too ill to remind you, remember that if you should hear that <u>Irvine</u> was dead and the South over - come never tell me, I could not hear it!" I have written so much to you about her because she always loved you and that her memory is cherished by you I know without being told - I have a small photograph of Florence cousin Laura sent us last summer. I shall write to my dearest Cousin Laura in a day or two - I have heard of the death of her husband and sympathize truly with her - I had so short a while to write this letter that I must hasten to close or it will not go with much love to you all I am your own

      Cousin Anna Bulloch[192]

Anna wrote to cousin William James Bulloch (1817-1865) and his mother Mary Young Bulloch (1782-1868). Mary was the widow of William Berringer Bulloch (1777-1852), Anna's great uncle on her father's side. At this time, William and Mary resided in Savannah. William died of typhoid fever in 1865, just a month or so after receiving this letter. He was buried in Laurel Grove Cemetery, where so many of his family, including his father, were laid to rest. Mary died in 1868 of a gastric complaint and was also interred in Laurel Grove. There is no stone marking either grave. Anna also mentioned Laura Jane Bulloch Locke (1812-unknown), daughter of William Bellinger Bulloch.[193]

The Year 1865

The Confederacy continued to fight until May of 1865. In the War's eastern theater, General Robert E. Lee surrendered his Army of Northern Virginia on 9 April at Appomattox Courthouse, Virginia. Other Confederate commanders surrendered later that day and on subsequent days. On 14 April, President Lincoln was assassinated in Washington, D.C.

The surrender of the Confederate departments of Alabama, Mississippi, and East Louisiana occurred on 4 May, followed by the Confederate District of the Gulf on 5 May. Confederate President Jefferson Davis was captured on May 10, along with other Confederate government departments. On 10 May, U.S. President Andrew Johnson declared the rebellion's armed resistance virtually ended.

However, the C.S.S. *Shenandoah* continued commerce raiding resulting in the capture and sinking or bonding of thirty-eight Union merchant vessels. Most of these were New Bedford whaling ships. It was not until 27 June 1865, sailing just below the Arctic Circle in the Pacific Ocean, that Captain Waddell learned from the captain of the captured *Susan & Abigail*, that General Robert E. Lee had surrendered his Army of Northern Virginia. The *Susan & Abigail's* captain produced a San Francisco newspaper about the end of the War. However, the newspaper also reported the Confederate government's flight from Richmond, Virginia, and President Jefferson Davis' proclamation to carry on the War. In response and disbelief, Waddell and his crew then captured ten more whalers in just seven hours. In all, she captured 38 vessels, destroying 34, and ransoming the remaining.[194]

Finally on 3 August, Waddell learned of the total surrender of all Confederate forces and the capture of Jefferson Davis. He lowered his flag and stowed it away along with his guns. He ordered the closing of his ship's ports and had the crew repaint her to look like a trading vessel. Sailing directly to Liverpool without hailing or speaking with another vessel, Waddell aimed to deliver his ship and crew to British officials.

When the pilot refused to guide him into port without a flag, Waddell once more raised the Confederate flag. On 7 November 1865, the *Liverpool Mercury* reported:

THE CONFEDERATE CRUISER SHENANDOAH IN THE MERSEY.

> Considerable excitement was caused on "Change" yesterday morning by circulation of the report that the Confederate cruiser *Shenandoah*, of whose exploits amongst the American whalers in the North Pacific so much has been heard, was passed about 8 o'clock by the steamer *Douglas* at anchor at the bar, of Victoria Channel, apparently waiting for high water. By many the report was discredited, it being thought that those on board the *Douglas* were in error, and had mistaken some other craft for the celebrated ex-Confederate cruiser. At half past ten, however, all doubts on the point were set at rest, with the *Shenandoah* steaming up the Victoria Channel with the Palmetto flag flying from her masthead.

Waddell surrendered his ship and crew. The *Liverpool Mercury* reported two days later:

THE SHENANDOAH. PAROLE OF THE CREW.

> . . . about 6 o'clock last night a telegram was received from Government by Captain Paynter, of her Majesty's ship *Donegal*, to whom the *Shenandoah* was surrendered, that the whole of the officers and crew, who were not British subjects were to be immediately paroled. Captain Paynter immediately proceeded to the Rock Ferry slip, and applied for a steamboat. The Rock Ferry steamer *Bee*

was placed at his disposal by Mr. Thwaites, in which he immediately proceeded alongside the *Shenandoah*. Captain Paynter went on board and communicated to the officers the object of his visit. The crew were mustered on the quarterdeck by the officers of the ship, the roll book was brought out, and the names of the men called out as they occurred. As each man answered to his name he was asked what countryman he was. In not one instance did any of them acknowledge to be British citizens. Many nations were represented among them, but the majority claimed to be natives of the Southern States of America or "Southern citizens". Several of those however, who purported to be Americans, had an unmistakably Scotch accent, and seemed more likely to have hailed from the banks of the Clyde than the Mississippi. Captain Paynter informed the men that by order of the Government they were all paroled, and might proceed at once to shore. This intelligence was received by the men with every demonstration of joy, and they seemed to be delighted at the prospect of leaving the craft in which they had hoped to be able to assist the Southern Confederacy. They commenced to pack up their bedding and other articles as fast as possible, and conveyed on board the *Bee*, which was to take them to the landing stage. Before leaving the vessel, however, they gave three lusty cheers, for Captain Waddell, their late commander. Captain Waddell, in feeling terms, acknowledged the compliment, and said that he hoped the men would always behave themselves, as brave sailors ought to do. The men then went aboard the *Bee*, and were conveyed to the landing stage. This separated the *Shenandoah* and her crew, and the vessel now rides at anchor in the Sloyne in charge of some men from the Donegal, under the command of Lieutenant Cheek.[195]

President Johnson formally declared the end of the War on August 20, 1866.

Epilogue

The Theodore Roosevelt collection holds many more Roosevelt letters, most from the many trips the family took to Europe. However, no additional letters could found from 1865. So, in a way, the Bulloch family story ended with Martha Stewart Elliott Bulloch's death. It seems a fitting place to leave our history. Nevertheless, we, the authors, felt the need to give you a brief narrative of what happened to our main characters.

In 1872, Hilborne West, Martha's executor, sold Bulloch Hall to Jason Sylvester Wood for only $1,000. Wood wanted to reactivate Roswell's woolen mill. Roswell, like most of the South, was still recovering from the effects of the War. About that time, Hilborne and Susan purchased for *Daddy* Luke approximately 40 acres in the Post Oak District of Cobb County, only a few miles from Bulloch Hall. *Daddy* Luke Monroe[196] appears in the 1880 U.S. Census. It states he is 94 years old (born circa 1786), widowed, and a farmer. Also at his residence were his grandsons, William, age 12, George, age 7, Samuel, age 2, along with his granddaughter Nancie, age 25 and his great granddaughter, Mary, age 8. *Maum* Grace Robinson was also listed in the Post Oak District. *Daddy* Luke lived to be over 100 years old and, at his request, was buried near James S. Bulloch.[197]

Mittie and Thee continued their lives in New York City, raising their four children first in the brownstone on 20th Street, and then, as their financial status climbed, they moved to a more prestigious home at 6 West 57th Street in late 1873. Mittie became one of New York's most important social icons, while Thee continued his work with the poor and needy.

Often the most accurate description of an historic person comes from someone who knew them personally. In

1911, in *Recollections Grave and Gay*, Mrs. Burton Harrison wrote of Mittie:

> . . . Mrs. Theodore Roosevelt seemed to me easily the most beautiful; and in the graciousness of her manner and that inherent talent for winning and holding the sympathetic interest of those around her, I have seen none to surpass her. . . This lady was of Southern birth, and many stories were whispered of her unhappiness during the war because of the fulminations of the Northern family into which she had married against her Confederate kin and sympathies. I remember her, first, in a small, inconspicuous house, one of a brownstone row in a street between Broadway and Fourth Avenue, where her afternoons at home seemed somehow to convey a waft of violets, of which blossoms she had many surrounding her; and the service of her door and tea-table was performed by neat little maids dressed in lilac print gowns, with muslin aprons and caps surmounted by bows of ribbon in the same shade. In the course of time the Roosevelts moved uptown into a handsome modern house in west Fifty-seventh Street. There a great ball was given, to which we went. I believe it was to celebrate the entrance into society of the eldest daughter, and the story was circulated that eleven hundred invitations had been sent forth.[198]

The family made trips to Liverpool, to see James and Irvine, and on to Europe and Egypt, with a trip up the Nile. Yet in late 1877, Thee grew ill. His condition worsened and then seemed to improve in the week after Christmas. However, on 9 February, Bamie, Ellie, and Cony sat at his side, and with Mittie kneeling beside him, he passed away from stomach cancer. The love story that began so many years ago, ended with Mittie's, "Darling, Darling, Darling, I am here."[199] While the family mourned, so did the citizens of New York.[200]

Obituary
Theodore Roosevelt

Mr. Theodore Roosevelt died at 4:45 P.M. on Saturday at his residence, No. 6 West Fifty-seventh street, from the effects of the disease which prostrated him about a month ago. A week prior to his death he was apparently in a fair way to recovery, but he had a relapse on Thursday, and rapidly failed. He died surrounded by his family and his brothers James and Robert B. Roosevelt. He was the youngest son of C.V.S. Roosevelt, brother of the late Judge Roosevelt, and was born in New York on 22 September 1831. Receiving liberal education from private tutors, he became, on attaining his majority, a partner in the firm of Roosevelt & Son, glass importers, which then occupied the building No. 94 Maiden-lane, and consisted of Mr. Roosevelt, Sr., and his son James. After the death of the father, the brothers continued in the business at No 92 Maiden-lane until January, 1876, when Mr. Theodore Roosevelt retired.

Soon after the outbreak of the late war, Mr. Roosevelt interested himself in the organization and work of the Allotment Commission, which went to the front to protect the interest of the Union soldiers and to induce them to send their money home to their families instead of squandering it in camp. In prosecuting this work Mr. Roosevelt and the other members of the commission found it necessary practically to abandon supervision of their own business affairs during the period of the war.

At the time of his death Mr. Roosevelt was one of the three State Commissioners of Public Charities, and since his retirement from business had been devoting his entire attention to investigating the various local charitable systems, with the view of checking abuses and instituting reforms in their management. In December, 1873, he was Chairman of the Committee of Nine appointed to superintend the affairs of the then newly-organized Bureau of Charities, the purpose of which was, not to give direct relief, but to gather and dis-eminate information as to the best mode of applying charity. . . . Mr. Roosevelt was a Trustee of the Children's Aid Society, and always manifested a warm interest in the Eighteenth-Street Lodging-house for Homeless Boys. On Sunday evenings, in all kinds of weather, he invariably visited that institution to give religious instruction to the inmates. Not content with this, he befriended the boys in many ways, regularly giving them Thanksgiving dinners. Through his efforts and those of his friends the lodging-house was purchased and presented to the Children's Aid Society.

Mittie lived to see three of her children marry and have children. Elliott married Anna Rebecca Hall (1863-1892) in 1880. She gave birth to Anna Eleanor Roosevelt on 11 October 1884. Two more children followed: Elliott Bulloch, Jr., in 1889 and Gracie Hall in 1891. On 29 April 1882, Corinne married Douglas Robinson, Jr. (1855–1918). Their four children all had the middle name Douglas: Theodore (1883), Corinne (1886), Monroe (1887), and Stewart (1889).

Teedie graduated from Harvard and married Alice Hathaway Lee (1861-1884). She delivered their first child, a girl, on 12 February 1884. Teedie arrived home from Albany to find Alice deathly ill of Bright's Disease, and upstairs Mittie lay close to death from typhoid fever. As Teedie moved from sick room to sick room, all looked dire. Mittie passed first at three in the morning, followed by Alice eleven hours later, both on Valentine's Day. After a joint service at the Fifth Avenue Presbyterian Church, Mittie and Alice Lee joined Thee in the Roosevelt plot at Brooklyn's Green-Wood Cemetery. Still unmarried, Bamie took baby Alice to raise, as Theodore, heartbroken, buried himself in his work.

After the War's end in 1865, Anna continued both her tutoring of Mittie and Thee's children and her courtship with James Gracie. So often, those familiar with the Bulloch family story have wondered at Anna's choice. Why did she marry a man from New York? However, a bit of research about the Gracie family painted a picture of a family very much like that of the Bullochs. James' father Archibald Gracie II (1795-1865) of New York had married the lovely Elizabeth Davidson Bethune of South Carolina, daughter of a plantation owner and of the South. Elizabeth was the third child of Angus Bethune of Scotland and Margaret Horton of London, who married in 1792 in Charleston, South Carolina. Archibald Gracie was a merchant who traded heavily in cotton, out of Mobile, Alabama, to American and British factories.

The family's southern connections continued with his oldest son, Archibald Gracie III (1832-1864), who studied at the University of Heidelberg (Germany) before returning to the United States and attending West Point. While at the Academy, he came to the attention of then West Point Commander Robert E. Lee, whom he greatly admired. After graduating in 1854, he served three years before resigning and joining his father's firm in Mobile, Alabama. By then Gracie had married Josephine Mayo (1836-1901). Confederate General Archibald Gracie died at the Seige of Petersburg.[201]

The War took more than just his brother. James Gracie lost his mother, Elizabeth on 11 April 1864 and his father one year later on 3 April. Again, here lies a story about a family divided by distance and allegiance, but not by love. So when Anna finally decided to accept a proposal of marriage, it came from a man who understood her background and her family.

Anna and James Gracie married on 6 June 1866 at the Church of Transfiguration (Episcopal)[202] located at 1 East 29th Street. Anna and James lived both in New York and their Oyster Bay home called *Gracewood* until Anna's death on 9 June 1893 of complications from routine surgery. After their marriage, James continued in the banking and finance business and served on numerous charitable boards with Thee. Additionally, he became very good friends with James and Irvine Bulloch. Gracie assisted James D. Bulloch financially on several occasions and upon his death left $10,000 each to Irvine Bulloch's wife Ella and James D. Bulloch's daughter Martha Louise.[203] His will also included large amounts for many of the Roosevelt children and grandchildren. James died on 23 November 1903. James and Anna never had children of their own.

Both Anna and then James were buried at Green-Wood next to Martha. Some have commented on her stone reading "Anna Bulloch" instead of Gracie. No longer can the engraved words below their names on any of the stones names be read. At one time, hers mostly likely read "Beloved wife of James K. Gracie" as was the custom of the time.

For many years, Susan and Hilborne West continued to live in Philadelphia, with Hill's parents. Hill's father, James, passed away on 1 April 1867. His mother Rebecca Coe West lived until 1882 and died in New York City. Her death was reported in the 22 June *Philadelphia Inquirer* and stated she was 97 at the time of her death. Her correct age was 91.

Susan and Hill never had children. They lived in Philadelphia until at least 1880. However, U.S. Census records show them residing in Morris County, New Jersey, by 1895 for at least part of the year. Susan passed away on 18 May 1905. Her very short obituary in the *New York Times* listed her as the half sister of the President's late mother.[204] Hilborne died after a brief illness on 22 January 1907 at the Paxton House in Morristown, New Jersey.[205] Susan and Hill lie buried side by side in Philadelphia's Laurel Hill Cemetery. Her stone reads "Susan A. Elliott" and "Wife of Hilborne West." There are five graves in this plot. Hill lies to the far

Tombstones of Anna Bulloch Gracie, James Gracie, and Martha Bulloch, Green-Wood Cemetery
Courtesy of Keith Muchowski

left with Susan next to him. Beside Susan is the grave of Eliza H. West who died on 28 October 1851. We have wondered many times if this grave could belong to an infant daughter of Susan and Hill. Next to this grave is one that is so eroded as to be illegible and is most likely that of James West. Rebecca Coe West lies on the far right.

West Family Graves at Laurel Hill Cemetery, Philadelphia
Courtesy of P. Eadie, Findagrave.com

James Dunwoody Bulloch and his family remained in Liverpool after the War. James and Harriott had a fifth child that year, Martha Louise, giving them three sons and two daughters. After the War, James became a cotton merchant and wrote his memoirs of service to the Confederacy in a two volume series entitled *The Secret Service of the Confederate States in Europe, or How the Confederate Cruisers were Equipped*.[206] First published privately in London, Theodore Roosevelt, James' nephew, helped arrange the New York printing. There are two excellent books on James D. Bulloch; each presents details of his life after the War and his interactions with the Bulloch/Roosevelt families.[207]

Irvine Stephens Bulloch, like James, decided to remain in Liverpool after the War. In *My Brother Theodore Roosevelt*, Corinne told of a clandestine visit Irvine made to the States to see Mittie and Anna, which probably occurred some two or three years after the end of the War.

> It was at Lowantaka,[208] at the breakfast-table one day, after my father had taken the train to New York—this was the second year of our domicile there, and the sad war was over—that my mother received a peculiar-looking letter. I remember her face of puzzled interest as she opened it and the flush that came to her cheek as she turned to my aunt and said: "Oh, Anna, this must be from Irvine!" and read aloud what would now seem like a "personal" on a page of the New York *Herald*. It was as follows:
> "If Mrs. Theodore Roosevelt and Miss Anna Bulloch will walk in Central Park up the Mall, at 3 o'clock on thursday afternoon of this week [it was then Tuesday] and notice a young man standing under the third tree on the left with a red handkerchief tied around his throat, it will be of interest to them."
> As my mother finished reading the letter she burst into tears, for it was long since the younger

brother had been heard from, as the amnesty granted to all those taking part in the Rebellion had not been extended to those who had gone to England, as had my two uncles, to assist in the building and the sailing of the Alabama, and letters from them were considered too dangerous to be received.[209]

Continuing the story, Corinne told of a short meeting between the sisters and Irvine, who had sailed in steerage under a different name, and had to return to England later that day.

Another source tells of Irvine during the War in Liverpool. It was late 1861 or early 1862, and the C.S.S. *Nashville* had sailed into England bearing the Confederate flag, the first to do so. While on leave the following took place:

> My brother [Clarence Cary, 1845-1911], in company with his close friend and fellow-midshipman Irvine Bullock, [sp] of Georgia, . . . ran up to London to see the sights, and two happier lads could not have been found. Drawing their pay in gold, petted and welcomed by sympathetic Britons, and having achieved the éclat of a notice in Punch, they described themselves as 'living like fighting chickens generally.'
>
> Irvine Bullock was declared by his comrades to be 'a tall stalwart fellow, the best in the world, and a splendid officer.'[210]

After the War, Irvine, like James, was not granted immunity under the initial pardon. Because the *Shenandoah* had continued to capture Federal ships long after the end of the War, many of its officers and men were reluctant to return to the United States. Irvine had at first desired to become a ship's captain, as James had before the War. Instead, he also became a cotton merchant living in Liverpool. Both James and Irvine became British citizens.

In 1869, Mittie, Thee, and their children traveled to Liverpool to see the "Uncles." James and Irvine, anxious to see their sister and her children, used a harbor tug to reach the *Scotia*, delayed by low tide. Their reunion must have been one to witness, so full of joy and sorrow. The Roosevelts stayed ten days, giving them a chance to meet Ella Clitz Sears (1849-1911), Irvine's fiancée. Mittie described her as the "freshest, dewiest pink rose bud, lovely eyes, dark, her picture is exactly like her, . . . soft white hands, blushing and affectionate."[211]

Ella had lived in Liverpool since the age of 12 with her parents and younger sister Harriet. Her father, a U.S. Army officer, Henry Beaufort Sears, was employed working on several dock projects, first in London, and by 1861 in Liverpool. Irvine and Ella enjoyed a long courtship, most likely due to Irvine's desire to establish himself before marriage. They did not marry until September of 1871. They took up *housekeeping* at 77 Canning Street next door to her parents. In 1872, Anna and James Gracie visited the couple. The story of the family's interactions over the coming years is well presented in *The Bulloch Belles*.[212]

On 14 July 1898, Irvine Bulloch died of cerebral hemorrhage at age 56. He and Ella had no children. James Dunwoody Bulloch followed his brother on 7 January 1901. Both Irvine and James were buried at Toxteth Park Cemetery in Liverpool.[213] Now only Susan, the longest lived of Martha's children remained.

In the nineteenth and early twentieth centuries, newspapers rarely printed obituaries for women. Therefore, it is often difficult to establish dates of death and other information that might be obtained from such articles. However, the deaths of such men as the Roosevelt brothers occasioned rather lengthy discourses on their achievements and details of their deaths. For example, the oldest brother, Silas Weir Roosevelt, passed in 1870 at 47 of a lengthy illness that left him barely able to walk. Mary followed in 1877. No obituary could be found.

The youngest Roosevelt brother, Theodore, died in 1878, followed by Cornelius Van Schaak, Jr., in 1887.

His obituary ended with: "Mr. Roosevelt was exceedingly charitable and was beloved by the poor. He employed many people, and made it a rule to pay higher taxes for service than was usually demanded."[214] Recognized as the Governor's [Theodore Roosevelt] aunt, Laura Porter Roosevelt's obituary was printed in the *New York Times* on 21 March 1900. The article states she had lived with her brother for 25 years at 13 East 48th Street in New York. It also listed her various charitable associations.

James Roosevelt followed Cornelius in death on 13 July 1898, one day before Irvine Bulloch died. James passed from a stroke on the Long Island train as he traveled to his country home. His obituary chronicled his death and subsequent details of the train's arrival at Oyster Bay and, like that of his brothers, then relates his many charitable works and associations, such as the Metropolitan Riding City Club and the Seawanhaka-Corinthian Yacht Club. The last line identifies him as the uncle of "Colonel Theodore Roosevelt."[215] James' wife Elizabeth Emlin Roosevelt passed on 13 April 1912. Her obituary was discovered under the headline "Mrs. J. A. Roosevelt Dead."[216] She, like her husband, was identified as to her relationship to Colonel Roosevelt. A subsequent article in several newspapers spoke to her will and estate of $1,843,955 left mostly to "her son's daughter and grandchildren."[217]

Robert Barnhill Roosevelt outlived all of his five brothers and his wife, Elizabeth Thorne Ellis, who died on 5 April 1887. Her brief obituary said she passed from apoplexy at her home in Sayville, New Jersey.[218] Robert lived until 1906 and also passed in Sayville. Robert's death occurred during Theodore's presidency, which was noted in the obituary's headline.[219] Unlike his wife's brief obituary, his listed his many achievements, offices, and the titles of his best known literary works, all having to do with game fish and game birds.[220]

Hilborne, who formed the bond between the Bulloch and Roosevelt families by marrying Susan Elliott, Martha Bulloch's daughter by her first husband, outlived them all. Hilborne connected one of Georgia's most prominent families to one of New York City's. He himself descended from one of

Philadelphia's original families. He witnessed so much of the nineteenth century: the rise of the United States, the Civil War, the Spanish American War, and his nephew by marriage, Theodore Roosevelt, serving as President of the United States. This legacy, this connection of families, brought about by a romance in 1849, created one of America's most beloved presidents and a First Lady, Anna Eleanor Roosevelt, known for her intelligence and philanthropy.

Endnotes

1. Factor: an agent entrusted with the possession of goods to be sold in the agent's name; a merchant earning a commission by selling goods belonging to others. Found at https://www.infoplease.com/dictionary/factor.
2. *Darien* (GA) *Gazette,* 22 September 1821.
3. Susan Ann Elliott, born 6 August 1820; Georgia Amanda Elliott, born 14 June 1822, and Daniel Stewart, born 20 November 1826.
4. *Savannah Georgian*, 11 September 1827. The obituary reads in part: "On the 8th inst. Charles William, son of the late John Elliott, age three." The Savannah Georgia Select Board of Health and Health Department Records 1824-1864 listed the date of his interment rather than his death.
5. *Savannah Daily Georgian*, 26 February 1831.
6. In the antebellum period, a sister-in-law or brother-in-law was considered a sister or brother.
7. Mary Telfair wrote of Martha and James' relationship as it would have been recognized by the social community. Betty Wood, ed., *Mary Telfair to Mary Few: Selected Letters 1802-1844* (Athens: University of Georgia Press, 2007),106-10.
8. Betty Wood ed., *Mary Telfair to Mary Few: Selected Letters 1802-1844* (Athens: University of Georgia Press, 2007),106-10: Charles Johnson, Jr., *Mary Telfair: The Life And Legacy of a Nineteenth-Century Woman* (Savannah, GA: Geor Frederic C. Beil, 2002), 93-94.
9. Ibid.
10. Ibid.
11. Named Martha for her mother, this child was apparently called *Mittie* from birth.
12. In the mid-1830s, Roswell King and his son, Barrington King, established a cotton mill at Vickery Creek in

upland Georgia. King invited investors to his "Colony of Roswell" to establish a town with the social and religious values befitting his social and economic status. By 1839, several prominent Savannah and Liberty County families had accepted King's offer and relocated to the village. Cf. Paulette Snoby *Georgia's Colony of Roswell: One Man's Dream and the People Who Lived It* (Crab Orchard, KY. Interpreting Time's Past, 2015).

13. Recently discovered documentation indicates his name may have been Monroe rather than Moumar or that he changed his name to Monroe when emancipated. 1880 U.S. Census and Georgia Agricultural Census for 1880.

14. Southern slave-holding families often gave honorary titles to their beloved house slaves, such as *Maum* (for Mama) and *Daddy*. The slaves mentioned here were called by these kinship terms in everyday speech and family letters by the Bulloch women.

15. Bulloch Hall is currently a house museum, owned by the City of Roswell, and funded, in part, by the Friends of Bulloch, Inc.

16. In 2017, Mimosa Hall was purchased by the City of Roswell.

17. Rebecca McLeod, "The Loss of the Steamer Pulaski," *Georgia Historical Quarterly* 3, No. 2 (1919): 88.

18. Walter E. Wilson and Gary L. McKay, *James D. Bulloch: Secret Agent and Mastermind of the Confederate Navy* (Jefferson, NC: McFarland, 2012), 16-17.

19. A. McElroy (compiler), *A. M'Elroy's Philadelphia Directory* (Philadelphia: Rackliff & Jones, 1837). Available online at: https://archive.org/.

20. John W. Jordon, ed., *Colonial Families of Philadelphia, Vol. I*, (New York: Lewis Publishing Company,1911), 2.

21. A. McElroy (compiler), *A. M'Elroy's Philadelphia Directory* (Philadelphia: Isaac Ashmead & Co. 1839). Available online at: https://archive.org/.

22. Christie Anna Farnham, *The Education of the Southern Belle: Higher Education and Student Socialization in the*

Antebellum South (New York: New York University Press, 1994), 65-67.

23. Mrs. I.M.E. Blandin, *History of Higher Education of Women in the South, Prior to 1860* (New York: Neale Publishing Company, 1909), 260-263.
24. Lynn Salsi and Margaret Sims, *Columbia: History of a Southern Capital* (Charleston, SC: Arcadia Publishing, 2003), 41-42.
25. James D. Bulloch to Anna Christie Stevens, 11 July 1849, James D. Bulloch Papers, Southern Historical Collection, Wilson Library, University of North Carolina, Chapel Hill.
26. A sixth son, William Weir, was born 20 September 1834 and died 18 December 1835.
27. National Archives and Records Administration (NARA); Washington D.C.; NARA Series: Passports Applications, 1795-1905; Roll #: 36; Volume #: Roll 036 - 07 Apr 1851-22 May 1851.
28. Hilborne West was not a physician when he met Mittie Bulloch. He did not study medicine until the late 1850s. See Koehler & Huddleston, *Between the Wedding & the War*, (Roswell, GA: Friends of Bulloch, Inc., 2016), 166-168.
29. Corinne Roosevelt Robinson, *My Brother Theodore Roosevelt* (New York: Scribner's Sons, 1921), 3.
30. *Savannah Republican*, 15 February 1851; Connie M. Cox and Darlene M. Walsh, *Providence: Selected Correspondence of George Hull Camp 1837-1907.* (Macon, GA: Indigo Publishing Group, 2008), 209.
31. Hermann Hagedorn, *The Boys' Life of Theodore Roosevelt* (New York: Harper & Brothers, 1918), 8.
32. For additional information on this year of courtship see Connie M. Huddleston and Gwendolyn I. Koehler, *Mittie & Thee: An 1853 Roosevelt Romance* (Roswell, GA: Friends of Bulloch, 2015).
33. H. Wilson, compiler, *Trow's New York City Directory*, (New York: John F. Trow, 1862). Accessed at https://

catalog.hathitrust.org/Record/100513654; House numbers in text reflect 1850s & 1860s references; Robert graduated from Harvard with a law degree in 1848.

34. H. Wilson, compiler, *Trow's New York City Directory*, (New York: John F. Trow, 1863). Accessed at https://catalog.hathitrust.org/Record/100513654.

35. Records found on Ancestry.com indicate James may have attended Columbia University, but that he did not graduate.

36. "After The Hickories: Roosevelt Park," Accessed 30 July 2017, https://www.durandhedden.org/archives/articles/after_the_hickories_roosevelt_park.

37. Koehler and Huddleston, *Between the Wedding & the War*.

Chapter 2:

38. The nearest telegraph to Roswell, Georgia, was most likely along the W & A rail line in Marietta, about 12 miles west of Roswell.

39. Walter E. Wilson, *The Bulloch Belles* (Jefferson, NC: McFarland. 2015), 112.

40. *Philadelphia Inquirer*, 25 January 1861.

41. *New York Times*, 24 January 1861.

42. Koehler and Huddleston, *Between the Wedding & the War*, 280-283.

43. Wilson and McKay, *James D. Bulloch*, 37.

44. Wilson, *The Bulloch Belles*, 104.

45. War Department Collection of Confederate Records. National Archives and Records Administration, Record Group: 109, Confederate Civilian Files, Roll: 0118.

46. Lucy was mistaken as Robert left $30,000 to James Dunwoody Bulloch.

47. Wilson, *The Bulloch Belles*, 104-105.

48. Last Will and Testament of Robert Hutchison, 26 April 1861, Accessed 4 April 2017, https://www.ancestry.com/.

49. *Frank Leslie's Illustrated Newspaper*, 15 July 1865, 269.

50. Wilson, *The Bulloch Belles*, 104, 108.

51. War Department Collection of Confederate Records. National Archives and Records Administration, Record Group: 109, Confederate Civilian Files, Roll: 0118.

Chapter 3:
52. Robert Manson Myers, *The Children of Pride: A True Story of Georgia and the Civil War (*New Haven, CT: Yale University Press, 1972), 1461-62.
53. Manassas was the Confederate name for the Battle of Bull Run.
54. Myers, *The Children of Pride*, 722.
55. Source of printer article enclosed with letter is unknown.
56. Wilson, *The Bulloch Belles*, 110.
57. To access the *Memphis Daily Appeal*, see Chronicling America at Library of Congress at: http://chroniclingamerica.loc.gov/lccn/sn83045160/.
58. Nathaniel Cheairs Hughes, *Yale's Confederates: A Biographical Dictionary* (Knoxville, TN: University of Tennessee Press, 2008), 62.
59. National Park Service, Civil War Soldiers and Sailors System. Accessed 16 January 2017, http://www.nps.gov/civilwar/soldiers-and-sailors-database.htm; Compiled Service Records of Confederate Soldiers Who Served in Organizations from the State of Georgia, The National Archives as found at www.fold3.com.
60. Verity Holloway, *The Mighty Healer: Thomas Holloway's Victorian Patent Medicine Empire* (Barnsely, UK: Pen and Sword History, 2016).
61. *Biographical Dictionary of the United States Congress: 1774 to Present*, s.v., McDougall, James Alexander." Accessed 17 January 2017, http://bioguide.congress.gov/scripts/biodisplay.pl?index=m000416.
62. The authors researched family trees using Ancestry.com. Names and dates were verified, when possible.
63. *Naval History and Heritage Command*, s.v., "C.S.S. Savannah." Accessed 17 January 2017, https://www.history.navy.mil/research/histories/ship-histories/

confederate_ships/savannah.html; *New Georgia Encyclopedia*, S.v., "C.S.S. *Savannah.*" Accessed on 17 January 2017, http://www.georgiaencyclopedia.org/articles/history-archaeology/css-savannah; Wilson, *The Bulloch Belles,* 113, 118.

Chapter 4:
64. Jenny Meade, "Genealogy Report: Descendants of Richard Sessions." Accessed 15 February 2017, http://www.genealogy.com/ftm/m/e/a/Jenny-Meade/GENE5-0002.html.
65. W. P. Breed, *West Spruce Street Presbyterian Church, of Philadelphia. 1856-1881,Quarter Century Anniversary, Organization of the Church, Pastorate of Rev. WM. P. Breed, D.D., The First and Only Pastor, April 3 and 4, 1881. (Philadelphia*: Sherman & Co. Printers, 1881), 15.
66. *New York Times,* 21September 1861, 23 September 1861, 24 September 1861.
67. United States War Department, *Revised United States Army Regulations of 1861, with an Appendix Containing the Changes and Laws Affecting Army Regulations and Articles of War to June 25, 1862* (Washington, D.C.: Government Printing Office, 1863).
68. Thee's journals are contained in a separate document file in the Theodore Roosevelt Collection, Houghton Library, Harvard, and these enclosures are not archived with the letters to Mittie in which they were originally enclosed.
69, Koehler and Huddleston, Between the Wedding & the War, 69-72.
70. Probably Hugh Lenox Hodge, but possibly Charles Hodge, brothers, born to Dr. Hugh Hodge and Mary Blanchard. Charles (1797-1878) was Presbyterian minister while Hugh Lenox (1796-1873) was a physician. Hugh married Margaret E. Aspinwall of New York. Myers, *The Children of Pride,* 1551.
71. According to the 1860 U.S. Census, the family consisted of Stephen age 42; Dorinda, age 40; Effingham

Townsend, age 23; Stephanie, age 21; Caroline, age 19; Melissa Augusta *Lillie*, age 16; and Stephen Jr., age 9. Stephen's obituary in 1879 said he had two sons and three daughters that survived him. Effingham was commissioned 1st Lieutenant in the 157th New York Volunteer Infantry on 23 July 1863.

72. Two of General James Samuel Wadsworth's sons served in the Civil War. Lt. Charles Frederick Wadsworth (1835-1899) served in the 116th New York Volunteers, and Craig Wharton Wadsworth (1840-1872) served on his father's staff for a short period of time.

73. At least three colonels named Davis served in New York Volunteer Regiments including Benjamin Franklin Davis of the 8th, Edwin Page Davis of the 153rd, and Uriah L. Davis of the 85th.

74. It was the 40th New York Volunteer Regiment that was known as the Mozart Regiment, not the 38th as Thee stated. Lt. Col. Farnsworth helped organize the 38th.

75. The 56th New York Volunteer Regiment served in General Silas Casey's division.

76. Wilson and McKay, *James D. Bulloch*, 56-59. This book provides a more detailed and exciting description of the C.S.S. *Fingal's* blockade run.

77. Ibid.

78. Ibid.

79. *Charlotte Democrat*, 10 December 1861.

80. *Vicksburg* (MI) *Weekly Citizen*, 30 December 1861.

81. James A. Morgan, III, *A Little Short of Boats: The Battle of Ball's Bluff and Edwards Ferry, October 21-22, 1861* (El Dorado Hills, CA: Savas Beatie, 2011).

Chapter 5:

82. "Cape Hatteras: The Civil War on the Outer Banks," National Park Service. Accessed 19 January 2017, https://www.nps.gov/caha/learn/historyculture/civilwar.htm.

83. The *Daily Ohio Statesman* was published in Columbus, Ohio. The article was found as a reprint in the *New York Tribune* 7 November 1861.
84. *Nashville Union and American* (Nashville, Tennessee) 17 November 1861.
85. This was John G. Nicolay, not Tom. Thee was incorrect.
86. James M. McPherson, *Battle Cry of Freedom: The Civil War Era* (New York: Oxford University Press, 1988), 364.
87. Elwood A. Corning, *Hamilton Fish*. (New York: Lanmere, 1918).
88. This is most likely Dr. John C. Chessman, who had treated Bamie during the late 1850s. See Koehler and Huddleston, *Between the Wedding & the War*, 188.
89. This is most likely John J. Charruand who taught dancing at 148 East 17th Street according to *Trow's* (1862) *New York City Directory*.
90. In Charles Dickens' *David Copperfield*, Wilkins Micawber was noted for his inability to work his way out of poverty.
91. *Reading* (PA) *Times*, 31 December 1861, 3.
92. Wilson and McKay, *James D. Bulloch*, 59-61.
93. The lines appear in various 19th century documents and literature, without a citation.
94. Robert Sobel and John Raimo, eds., *Biographical Directory of the Governors of the United States, 1789-1978, Vol. 1*, s.v., William Albert Buckingham (Westport, CT: Meckler, 1989); Patricia F. Staley, *Norwich and the Civil War* (Charleston, SC: The History Press, 2015), 22.
95. Kerrigan was elected to the House of Representatives as an Independent Democrat, and he served from 4 March 1861 - 3 March 1863, at the same time as serving as a colonel in the volunteers. Kerrigan's absence, as noted by Thee, resulted from the following encounter with General Martindale. Martindale visited the regiment's camp on 18 October "for the purposes of examination and instruction" and found the soldiers dirty, their

weapons foul, and the camp in a state of chaos. When Martindale assembled the officers to lecture them, Kerrigan walked away, apparently bored with the meeting. Martindale ordered Kerrigan to come back, but Kerrigan "did willfully and positively refuse to obey said command and order," according to the charges, which also specified Kerrigan allowed his soldiers "to appear on parade in a state of unseemly disarray and filth -- their pants unbuttoned and their underclothes and persons exposed." Thomas P. Lowry, *Curmudgeons, Drunkards, and Outright Fools: Courts-Martial of Civil War Union Colonels* (Lincoln NE: Bison Books, 2003), 94-95.

Chapter 6:
96. Robinson, *My Brother Theodore Roosevelt*, 22-23.
97. "Civil War Facts: 1861-1865," National Park Service. Last updated 6 May 2015, www.nps.gov/civilwar/facts.htm.
98. Albert Bernhardt Faust, *The German Element in the United States* (Boston: Houghton Mifflin, 1909).
99. Probably Stewart Brown, a Wall Street banker. *Trow's New York City Directory*, 1862.

Chapter 7:
100. Wilson and McKay, *James D. Bulloch*, 47.
101. Thurston Rowland Bloom died on 8 February 1869 in New York, New York, at the Fifth Avenue Hotel. The following appeared on 17 February 1869 in *Pomeroy's Democrat* (from *New York Democrat*, Feb. 9): Thousands of our Southern readers will be shocked at the announcement we are pained to make this morning of the death of Thurston R. Bloom, Esq., who died yesterday afternoon at the Fifth Avenue Hotel in this city. Mr. Bloom was a resident of Macon, Georgia, and a gentleman well known throughout most of the South. He was a native of New York State, but going to Georgia in early boyhood, grew to be largely identified with the commercial and trade interests of the South,

especially giving his attention to cotton, its production and sale, and was known as one of the best financiers, as he was a leading business man of the South. Only a few weeks ago, by a fine stroke of financial strategy and foresight, for which he was so well qualified, Mr. Bloom made for himself and two partners nearly a million dollars in one transaction, and while it made for them, it also enhanced the value of the cotton crop at that time in the hands of planters upward of thirty millions of dollars, making the South just so much more wealthy. Mr. Bloom had been in New York a little more than a week, and was negotiating for the investing of some moneys in Western interests, when he was taken down with the lung fever, which resulted fatally. His stricken wife, who had been sent for, was at his bedside during his last hours, and she has the earnest sympathy of scores of friends in her affliction. Mr. Bloom was about forty-five years of age, of fine address, indomitable pluck and perseverance, and was possessed of rare business tact. His family consisted of himself, wife, and one child, and they had one of the happiest homes in the whole Southland.

102. *Macon* (GA) *Daily Telegraph*, 23 February 1860.
103. *The Liberator* (Boston), 28 February 1862.
104. *Joliet Signal* (Joliet, Illinois) 25 February 1862.
105. Sephardic refers to Jews from Spain or Portugal or their descendants.
106. *New York Times*, 6 January 1862, 5.
107. *New York Times*, 19 February 1862, 5.
108. Joy Lumsden, "Jamaicans Abroad - Raphael De Cordova 1822-1901." Accessed 8 February 2017, http://jamaicansabroad.weebly.com/-raphael-j-de-cordova.html; Hawthorne Quinn Mills, "American Zionism and Foreign Policy" Thesis for M.A. in Political Science University of California, Berkeley 1958.
109. *Syracuse* (NY) *Daily Courier and Union* (New York), 7 February 1862, 2.
110. The purchase of the war materials for the Fingal are

described in Stephen Chapin Kinnaman's *Captain Bulloch: The Life of James Dunwoody Bulloch Naval Agent of the Confederacy* (Indianapolis, IN: Dog Ear Publishing, 2013), 267-273. References to profits from the sale can be found in Wilson and McKay, *James D. Bulloch*, 59.

111. At this time, the colonels for the 44th New York Infantry Regiments (also known as Ellsworth Avengers; People's Ellsworth Regiment) were Stephen W. Stryker, James C. Rice, and Freeman Conner. Refer to *The Union Army: A History of Military Affairs in the Loyal States, 1861-65 -- Records of the Regiments in the Union Army -- Cyclopedia of Battles -- Memoirs of Commanders and Soldiers, Vol. II* (Madison, WI: Federal Pub. Co., 1908). https://babel.hathitrust.org/cgi/pt?id=uva.x001496379;view=1up;seq=79.

112. Elizabeth Keckley, *Behind the Scenes, or, Thirty Years a Slave and Four Years in the White House* (Rockville, MD: Wildside Press, 2013), 101-104.

113. Cox and Walsh, *Providence*, 646, notes 884, 886.

114. Nancy Alderman, "A Biography of Charles Green," The Savannah Biographies, Special Collections. Lane Library, Armstrong Atlantic State University, Savannah, GA, http://library.armstrong.edu/Green_Charles.pdf.

115. Gladys Shults, *Lady From Savannah* (Philadelphia: Lippincott, 1958) 126-27.

116. Wilson and McKay, *James D. Bulloch*, 53-57.

117. Wilson and McKay, *James D. Bulloch*, 105.

Chapter 8:

118. Russell Beatie, *Army of the Potomac: McClellan's First Campaign, March - May* (El Dorado Hills, CA: Savas Beatie, 2007), 291–95.

119. *Woods' Baltimore City Directory Ending Year 1860*, Baltimore, 186, Accessed at https://archive.org/details/woodsbaltimoreci1860balt; *Waldonia [sic]*, "StereoView of Barnum's Hotel by William Chase," Photographicus Baltimorensis (blog). [n.d.], https://19thcenturybaltimore.

wordpress.com/2012/02/27/stereoview-of-barnums-hotel-by-william-chase/.

120. *Trow's* (1862) *New York City Directory*, 51.
121. The family was identified using *Trow's* (1863) *New York City Directory*, and U.S. Census records accessed on Ancestry.com.
122. "Abraham Lincoln Autograph Letter Signed 'A Lincoln' as President, one page, 5" x 7.75" [,on] Executive Mansion," Heritage Auctions. Accessed 14 February 2017, https://historical.ha.com/itm/autographs/u.s.-presidents/abraham-lincoln-autograph-letter-signed-a-lincoln-as-president-one-page-5-x-775-on-executive-mansion-washingto/a/658-25144.s; The Peerage, s.v. "Maj.-Gen. Charles Frederick Havelock" Accessed 14 February 2017, http://www.thepeerage.com/p1586.htm.
123. Koehler and Huddleston, *Between the Wedding & the War*, 113, 118, & 129.
124. "Good and upright is the LORD: therefore will he teach sinners in the way." Ps 28:5 (KJV).

Chapter 9:
125. *The Recreations of a Country Parson* was first published in London by J.W. Parker and Son in 1860-1861. By 1866, an America publisher/printer Ticknor & Fields of Boston had also published an edition that can be found on Google books, https://ia600207.us.archive.org/32/items/recreationsofcou04boyd/recreationsofcou04boyd.pdf. The illustration in this text is from the American 1866 version.
126. "Woman in White, The" in The Oxford Companion to English Literature, edited by Dinah Birch (Oxford: Oxford University Press, 2009), Accessed 28 February 2017: http://www.oxfordreference.com/view/10.1093/acref/9780192806871.001.0001/acref9780192806871-e-8185.
127. Tope, a verb, means to drink to excess. English, Oxford Living Dictionaries, Accessed 20 July 2017, https://en.oxforddictionaries.com/definition/tope.

128. For more infomation on the Enchantress Affair, see http://48thpennsylvania.blogspot.com/2007/08/little-known-civil-war-story-of.html.
129. From *Picturesque America. New York:* D. Appleton and Co., 1873. One of the most important 'view books' of the nineteenth century was *Picturesque America,* an impressive work which contained steel and wood engravings, along with text, illustrating natural wonders of America from the east to the west and from north to south. Not surprisingly, Niagara Falls was one of the featured sites.
130. "N. L. Rice, 1807-1877," Presbyterians of the Past: The Lives, Places and Events of Reformed History." Accessed 7 March 2017, http://www.presbyteriansofthepast.com/2015/09/19/n-l-rice-1807-1877-part-1/.
131. Wilson and McKay, *James D. Bulloch*, 103.

Chapter 10:
132. Myers, *The Children of Pride,* 1594; U. S. Census of 1860, Accessed on Ancestry.com.
133. *Philadelphia Inquirer,* 17 November 1862; 4 December 1862
134. *Philadelphia Inquirer,* 12 November 1862.
135. *The Liberator* (Boston), 5 December 1862.
136. Refers to family of deceased friend George Morris. See Koehler and Huddleston, *Between the Wedding & the War,* 192.
137. A search of period newspapers on Newpapers.com revealed a Buffalo, New York, man named Colden C. Tracy who was imprisoned and was the nephew of Supreme Court Justice Gould. However, it is doubtful this is the correct identification for the Mr. Tracy in this letter. *Evening Courier and Republic* (Buffalo, New York), 17 December 1862.
138. Measuring Worth.com, Found at: https://www.measuringworth.com/uscompare/relativevalue.php.
139. This is probably Dr. William Pratt Wainwright, see Appendix B.

140. Teresa Griffen Viele (1831-1906).
141. Koehler and Huddleston, *Between the Wedding & the War*, 218.
142. See for example, *Baltimore Sun*, 25 October 1862.

Chapter 11:
143. *Brooklyn Daily Eagle*, 26 January 1863.
144. Walter E. Wilson, personal communication, states this letter was written by an enlisted petty officer, an enlisted man, who cannot be identified. Wilson found the original letter in the *Liverpool Mercury* (9 December 1862) where it states: "The following is the principal portion of an interesting communication from a petty officer of much intelligence and ability who has been aboard the Alabama since she sailed from Liverpool . . ."
145. *Philadelphia Inquirer*, 17 February 1863.
146. *Brooklyn Daily Eagle*, 7 November 1898.
147. James McIntosh Kell, *Recollections of a Naval Life: Including the Cruises of the Confederate States Steamers "Sumter" and "Alabama"* (Washington, D.C.: Neale Co. 1900), 41-42.
148. *Nancy* must have been Irvine's pet name for Anna.
149. *Philadelphia Inquirer*, 19 February 1864.

Chapter 12:
150. Koehler and Huddleston, *Between the Wedding & the War*, 242.
151. *Hillsborough* (NC) *Recorder*, 22 July 1863; *Daily Progress* (Raleigh, NC) 25 June 1863.
152. See, for example, *Brooklyn Daily Eagle*, 24 June 1863; *Janesville* (WI) *Daily Gazette*, 27 June 1863; *The Liberator* (Boston) 3 July 1863.
153. *Pittsburgh Gazette*, 26 June 1863.
154. A vault or chamber, especially in a rampart, with embrasures for artillery. Dictionary.com, Accessed 20 July 2017, http://www.dictionary.com/browse/casemate.
155. Brig. General Johnston Pettigrew (1828-1863) of North

Carolina, was wounded at the Battle of Seven Pines (31 May-1 June 1862), taken prisoner, exchanged two months later, recovered from his wounds, and returned to service. He was mortally wounded at Gettysburg and died from his wounds on 17 July during the retreat to Virginia.

156. Dale Fetzer and Bruce Mowday, *Unlikely Allies: Fort Delaware's Prison Community in the Civil War*, (Mechanicsburg, PA: Stackpole Books, 2000), 108-116; Jocelyn P. Jamison, *They Died at Fort Delaware 1861-1865: Confederate, Union and Civilian*, (Delaware City, DE: Fort Delaware Society, 1997), 85-90.

157. Isaac W. K. Handy, *United States Bonds Or Duress By Federal Authority: A Journal Of Current Events During An Imprisonment Of Fifteen Months, At Fort Delaware*, (Baltimore: Turnbull Brothers, 1874). https://babel.hathitrust.org/cgi/pt?id=nyp.33433081800959;view=1up;seq=13.

158. Henry R. Berkeley, *Four Years in the Confederate Artillery: The Diary of Private Henry Robinson Berkeley.* (Richmond: Virginia Historical Society, 1991), 129.

159. Measuring Worth.com. Found at: https://www.measuringworth.com/uscompare/relativevalue.php. Accessed: 16 March 2017.

160. Myers, *The Children of Pride*, 1682.

161. Koehler and Huddleston, *Between the Wedding & the War*, 10-12, 14,179-180; Huddleston and Koehler, *Mittie & Thee*, 141, 148, 161, 166, 189, 198, 206.

162. For Major Alexander's obituary, refer to: https://www.findagrave.com/cgi-bin/fg.cgi?page=gr&GRid=91163895&ref=acom.

Chapter 13:

163. Delaine was any high-grade woolen or worsted fabric made of fine combing wool and was considered a high-quality women's wear dress material in the mid-1800s.

164. Foolscap, so called because in the 1700s it had a fool's cap watermark, is paper cut to the size of $8^{1/2} \times 13^{1/2}$ inches

and was the traditional paper size used in Europe and the British Commonwealth during this period. http://www.innovateus.net/innopedia/what-foolscap-paper

165. Tammy Harden Galloway, ed., *Dear Old Roswell: The Civil War Letters of the King Family of Roswell, Georgia* (Macon, GA: Mercer University Press, 2003), 48.
166. "Wrong Place at the Wrong Time," Chickamauga Blog: Chickamauga, the Civil War, and Sometimes, Just Life (blog). Accessed 2 February 2017, https://chickamaugablog.wordpress.com/2011/06/20/the-wrong-place-at-the-wrong-time/. Accessed: 2 February 2017; Paulette Snoby, *Georgia's Colony of Roswell* (Crab Orchard, KY: Interpreting Time's Past, LLC, 2015).
167. *New York Times*, 5 Nov 1863.

Chapter 14:

168. The Nicolay Version, named for John G. Nicolay, President Lincoln's personal secretary, this is considered the "first draft" of the speech, begun in Washington on White House stationery. The second page is written on different paper stock, indicating it was finished in Gettysburg before the cemetery dedication began. Lincoln gave this draft to Nicolay, who traveled to Gettysburg with Lincoln and witnessed the speech. The Library of Congress owns this manuscript.
169. Examples include articles in the *Daily Milwaukee News*, 14 November 1863 and the *Pittsburgh Daily Commercial* 12 November 1863.
170. *Harper's Weekly* often used the fictional Shoddy family as satirical characters in such editorial pieces as this one. The Shoddys were Irish, wealthy, and lacking in social graces. J. Matthew Gallman, *Defining Duty in the Civil War: Personal Choice, Popular Culture, and the Union Home Front* (Chapel Hill, NC: University of North Carolina Press, 2015), 109.
171. *Harper's Weekly*, 21 November 1863, 1-2, 11-12.
172. Florence Hartley, *The Ladies' Book of Etiquette, and*

Manual of Politeness: A Complete Hand Book for the Use of the Lady in Polite Society (Boston: G.W. Cottrell, 1860), 32-33.
173. Thomas Hamilton, "Stevenson, William Fleming," *Dictionary of National Biography, 1885-1900*, vol. 54 (London: Smith, Elder & Co., 1898).
174. Psalms 116, *The Bible*, (KJV).
175. Mrs. James Patterson lived at 229 W. 21st. James was an agent according to *Trow's* (1863) *New York City Directory*, 679.
176. On 28 March 2017 more than 2,500 articles could be found on Newspapers.com that related directly to the *Alabama* and other Confederate privateers.
177. *Evening Star* (Washington, D.C.) 10 August 1863.
178. Ibid.

Chapter 15:
179. Robinson, *My Brother Theodore Roosevelt*, 20-21.
180. McCullough, *Mornings On Horseback* (New York: Simon & Schuster, 2001), 28.
181. Two related, upper-class families named Adams resided in Roswell in 1864. Refer to *Providence* (Connie M. Cox and Darlene M. Walsh). However, no one in either family was married to someone with the last name Leagare or Légare. These families did have relatives living in the North.
182. *New York Times*, 2 February 1864.
183. An exhaustive search for a man named John Elliott, from Georgia, who fought in the Civil War, revealed numerous such men. A 2nd Lieutenant John B. Elliott served in Maxwell's Regular Light Artillery and was most likely Johnnie's father. Maxwell was a common name in Liberty County, Georgia, and related, by marriage, to the Elliott family. Additionally, little Johnnie Bugs was sent to relatives in the North indicating a certain degree of wealth within the family. Most often men of weatlh held officer's ranks during the Civil War.

184. James Tertius deKay, *The Rebel Raiders: The Astonishing History of the Confederacy's Secret Navy* (New York: Ballantine, 2002), 192-193.
185. Ibid., 191-203; Stephen Chapin Kinnaman, *The Most Perfect Cruiser* (Indianapolis: Dog Ear Publishing, 2009), 247; Wilson and McKay, *James D. Bulloch*, 165-166.
186. Ibid.
187. Wilson and McKay, *James D. Bulloch*, 165-166.
188. Suggested books include: Michael D. Hitt, *Charged with Treason: ordeal of 400 mill workers during military operations in Roswell Georgia, 1864-1865* (Monroe, NY: Library Research Associates, 1992); Mary Deborah Petite, *The Women Will Howl: The Union Army Capture of Roswell and New Manchester, Georgia, and the Forced Relocation of Mill Workers* (Jefferson, NC: McFarland, 2008); Snoby, *Georgia's Colony of Roswell*; Darlene Walsh, ed., *Roswell: A Pictorial History* (Roswell, GA: Roswell Historical Society, 1994).
189. "Blessed" was a family term of endearment for Martha often used by her children.
190. In *The Rise of Theodore Roosevelt*, Edmund Morris states that Thee purchased a home, called Loantaka, in Madison, New Jersey, in 1863. He wrote that the family spent the next four summers there. Their letters indicate the family summered at Long Branch, New Jersey, in 1863 and returned there on 7 June 1864. As there are no additional letters from the family that summer, it is possible they moved to Loantaka during the summer, and that Martha remained after the family's return to New York. See Edmund Morris, *The Rise of Theodore Roosevelt* (New York: Random House, 2010), 16-17; Corinne Roosevelt Robinson, in *My Brother Theodore Roosevelt*, states that the family did summer at Loantaka for several summers, but indicates these were in the years immediately following the War. See Robinson, *My Brother Theodore Roosevelt*, 34-35.
191. Breed, *West Spruce Street Presbyterian Church*, 15, 44.

192. "Letter from Anna Bulloch to William Bulloch, dated 23 January 1865" Southern Historical Collection, Louis Round Wilson Special Collections Library, University of North Carolina at Chapel Hill.
193. Laura married Joseph Lorenzo Locke in 1843. Locke graduated from West Point in 1835 and was stationed in Savannah with the artillery. He later resigned his commission and worked as an engineer for the Brunswick and Altamaha Land Company before purchasing the *Savannah Republican* newspaper in 1839. As editor, Locke became a respected writer and citizen of Savannah. With the beginning of the War, he offered his services to the Confederate States military and served as a major and Chief Commissary Officer of the Military District of Georgia. He died on 5 October 1864 and was buried in Laurel Grove Cemetery.
194. Cornelius E. Hunt, *Shenandoah : or, the Last Confederate Cruiser* (Charleston, SC: Nabu Press, 2010), 267; J. Thomas Sharf, *History of the Confederate States Navy: From Its Organization to the Surrender of Its Last Vessel* (The Fairfax Press, 1978), 809-812.
195. *Liverpool Mercury*, 9 November 1865.

Epilogue:
196. Luke Monroe was formerly identified as Luke Moumar. He registered to vote in 1867 as Luke Monroe. Georgia Voter Registrations records accessed on Ancestry.com.
197. *Atlanta Constitution*, 8 October 1905.
198. [Constance Cary] Burton Harrison, *Recollections Grave and Gay* (New York: Charles Scribner's Sons, 1911), 276-279.
199. McCullough, *Mornings on Horseback*, 184.
200. *New York Times*, 11 February 1878.
201. At the outbreak of the War, Archibald Gracie enlisted in the Confederate Army, first serving as a major with the 11th Alabama Regiment. He rose quickly through the ranks, and by the Battle of Chickamauga had earned the

rank of general. His unit lost over 700 men in that battle. He next served with General Longstreet and was wounded at the Battle of Bean's Station. At the Siege of Petersburg, between July and December 1864, Gracie served in the trenches. On 1 December, his 32nd birthday, his second child, a girl, was born. On 2 December an exploding artillery shell ended his life - the day before he was to take leave.

202. Anna's friend, Stephanie Hyatt married Horace Porter, one day later in the same church.
203. Wilson and McKay, *James D. Bulloch*, 289.
204. *New York Times*, 22 May 1905.
205. *Philadelphia Inquirer*, 26 January 1907; The Paxton House was a resort-type boarding hotel.
206. James D. Bulloch, *The Secret Service of the Confederate States in Europe, or How the Confederate Cruisers were Equipped* (New York: G.P. Putnam's Sons, 1884).
207. For further information of James D. Bulloch, see Kinnaman, *Captain Bulloch*; Bulloch, *The Secret Service of the Confederate States;* and Wilson and McKay, *James D. Bulloch*.
208. Spelled "Loantaka" in other references.
209. Robinson, *My Brother Theodore Roosevelt*, 36-37.
210. Harrison, *Recollections Grave and Gay*, 74-75.
211. Cited as found in Wilson, *The Bulloch Belles*, 151.
212. Ibid, 159-164.
213. Pictures and information about James and Irvine's graves can be found at http://www.csa-dixie.com/liverpool_dixie/newlinksab.htm.
214. *New York Tribune*, 1 Oct 1887.
215. *Brooklyn Daily Eagle*, 16 July 1898.
216. *New York Times*, 14 April 1912.
217. *Washington Herald*, 5 December 1912.
218. *New York Times*, 6 April 1887.
219. [Rochester, New York] *Democrat and Chronicle*, 15 June 1906.

220. *Minnie* O'Shea. After the death of Elizabeth Ellis, Robert Roosevelt married his mistress, Marion Theresa *Minnie* O'Shea, who had lived very near Robert's home for many years, under the name Fortescue. Together they had three or four children, who maintained the Fortescue name throughout their lives. Refer to McCullough, *Mornings on Horseback,* 22, 365.

Bibliography

Alderman, Nancy. "A Biography of Charles Green." The Savannah Biographies, Volume 4. Special Collections, Lane Library, Armstrong Atlantic State University, Savannah, GA, 1980.

Beatie, Russell. *Army of the Potomac: McClellan's First Campaign, March - May.* Savas Beatie, LLC, El Dorado Hills, 2007.

Berkeley, Henry R. *Four Years in the Confederate Artillery: the Diary of Private Henry Robinson Berkeley.* Virginia Historical Society, Richmond, 1991.

Blandin, I.M.E. (Mrs.). *History of Higher Education of Women in the South, Prior to 1860.* The Neale Publishing Company, New York, 1909.

Boyd, Andrew Kennedy Hutchison. *The Recreations of a Country Parson.* Ticknor & Fields, Boston, 1866.

Breed, W.P. *West Spruce Street Presbyterian Church, of Philadelphia. 1856-1881.* Sherman & Co. Printers, Philadelphia, 1881.

Bryant, William Cullen, ed., *Picturesque America.* D. Appleton and Co., New York, 1873.

Bulloch, James D. *The Secret Service of the Confederate States in Europe, or How the Confederate Cruisers were Equipped.* G.P. Putnam's Sons, New York, 1884.

Corning, Elwood A. *Hamilton Fish*. The Lanmere Publishing Company, New York, 1918.

Cox, Connie M. and Darlene M. Walsh. *Providence: Selected Correspondence of George Hull Camp 1837-1907, Son of the North, Citizen of the South*. Indigo Publishing Group, Macon, GA, 2008.

deKay, James Tertius. *The Rebel Raiders: The Astonishing History of the Confederacy's Secret Navy*. Ballantine Books, New York, 2002.

Farnham, Christie Anna. *The Education of the Southern Belle: Higher Education and Student Socialization in the Antebellum South*. New York University Press, New York, 1994.

Faust, Albert Bernhardt. *The German Element in the United States*. Houghton Mifflin, Boston, 1909.

Gallman, J. Matthew. *Defining Duty in the Civil War: Personal Choice, Popular Culture, and the Union Home Front*. University of North Carolina Press, Chapel Hill, 2015.

Galloway, Tammy Harden (ed.). *Dear Old Roswell: The Civil War Letters of the King Family of Roswell, Georgia*. Mercer University Press, Macon, GA, 2003.

Hagedorn, Hermann. *The Boys' Life of Theodore Roosevelt*. Harper & Brothers Publisher, New York, 1918.

Hamilton, Thomas. "Stevenson, William Fleming" *Dictionary of National Biography 1885-1900, Volume 54*. Smith, Elder & Co., London, 1898.

Handy, Isaac W. K. *United States Bonds or Duress By Federal Authority: A Journal of Current Events During An Imprisonment of Fifteen Months, At Fort Delaware*. Turnbull Brothers, Baltimore, 1874.

Harrison, Burton (Mrs.). *Recollections Grave and Gay.* Charles Scribner's Sons, New York, 1911.

Hartley, Florence. *The Ladies' Book of Etiquette, and Manual of Politeness: A Complete Hand Book for the Use of the Lady in Polite Society.* G. W. Cottrell, Boston, 1860.

Hitt, Michael D. *Charged with Treason: Ordeal of 400 mill workers during military operations in Roswell, Georgia, 1864-1865.* Library Research Associates, Monroe, NY, 1992.

Holloway, Verity. *The Mighty Healer: Thomas Holloway's Victorian Patent Medicine Empire.* Pen and Sword History, Barnsely, UK, 2016.

Huddleston, Connie M. and Gwendolyn I. Koehler. *Mittie & Thee: An 1853 Roosevelt Romance.* Friends of Bulloch, Inc., Roswell, GA, 2015.

Hughes, Nathaniel Cheairs. *Yale's Confederates: A Biographical Dictionary.* University of Tennessee Press, Knoxville, 2008.

Hunt, Cornelius E. *Shenandoah: or, the Last Confederate Cruiser.* Nabu Press, Charleston, SC. 2010.

Jamison, Jocelyn P. *They Died at Fort Delaware 1861-1865: Confederate, Union and Civilian.* Fort Delaware Society, Delaware City, DE, 1997.

Johnson, Charles, Jr. *Mary Telfair: The Life and Legacy of a Nineteenth-Century Woman.* Geor Frederic C. Beil Publisher, Savannah, 2002.

Jordan, John W. (compiler). *Colonial Families of Philadelphia, Vol. 1.* Lewis Publishing Company, New York, 1911.

Keckley, Elizabeth. *Behind the Scenes, or, Thirty Years a Slave and Four Years in the White House.* Wildside Press, Rockville, MD, 2013.

Kell, John McIntosh. *Recollection of a Naval Life Including the Cruises of the Confederate States Steamers "Sumter" and "Alabama."* The Neale Company, Publishers, Washington, D.C., 1900.

Kinnaman, Stephen Chapin. *Captain Bulloch: The Life of James Dunwoody Bulloch Naval Agent of the Confederacy.* Dog Ear Publishing, Indianapolis, 2013.

——— *The Most Perfect Cruiser.* Dog Ear Publishing, Indianapolis, 2009.

Koehler, Gwendolyn, I. and Connie M. Huddleston. *Between the Wedding & the War: The Bulloch/Roosevelt Letters 1854-1860.* Friends of Bulloch, Inc., Roswell, GA, 2016.

Lowry, Thomas P. *Curmudgeons, Drunkards, and Outright Fools: Courts-Martial of Civil War Union Colonels.* Bison Books, Lincoln NE, 2003).

McCullough, David. *Mornings on Horseback.* Simon & Schuster Paperbacks, New York. 2001.

McElroy, Archibald (compiler). *McElroy's Philadelphia City Directory, 1837.* Rackliff & Jones, Philadelphia, 1837.

McElroy's Philadelphia City Directory, 1859, Isaac Ashmead & Co., 1859.

McLeod, Rebecca. "The Loss of the Steamer Pulaski," *The Georgia Historical Quarterly* 3:2 (1919).

McPherson, James M. *Battle Cry of Freedom: The Civil War Era*. (Oxford History of the United States Book 6). Oxford University Press, New York, 1988.

Morgan, James A., III. *A Little Short of Boats: The Battle of Ball's Bluff and Edwards Ferry, October 21-22, 1861*. Salvas Beatie, El Dorado Hills, CA, 2011.

Morris, Edmund. *The Rise of Theodore Roosevelt*. Random House Trade Paperbacks, New York, 2001.

Mowday, Bruce and Dale Fetzer. *Unlikely Allies: Fort Delaware's Prison Community in the Civil War*. Mechanicsburg, PA, Stackpole Books, 2000.

Myers, Robert Manson. *The Children of Pride: A True Story of Georgia and the Civil War*. Yale University Press, New Haven and London, 1972.

Rixey, Lilian. *Bamie: Theodore Roosevelt's Remarkable Sister*. David McKay Company, Inc., New York, 1963.

Robinson, Corinne Roosevelt. *My Brother Theodore Roosevelt*. Charles Scribner's Sons, New York, 1921.

Salsi, Lynn and Margaret Sims. *Columbia: History of a Southern Capital*. Arcadia Publishing, Charleston, SC, 2003.

Sharf, J. Thomas. *History of the Confederate States Navy: From Its Organization to the Surrender of Its Last Vessel*. The Fairfax Press, New York, 1978.

Shults, Gladys. *Lady From Savannah*. Lippincott Company, Philadelphia and New York, 1968.

Smith, Derek. *The Gallant Dead: Union and Confederate Generals Killed in the Civil War*. Stackpole Books, Mechanicsburg, PA, 2005.

Smith, William Prescott. *The Book of the Great Railway Celebrations of 1857*. D. Appleton & Co., New York, 1858

Snoby, Paulette. *Georgia's Colony of Roswell: One Man's Dream and the People Who Lived It*. Interpreting Time's Past, LLC, Crab Orchard, KY, 2015.

Sobel, Robert and John Raimo (eds.). *Biographical Dictionary of the Governors of the United States, 1789-1978, Vol. 1*. Meckler, Westport, CT, 1989.

Staley, Patricia F. *Norwich and the Civil War*. The History Press, Charleston, SC, 2015.

────── *The Union army: a history of military affairs in the loyal states, 1861-65 -- records of the regiments in the Union army -- cyclopedia of battles -- memoirs of commanders and soldiers, Volume II*. Federal Publishing Co., Madison, WI, 1908.

United States War Department. *Revised United States Army Regulations of 1861, with an Appendix Containing the Changes and Laws affecting Army Regulations and Articles of War to June 25, 1862*. Government Printing Office, Washington, D.C., 1863.

Walsh, Darlene M. (editor). *Roswell: A Pictorial History*. Roswell Historical Society, Roswell, GA, 1994.

Wilson, H. (compiler). *Trow's New York City Directory, 1862*. John F. Trow, New York, 1862.
 Trow's New York City Directory, 1863. John F. Trow, New York, 1863.
 Trow's New York City Directory, 1864. John F. Trow, New York, 1864.

Wilson, Walter E. *The Bulloch Belles: Three First Ladies, a Spy, a President's Mother, and Other Women of a 19th Century Georgia Family*. McFarland & Company, Inc. Publishers, Jefferson, NC and London, 2015.

Wilson, Walter E. and Gary L. McKay. *James D. Bulloch: Secret Agent and Mastermind of the Confederate Navy*. McFarland & Company, Inc. Publishers, Jefferson, NC, and London, 2012.

Wood, Betty (editor). *Mary Telfair to Mary Few: Selected Letters 1802-1844*. The University of Georgia Press, Athens, 2007.

―― *Woods' Baltimore City Directory Ending Year 1860*. John W. Woods, Baltimore, 1861.

Newspapers (unless stated) and Magazines:

Baltimore Sun
Brooklyn Daily Eagle
Buffalo Commercial (NY)
Charlotte Democrat
Daily Appeal (Memphis)
Daily Milwaukee News
Daily Ohio Statesman (Columbus)
Daily Progress (Raleigh)
Darien Gazette (Georgia)
Democrat & Chronicle (Rochester, NY)
Evening Star (Washington, D.C.)
Frank Leslie's Illustrated Newspaper
Harper's New Monthly Magazine
Harper's Weekly
Hillsborough Recorder (North Carolina)
Illustrated London News
Janesville Daily Gazette (Wisconsin)
Juliet Signal (Illinois)
Liberator (Boston)
Liverpool Mercury (UK)

Macon Daily Telegraph
Nashville Union and American (Tennessee)
New York Democrat
New York Herald
New York Times
New York Tribune
Peterson's Magazine
Philadelphia Inquirer
Pittsburgh Gazette
Pittsburgh Daily Commercial
Pomeroy's Democrat (New York City)
Reading Times (Pennsylvania)
Savannah Daily Georgian
Savannah Georgian
Savannah Republican
Syracuse Daily Courier and Union (New York)
Washington Herald (Washington D.C.)

List of Persons

Adams, Theodore Dwight (1829-1901): storekeeper at the Roswell Manufacturing Company and assistant postmaster.

Bulloch, Anna Louise (1833-1893): daughter of Martha and James Stephens Bulloch.

Bulloch, Elizabeth "Lizzie" Euphemia Caskie (1831-1854): of Richmond, Virginia, sister to Mary Edmonia Caskie (second wife to Robert Hutchison) married James Dunwoody Bulloch in 1851.

Bulloch, Henry Dunwoody (1861-1871): second son of James and Harriott Bulloch.

Bulloch, Irvine Stephens (1842-1898): son of Martha and James Stephens Bulloch.

Bulloch, James Dunwoody (1823-1901): son of Hester Elliott and James Stephens Bulloch, married Lizzie Caskie in 1851. Often referred to as *brother Jimmie*.

Bulloch, James Dunwoody, Jr. (1858-1888): first son of James D. Bulloch and Harriott Cross Foster.

Bulloch, James Stephens, Major (1793-1849): grandson of Georgia's first governor, Archibald Bulloch, veteran of the War of 1812, invested in Roswell Manufacturing Company, built Bulloch Hall. Married first to Hester Amarintha Elliott (1797-1831) in 1817, son James Dunwoody Bulloch (1823-1901) lived to maturity. Second marriage to his stepmother-in-law, Martha Stewart Elliott in 1832, children include Anna

(1833-1893), Martha *Mittie* (1835-1884), Charles Irvine (1838-1841) and Irvine Stephens (1842-1898).

Bulloch, Jessie Hart (1860-1941): first daughter of James D. Bulloch and Harriott Cross Foster.

Bulloch, Martha Louise (1865-1947): second daughter of James and Harriott Cross Foster Bulloch.

Bulloch, Martha Stewart Elliott (1799-1864): daughter of American Revolutionary General Daniel Stewart. Married first John Elliott in 1818, children include John Whitehead (1818-1820), Susan Ann (1820-1895), Georgia Amanda (1822-1848), Charles William (1824-1827), and Daniel Stewart (1826-1862). Married second, in 1832, James Stephens Bulloch (her step-son-in-law), children include Anna Louise (1833-1893), Martha *Mittie* (1835-1884), Charles Irvine (1838-1841) and Irvine Stephens (1842-1898).

Bulloch, Stuart Elliott (1863-1939): third son of James and Harriott Bulloch.

Bulloch, William Gaston, Dr. (1815-1885): cousin to James Stephens Bulloch, resident of Savannah, Mittie's second cousin.

Caskie, Ellen Laura (1836-1858): resident of Richmond, Virginia, first cousin to Robert Hutchison's second wife and Lizzie Bulloch.

Although most Dunwoody family documents from this period use only one "o" in the name, we have used the more familiar Dunwoody spelling for consistency.

Dunwoody, Charles Archibald Alexander (1828-1905): son of John Dunwoody, married Ellen Rice (1827-1895) in 1852.

Dunwoody, Ellen Rice (1827-1895): married Charles Dunwoody in 1852.

Dunwoody, Henry Macon (1826-1863): fourth child of John and Jane Dunwoody.

Dunwoody, James Bulloch (1816-1902): son of John and Jane Dunwoody. A Presbyterian minister who served from 1845 to 1855 in Pocotaligo, South Carolina. He married Mittie and Thee. Married Laleah Georgianna Wood Pratt (1823 to 1853) who died about 1 October giving birth to a son.

Dunwoody, Jane Irvine Bulloch (1788-1856): wife of John Dunwoody of Roswell.

Dunwoody, John (1786-1858): planter in Liberty County, Georgia, before moving to Roswell, Georgia, married Jane Bulloch in 1808, brother-in-law to Martha Bulloch.

Dunwoody, John, Jr., Colonel (1818-1903): second child of John and Jane Dunwoody, served eight years in Georgia militia, fought in Mexican War (1846-1848), served as government surveyor in Kansas, and later in Confederacy, married Elizabeth Clark Wing.

Dunwoody, Laleah *Lilly* Georgianna (1844-1919): daughter of Reverend James and Laleah Dunwoody.

Dunwoody, Marion Stanhope Glen (1821-1885): fifth child of John and Jane Dunwoody, married for second time in 1851 to William Glen.

Dunwoody, Ruth Ann Atwood (1826-1899): married to Dr. William Elliott Dunwoody, mother of three children by 1853.

Dunwoody, William Elliott, Sr. Dr. (1823-1891): son of John and Jane Dunwoody.

Elliott, Daniel Stewart (Stuart) (1826-1862): son of Martha Stewart and John Elliott, often referred to as *brother Dan*. Daniel Stewart Elliott officially changed his name to Stuart Elliott in December of 1853. The official notice did not give a reason for this change.

Elliott, John (1773-1827): planter, lawyer, and U.S. Senator. Married in 1795 to Esther Dunwoody (d. 1815), children included Caroline Matilda (1796-before 1827), Hester Amarintha (1797-1831), John (1801-1803), Rebecca Jane (1803-1804), John (1807-1813), Jane Elizabeth (1809-1829), Corinne Louisa (1813-1838) and Charles James (1815-1817). Second marriage to Martha Stewart in 1818, children included John Whitehead (1818-1820), Susan Ann (1820-1895), Georgia Amanda (1822-1848), Charles William (1824-1827), and Daniel Stewart (1826-1862).

Elliott, John Stuart (1859-1913): son of Daniel Stewart/Stuart Elliott and Lucinda Ireland Sorrel.

Elliott, Lucinda *Lucy* Ireland Sorrel (1829-1903): married Daniel Stewart/Stuart Elliott in 1858.

Elliott, Matilda Moxley (1860-1910): daughter of Daniel Stewart/Stuart Elliott and Lucinda Ireland Sorrel.

Emlen, George (1814-1853): wealthy Philadelphia merchant and brother-in-law to James Alfred Roosevelt.

Emmet, Catherine Rebecca Duncan (1825-1905): wife of Dr. Thomas Addis Emmet, married in Alabama in 1854.

Emmet, Dr. Thomas Addis (1828-1919): well respected and published gynecologist and Roosevelt family physician, married to Catherine Rebecca Duncan, Martha's friend.

Henop, Julia Dickson (1814-1887): fellow Southerner, Martha's friend, and wife of Frederick Lewis Henop.

Hutchison, Robert (1802-1861): Scottish born, wealthy Savannah merchant, married first in 1832 Corinne Louisa Elliott, Martha Bulloch's stepdaughter. Corinne and their two daughters died in the sinking of the steamer *Pulaski* in 1838. Hutchison married second Mary Edmonia Caskie of Virginia in 1848. Mary died of consumption in 1852. Hutchison remained a friend of the family and was executor of James Stephens Bulloch's estate. He married a third time, on 23 April 1857, Ellen Laura Caskie (1836-1858), who was the first cousin of his second wife.

Hyatt, Caroline *Caddie* (1841-unknown): daughter of Stephen and Dorinda Hyatt.

Hyatt, Melissa Augusta *Lillie* (1843-1915): daughter of Stephen and Dorinda Hyatt.

Hyatt, Stephanie *Phanie* (1844-unknown): daughter of Stephen and Dorinda Hyatt.

King, Barrington (1798-1866): son of Roswell King and co-founder of Roswell Manufacturing Company, married Catherine Margaret Nephew. Lived in Barrington Hall, adjacent to Bulloch Hall.

King, Barrington Simeral (1833-1865): fifth son of Barrington and Catherine King, grandson of Roswell King (Roswell's founder)

King, Clifford Alonzo (1842-1911): youngest surviving child of Barrington and Catherine King, grandson of Roswell King (Roswell's founder), lived at Barrington Hall.

King, James Roswell (1827-1897): son of Barrington and Catherine King, grandson of Roswell King (Roswell's founder), married Elizabeth Frances *Fanny* Hillhouse Prince (1829-1881) in 1851.

King, Ralph Browne (1835-1900): son of Barrington and Catherine King, grandson of Roswell King (Roswell's founder), lived at Barrington Hall.

King, Thomas *Tom* Edward (1829-1863): son of Barrington and Catherine King, grandson of Roswell King (Roswell's founder). Married Mary (Marie) Read Clemens of Huntsville, Alabama, on 30 November 1854.

King, William Nephew, Dr. (1825-1894): son of Barrington and Catherine King, grandson of Roswell King (Roswell's founder), lived at Barrington Hall, William studied at the New York College of Physicians and Surgeons before studying surgery for three years in Paris.

Low, Mary Cowper Stiles (1832-1863): sister of William Henry Stiles II, daughter of William Henry and Eliza Anne Stiles of Savannah, married Andrew Low of Savannah.

Pratt, Nathaniel Alpheus, Reverend (1796-1879): first minister of the Roswell Presbyterian Church, schoolmaster, married Catherine Barrington King in 1830.

Roosevelt, Anna *Bamie* (1855-1931): first child and daughter of Mittie Bulloch and Theodore Roosevelt.

Roosevelt, Corinne (1861-1933): second daughter and fourth child of Mittie Bulloch and Theodore.

Roosevelt, Cornelius Van Schaak (1794-1871): married Margaret Barnhill (1790-1861) in 1821.

Roosevelt, Cornelius Van Schaak, Jr. (1827-1887): married Laura H. Porter (1833-1900) in 1854.

Roosevelt, Elizabeth *Lizzie* Thorne Ellis (1833-1887): married to Robert Barnhill Roosevelt.

Roosevelt, Elizabeth *Lizzie* **Norris Emlen** (1825-1912): married James Alfred Roosevelt in 1847.

Roosevelt, Elliott (1860-1894): third child and second son of Mittie Bulloch and Theodore Roosevelt

Roosevelt, James Alfred (1825-1898): married Elizabeth Norris Emlen in 1847, often called *Jim*.

Roosevelt, John Ellis (1853-1939): first child of Robert and Lizzie Roosevelt.

Roosevelt, Laura H. Porter (1833-1900): of Lockport, New York, married Cornelius Jr., in 1854.

Roosevelt, Margaret Barnhill (1799-1861): married Cornelius Van Schaak Roosevelt, Sr. in 1821.

Roosevelt, Margaret Barnhill (1851-1927): daughter of Robert and *Lizzie* Ellis.

Roosevelt, Martha *Mittie* **Bulloch** (1835-1884): daughter of Martha and James Stephens Bulloch.

Roosevelt, Mary West (1823-1877): wife of Silas Weir Roosevelt, Hilborne West's sister.

Roosevelt, Robert Barnhill (1829-1906): married to *Lizzie* Ellis in 1850, most often called *Rob*.

Roosevelt, Silas Weir (1823-1870): married Mary West in 1845.

Roosevelt, Theodore (1831-1878): married Mittie Bulloch in 1853.

Roosevelt, Theodore (1858-1919): first son and second child of Mittie Bulloch and Theodore Roosevelt, 26th president of the United States.

Smith, Archibald (1801-1886): resident of Roswell, married Ann Margaret Magill.

West, Hilborne, Dr. (1818-1907): of Philadelphia, married Susan Ann Elliott in 1849.

West, James (1785-1867): of Philadelphia, married Rebecca Coe in 1816, father of Mary, Hilborne, and Lewis.

West, Lewis *Lew* (1829-1867): of Philadelphia, officer in the U.S. Navy, younger brother of Hilborne and Mary West.

West, Rebecca Coe (1791-1882): of Philadelphia, wife of James West, mother of Mary, Hilborne, and Lewis.

West, Susan Ann Elliott (1820-1895): daughter of Martha Stewart and John Elliott, married Hilborne West in 1849.

Roosevelt Family Servants (New York):
Ann Butler
Annie
Bessie
Bridget - Elliott's nursemaid
Delia
Dora
Mary Ann
Mrs. Riley - wet nurse for Corinne
Nora - Irish nursemaid to Anna *Bamie*

West Family Servants (Philadelphia):
Hannah Crone
(In 1860 James and Rebecca West had three Negro female servants, all from Maryland. In 1870, Hilborne and Susan lived with Rebecca and had three female Irish servants and one female servant born in Pennsylvania. Hannah Crone is listed in 1860 at Hilborne and Susan's home in Philadelphia, but not in 1870).

Appendix A:
A Brief History of Bulloch Friends and Family Who Served the Confederacy

Roswell, Georgia

Although Irvine struggled with whether to join the Confederate Army or Navy, other young men of Roswell made, what was to them, the obvious choice. Of Barrington King's sons, Dr. William Nephew King (1825-1894) served as a staff surgeon. At their own expense, James Roswell King (1827-1897) and Thomas Edward King (1829-1863) formed a cavalry company named the Roswell Battalion. Until 1864, James stayed in Roswell and ran the company's mills which made a gray, wool-blend cloth used for Confederate uniforms. He served in the Confederate Army as a captain and after the destruction of Roswell's mills during Sherman's March to the Sea. Later he campaigned with the Roswell Battalion before being detailed to oversee railroad construction for the Confederate military. James served until surrender in 1865.

Thomas, known to all as *Tom*, was wounded at the First Battle of Manassas (First Battle of Bull Run 21 July 1861). Tom returned home to recover from his wounds, which included a shattered ankle. However, on 14 September 1863, Tom hopped a train north, determined to rejoin the War in any capacity, as he still hobbled with a cane. Arriving on the morning of 19 September, he joined the staff of Brigadier General Preston Smith at Chickamauga as an aide-de-camp. That night, the 19th of September 1863, General Smith and several aides accidently crossed enemy lines and were fired upon by members of the 77th Pennsylvania. General Smith and Captains Tom King and John Donelson all died during the ambush. His family later moved his body to Roswell's Presbyterian Cemetery.

Barrington Simeral King (1833-1865), a homeopathic physician, joined Cobb's Legion, Confederate Army of Northern Virginia, as a lieutenant colonel and moved his family to Virginia as the War began. Barrington served throughout the War in the Cobb's Legion, fighting in most of the battles on that front. While leading a charge at the Battle of Averasborough (or Averasboro) on 16 March 1865, Barrington suffered a fatal wound and died on the battlefield, less then one month before the War's end. Like that of his brother Tom, his family later moved his body to Roswell's Presbyterian Cemetery.

Ralph Browne King (1835-1900) enlisted and served as a lieutenant under General W. J. Hardee and as a member of the Chatham County (Savannah) Artillery. He reached the rank of captain in the home guard. He suffered a severe wound and never completely recovered.

Joseph Henry King (1839-1917) joined early, even before Georgia's secession. He signed up as a private at Fort Pulaski and served under General Bartow and General Joseph Johnston. Like his older brother Tom, Joseph was wounded at the First Battle of Manassas. He never returned to service.

In 1859, Irvine Bulloch's best friend Clifford Alonzo King enlisted as a cadet at West Point. It seems he stayed only one year. His commander was Colonel William Joseph Hardee of Georgia. On 20 September 1861, at age 20, Clifford (1842-1911) enlisted in 3rd Battalion Georgia Infantry and was sent to Greenville, Tennessee, and later Cumberland Gap, Kentucky. Early 1862 found Clifford absent on medical leave from 9 February until 28 April and after that listed as *absent without leave*. On all records from this early part of the War, Clifford is listed as *Cadet*, meaning an officer who had not reached his *majority* or legal age to be an officer. In September of 1863, Clifford requested a transfer and relief from field service to staff service under General Hugh W. Mercer in Savannah, due to severe dysentery. As required by regulations, a surgeon's note attached to the letter was signed by William Nephew King, Staff Surgeon and Clifford's older brother. Clifford signed his letter 2nd Lieutenant, as he had now reached legal age. Clifford married Mary Eliza Hardee, niece of General Hardee, on 3 March 1864 and remained in Savannah until its fall in December of that year. In early 1865, Hardee requested Clifford's promotion to 1st Lieutenant, as he then served on Hardee's staff.

Of their cousins the Dunwoodys, four sons served the Confederacy. The Rev. James Bulloch Dunwoody (1816-1902) served briefly as an army chaplain. Lt. Col. John E. Dunwoody, Jr. (1818-1903), once a West Point cadet, served eight years in the Georgia Militia as chief of staff for General Walter Echols. He fought in the Mexican War, and later served as a government surveyor in Kansas. He accepted the rank of major in the 7th Regiment Georgia Infantry in May of 1861 and a promotion to lieutenant colonel in December. When his commission ended, John continued to serve as a major, and a disbursing agent.

Henry Macon Dunwoody (1826-1863) accepted appointment as a captain of the 51st *Early (County) Volunteers* Georgia Infantry on 4 March 1862. He saw action at Seccessionville, South Carolina, South Mountain, Sharpsburg, Fredericksburg, and Chancellorsville. Henry received a promotion to major just prior to their march into Pennsylvania, where he was killed in the Battle of the Wheatfield at Gettysburg. Henry left behind his wife Matilda Elizabeth Maxwell (1829-1902) and three children, Althea (1853-1866), Edward Maxwell (1856-1873), and Corinne Elliott (1860-1875). They were buried in a Dunwoody plot at Roswell's Presbyterian Cemetery. Henry's remains may have been returned to Roswell after the War. Matilda outlived her immediate family and served as a nurse in Savannah according to the 1880 census. By 1900, she had returned to Roswell where she rented a house.

Charles Archibald Alexander Dunwoody accepted a commission as a first lieutenant in the Roswell Guard in May of 1861. He served in Longstreet's Corps and with General Bee's army at the Battle of First Manassas where he was wounded in the hip. Although he resigned his commission, Charles returned to service twice. In the Spring of 1862, Charles became the commanding officer with the rank of major at the instructional camp at Calhoun, Georgia. He returned to active duty once again on 28 June 1863, as a private with the Roswell Battalion Georgia Cavalry, but resigned again on 8 December of that year for health reasons.

Archibald and Anne Smith had two sons. William S. *Willie* (1834-1865) enlisted in the Savannah Volunteer Guards and remained in service in Savannah until its fall in December of 1864. His unit retreated with troops under General Hardee, to whose staff he was attached. Willie succumbed to a variety of illnesses after a long period of hospitalization in North Carolina. His brother, Archibald, called *Archie,* (1844-1923) enrolled in the Georgia Military Institute in Marietta in 1862. By 1864, both Smith sons served in Savannah. They met briefly during the evacuation of that city. Archie returned home safe and sound and lived out his life in LaGrange, Georgia.

The Reverend Nathaniel Alpheus Pratt and his wife Catherine Barrington King had five sons at the beginning of the War. Horace A. (1830-1870) possibly served in the 3rd Regiment, 2nd Battalion, Georgia State Troops, while Henry Barrington (1832-1912) served in the 42nd Regiment, Georgia Infantry.

Nathaniel Alpheus Pratt (1834-1906) studied medicine and chemistry and served as a professor of chemistry and geology at Oglethorpe University at the outbreak of the War. *Nat* organized his own company of Jordan Grays, but the Confederate government had other plans and made him assistant chief of the Confederate States Niter and Mining Bureau with the rank of captain. Nathaniel never saw active duty.

Charles Jones Pratt (1842-1924) attended the Georgia Military Institute at Marietta and enlisted as a private on 2 May 1862 in the Savannah Volunteer Guards, Company A, 18th Battalion Georgia Infantry. On 16 June, he accepted an appointment as drillmaster with the rank of 2nd lieutenant and was transferred to the instructional camp at Macon. Charles resigned in early 1863 and took up employment as an engineer on the proposed Atlanta & Roswell Railroad. Later that year, on 11 August, he once again signed up as a junior 1st lieutenant in Company B, Roswell Battalion, Georgia Cavalry. Early the next year, Charles joined Morgan's command as a private in Company B, 1st Regiment Kentucky Cavalry. He was taken prisoner on 4 September in Green County, Tennessee, sent to Chattanooga, and exchanged at Rough & Ready, Georgia, on the 22nd of that same month. Charles did not return to service after his release.

William Nephew Pratt (1848-1935) was only 13 when the War began; however, it appears that William did join the Company A, Roswell Battalion, Georgia Cavalry, at some point before the War's end.

Richmond, Virginia

Robert Alexander Caskie (1830-1928) enlisted and was commissioned as a captain on 9 June 1861 with Company A, Virginia 10th Cavalry Regiment. Rob received a promotion to full lieutenant colonel on 11 September 1863. The unit served in Hampton's, W.H.F. Lee's, Chambliss' and Beale's Brigade, Army of Northern Virginia. They fought in the Seven Days Battles, Antietam, Fredericksburg, Brandy Station, Upperville, Gettysburg, Bristoe, and Mine Run. The regiment was involved in the Wilderness Campaign, the defense of Richmond and Petersburg, and at Appomattox Courthouse. Robert's name appears on the list of parole passes given out after Lee's surrender at Appomattox Courthouse.

Rob's Associated Press obituary states he was the officer and organizer of the Richmond Grays, organizer and leader of the Caskie Rangers, a band of cavalry. It also states he became a liaison officer serving Generals Lee, Jackson, and Stuart and "once was seriously wounded." Records show Rob was listed as *Wounded in Action* at Reams Station on 23 August 1864 and was on limited action for several months thereafter. Jeb Stuart nicknamed him "Old Joshua."

Rob married Amanda Wallace Gregory (1844-1902) and had two sons: William Armisted (b. 1860) and Edmund William (b. 1861). They added four more children after the War and moved to Rocheport, Missouri, where Robert continued the family business of buying and selling tobacco.

William *Willie* Henderson Caskie (1834-1900) enlisted and was commissioned as a 2nd lieutenant on 11 May 1861. Willie served in Company C, Virginia 38th Light Artillery Battalion, also known as *Read's*. The unit was assigned to the Army of Northern Virginia and was active from the Seven Days battles to Gettysburg. They then moved to North Carolina and were later involved in the Plymouth expedition. Upon their return to Virginia, his battery fought on the Bermuda Hundred line, at Cold Harbor, and participated in the defense of Petersburg. Willie was promoted to captain on 21 April 1862 and served until 9 April 1864. He re-enlisted that same day and was promoted to major. His unit served until Appomattox.

Civil War era records show Willie at the hospital in Richmond on 19 September 1864. He was released the next day to recuperate at home. He also received a five month furlough in November of 1864, but reported back on 1 February 1865, near Petersburg. It is possible Willie was present at General Lee's surrender; however his name does not appear on the list of officers who received parole passes to return home after the surrender.

When the War started, Willie was married to Mary Augusta Ambler (1838 -1918). They had four children Ambler (1856-1934), John (1857-1915), Gay (b. 1859), and Robert A. (born 1861). Only the first two are listed on Willie's tombstone in Galveston, Texas. In Texas, Willie illustrated for various magazines, periodicals, and comics for the *Texas Siftings*. In later years, he served as an office deputy in Galveston. He continued to produce pen and ink illustrations, and painted notable scenes from his memories of the Civil War.

Appendix B:
Relevant Union and Confederate Officers and Leaders

Army ranks:
General
Lieutenant General
Major General
Brigadier General
Colonel
Lieutenant Colonel
Major
Captain
First Lieutenant
Second Lieutenant
Sergeant
Corporal
Private

Union* Navy Ranks & Ratings
Rear Admiral
Commodore
Captain
Commander
Lieutenant Commander
Lieutenant
Master
Ensign
Midshipman
Master's mate
Master's Mate (rated senior petty officer
Petty Officer
Ordinary Seaman
Landsman
Boy

*Confederate Navy ranks and ratings were similar to those of Union Navy.

Each entry gives the person's name, rank (if applicable), year of birth and death, state of birth, relevant comments and page number of mentions. Listed in alphabetical order with Union first followed by Confederates.

United States of America

Adams, Col. Julius Walker, 1812-1899, New York, born in Mass., wounded at Fair Oaks/Seven Pines, 72

Alberger, Lt. Col. William Clendenin, 1837-1925, New York, wounded at Antietam, 76.
Augur, General Christopher Columbus, 1821-1898, New York, Commandant at West Point at outbreak of War. 125-127.
Bartlett, Col. Joseph Jackson, 1834-1893, New York, rose to rank of Brigadier General then Brevet Major General, 79.
Banks, Major General Nathaniel, 1816-1894, Massachusetts, nicknamed Bobbin Boy Banks as he once worked in cotton mills, self-educated, 154-155, 198.
Bendix, Col. John E., 1818-1877, New York, wounded at Fredericksburg, Brevet Brigadier General during War, 138-139.
Bidwell, Col. Daniel Davidson, 1819-1864, New York, promoted to Brigadier General in Aug. 1864, killed Oct. 19, 1864 at Battle of Cedar Creek, 76.
Blair, Representative Francis Preston, Jr., 1821-1875, Kentucky, represented Missouri, Chairman of Military Affairs Committee. Also a colonel in the volunteer army, 92-93, 96, 109.
Blenker, Brigadier General Louis, 1812-1863, Worms, Germany, raised 8th NY Volunteers, mustered out in 1863, died of injuries sustained while in army, 79.
Bronson, Theodore Bailey, 1830-1881, New York, named commissioner later in year, served as Provost Marshall of New York, 120-121, 130, 133, 146,-147, 150, 164, 170, 198-199, 201-202, 204, 221, 223, 225-227.
Brown, Ezekiel, 1823-1888, unknown, Secretary of Statistical Bureau of the Sanitary Commission, 67.
Buckingham, Govenor William Albert, 1804-1875, Connecticut, 113.
Burke, Lt. Col. John Timothy, 1838-1914, Ireland, court martialed after Battle of Antietam for cowardice, 79.
Burnside, Major General Ambrose Everett, 1824-1881, Rhode Island 121, 211.
Butterfield, General Daniel Adams, 1831-1901, New York, Medal of Honor winner, wrote or rewrote *Taps*, 106-107, 112, 151, 313, 315, 322.

Cameron, Secretary of War Simon, 1799-1889, Secretary of War from March 1861 to January 1862 (resigned), 89-90.
Casey, General Silas, 1807-1882, Rhode Island, Graduated West Point 1826, served in Mexican War and Pig War, 80
Chamberlain, Dr. William M., 1826-1887, New Jersey, inspector for the Sanitary Commission, 73.
Chase, Salmon Portland, 1808-1873, New Hampshire, Secretary of the Treasury, 97.
Colgate, Lt. Col. Clinton Gilbert, 1834-1886, New York, 15th New York Engineers' Regiment, promoted to Col. Dec of 1862, 69.
Cone, Col. Spencer Wallace, 1819-1888, Virginia, New York lawyer and poet, Brevet Brigadier General after the War, 80.
Cochrane, Col. John, 1813-1898, New York, lawyer, resigned in 1863, 72.
DeTrobriand, Col. Philippe Regis Denis de Keredern, 1816-1897, New York, native of France, 66-68.
Dickel, Col. Christian Frederich, 1808-1880, Germany, Dickel's Mounted Rifles, owned a riding academy on 43rd Street, New York, 78.
Dix, Major General John Adams, 1798-1879, New York, former governor of New York, 100, 166, 168, 198, 212, 225.
Dodge, Major Charles Cleveland, 1841-1910, New York, would be later promoted to Brigadier General, received his commission at age 21, brother of William E., 138-139, 224-226
Dodge, William Earl, Jr., 1832-1903, New York, Allotment Commissioner for New York, brother of Charles C., 63-64, 69, 89, 92-95, 98-101, 103, 111-115, 119-123, 130, 133, 138-139, 142, 147, 150, 153-154, 176.
Fardella, Col. Enrico, 1821-1892, Sicily, Brevet Brigadier General, lived in New York, 172, 174.
Farnsworth, Lt. Col. Addison, 1825-1877, New York, 38th NY Volunteers, wounded at 1st Bull Run, Brevet Brigadier General, 79.
Fessenden, Senator William Pitt, 1806-1869, Maine, 92.
Fish, Governor Hamilton, 1808-1893, New York, governor from 1849 to 1850, 99-100.

Foster, Capt. George, New York, rose to rank of Lt. Col., Dismissed in Oct. 62 for disability, 72.
Fowler, Col. Edward Brush, 1828-1896, New York, wounded at Second Bull Run, Brevet Brigadier General after War, 77.
Garrard, Brigadier General Kenner, 1827-1879, Kentucky, Graduated West Point 1851, two brothers also Union generals, 332.
Grant, General Ulysses S., 1822-1885, Ohio, Graduated West Point 1843, 129, 166, 235, 271, 319.
Halleck, Major General Henry Wagner, 1815-1872, New York, Graduate West Point 1839, 121, 166.
Hardie, Col. James Allen, 1823-1876, New York, worked for Gen. Thomas Williams, 66-67.
Harris, Senator Ira, 1802-1875, New York, organized Harris Light Cavalry, 93-94, 112, 164, 173.
Hawkins, Col. Rush Christopher, 1831-1920, Vermont, 110-111.
Hay, John, 1838-1905, Springfield, Illinois, Lincoln's personal secretary. Sec. of State under Theodore Roosevelt, 66, 69-70, 72, 74, 89, 93, 98, 147-148, 158.
Heintzelman, Major General Samuel Peter, 1805-1880, Pennsylvania, Graduated West Point 1826, career military, wounded at 1st Bull Run, returned to duty, 79.
Hooker, Major General Joseph, 1814-1879, Massachusetts, Graduated West Point 1827, 235,253.
Hooper, Representative Samuel, 1808-1876, Massachusetts, 93-94, 98.
Innes, Col. Charles H., 1823-1888, New York, served in and wounded twice in Mexican War, 36th New York, 72.
Jenkins, Dr. John Foster, 1826-1882, unknown, first General Secretary of the Sanitary Commission, 67.
Johnson, Col. Charles Adams, 1826-1891, New York, wounded at Hanover Court House, Brevet General after the War, 77.
Ketchum, Captain William A., unknown, New York, entered as a Capt. in 1861, resigned as a Lt. Colonel in 1865, 69.

Keyes, General Erasmus Darwin, 1810-1895, Massachusetts, Graduated West Point 1832, career military, 77, 93-94, 97, 173, 197.

King, Senator Preston, 1806-1865, New York, 112.

King, Captain Rufus, 1838-1900, New York, Medal of Honor winner, 302, 305.

Lansing, Col. Henry Seymour, 1823-1882, New York, Brevet Brigadier General at end of War, 76, 120.

McClellan, Major Gen. George B., 1826-1885, Pennsylvania, briefly general-in-chief, 41, 92-94, 121, 128, 155-156, 159, 165-166, 174, 189, 211, 319.

McCunn, Col. John H., 1820-1872, Ireland, Brevet Brigadier General, judge, involved in Tweed Ring after the War, 79.

McDowell, Major General Irvin, 1818-1885, Ohio, Graduated West Point 1838, 41.

McQuady, Col. James, 1829-1885, New York, Brevet Major General at end of War, 77.

Mansfield, Brigadier General Joseph King Fenno, 1803-1862, Connecticut, killed at Battle of Antietam, 145-147.

Marcy, Brigadier General Randolph Barnes, 1812-1887, Massachusetts, Brevet Major General, 134, 155.

Martindale, Brigadier General John Henry, 1815-1881, New York, Graduated West Point 1835, resigned in 1864 due to poor health, 77, 106-107.

Meade, Major General George Gordon, 1815-1872, Spain, Graduated West Point 1835, 253-254.

Morgan, Govenor Edwin Denison, 1811-1883, New York, Governor from 1859-1862, U.S. Senator from 1863 to 1869, 79, 99.

Morrell, Brigadier General George Webb, 1815-1883, New York, 1st in class at West Point in 1835, 77.

Morris, Lt. Col. Thomas Ford, 1829-1886, possibly New York, wife died March 1862, 76.

Nicolay, John George, 1832-1901, Bavaria, Lincoln's personal secretary, 93-94, 112.

Olmstead, Frederick Law, 1822-1903, New York, 1 of 6 founding members of New York's Union League Club, Executive Director of Sanitary Commission, 79.

Palmer, General Innis Newton, 1821-1900, New York, Graduated West Point 1846, 93-94.
Peck, Major General John J., 1821-1878, New York, 66, 198, 225.
Pettus, Lt. Col. William Henry, 1815-1880, New York, born in Vermont, 15/50th New York Stuart Engineers, 69.
Porter, General Andrew, 1820-1872, Pennsylvania, attended West Point, Mary Todd Lincoln's second cousin, 106-107, 112, 153.
Pratt, Col. George W., abt 1842-1862, New York, 20th Ulster Guards, wounded at Second Bull Run, died at home the next month, 78, 125, 127.
Randall, Governor Alexander Williams, 1819-1872, New York, Governor of Wisconsin (1858-1862), Lincoln supporter, Appointed Ambassador to the Papal States in 1861, 80.
Riker, Col. J. Lafayette, 1828-1862, New York, Anderson Zouaves, died at Fair Oaks, Peninuslar Campaign 31 May 1862, 68.
Ripley, Brigadier General James Wolfe, 1794-1870, Connecticut, delayed putting repeating rifles into the arsenals, 155.
Rice, Lt. Col. James C., unknown, unknown, 44th Ellsworth Avengers, 77, 152.
Schoepf, Brig. General Albin Francisco, 1822-1886, Poland, commander at Fort Delaware POW camp beginning in April 1863, 313.
Scott, Brevet Lt. General Winfield, 1786-1866, Virginia, fought in War of 1812, 41, 75.
Seward, Major Augustus Henry, 1826-1876, New York, Brevet Colonel, 138-139, 148.
Seward, Assistant Secretary of State Frederick William, 1839-1928, New York, uncovered an early attempt on Lincoln's life, 139.
Seward, Secretary of State William Henry, 1801-1872, New York, responsible for purchase of Alaska, 133, 138-139, 148.
Sherman, General William Tecumseh, 1820-1891, Ohio, Graduated West Point 1840, 319, 332.

Slocum, Gen. Henry Warner, 1827-1894, New York, Graduated West Point 1852, 79.
Stanton, Secretary of War Edwin McMasters, 1814-1869, Ohio, 64, 89, 130, 133, 150-151.
Stryker, Col. Stephen W., 1836-1897, New Jersey, 77.
Stuart, Col. Charles B., 1814-1881, New York, 15th NY, Stuart's Engineers; Independent Engineers; Sappers, Miners And Pontoniers, 69.
Sullivan, Col. Timothy, abt. 1821, New York, Oswego Livestock dealer, 77.
Taylor, Col. Robert F., abt. 1826-unknown, New York, 76.
Thomas, Lt. Col. Gordon F., ?-1862, New York, died at Second Bull run in Aug. 1862, 77.
Van Allen, Col. James H., unknown, New York, 3rd New York Volunteer Cavalry, Van Allen's Cavalry, 170.
Van Vliet, General Stewart, 1815-1901, Vermont, Chief Quartermaster of the Army of the Potomac, 112-113.
Vinton, Col. Francis L., 1835-1879, Maine, Graduated West Point 1856, promoted to Brigadier Gen. in Sept 1862, wounded at Fredericksburg, 76.
Wadsworth, Craig Wharton, 1840-1872, Pennsylvania, served on his father's staff at beginning of War, 63, 78.
Wadsworth, Brigadier General James Samuel, 1807-1864, Pennsylvania, killed in Battle of the Wilderness, 6 May 1864, brevet Major General, 77, 125-126, 172.
Ward, Marcus Lawrence, 1812-1884, New Jersey, 21st Governor of New Jersey from 1866 to 1869, 69, 73.
Wightmand, Mayor Joseph M., 1812-1885, Massachusetts, Mayor of Boston, 1861-1863, Allotment Commissioner, 69.
Williams, Brigadier General Thomas, 1815-1862, New York, Died at Battle of Baton Rouge, 66.
Wilson, Senator Henry, 1812-1857, New Hampshire, Massachusetts Senator, later 18th Vice President of USA, 92-93, 96, 99.
Wool, Major General John Ellis, 1784-1869, New York, served in three consecutive wars; War of 1812, Mexican-American, and Civil War, 138-139, 221.

Confederate States of America

Anderson, Major Edward Clifford, 1815-1883, Georgia, U.S. Navy Officer prior to War, 82.
Beauregard, General Pierre Gustave Toutant, 1818-1893, Louisiana, Graduated West Point 1838, 41, 107, 166.
Bragg, General Braxton, 1817-1876, North Carolina, resigned command of the Army of Tennessee in Dec. 1863, 269.
Dunwoody, Major Henry Macon, 1826-1863, Georgia, killed at Gettysburg, at the Wheatfield, 265, 273.
Huger, Major General Benjamin, 1805-1877, South Carolina, Graduated West Point 1825, 131.
Jackson, Lt. General Thomas Jonathan *Stonewall*, 1824-1863, West Virginia, Graduated West Point 1846, 189, 217, 253, 256, 397.
Johnston, General Joseph Eggleston, 1807-1891, Virginia, Graduated West Point 1829, 41, 166, 174, 269, 394.
Johnston, General William Sidney, 1803-1862, Kentucky, Graduated West Point 1826, served in Texas War for Independence, died at Shiloh, 166.
Kell, Lt. John McIntosh, 1823-1900, Georgia, U.S. Navy officer before the War, Executive Officer on the C.S.S. Alabama, 243, 248, 270.
Lawton, Brig. General Alexander Robert, 1818-1896, South Carolina, Graduated West Point 1839, Quartermaster General of CSA, 30, 37, 270.
Lee, General Robert Edward, 1807-1870, Virginia, Graduated West Point 1829, 166, 189, 211, 217, 253, 337, 345, 397.
Mackall, Brigadier General William Whann, 1817-1891, Washington, D.C., Graduated West Point 1837, 269.
Maffitt, Commander John Newland, 1819-1886, born at sea, raised in North Carolina, called Prince of Privateers, 29.
Pettigrew, Brig. General Johnston, 1828-1863, North Carolina, mortally wounded at Gettysburg, 264.
Semmes, Captain Raphael, 1809-1877, Maryland, U.S. Navy officer before the War, Captain of the C.S.S. Alabama, later promoted to Admiral, 210, 245-248, 261, 311, 330-332.

Walker, Secretary of War LeRoy Pope, 1817-1884, Alabama, 1st Confederate Secretary of War, 29-30, 40.
Wise, Brigadier General Henry Alexander, 1806-1876, Virginia, lawyer, plantation owner, 142, 145.

Battles Commonly Known by Two Names

Date	Southern Name	Northern Name
21 July 1861	First Manassas	First Bull Run
10 Aug 1861	Oak Hills	Wilson's Creek
12 Oct. 1861	Leesburg	Ball's Bluff
19 Jan. 1862	Mill Springs	Logan's Cross Roads
7-8 March 1862	Elkhorn Tavern	Pea Ridge
6-7 April 1862	Shiloh (Church)	Pittsburg Landing
31 May 31- 1 June 1862	Seven Pines	Fair Oaks
26 June 1862	Mechanicsville	Battle of Beaver Dam Creek
27 June 1862	Gaines's Mill	Chickahominy River
29-30 Aug. 1862	Second Manassas	Second Bull Run
1 Sept. 1862	Ox Hill	Chantilly
14 Sept. 1862	Boonsboro	South Mountain
14 Sept. 1862	Burkittsville	Crampton's Gap
17 Sept. 1862	Sharpsburg	Antietam
9 Oct. 1862	Perryville	Chaplin Hills
31 Dec. 1862 - 2 Jan. 1863	Murfreesboro	Stones River

407

Appendix C:
Undated Notes from Mrs. Abraham Lincoln

Two notes, both undated, indicate that Mrs. Lincoln corresponded with Thee and Mittie while visiting New York City. In the first note, Mrs. Lincoln declines an invitation from Thee, and in the second, one from Mittie.

Mr Rosevalt
 It would afford me much pleasure to accompany you to Central Park this afternoon, yet having received one or two previous invitations, I fear I will have to decline. Being better acquainted ^{yourself there} with the other parties. I should otherwise, be most happy to accept your invitation
 Very Truly &
  Mrs Lincoln —

  Tuesday Noon
 Mrs Lincoln's Compliments to Mrs Roosevelt, and regrets being unable to accept her kind invitation for Wednesday eve at 9 o'clock – Visiting New York very quietly, must as {her/my} apology, for being compelled to decline the polite attentions of her friends.

Appendix D: Daniel Stuart Elliott's Will

State of Georgia
Cobb County
I Stuart Elliott of the county of Chatham in said state, being of sound and disposing mind and memory, but physically quite feeble, desirous of directing the disposition of my estate, do make, ordain, publish and declare the following as my last will and testament, revoking all others.
Item 1st I give and bequeath unto my beloved wife Lucy Ireland Elliott during her natural life, subject only to the conditions hereinafter limited, and for the uses hereinafter designated, the whole of my estate of every character whatsoever, real, personal and mixed, the annual profits thereof in every manner accruing to be used by her in her discretion, in her own maintenance and support, and in the maintenance, support and education of our children, confidently relying upon her maternal affection and her discretion, for the judicious application of the funds.
Item 2nd I give and bequeath to my beloved children John Elliott and Matilda Moxley Elliott all of my estate of every kind whatsoever, real, personal and mixed, subject only to the life estate herein before given my wife.
Item 3rd Should my wife again marry, then and from that date, I will that her life estate in item number 1 given, cease and determine, and in lieu thereof, I will that my estate be then divided into three equal parts, by commissioners to be appointed by the Court of Ordinary for that purpose, and that she take in fee simple her own right one third, and our children the other two thirds of my estate.
Item 4th I direct that after the extinguishment by my Executors of any and all just debts I may owe at the time of my decease, the remaining Cash on hand or in bank be invested, in the best discretion of my Executors, regarding in such investments,

first, the security, and secondly, the annual profits thereof.
Item 5$^{\underline{th}}$ I nominate my friends Maj. Anthony Porter, Wallace Cumming & A J Hansell as Executors of my will, and solicit their acceptance of the trust. In testimony whereof I have hereto set my hand and seal, this 31st day of July A. D. 1862.
      Stuart Elliott.
Signed, sealed and declared by the Testator, as and for his last will and testament, in our presence, who at his request and in his presence and that of each other, have signed the same as attesting witnesses.
      Carl Epping
      J. C. Levy
      {J ? } S. Wright

      August 1st 1862
Mem. I request my wife to present my beloved mother Mrs Martha Bulloch and my sister Mrs Susan West, each some memento for me, chargeable to my estate--
 And to present to my mother's faithful old servant Luke, the sum of fifty dollars- also charging same to my estate
      Stuart Elliott
attest
A J Hansell
 I Dominick A O'Byrne Ordinary of Chatham County, and ex officio clerk of my own district Court, do hereby certify the above and foregoing instrument of writing, to be a true and faithful copy of the original last will and Testament of Stuart Elliott, on file and of record in my office.
 In witness whereof I have hereunto set my hand and official seal this Twenty Seventh day of January A. D. 1863
      Dominick A. O'Byrne
      ex officio clerk C, o, c, c,

Index

Adams, Dr. James 75, 101, 208, 217, 281
Adams, Theodore Dwight 322
Alexander, Adam 268
Alexander, Felix 268
Atlanta, GA xv, 49, 319, 332
Augusta, GA 6, 56, 131

Baldwin, GA 49
Ball, Willis 7
Ballard, Dr. Charles W. 172
Baltimore, MD 133, 147, 166, 168-169, 171, 197, 212-214, 216, 221-224, 227, 242-242, 263, 281, 308, 315, 322
Barham, Jane 10
Barhamville, SC 9
Barnum's City Hotel 168, 222
Barnum, P.T. 240
Bartow, Francis Lloyd Stebbins 44
Bartow, Theodosius 44
Beaufort County, SC 30
Benjamin, Asher 7
Bibb County, GA 132
Bishop, David 85
Blair, Preston Francis, Jr. 93
Bonar, Horatius 186
Boyd, Andrew Kennedy Hutchison 187
Boynton, Cornelia Sessions 62, 159, 177-178, 180-181, 201, 258, 263, 302, 308, 311, 323-325
Boynton, John 62
Brown, Governor Joseph M. 32, 44
Brownrigg, Claude 206-208, 210 215
Brownrigg, Dr. John Henry 210
Bugs, Johnnie 328

413

Bulloch, Archibald 2
Bulloch, Elizabeth *Lizzie* Euphemia Caskie 21, 145
Bulloch, Harriott Cross Foster 21, 42-43, 46, 56, 81-82, 127, 160, 163, 171-172, 183, 206-207, 212-214, 220, 222-223, 239, 248-249, 251, 257, 267, 279-282, 302, 314-315, 348
Bulloch, Henry Dunwoody 13, 257, 273, 282, 298
Bulloch, Hester Elliott 2
Bulloch, Irvine Stephens 7, 21, 25-27, 29-31, 35, 37-38, 40, 42, 48-49, 53, 55-58, 74, 81, 83, 85, 127, 132, 160, 171, 182, 188, 190-191, 207, 210, 215, 217-218, 243, 245-252, 261, 268, 310-311, 314, 330, 333-336, 342, 346, 348-351
Bulloch James Dunwoody 2, 6, 8, 10, 21, 24, 29, 37, 61, 81, 84, 149, 162, 209, 242, 248, 251, 348, 350
Bulloch, James Dunwoody, Jr. 13, 183, 207, 257
Bulloch, James Stephens xi, 1, 9, 256
Bulloch, Jessie Hart 13, 21, 257
Bulloch, Martha Louise 13, 346
Bulloch, Mary 304, 336
Bulloch, Stuart Elliott 13, 257
Bulloch, William Bellinger 304, 336
Bulloch, William Gaston 31, 384
Bulloch, William James 301, 304, 336
Burke County, GA 2
Burnside, Mary Richmond Bishop 120
Butler, Ann 141, 143, 325
Butterfield, Edgar Burgh 315
Butterfield, Julia Elizabeth Brown 313-315

Caskie, Alexander Lawton 37
Caskie, Ellen Laura 36
Caskie, Fanny 205
Caskie, James and Mrs. 37, 239, 241?
Caskie, James K. 37, 239, 241?
Caskie, Robert Alexander 145
Caskie, William *Willie* Henderson 142, 145
Charleston, SC 4, 23, 131, 222, 241, 243, 245, 345

Chase, Catherine Jane 96-97
Cobb County, GA 341, 411
Columbia, SC 9
Columbus, GA 49
Cross, Edwin Bathhurst 163
Cross, Julia Duvall vonSchaumburg 163
C.S.S. Agrippina 311
C.S.S. Alabama 243, 245-248, 260-261, 270, 311-312, 330-332, 334, 349
C.S.S. Bahama 210
C.S.S. Fingal 82-83, 111, 149, 163
C.S.S. Nashville 82, 349
C.S.S. Savannah 29, 38, 57
C.S.S. Shenandoah 334, 337-339, 349
C.S.S. Sumpter 248
C.S.S. Virginia 165, 227

Danville, KY 208
Darien, GA 248, 254, 258-259
Davis, Jefferson 23, 337
DeCordova, Raphael J. 143-144
Dix, Catherine 168
Dix, Charles Temple 167-168, 197-198, 224
Dix, John 100, 167
Dix, Lt. Col. Roger Sherman 163
Dunwoody, Henry Macon 265, 273
Dunwoody, Jane 45
Dunwoody, Jane Marion Stanhope Glen 270, 276

Early County, GA 270
Elliott, Caroline Matilda 2
Elliott, Charles William 3
Elliott, Corinne Louise 2
Elliott, Daniel Stuart xiii-xvii, 21, 25, 27-28, 32-36, 37-38, 42-44, 48-52, 55-57, 69, 74, 81, 127, 131, 139, 143, 160, 171, 177-178, 183-184, 190-191, 207, 209-210, 215, 220, 239, 248-249, 251, 256-257, 276, 298, 310, 314, 334, Appendix D

Elliott, Fred 274
Elliott, Georgia Amanda *Daisy* 3, 60
Elliott, Jane Elizabeth 2
Elliott, John 2-3, 5, 36, 256, 328, 253
Elliott, John Stuart 21, 35
Elliott, John Whitehead 2-3
Elliott, Julia 97, 141
Elliott, Lucinda *Lucy* Sorrel xiii, xv, 25, 35-37, 127, 139, 177-178, 180, 200, 212, 214-216, 220, 222, 229, 231, 239, 241-243, 251, 264, 268, 269-277, 279-281, 290, 298, 302, 310, 335
Elliott, Matilda Moxley 21, 35
Ellis, John 18, 250
Emmet, Catherine Rebecca Duncan 230, 305-306, 322, 324-326
Emmet, Dr. Thomas Addis 230, 305, 322
Eutaw House 221-222, 224
Excutive Mansion 70, 72, 74, 98, 148

Few, Mary 5
Fortress Monroe 54, 127-128, 130, 132-133, 138, 140, 145-146, 148, 167, 198-199, 212, 223, 225-226, 230 278
Fort Wagner, SC 254

Garrard County, KY 208
Gebhard, William 85
Georgia iii-iv, ix, xi, 1-3, 6, 10, 18, 28, 32, 34, 38, 44, 48-49, 56-57, 131-132, 162, 167, 172, 209-210, 248, 254, 256, 259, 268-271, 276, 290, 319, 332
Georgia Military Institute 396
Gilliam, James Skelton 268
Gilmer, Louise 37
Gracie, Archibald II 345
Gracie, Archibald, III 345
Gracie, Elizabeth Davidson Bethune 345
Gracie, James 176, 345-346, 350
Green, Charles 160, 162

Gurley, Rev. Phineas 71

Hagadorn, Hermann 18
Halsey, Minny 51
Hancock, Thomas 275
Harvey, David 243
Henop, Frederick Lewis 172
Henop, Julia Dickson 171-172, 308
Henop, Louis Phillips 172
Henop, Miss 291, 301, 305-306, 308, 315, 322
Henop, Sidney 172,
Homer, Winslow 292, 295-296
Hooper, Sam 93-94, 98
Hunter, James and Mrs. xv
Husbert, Thomas 95
Hussey, William 222
Hutchison, Ellen L. 36
Hutchison, Nannie C. 36
Hutchison, Robert 4, 7-9, 36-37, 50, 145, 209
Hutton, Aston 142
Hyatt, Caroline *Caddie* 75, 78, 93. 97-98, 153, 175, 255
Hyatt, Melissa Augusta *Lillie* 75, 270
Hyatt, Stephanie *Phanie* 75, 93, 97-98, 101, 104, 109, 142, 153, 175, 328

Jackson, MS 49
Jeffers, William H. 273, 275
Jenkins, Dick 320
Jones, Charles Colcock 45, 208

Kell, John McIntosh, 243, 248, 270
Kell, Julia Blanche Monroe 268, 270
Ketchum, Morris 69, 99-100, 111, 121
King, Augustus Fleming 192
King, Barrington 6-7, 45, 56, 58, 162, 332-333
King, Charles 191-192
King, Henrietta Liston Low 192
King, Clifford Alonzo 278

King, James Roswell 333
King, Joseph Henry 45
King, Roswell 6
King, Thomas *Tom* Edward 36, 45, 58, 278-279
Knox, Augusta, 176
Knox, Isaac 176

Laird, Samuel 38, 43, 47, 176, 178-179, 183-184, 186, 190-192
Lansing, Mrs. Henry S. 120
Law, John Stevens 4
Lehigh Canal, PA 55
Lewis, Dr. Francis West 26
Lewis, George C. 304
Lewis, John Adams 304
Lewis, Mordecai D. 26
Lewis, Robert Adams 304, 321
Lewis, Robert Adams, II 304
Lewis, Robert H. 304
Lewis, Sarah Francis 28
Leydan, Charley 223
Liberty County, GA 1-4, 6, 9, 45, 162, 208, 232, 259, 270
Lincoln, Abraham 23-24, 41, 64, 71-72, 83, 89-90, 93-94, 113, 134, 148, 159, 165-166, 174, 189, 199, 211, 235, 240, 253, 271, 289, 319, 337
Lincoln, Mary Todd xvii, 79, 93-94, 133-135, 137, 155, 173, 240, Appendix C
Lincoln, Tad 157
Lincoln, William *Willie* 135, 155, 157
Liverpool, England 29, 37, 43, 46, 82, 111, 127, 131, 162-163, 209-210, 213, 220, 245-246, 251, 257, 333-335, 337-338, 342, 348-350
London, England 207, 307, 327, 332, 345, 348-350
Locke, Laura Jane Bulloch 336
Low, Andrew 82, 162, 268-269
Low, Charley 267
Low, Mary Cowper Stiles 267-268

McClellan, Mary Ellen *Nelly* Marcy 155
McConnell, Lillia 55
McConnell, Marilla 55
McConnell, May 55
McDougall, Senator James Alexander 55
McDougall, Mrs. 54
McIntosh County, GA 248
McIntosh, Nettie 280
Mackall, Dr. Leonard and Mrs. 212-213, 214
Mackall, Amita Elizabeth Douglas Sorrel 269
Macon, GA 131-132, 160, 265, 268
Makin, John 82
Marietta, GA xiii, 21, 28, 32
Markoe, Dr. 297
Marks, Dr. 9-10
Memphis, TN 48-49
Metcalf, Dr. John T. 200, 205
Milton, John 45
Mississippi 49, 62, 83, 166, 210, 235, 247, 254, 337, 339
Mitchell, Sam 173
Montgomery, AL 23, 29, 49, 228, 230, 261, 305
Morris, Reuben 85
Moumar/Monroe, *Daddy* Luke 6, 34-36, 58, 216, 341
Moxley, Dr. Benjamin Gustavus 213
Moxley, Matilda Amita Douglas 268

Newberry, Susan 186, 193, 206
New York Avenue Presbyterian Church 71
Nicoll, Georgia Clifford 267-268

Opdyke, George 145
Opdyke, Nancy 145
Oxford, MA 321

Palmetto Bluff, SC 7
Pennsylvania 55, 107, 241, 253, 258-259
Phelps, Anita 142, 144

Phelps, Royal 144
Philadelphia, PA 3, 8-9, 17-18, 21, 26, 28, 33, 62, 94, 97, 172, 179, 197, 212, 223, 230, 241-242, 245, 252, 325, 329, 334, 346-347, 352
Phillips, Dr. William Wurt 143
Pocotaligo, SC 385
Porter, Louise 37
Pratt, Charles 301, 304
Pratt, Rev. Nathaniel Alpheus 7, 304
Pratt, Nathaniel 301, 304
Pruyn, Margaret 268

Rice, Rev. Nathaniel L. 207-208, 211, 237-238
Richmond, VA 21, 37, 44, 48, 54, 56-57, 83, 121, 131, 142, 145, 160, 162, 165-166, 173, 185, 212-214, 243, 246, 252, 316, 319, 337
Robert, Mary xv
Robinson, Douglas 344
Roosevelt, Anna *Bamie* 18, 25, 31, 33, 48, 50-52, 57, 75, 81, 86, 95, 97, 100-102, 114, 141-143, 153, 175-176, 179-180, 182, 193, 200, 205, 213, 217, 219-220, 224, 229-233, 236, 239, 248, 255-257, 267, 272, 274, 278, 281, 291, 298, 301, 302, 308, 312, 314, 320, 324, 326-328, 342, 344-345
Roosevelt, Anna Rebecca Hall 344
Roosevelt, Corinne 17-18, 56, 62, 81, 95, 119, 141, 151, 154, 175-176, 179, 181-182, 185, 190, 200, 205, 213, 217-219, 224, 229-232, 236, 262, 272, 274, 276, 279, 281, 291, 298, 301, 308, 312, 325, 328, 342, 344, 348-349
Roosevelt, Dr. Cornelius J. 268
Roosevelt, Cornelius Van Schaak (b. 1794) 15, 19
Roosevelt, Cornelius Van Schaak (b. 1827) 15, 19, 257, 350-351
Roosevelt, Elizabeth *Lizzie* Thorne Ellis 18, 98, 101-102, 141, 143, 232, 308, 351
Roosevelt, Elizabeth *Lizzie* Norris Emlen 19, 95, 113, 209, 217, 230, 232, 308

Roosevelt, Elliott 18, 47-48, 52-53, 57-62, 70, 73, 75, 100, 102, 108-109, 114, 132, 141, 151, 160, 170-171, 178-179, 181-183, 185, 193, 196, 200, 206, 213, 218-219, 224, 229-230, 232-233, 239, 255, 258, 291, 301, 308, 312, 325-326, 342, 344
Roosevelt, James Alfred 15
Roosevelt, John Ellis 18, 251
Roosevelt, Laura H. Porter 19, 102, 336, 351
Roosevelt, Margaret Barnhill (B. 1799) 15, 19, 28, 43, 212
Roosevelt, Margaret Barnhill (b. 1851) 18
Roosevelt, Mary West, 18, 56, 205, 230, 244, 257
Roosevelt, Robert Barnhill 15, 18-19, 62, 79, 102, 114, 125, 141-143, 148, 152-154, 159, 223, 230, 343, 351
Roosevelt, Silas Weir 15, 18-19, 145, 183, 209, 230, 245, 257, 350
Roosevelt, Theodore, (b. 1858) 18, 30-31, 33, 48, 57-58, 61-62, 70, 75, 81, 86, 95, 97, 100-101, 114-115, 118-119, 122, 125, 141, 153, 160, 170, 174-175, 179, 181-182, 185, 190, 192-193, 200, 205, 208-209, 213, 219, 229-230, 232-233, 248, 251-252, 255, 258, 261, 272-273, 281, 291, 301, 308, 310, 328, 344-345
Roswell, GA iv, xi, xv, 6-9, 15, 17-18, 21, 28, 33-35, 38, 40, 45, 72, 162, 209, 213, 256, 262, 265, 278, 304, 321-322, 332-333, 334, 341

Savannah, GA xiv-xv, 1-9, 21, 28-31- 36-38, 44, 82-83, 111, 162, 259, 267-269, 276, 278, 304, 319, 335-336
Semmes, Dr. Marion 26, 81, 206
Sessions, Eliza Ann 62, 178, 180-181, 201, 302, 311
Scott, John Doughty 142-145
Scott, Nancy 143, 145
Shelton, Adelle 210
Shelton, Elizabeth Martha Haskins Brownrigg 210, 213, 238
Shelton, Mr. 207-208, 210, 238

Smith, Archibald 7
Sorrel, Agnes Eugenie 269
Sorrel, Annie M. 269
Sorrel, Francis 268, 276
South Carolina 1, 4, 7, 9, 30, 23, 27, 57, 254, 268, 345
Sparta, GA 10
Stevenson, Rev. William Fleming 300
Stewart, General Daniel 1, 4
Stiles, Frank 183
Stiles, Rev. Joseph Clay 162
Sturges, Ed 173

Telfair, Mary 5
Thumb, General Tom 240
Todd, Lockwood 157

Unionville, SC 268
University of Pennsylvania 21, 26
U.S.S. Ariel 246
U.S.S. Congress 165, 227
U.S.S. Cumberland 165, 227
U.S.S. Hatteras 247, 311
U.S.S. Kearsarge 330
U.S.S. Merrimack 227
U.S.S. Monitor 165

Wainwright, Dr. 223
Wallack, Lester 327
Warren, Lavinia 240
Warren, Reamey 93
Washington, D.C. 3, 41, 63, 65, 69-73, 76, 78, 80, 85-86, 89, 92, 94-96, 98, 103-104, 108-109, 111, 115, 117, 119, 121, 124-125, 127, 130, 132, 135, 138-139, 147, 149, 154, 158-159, 162-163, 166-167, 169, 172- 174, 181, 189, 197, 212, 219-220, 227, 229, 263, 315, 337

West, Dr. Hilborne 8-9, 17-19, 21-22, 25-28, 31, 33, 43, 48-50, 53, 56-58, 61-62, 132, 161, 171, 175, 179-181, 185, 190, 196-197, 201, 215, 217, 219, 222-223, 231, 236-237, 239-242, 244, 251, 256-257, 273, 281, 298, 302, 309, 311, 315, 319, 321, 323, 327-329, 334, 341, 346-347, 351
West, James 9, 28, 347
West, Lewis *Lew* 201
West, Rebecca Coe 9, 28, 244, 346-347
Willard's Hotel 169, 197
Wilson, Walter E. 38
Winston, Frederick Seymore 162
Winston, Susan 155, 159, 162, 278

About the Authors

Award-winning author **Connie M. Huddleston** (left) now spends most of her time writing historical fiction. She published a biography of James Stephens Bulloch in 2020 along with a biography of Jemima Boone written in novel form. Learn more at www.cmhuddleston.com.

Bulloch Hall Education Director **Gwendolyn I. Koehler** (right) is now working on a post-1865 Bulloch and Roosevelt family project. While she continues to volunteer at Bulloch Hall, Gwen is now retired and enjoying life, cruises, and travel with her husband.

www.ingramcontent.com/pod-product-compliance
Lightning Source LLC
Chambersburg PA
CBHW070714160426
43192CB00009B/1187